Hitchcock's Cryptonymies

Hitchcock's Cryptonymies

Volume I. Secret Agents

Hitchcock's Cryptonymies

Tom Cohen

University of Minnesota Press
Minneapolis • London

Published by the University of Minnesota Press
111 Third Avenue South, Suite 290
Minneapolis, MN 55401-2520
http://www.upress.umn.edu

Library of Congress Cataloging-in-Publication Data

Cohen, Tom, 1953–
    Hitchcock's cryptonymies / Tom Cohen.
        p.   cm.
    Includes bibliographical references and index.
    ISBN 0-8166-4205-2 (hc : alk. paper) — ISBN 0-8166-4206-0 (pb : alk. paper)
    1. Hitchcock, Alfred, 1899–1980—Criticism and interpretation.   2. Spy films—History and criticism.   3. War films—History and criticism.   I. Title.
    PN1998.3.H58C62 2005
    791.4302'33—dc22

                                                                    2005001127

Printed in the United States of America on acid-free paper

The University of Minnesota is an equal-opportunity educator and employer.

12 11 10 09 08 07 06 05   10 9 8 7 6 5 4 3 2 1

For Helen Elam

Contents

Acknowledgments

This work was originally proposed by Douglas Armato during a luncheon discussion a number of years ago. Over the long interim, he reengaged its development and provided invaluable support. This book and the companion volume, *Hitchcock's Cryptonymies, Volume II. War Machines,* owe their existence to his interest and patience.

Many others also influenced the course of this project with their intellectual and personal support. I would like particularly to thank Helen Elam, to whom this volume is dedicated in esteem and friendship. Among others whose stimulus and work have nourished this project, I am indebted to Barbara L. Cohen, Eduardo Cadava, Werner Hamacher, Mike Hill, Geoff Manaugh, J. Hillis Miller, Avital Ronell, Henry Sussman, Ivana Tieman, McKenzie Wark, and Jennifer Wesley for her assistance and criticisms.

I also thank Vice President William Hedberg of the University at Albany, State University of New York, for university support during the period of composition. Finally, my gratitude to the copy editor of this book for her patience and intimate work with the manuscript, and to Laura Westlund for her oversight and support on the logistics of production.

Preface

Is the age of the spread of the American way of life inscribed on
its films throughout the world the same age as Hitchcock's, or a
subsequent one, an underlying one? Might Hitchcock only be
an epiphenomenon in the process of its ineluctable advance?
—**George Collins, "Incidence of Instant and Flux"**

What I call in this study Hitchcock's "secret agents" alludes not to
characters linked to espionage in various political thrillers. Rather, the
term refers to more or less "secret" visual elements, graphic riddles, letteration, and cryptonymies that traverse all of his works, linking each to
each in perpetual if active interface. Agents are secret if unseen, outside
certain assumptions about the eye or sight; secrets become agents when
they transform the perceptual grid or sabotage it or rewire its memory
system. In this sense, this study began as an examination of what can
be called secret writing systems that traverse this work. Yet in pursuing a relatively minor formal question I was drawn repeatedly into more
extensive implications—both for what we call "Hitchcock" and for the
histories of contemporary telepoetics. I had wandered into a crypt, it
seemed to me, in the archaeology of the telemediatized present that had,
strangely enough, been left almost undisturbed by the critics. Why?

As an amateur close reader, I first approached the question of writing
systems in Hitchcock in the spirit of an interesting puzzle; after all, in
a medium devoted to the seductions of the visual, things like signature
effects and citational rebuses would at best serve supporting or minor
roles in an already brilliant critical repertory. They are, we know, formal
accoutrements to the plenitude of images, the deviance of narrative, the
complicities of psychology, the star's face or the interpreter's agenda. I
had wandered into "Hitchcock" with a question—how does this cinema
experience the transition from the era of the Book into the teletechnic

era it also invents?—only to be drawn into a constellation of performative citations, signature effects, treatments of language, speculations on the powers of cinema. It was not that Hitchcock's oblique deployment of Shakespeare and the Greeks, Egyptian motifs and Poesque runes locates his practice within the histories of writing, or even usurps the latter. One finds oneself drawn into a prehistory of the afterlife of the present, a zone of unfinished epistemo-political wars, still-contested histories, teletechnic events not yet grasped. "Hitchcock" from this perspective appears less an oeuvre in film history—more or less "modernist," more or less auteurist—than an unsettled event within the archaeology of "global" image culture.[1]

Thus the position I found myself in involved a curious blockage, given that the long-held premise of cinema studies has been predicated on privileging a visual ideology, an aesthetic ideology. I found that Hitchcock's signature systems, counter to expectation, leave few ocularcentric or auteurist assumptions in place. How, then, does one contribute an insight to a critical community whose projects seem, in discrete ways, premised on its occlusion or dismissal? This Hamletian position corresponds to that of many Hitchcock characters or ciphers. They know too much (or too little) to speak, like Iris Henderson in *The Lady Vanishes,* with her ocular name and insistence on a knowledge of something not visible, of memory, and denied by everything and everyone on the cinematic train. The tracker of cryptonyms can feel like Iris, locked in a mute position before the brilliant projects and aquarium of critical styles that have made "Hitchcock" the premier theoretical testing ground of critical insight. That networks of repetitions, insignia, signature effects, and language experiments down to preletteral and numerical logics run across this work is not unknown, but it has for perhaps too good a reason been deemed a marginal prop for interpretation. Often enough, a commentator stops to question how or why certain figures recur while seeming to void any one "content" or symbolic use (spectacles, the white milk, the letter M)—as if each were part of a vaster postal system that shuttles between aural and visual puns and citational revisions. Slavoj Zizek stops his neo-Lacanian weaving to reflect on just these secret agents and proposes, briefly, to call them *sinthomes*—before the effort is suspended; Gilles Deleuze, moving too briskly altogether, denaturalizes any symbolic logic by calling them *demarks*. In each case the vista closes again.[2]

Walter Benjamin suggested that cinema arrived as a virtual "shock" to socialized memory systems and that it implied the destruction of what he calls *aura*. This term, aura, has been assumed at times to name the originary presence lost through *technische* reproduction, yet it is allied, in Benjamin, with personification as such, as well as with the metaphoricity of "light," and more generally Enlightenment figures. What we call film studies, by keeping the mimetic promise of photography dominant, has constituted a sort of retreat from Benjamin's edgy assertion—as though, all along, even innocently, the dominant criticism labored to reconstitute the simulacrum of an aura perhaps vacated a bit too suddenly. Hitchcock plants in his early works a political fable for this: the uprising of various cinematic "villains" against the aesthetic state of England—an uprising that, were it to succeed, would rewire cognition and alter histories. The study of cryptonymies in cinema irreversibly drifts into unsettled literacies and sensorial programs. The very definition of the "aesthetic" changes, as it were, once a machine of memory is openly introduced, atomizing the visual order and rendering external everything that had been mythologized, during a supposed era of the Book, as interiority and experience. If it had been defined as representing the real, as mimetic, cinema is now determined as the site in which the world is mnemonically programmed, among other things, through phenomenalizing inscriptions, through the senses, or in their construction. Hitchcock treats the image not as a visual template but as a citational fabric that perpetually speculates on and marks its own teletechnic powers as an intervention in the histories of perception and writing.

Diverse media and typographical machines traverse this work: giant mills and presses, vehicles of transport and telegraphics of all kinds turn up. Hitchcock was the first "master" of global media: and it turned, in its advertising logics, around his signature, his cameo, his marketing devices. Jean-Luc Godard would remark that at one point the director exercised more real power over the globe than imperial conquerors such as Napoleon or Hitler. Yet this empire identifies with its own resistance. The uprisings in the British thrillers seem early variants of what Hitchcock later calls the "bird war"—poised against the human enclave as defined. What began as the state of "England" is reduced to the disinteriorized clapboard Brenner house, from which the ersatz family is driven. That war involves an attack by teletechnic agents on the anthropomorphic as such—on the house as aura, on the family as ocularcentric breeding ground, on the schoolhouse as a site of memorization and programming. These birds seem allied not to animals but to animation and teletechnics. Flying up over telegraph wires, they attack by pecking out eyes. This nonapocalyptic "war" is waged already in *The 39 Steps,* perhaps, by what is simply called "a certain foreign power"—foreign in the sense of being without aura, without personification. In its understated way, the bird war occurs within definitions of alterity and technology, and it overrides the wars of twentieth-century nation-states, subsuming "world wars" in which, at a certain point, both sides appear at various ends of the *same* cruel Enlightenment episteme. This structural war goes to the core of how memory has functioned, the human been defined, cognition determined by programs like ocularcentrism. When one approaches an oeuvre that has implanted itself at the very heart of a canonical nervous system, and then discloses itself as alien to the contracts and assumptions that surround it, it can operate like sabotage or a delayed time bomb, a familiar cinematic trope for Hitchcock. What would be dispossessed is all interiority of the home state, the house, monolingualism, gender identity, memory as perpetual artifice, mimetic and identificatory reflexes. But what does one do with a cinematic practice that attacks ocularcentrism and pecks out the "eye" as a trope? The rewriting or rewiring of "Hitchcock"—at the core of the cinematic canon—involves similar repercussions, since it potentially alters and sends tremors through entire critical and cultural histories and their innumerable extensions.

In a well-known train scene in *The Lady Vanishes,* Iris Henderson, trying to locate her vanished companion, the governess Miss Froy, finds the latter's existence denied by everyone—challenging what she "knows," her sanity and memory. She does not know that this total denial is orchestrated by the sweetly vampiric Dr. Hartz, the charming surgeon who is an agent for an imaginary Balkan, yet also cinematic, state, which has its own imaginary language. Both nation and language are named *Band*riki (suggesting celluloid bands).[3] In the dining car, Iris looks out the window as the cinematic train enters a tunnel and the rectangular surface fogs up. Briefly, the signature *FROY* appears spelled out on the glass from an earlier scene, when the lady spelled out her name for Iris. The letters seem to peel away the pretense of a Freudian unconscious with a *fröhliches Wissenschaft* of sheer inscription. The signature confirms Iris's denied knowledge, yet it is instantly erased as the train passes through another tunnel. It is like madness: Iris pulls the brake, stopping the succession of images, and blacks out. Something that Iris—that is, in some sense, the eye—knows is attested to by an inscription on befogged glass that flashes up and is erased. That is, rather as Hitchcock's signature effects do through a churning web of citational objects, letters, gestures, figures, or marks. It cannot, after the frame passes, be seen or pointed to. Iris's "knowledge" is referenced to inscriptions that flash on the rectangular glass itself, a medium drawing brief attention to *itself*. But why is it Iris, a figure of the ocular, who knows something that is not, so to speak, before her eyes at all? Is the eye (Iris) a product of mnemonic inscription or the passive recipient of what is in fact before it?[4] In Hitchcock's early thrillers all variety of secret codes and covert postal relays are on display.

In *Secret Agent,* Hitchcock offers us a sort of model for just this postal system (he even calls it the "spies' post office"), except that he places it in the midst of elaborate intrigues over the destiny of history and world war. The title of that film, like the borrowed one of this volume, does not reference quite the official MacGuffin of the plot—John Gielgud and Peter Lorre's assignment to identify and eliminate a double agent during the first world war: an agent who, if allowed to reach Constantinople by train, could (retrospectively) alter the map and outcome of a world war. It is a work obsessed with Babelesque language experiments, translation, and deafening aural signifiers that highlight the ear—and these too are encompassed by the term secret agent. What, then, is secret, or what agency is in question? Is it the "act" of the cinematic trance itself, or the agents of a different writing system that could alter the temporal map? When the "secret agent" (Robert Young's "*Mar*vin") is identified, the name resonates with marking systems, and it is disclosed during the buffo visit to a giant chocolate factory, which is disclosed as a front for a "spies' post office."[5] Its giant gears mime cinematic production, an automated factory cranking out excremental dark candies—the bonbons of film as entertainment—which contain in their wrappers transcribed messages to other agents. From the spies' post office, one could infer, signature systems issue that connect not only all of Hitchcock's works past or to come (as the cameos are thought to do) but also the manner in which cinema intervenes, in Hitchcock's purview, in the teletechnic histories and global wiring to come. We do not need to be reminded that what we call "Hitchcock" involved a certain totalized approach to the artifice of cinema: that all the shots and markers would be as if planned in advance, that he complained about the tedium, after that, of having to shoot the actual film (and lose a percentage of the ideas).

The definition of signature used here diverges from how the word is sometimes used to uphold auteurial logics. For the latter, on occasion, the term would provide a kind of authorizing self-inscription that can help secure a "Hitchcock" to speak for or through. Yet it is these signature systems that seem in rebellion against just this model, since, among other things, they know quite well that what we call Hitchcock is in varying degrees the product of their work. There is a direct link between the moralist readings of the early auteurist critics and the ocularcentric habits, even, of identity politics and those deploying "the gaze" as an ontological anchor. From an auteurist perspective "signatures" would testify to mastery and control, and they would tend to authorize mimetic, moralist, or identificatory interpretation. The model is ocularcentric. But when auteurists use the term signature and suppose the director to be leaving his mark, gathering all into a field of authorization, they misread its implications—opening a Pandora's box of citational powers. Hitchcock's signature effects traverse his works and *re-mark* themselves as letters, body parts, citational networks, numerical ciphers, and so on. But even these figures seem possible to channel back into familiar semantic preserves. As if to remind us of this, another signature effect eventually surfaces that, unlike the cameos with their bodily form, is shorn of any possible anthropomorphic guise or mimetic front (such as what we call "Hitchcock"). Indeed, it seems to drain the entire texture of the medium of any metaphor, recalling the experience of cinema to the conditions of its conjuring. Leave it to an arch auteurist to stumble upon this effect, which by itself would doom his or her program.

William Rothman spotted just this pattern in what he called the "bar series" that appears in every Hitchcock work. He termed it Hitchcock's premier signature. While perhaps the most significant insight into Hitchcock of its time, the critical tradition since has been to, with reason, dutifully ignore it. Rothman, in his linear frame-by-frame analyses, observed that *a series of vertical bars* turns up frequently—say, as occurs in a banister, a spiked fence, a row of trees, parallel lines in a fabric, musical bars in a score—and that these have their *aural* analog in a series of syncopated knocks or taps. Does this effect mime a stuttering citation, a viral cut preoriginary to any perception whatsoever, an imitation of divided celluloid frames, a serial repetition, differential spacing, the faux origin of number or rhythmics? Rothman reproduces this pattern of serial slashes typographically as / / / /. Preletteral, self-dividing, composed of or by interval, the pattern of parallel bars is without any possible mimetic value:

> The view is through the bars of the banister, and the frame is dominated by the bars in the foreground. I call this pattern of parallel vertical lines Hitchcock's / / / / sign. It recurs at significant junctures in every one of his films. At one level, the / / / / serves as Hitchcock's

signature: it is his mark on the frame, akin to his ritual cameo appearances. At another level, it signifies the confinement of the camera's subject; we might say that it stands for the barrier of the screen itself. It is also associated with sexual fear and the specific threat of loss of control or breakdown.[6]

Emerging briefly to view, Rothman cannot refrain from assigning this bizarrely classic and disarticulating "signature" a content, a corollary, a subjective space of familiarity—even if that is the "threat of . . . breakdown." But the figure's seriality (if it is a figure) precludes containment. *It* is without analogy or metaphor, although it will proclaim or generate both. *It* perhaps recalls the alternacy of waves preinhabiting "light." *It* cannot be the "signature" of Hitchcock as such, even if such a bar occurs seven times across the letters of his name. Out of *it* space and temporalities seem conjured. *It* can interrupt any memory band, traverse works, suspend identification. *It* precedes the coalescence of perception, image or sound, or even letter. If Rothman stumbled into the bar series hoping to pile up another auteurist coup, he touched the third rail of a "signature system" that nullifies and voids the auteurist approach *tout court*.

What we call Hitchcock does not leave "his" signature; rather, "he" is the product of a system of signature effects. To underscore this point, he ceaselessly references cinematic machines and teletechnic devices that are absorbed into or by cinema more generally. To find that this oeuvre assaults ocularcentrism in all its extensions suggests that Hitchcock plotted sabotage at the heart of modernity's archive—which is to say, in the construction of the contemporary.

The frames below are all images in Hitchcock that expose or attack any natural assumption of the eye as perceptual organ. By extension, each could be said to assault or suspend the ocularcentric premises upon which, to some degree, cinema seems founded. Instead, the eye appears as if preinhabited by graphics and mnemonics, a cut, or else it is aggressively extinguished. One could add to this portfolio of shots many others: the suicidal cinematic gunshot into the camera's eye in *Spellbound*; "Mother's" extinguishing a cigarette into a sunny-side-up egg in *To Catch a Thief*. In the images here the eye is assaulted or, if one prefers, exposed as an imaginary organ of light or transparency. Each comments on this differently. In the first shot, the eye of a woman is focused on in the credit sequence preceding *Vertigo*, and it is preinhabited by graphics and mnemonic coils in Möbius strip–like bands—this, after tracking up *first* from the lips, site of partition and speech. In the second, Dalí's dream sequence from *Spellbound* scissors a placardlike eye, citing for its own purposes the cinematic gesture from *Un chien andalou*. Behind the inert cut eye is reproduced another. In the third shot, from *Shadow of a Doubt,* there does not appear to be an eye. Yet Uncle Charlie, who will be identified with smoke rings and cinematic "O's," and who refuses photos of himself, here dissolves into networks of teletechnic media—the spool-like daisy wheel of the telephone, the wires of telegraphs. Charlie, who has the teletransporting powers to stand outside the visible frame and enter it, at will, dissolves into sheer teletechnicity and machinal links.

The fourth image is taken from the Riviera fireworks scene in *To Catch a Thief.* It is the background of a seduction scene and comes to the fore as if to affirm *jouissance.* Yet the cold pyrotechnic will finally burn out the screen, as if plunging an ember into the touristic eye of

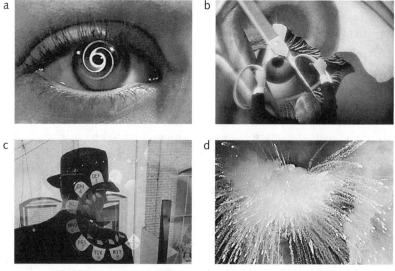

Figure 1. (a) Female eye inhabited by graphic vortex—shortly dissolved into Möbius strip–like coils of memory—opens the credit sequence of *Vertigo*; (b) Dismembered giant eye on a curtain is scissored in the Dalí dream sequence in *Spellbound,* cutting the ocularcentric facade; (c) Uncle Charlie, a.k.a. the "Merry Widow" serial killer in *Shadow of a Doubt,* is identified with telephones and telegraphics; (d) One of the most "beautiful" sights on *To Catch a Thief*'s Riviera: pyrotechnics scorching out the screen—or viewer's Cyclopean eye.

the viewer and obliterating mimetic seductions. It mimes a nocturnal sun as the effect of technics and, while burning up in its showering excess, whites out vision. In the first and third frames, the "eye" is identified with mnemonic bands and telegraphics that program it. In the second and fourth, the "eye" will be sliced or actively blinded—disinhabiting, in the process, the ocularcentric order that seeks in cinema confirmation.

Hitchcock uses diverse fronts in his plots to dissimulate and present the implications of his practice. In his final film, *Family Plot,* he offers it as a séance, a trance in which the voices of the dead speak through the living to unriddle, or recast, a future. Or rather, he offers it as a con man's séance with Mme Blanche allo-ventriloquized through her male medium, "Henry." The cinematic operates as a catabasis. It is essential to access the memory of the dead, Julia Rainbird tells Mme Blanche, if the Rainbird name and family fortune are to have a future. A plot in every sense is attached to the logics of the "family," which is also attached to the rectangular plot, as it were, of the screen's faux familiarity. In séancing this side of Hitchcock we seem to séance the ghost and advent of the cinematic, as if from "today," embedded in the networks it legislates and anestheticizes as a global teletechnic era, asking new questions of Mr. Memory.

This monograph raises the issue directly of what writing on the image entails or does as a process of unweaving, reading, citation, and *conflicting*

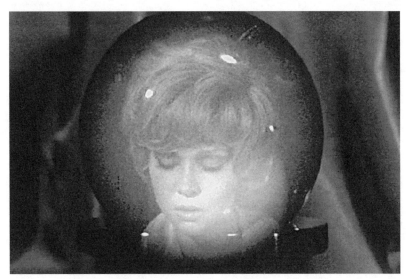

Figure 2. Mme Blanche's encircled face séancing a "family plot."

legibilities. In this case, the writing puts new archival markers into play, highlights figures that lapse into the invisible, induces a certain mobile-effect across its pages—tracing and returning to fractal agents, differently. The readings enter into a contract of accelerations and back loops and slow-motion replays, probing what can be called cryptonymic networks. The style might be called faux cinematic by default, only in part because of its alliance with the figure of the circle or *backspinning* wheel, a Nietzschean topos.

Introduction: The Blind of Ocularcentrism

> If I play on the orthography of his name, at least five current "Hitchcocks" can be characterized: there is HitchCOCK (feminist critiques), HITCHcock (the de Lauretis sort of deconstruction), HITCHCOCK (Wood's or Rothmanesque auteurism), hitchcock (Modelski's ambiguous use of him), Hitchcock (Jameson, the H standing as well, of course, for History), and hitchcocK (Zizek, where the last K will signal his gleeful use of Kafka and Hitchcock as neither mass culture nor high art).
> **—Clint Burnham, *The Jamesonian Unconscious***

> He has a dozen names. He can look like a hundred people. But one thing he can't disguise. This part of his little finger is missing.
> **—*The 39 Steps***

As cinema dies, its ghost emerges, but it is no different from the way, say, that the "dead" Madeleine haunts the supposedly living Scottie in *Vertigo,* as if he were a film viewer, haunts him to madness, even though technically she, "Madeleine," never existed as such, never was alive to begin with. *First impasse:* "cinema" was supposed to guard representation, assure the eye's domain and its mimetic transparency, be "coded as the real, the locus of truthful representation" (Rodowick), yet, constituted by etched marks and shadow play on a translucent band, *it* above all exemplifies the priority of inscription over perception, memory over phenomenalization. It renders sight, perception, and ideation mnemonic *fables* that seek, in turn, to repeat and replicate. *Second impasse:* "cinema" was supposed to uphold ocularcentrism, the centrality of the eye to cognition (going back to the Greek fusion of the two in the verb *eidein*), yet cinema precedes "sight" as an effect of cutting rendering, again, the "eye" a mnemonic fable. *Third impasse:* cinema arrives on the scene,

1

Benjamin tells us, as the revocation of *aura*—or at the very least literalizing that revocation. It is an "aura" defined as personification, as anthropomorphism, as taking "light" to be originary or natural or true; it is an "aura" that oversees, still, the most familiar logics used by criticism: identification of the viewer with a face, the personifying gaze, indexing the real, the auteur, and so on. As cinema dies, its ghost becomes more visible, even if it never "existed" quite that way as such, even if it cannot, technically, die as such.

This study takes "Hitchcock" as a Rosetta stone for this double event: that of cinema's advent, its accelerating role in a teletechnic revolution, and its presumed death, *as if* at the hands of new media. Indeed, if Hitchcock can be used, today, to reopen the question of a cinema without aura (a redundant phrase for Benjamin), his reception tells us something about how that has been guarded against, how cinema is reauratized. It is Fredric Jameson who brushes up against this rift when he speaks, in an attempt no doubt to implement a variant of Benjaminian "allegory," of aiming for a reading of Hitchcock that would do "away with consciousness, 'character,' and the anthropomorphic."[1] Why would these favored domains need to be bracketed—and with them, an entire dossier of critical insights? Is ocularcentrism so easily bracketed? Is it understood that a certain notion of the visual is not innocent, nor was for Hitchcock, in the programming of truth, identity, time, gender, and politics, as Hitchcock's early British thrillers can be read as knowing.

Figure 3. Spellbound eyes line gambling dream of ocular night in Dalí sequence.

Thomas Elsaesser has recently described a certain deocularization of "film studies" as almost routine today, though he does so in a manner that puts it into question as well: "Rather than continue to think about the cinema as an ocular-specular phenomenon, whose indexical realism we celebrated or whose illusionism we excoriated (which was the case in classical film theory and, subsequently, during the decade when psychosemiotic apparatus theory held sway), scholars now tend to regard the cinema as an immersive perceptual event. Body, sound, and kinetic-affective sensation have become its default values, and not the eye, the look, and ocular verification."[2] Elsaesser references as given a supersession of an "ocular-specular phenomenon," yet the description is unconvincing and ironic—as if things would soon, indeed, spring back. One is said to be immersed, for instance, in a fully *perceptual* event," as if the "body" were not a cinematic invention; immersed, that is, not in a mnemonic and telesthenic sensorium but in something perceptually immediate. The term *ocular* is preserved and hedged, then, should one want to return to its hegemony in the future (which one never really believed was broken). The critic uses specularity to describe this ocularcentrism (the "ocular-specular"). As if all one gave up, and that tentatively, were "indexical realism." These assumptions are punched in like newly entered "default values," while one awaits their demystification.

If one peels away some of the investments that have sustained the *ocularcentric* use of cinema, taking Hitchcock's reception as a cipher, one may again ask what is, or was, a cinematics without aura? What would a *spectrographic* reading of Hitchcock, for instance, look like—if we may coin a term for the prehistory of cinema's afterlife, which aims, as does Benjamin's "materialistic historiography," at a certain performative event that Hitchcock, in the early British thrillers, likens to a saboteur's time bomb, the epistemological atomization or dematerializing of installed programs of time and the senses, and this in the name at times of a "certain foreign power"? What if many of the techniques we take for critical innovations, auratic strategies to anthropomorphize cinema, were all along attempts to roll back or cover up something that cinema abandoned at its advent?

Telehistories

A recent effort to historicize the shifting roles of cinema, Philip Rosen's *Change Mummified: Cinema, Historicity, Theory,* situates them among different representational modes, among them documentary, digital, and analogic partitions.³ While stretching a historical model into corners of media development, Rosen brings us to a point where that model itself would be transformed. What model of history situates a medium that has produced, accelerated, and altered the definitions of "history"? How would one write the history of a medium (or media) that contains the measure to which it is supposed to be held? Cognitive models can be said to have been installed or erased from this medium, "experience" conjured or programmed, identifications legislated. Rosen uses the term historiography here, yet that occurs most decisively in the final pages when he fully turns to Benjamin's use of the term—as in the latter's materialistic historiography with its proposed "transformation of historical time." That is, the prospect arrives as a next step or point of future departure: "Whether one regards this as an aporia or a dialectic, coming to grips with it might enable a new history, and new practices, of 'new media'" (359). What is aimed at, then, is a transformation of the premises of the historial and of its performative effects—even if that prospect, arriving at the exhaustion of historicizing techniques, will be deferred.

And yet, to the degree that Hitchcock can appear a cipher for the event or advent of cinema, his practice could in very specific ways be called "Benjaminian" from the first. That is, it takes account of itself as a suspension of and assault preceding perceptual programs. One can read in its plots and MacGuffins a potential intervention in mnemonics. Hitchcock's early thrillers are always epistemo-political in specific ways, and always informed by cryptonymies, marking and signature systems, performative and citational networks that assault ocularist viewing in a parallel fashion. In each, as with Benjamin's materialistic historiography, the turning point is an "event" that would reconfigure history and the world order through an assault on representational and mnemonic regimes. These assaults are indicated and mapped out on micrological levels, and their agents are, as again seems clearer today, entirely void of "aura"—as much, say, as the saboteur Verloc's blackout of London that opens *Sabotage*.⁴

Histories such as Rosen's admirable attempt appear, or tend to, at the end of a cycle—as if after the death of its subject has been tacitly assumed, such as cinema, today, before "new" media, analogic technology retired before the digital shattering of all into numeration and pointillist calculation. Yet *cinema's* death is redundant. For one thing, the term was never decisively affiliated with one technology or another, and second, its death seems to coincide with its totalization as a perceptual model: events are experienced and generated, including wars, through cinematic manipulations ("Iraq"); policies of preemption run like Spielberg's precogs in *Minority Report,* cinematic memory as if unspooled forward to cut off "future" eventualities. The political and philosophical strategy of marginalizing *the aesthetic* as play is, however, inverted in the process, installed as a mediatric program in advance of or generating ideation—as if, in Hitchcock's tropes, reaching into, stealing from, raping, installing, anestheticizing what would then be called "consciousness." This is one of the things Godard meant, perhaps, by asserting that at a certain moment Hitchcock had absolute "power" over the world, more than Hitler or Napoleon. It is at this point that cinema appears one last time in its Benjaminian revision, as a precursor to "materialistic historiography," the placing in suspension and alteration of inscriptions.

Particles, Photons, Atoms

Perhaps the defining dossier in Hitchcock criticism was launched by Claude Chabrol and Éric Rohmer's work, rehearsing theological inflections that run through Zizek. In various ways, widely differing key interventions in the construction of Hitchcock are marked by auteurial premises whose attributes are shared: an occlusion by and large of an entire order of signifying agents and writing experiments that anchor this work, the dominance of ocularcentric and identificatory response (pro and con), an alliance between thematic and Oedipal modes, historicism and various rhetorics of "gaze." From new critical auteurism like Rothman to feminist assaults and, to a degree, neo-Lacanians, the brilliance of this tradition has been marked by an ocularcentric subterfuge. But if Hitchcock's practice assumes a *graphematics* that precedes the perceptual and mnemonic effect, an entire series of epistemological prejudices goes into partial default.

One might group certain auteurist, humanist, "modernist," mimetic, and historicist projects as among the most decisive writings on film or Hitchcock. Yet the theological inflections introduced by Rohmer and Chabrol's work will echo in the *ludic* or aestheticized strategy of the auteur playing "games" of control with his viewers (Thomas M. Leitch's *Find the Director and Other Hitchcock Games*) or, polemically, in Tania Modleski's rewriting of Hitchcock as the ambiguated guilty patriarchist. Even studies of Hitchcock's technical motifs have been restricted, as in Elisabeth Weis's essentially thematic analysis of "sound." It is not accidental that the wayward methodology affiliated with the "hieroglyphic" project of Marie-Claire Ropars suggests one limit to available methods—though one that itself is not adequate to engage Hitchcock's own signature system or what I have suggested is its Benjaminian impetus or logic, since the latter asks that one grasp Hitchcock's deauratic cinema not only as in excess of the auteurist model *tout court,* but as posing the question of an intervention or transition to another epistemo-political model it can neither quite affirm nor return from. For one thing, a deauratic "Hitchcock" runs into the following trouble: if it is not ocularcentric, not anthropomorphic, and not necessarily visual, what did "pure cinema" mean and why, today, would a portmanteau term like *spectrographic* reorient us to the event nature of this intervention?[5]

What Hitchcock called "pure cinema" was supposed to denote the purely visible, but turns out to name semiotic violations and matrices that are technically invisible. In part, the promulgation of the auteur reflected the most decisive defense before a dismembering signature system whose circuitry perpetually reconfigures the work. Even deployments of the Lacanian "gaze" could not function without a recuperative personification that includes Zizek's locating in *Psycho* of a *subject beyond subjectivity.* Thus the trope of "signature" has appeared to anchor the perpetually constructed auteur, emerging in the case of Rothman's "bar series" as precisely what might undo it in fact.[6] Thus Flitterman-Lewis will comfortably reference that "consummate auteur and exemplar of patriarchal power, Alfred Hitchcock."[7] Kaja Silverman endorses this inversion: "Hitchcock has posed a consistent challenge to those theories that seek to dissolve authorship, both because of his cameo appearances in his own films, and because of the sophisticated verbal apparatuses that he has put in place around those films through interviews and publicity statements."[8]

Laura Mulvey's once influential argument for an institutionally dominant *male* gaze assumed an ideology so entrenched in Hollywood cinema that, for the spectator, "pleasure" in viewing itself involved participation in the performative erasure of woman (prime examples were to have been *Rear Window* and *Vertigo*). While the monolithic argument has been displaced or revised (among others, by Mulvey herself), the gendering of ocularcentric power also morphed.[9] Modleski's *The Women Who Knew Too Much* sought alternative positions for a female spectator, arguing that woman in Hitchcock is in general a figure of bisexuality who must be actively repressed before the prospect of exposing the male's own bisexuality. This requires restituting "Hitchcock" as ambiguated patriarchal monster, auteurial agent-father. In "Mother's" vocal castigation of Norman in his *cell* within his head, as the fly lights on his hand, she strategizes against him as if he were setting her up to take the blame for the murders—alert to another eye watching before which she must, too, dissimulate, as before the psychiatrist. Modleski's *identification* is complete:

> ["Mother"] speaks through her son's body to protest her innocence and place the blame for the crimes against women on her son. I think she speaks the truth. As I will argue, the sons are indeed the guilty ones, and, moreover, it is my belief that the crime of matricide is destined to occur over and over again. (15)

Modleski, personifying "Mother," feels "forced to relinquish the more facile notions about Hitchcock's self-reflexivity and his critiques of voyeurism" (14), turning toward a resolutely identificatory model. Yet the argument, reiterated by Silverman, that Hitchcock's "authorial system may be far more heterogeneous and divided than Bellour could ever have imagined, and it may, in fact, contain a female voice as one of its constituent although generally submerged elements" (210–11), is timid. The voice called "Mother" alludes to herself as the stuffed *thing*, is radically other than an extricable victim or necessarily a she, dead in advance while impersonating itself as gendered. At odds with Mulvey's hypostasization or Bellour's generalization of a panoptical "male" gaze, Hitchcock's women (if they are that) may occupy ocular tropes too precisely: Iris Henderson linked to the train (cinema as motion, as relay), Mrs. Paradine called "the eyes" of the (already) dead blind man, Judy Barton taunted as an "apt *pupil*" by Scottie.

Joan Copjec criticized routine deployments of the gaze in film theory for implicitly using a Foucauldian notion of the panopticon (as in the power of a male gaze), rather than Lacan's, for whom "gaze" would conjure an otherness that cannot be anthropomorphized—yet this orthodoxy can seldom be enforced (as Zizek's surrogate phallophanies display). A casual use of gaze closer to that of a linguistic effect occurs in Anne Friedberg's *Window Shopping: Cinema and the Postmodern*, under the aegis of a Benjaminian project.[10] Friedberg announces a "*virtual* gaze" along the model of the flaneur in the arcades, as a kind of movement-writing:

> Rather than proclaiming a single distinct moment of rupture—when the modern ended and the postmodern began—I suggest a gradual and indistinct epistemological tear along the fabric of modernity, a change produced by the increasing cultural centrality of an integral

feature of both cinematic and televisual apparatuses: a *mobilized "virtual" gaze*. The *virtual gaze* is not a direct perception but a received perception mediated through representation. . . . The *mobilized gaze* has a history, which begins well before the cinema and is rooted in other cultural activities that involve walking and travel. (2)

A virtual gaze is mobilized, which means it is subjected to fields and circuits of repetition, of *re-marking,* though virtuality would be read in a proactive sense rather than registering the position of an always vicarious gaze. Thus: "Benjamin was attracted by the arcade's curious temporality, its embrace of 'the new, the already past, the ever-same.' Like the arcade, the cinema embodies this conflated temporality" (184). Retaining the privilege of the ocular even where mobilized and rendered virtual, Friedberg approaches a topos of inscription that would imply the abandonment of that same metaphorics.

Cinema suspends in advance the promised mimeticism literalized in the critical tradition's major trends (humanist, identificatory, Oedipalist, historicist, auteurist), as though replacing it with webs of cross-relays and trace chains.

Ropars in *Le Texte divisé* and subsequent work pioneered an altered concept of *visibility* predicated on where Derridean *différance* (one implication of the bar series) leads to variant *hieroglyphic* readings, in which once excluded markers and signifiers interlace as if between visual and aural registers, anagrams and patterned or citational inflection.[11] Ropars discloses a contested interface that traverses visual and aural signifying surfaces, anagrams and phonemic chains, converting the "cinematic" into a totalizing confluence of inscriptions.[12] Tom Conley observes that implicit "in the concept of the camera style is a film hieroglyph, a writing that unites and divides word and image; that invokes memory to recall analogous forms of legibility and meaning."[13] In contrast to tracing rules of the game or reading strategies to evade the institutional error of a divide between the visual and the scriptive, image and text, Hitchcock's recasting of marks, language, and teletechnics at the core of the cinematic redefines an entire set of performatives that include gender, memory, agency, and time.[14]

Suspense, Suspension

The signature machines of Hitchcock do not stamp a stable authorship or secret content. They initiate and anticipate readings that have yet to arrive, readings "to come." In these, all trace chains, linguistic histories, aesthetic variables are at risk, much as Jameson speaks of something "draining off the generic sign system itself and transforming the latter's signifiers into some new autonomy of the sign in its own right."[15] At that point the covering mantle of the "auteur" drops away as a MacGuffin.

Any spectrographics would already have moved a step beyond any metaphorics of the eye, alert to what Hitchcock in *Number 17* calls *footsteps without feet,* but it would still differ from a hieroglyphic logic. Indeed, the hieroglyphic itself will have been as if preceded by a signifying agent to which Hitchcock gives many names and faces, sometimes cat, sometimes black sun, sometimes chocolate, sometimes finger or sound, which precedes the monumental histories of representational forms and logics. "Cinema," in this practice, once activated, finds itself, among other things, in any and all phenomenal forms it assumes—what keeps it, the instant there are two frames, perpetually from being in any way documentary or indexing or mimetic. And in the same way it cannot acknowledge borders: of living and dead, of actors and characters, of any out-of-frame once that is marked as premise. (In the case of the literal "actor," who is indelibly inscribed and altered as a signifying constellation in fact and for the public, *Murder!* will call that being *"half-*cast[e].") Hieroglyphic premises accelerate the infraspace of grapheme and trace, yet remain to engage where just this totalization platforms or partakes of an archival intervention.[16]

In Hitchcock hieroglyphics as an Egyptian notation is itself preceded by a nameless trace that cannot be historicized or even find its origin in that "birth" of writing. Indeed, judging from the ending of *Blackmail,* in which there is a chase through the Egyptian wing of the British Museum, "Egypt" itself is just another monumentalized dossier in cinematic logics (not the reverse). Cinematic "shock" in *Blackmail* antedates the monumentalism of museums, which display papyrus behind glass. Christopher Morris observes: "Although *Vertigo* seems primarily a love story of untenable points of view, its political allegory narrates the public catastrophes of Western civilization, thereby calling into question meliorist theories of history and the 'monumental' art that celebrates it."[17] The decimating and atomizing power of the cinematic has to do with dematerializing what is, as it were, *shot,* the citation breaking the cited into innumerable suspended points, like fog, disinscribing what has come into a viewfinder.[18]

Any *spectrographics* one might speak of to shed the remnants of auratic habits (identification, for instance) remains affiliated, here, with signature systems and even "cameo" effects. It departs from the micrologic

effects, "pieces of film," in all its denominations. It is alert to a fundamental inversion that is as obvious as machinal forms of mnemonic
storage, and thus participates in the effaced scene of production, or
projection, of the cinematic. This cinema marks itself as inscribing the
effects of "life" into a semiomorphic band without a beginning outside
of such inscriptions or media—going back to, and before, Egypt. This
requires of Hitchcock that every work mark not only the irreducible
premises of the visible (such as the pattern of parallel lines in *Spellbound,*
or the *Mar-* names generously dispersed) but also the contract between
the screen wraiths and the viewing public, unaware that "life" and its
cognitive rituals derive from the deauratic bands of pure inscription as
well, that what they deem *life* is an inscribed and cinematic effect, and
that the cinematic would further install itself as a dominant epistemomnemonic or tele-archival mode in an always coming "global" time-
scape. A "secret *clause*" is used in a treaty as a world-altering political
MacGuffin in *The Lady Vanishes* and *Foreign Correspondent,* one inserted into an official global manipulation. Hitchcock's *anarchivists* represent
resistance to a "globalized" media order and the possibility of alternative
futures.

Jameson turns to Hitchcock, and not a literary work, when probing
how to reclaim Benjaminian allegory for performative analysis, and although he is committed to a "modernist" rhetoric, the attraction of these
two instances (Hitchcock and Benjamin) is consistent. Benjaminian
"allegory" does not define itself as *representing.* Rather, for Benjamin,
"[allegory] means precisely the *non-existence* of what it (re)presents";
that is, it alters or deforms the terms by which the world or the senses
are programmed, pasts and futures designated or occluded. It actively
decimates the phantasm it turns upon and against, which, in the case
of what is called allegory, is the "symbolizing" character or signifying
agents it encounters. It turns on the formal not to abstract itself from
historical conflict but precisely to alter the model of the historial, "experience," horizons of the possible.[19] It is only by negating an installed
program that a predictable future can be interrupted, vaporized, put
into play otherwise—and, for Benjamin, the "enemy" is not one or
another political ideology as such but an epistemological practice, historicism, the assemblage of "facts," like what Mr. Memory is said to do
in entertaining his audience in the Music Hall opening scene of *The 39
Steps.* Jameson would empty the "contents" of auteurial interpretation
tout court, and it is here that something like "form" returns.

What Jameson does not have access to in his address of "space" is the micrological order of Hitchcock's signifying agencies—interestingly presented in *North by Northwest,* the work Jameson analyzes, as what the entire plot turns on, the "microfilm" concealed in the pre-Columbian *figure,* as it is called. That is, something *ante*figural, micrological, like the facticity of the celluloid snippets that Hitchcock briefly shows as the figurine shatters. It is nonetheless curious here that Jameson turns to what Rothman calls Hitchcock's signature, the bar series effect, a discovery that the critical literature has left largely untouched for two decades. Rothman identifies this marking system as irreducible and traversing every work of Hitchcock's, hence the term *signature,* but he must fill in symbolic contents for what, clearly, rattles the auteurist premise that the term signature was meant to uphold. A sort of $N + 1$ effect that projects movement, even its imaginary translation is propelled into a series ("*also* associated with"). In turning to *North by Northwest,* Jameson aims at what can be termed a deauratic mode.[20] Yet this $N + 1$ effect does not, strictly, signify any *thing*: it does not symbolize ("sexual fear"), nor is it "associated with" a content; it is, among other things, nothing at all, yet it revokes "light" as other than an effect of such alternation. Jameson's return to *allegory* dovetails with this closure of anthropomorphism and, he suggests, points "not towards Hitchcock's genius or his libido, but rather towards the history of form itself" (48)—or, one might add, the intervention of "form" in the cast of historiality:

> But [the scene in the pine woods] is not the only feature of the empty-field sequence which "rhymes" with scenes and spaces elsewhere in the film. We must also note the peculiar inscriptions, here, which streak both versions of the empty surface of space—the expanse of the sky fully as much as the expanse of the empty land below. Both are furrowed with a set of parallel lines that is not without some distant affinity with the "trauma" of *Spellbound*: the fateful ski tracks in the snow, reproduced by Gregory Peck's fork upon the white linen of the dining-table. The plane leaves its ephemeral traces on the sky fully as much as the empty fields retain the serrated grooves of tractor and plow. (64)

Jameson uses this bar series to cut a way out of the auratic and auteurial tradition—the play of shadow precedes not only face, it appears, but a prosthetic *earth.* He terminates a cycle of reception inaugurated by Rohmer and Chabrol's work. This impenetrable surface *upends* vertically, then dispossesses any anthropomorphic valence. Jameson deploys the pattern of parallel lines as if to emerge from the auratic and auteurial tradition ("consciousness, 'character,' and the anthropomorphic"), but in the process precedes not only face but earth as a figure: "Here, far more abstractly, we confront the same grid of parallel lines, systematically carved into the rock surface like a strange Mayan pattern. Again, what is confirmed by this pattern, and scored into the space of the scene, is the primacy of surface itself: the earth as a surface upon which the ant-like characters move and agitate, the sky as a surface from which intermittently a mobile and deadly technological mechanism dips; and here finally the upending of the surface into the vertical monument, prodigious bas-relief which has no inside and cannot be penetrated" (64).

The most mimetic of media appears undone by what precedes figuration, or the referential ideology of the state. The allegorical or allographic, here, which would bar anthropomorphism, might come at the cost of the trope of "modernism." It is as far as one can go, at least, coming out of the auteurial fold Jameson relinquishes as auratic, even if the parallel line pattern opens networks of signifying agencies that cannot be termed, simply, spatial or surface, since their networking at this point is teletechnic. One can hypothesize that Jameson's engagement of the "spatial" as the last avatar of ocularcentrism as such turns upon itself, the way Murchison's revolver does against the camera's own eye at the conclusion of *Spellbound*.

Cinema with its irreducible materiality ("microfilm") is disclosed as a *technē* in a battle against mimetic media's representational humanism ("pictures of people talking"). A *spectrographic* cinema would alter the very program out of which reference is produced and anteriority managed.

Kaleidoscopia

What has escaped notice is not only Hitchcock's micrological treatments of language, nor his precise treatises on mnemonics, nor how the *mark* suffuses proper names, and so on. What escapes criticism is how preserves of machines and teletechnics score these bands, operate as secret agencies within the works.[21]

As the Captain says in *The Trouble with Harry* with the middle-aged maid Miss Gravely in mind, "Preserves must be opened." In "The Task of the Translator," Benjamin hypothesizes a so-called pure language *(reine Sprache)*, a differential field of marks and phonemes void of content yet fractally in flux. It is like Hitchcock's Alpine Babel scenes, where all languages are spoken yet reduced to sound. Contents are voided, steps or feet rise to the position of the head, turning "the *symbolizing*"—that is, the transporting media of the vehicle, letter, mark, phoneme—"into the symbolized."[22] Exposed as mute and without mimetic referent, the image accelerates what Jameson called its *formal* properties—eviscerating personifications. In elaborating the logics of the spectral in *Specters of Marx,* Derrida stops at one point for a sort of totalizing résumé of its contamination and virulent conversions:

> Two conclusions, then: (1) the phenomenal form of the world itself is spectral; (2) the phenomenological ego (Me, You, and so forth) is a specter. The *phainesthai* itself (before its determination as phenomenon or phantasm, thus as phantom) is the very possibility of the specter, it brings, it gives death, it works at mourning.[23]

The spectral for Derrida is heir to the logics of the trace but assumes the powers of allomorphic incorporation and inverse embodiment. Locating a practice of cinema within this site has two immediate consequences that cannot be shed, disavowed, and bracketed. First, the Hitchcockian practice (which is not a unique style so much as the hyperformalization of the medium) inscribes the "world" (cipher character, viewer, tourist, "half-cast[e]" actor) as a type of animation, which might then be called "life" or which, at least, renders "death" a horizonless semaphoric plane of speeds and intensities. And second, it confronts in different modes its own status as virtual "event" or intervention within the histories it serves as regenerative station and transit point to. It does this by devolving to its epistemo-political premises—the marking system, say, that haunts *Spellbound* and perhaps gives that work its title. In the British "political" thrillers this will take the form of a world-altering intervention, a history-transforming plot, uprising, or assault on the hermeneutic state. And yet, unlike Derrida's reinscription of the spectral, this cinema seems to occur from a site *beyond mourning,* the perspective, say, of the birds. And if the logic of the image is familial or appears to be, it is involved in the backloops of a perpetual family plot, expropriating the familiar. Thus in *Family Plot* Hitchcock risks a Benjaminian trope for this *cinematics,* that of the faux séance, in which undecided legacies and futures are convoked.

It would appear that what we now call "Hitchcock," lodged at the center of the cinematic canon, represents a strange rejection of much that canon is thought to be held in place by. That is, "Hitchcock" would be demonstrably the opposite of ocularcentric: he does not believe in "light" and does not assume the existence of what is called the "eye," since that is itself a mnemonic effect. He irradiates signature effects, but these do not mark auteurial dominance. He is deauratic, nonanthropomorphic, rejecting cinema as "pictures of people talking." Pure cinema does not name a pure visuality, if such existed, but instead something to do with mnemonic or semaphoric networks. But there is more: linguistic impasses and teletechnic figures overrun this work, from postal relays to language lessons, Babelesque scenarios to letteration, machines and media (newsprint, wireless, telegrammatics). They form patterns and critiques, interface teletechnic variants and machines, appear in MacGuffins and inform plots. To understand whatever was going on in this spectral medium and its import as a prehistory of the "present," a reading of these elements and the political (and Benjaminian) motives that mobilized them is key.

There is more still: the fabled divide between text and image, visual arts and literary topoi is entirely vaporized, not even acknowledged, unless in continuing meditations on the fate of the book within mass media. For Hitchcock, the visual is a web of blinding fronts for other operations, much as Verloc's Bijou movie house hosts a saboteur's cell. Moreover, letters and faces are atomized by differential marking systems, of which the pattern of parallel lines may be an irreducible instance that renders even black and white coextensive, indistinguishable at times. If anything, the cinematic *trace* traverses picture and letteration, articulate phonemes and face. Hitchcock devotes entire films to tracking this agency; indeed, with slight adjustments, one could say as much of *Blackmail, Secret Agent,* even *Spellbound.*[24] Thus time and again, in the early "thrillers," what is delved into is cinematic mysteries and their deceptive fronts—the anesthetizing dentist's office, the "mysteries of the sevenfold ray" in the temple of sun worshippers, the "thirty-nine steps" and Mr. Memory's mission, the inner sanctum of the Bijou behind the movie screen, where plans are hatched. And *this* trace assumes different names yet appears to precede phenomenalization altogether. It will appear as a black sun, a dog, a prowling cat, a piece of chocolate, a desemanticized clang or crash; and it will have some sort of relation to the parallel bar pattern, although not by way of overt analogy. It will blackmail by virtue of its bond with sheer anteriority, and it will eviscerate. It will precede recorded or monumental history (as if such were always museums), and it is connected to wars; indeed, the trace does not so much take sides in these "wars," as it sometimes seems, as expose and almost wed these two sides to one another by positioning itself against the programs that lock them into a specular impasse.

Friedrich A. Kittler links the typewriter to cinema's advent and identifies this confluence as a site where something termed *inscription* occurs.[25] Hitchcock's signifying agents counter and resist the very teletechnic empire they derive from. The question of what "cinema" was—and if it is now dead, the spectral as such—remains a dark site in the core of contemporary epistemological programs and the horizonless "globalization" of the coming last man of the tele-image. If the analogic or mimetic proved to have been a state fiction, one in the service of a certain regime of memory and naming, perception and the aesthetic itself, marketing and consumption, "Hitchcock" performs as a prehistory of the afterlife of "cinema." The hieroglyph is but one logic of the cinematic, which would precede or contain among its variants all histories of (picture) writing. At the telltale heart of the image is an old mole, blind, mute, like a black sun. The citational structures that ruin the image as representation empower it otherwise, as Eduardo Cadava reminds us:

> The historical index of an image always claims the image for another time—for another historical moment (itself plural, and composed of several other moments) and for something other than linear, chronometric time (which would be, for Benjamin, "purely temporal" and "continuous"). This is also why Benjamin's understanding of the historical index *cannot be understood as either indexical or referential*: it can never index or refer to a single historical moment or event. . . . It is because the traces carried by the image include reference to the past, the present, and the future, and in such a way that none of these can be isolated from the other, that the image cannot present the traces it recalls—without at the same time exploding, or bursting, its capacity to (be) present.[26]

War is always also by and over an archive, its legacies and futures, its territorial ambitions.[27] Like the home state of England and the anarchival usurpers representing cinematic powers in Hitchcock's early thrillers, this epistemo-political war can take place in the background, on the stage of a public music hall, yet has as its turf the whole of monumental memory—say, the hallowed rooms of the British Museum, assembled world of an empire, down to its universal reading room *(Blackmail)*.[28] An image has access to all that has been marked and stored, inscribed or projected by that site, its memory, and its virtual futures. The archival is traversed by all its possible pasts and futures. It broods from and over an outside to the "Enlightenment" protocols it "knows too much" about.

Departing from familiar interpretive programs, McKenzie Wark deploys a Deleuzian figure of the "vector" to name a *dual* empire" of the mediatrix, a sort of contemporary mapping for the state(s) of the image. In Hitchcock, these global maps have allegorical coordinates: London, "Bandriki," Nice, San Francisco, Phoenix, New York. For Wark, a CNN report conveys and generates a global event simultaneously, summarizing and neutralizing the archiving archive. He thus recirculates what had been for Benjamin figures of disruption, *lightning blasts* and *thunderclaps,* as casual occurrences: "How are we to avoid being stupefied by these events (without narrative contexts)? . . . By being prepared, when the event happens, not to look at the lightning strike of images, nor to wait for the thunderclap of explanation."[29] The once romantic blitz is commodified as anesthetizing effect, rather than as strike and intervention—something one becomes nervously addicted to in its normalization of the catastrophic. To shift from the historicism and ocularcentric blind of the critical traditions surrounding "film" to a hypothetical spectrographics or allographics in Hitchcock's case implies reengaging the epistemo-political skirmishes he mounted at the advent of the cinematic era.

Such an attempt encounters a performative clash at the site where perceptual programs are installed or set—a clash whose outcomes, these works suggest, alter time and political horizons, gender definitions and terrestrial consumption (the way reference is constituted, anthropomorphisms legislated). What is interesting, simply as a proposition, is not only that these conflicts are staged in "formal" terms bearing on the definition of the eye and light, memory and the visual—everything implied by the reassuring phantom of the *aura*—but also that they are played out, in the exemplary case of Hitchcock, through micrological and micrographic agents. Yet it seems in retrospect obvious that the cinematic, at its advent, arrives as a devastating exposure of the eye's prosthetic fiction, a critique implied in its totality from, say, the opening shot of the screaming face of the blonde victim in *The Lodger.*

I. Police, Criminals, and the Mediatric State

1. The Avenging Fog of Media: The Lodger as Host

[The number 3] can even be seen as the first "real" number, and the first to produce a geometrical figure: since three points enclose the triangle, it is the first plane figure that can be perceived by our senses.
> —Anne-Marie Schimmel, *The Mystery of Numbers*

"Practice the triangle!"
> —Philip Martin, blind man, *Saboteur*

Nietzsche's notion of *inscription* . . . has validity only within the framework of the history of the typewriter. It designates the turning point at which communications technologies can no longer be related back to humans. Instead, the former have formed the latter.
> —Friedrich A. Kittler, *Gramophone, Film, Typewriter*

The Lodger might be approached, today, as a peculiar and fateful incision—not only opening the signature of "Hitchcock" to the immense line of credit it will assume (one by no means depleted), and not only establishing this through the insertion of the first two cameos that, in a sense, will govern, as if between them, all others. We know its too simple premise: the lodger in pursuit of the unknown strangler, whom he is taken for, who he might *be* from the point of view of the family of the house in which he is a guest, moved to avenge himself against that Avenger—tracking, pursuing in a double chase, setting aside for the moment the ancillary players, the sexually arrested detective, the almost incestuous beloved (Daisy), with the faux triangle between them, the personified house itself with rooms and clocks made up like faces. It would not take much to focus more acutely on what seems interwoven here. One has only to remark upon the Hughes brothers' recent adaptation of the Alan Moore graphic novel, *From Hell,* which cannot stop citing *The Lodger* as the opening of the cinematic era and which links it, in no uncertain terms, to the dawn of techno-genocides and world wars to come. That work expends itself on this insight by returning to the trope of Jack the Ripper that mobilizes cinema's advent in *The Lodger,* whose extended title will have to be unpacked: *A Story of the London Fog.* Linking the surgically dismembering murders of the Ripper to the epistemological cuts and implied dehumanization of the cinematic—not to mention the dawn of telemarketing and the link between photography and techno-weaponry—*From Hell* is canny enough to package the whole in a royalist intrigue and suppression, in the conspiracies of the CEO class, erasing finally Johnny Depp's inspector, whose cinematic opium trances move across pasts and futures. The fatality of the urtext of which the latter is a minor reading is, nonetheless, marked.

But the "event" of *The Lodger* resonates in two other manners I will attempt to isolate. The first is the installation of the "cameo" logic—and its recurrence, its fatal re-marking, as if no "first" could occur outside of

Figure 4. Inaugural cameo in *The Lodger*: news editor in glass booth, back to us, before a succession of telemachines (print, wireless) disseminating the report of the Avenger appears.

a reversible repetition. The second involves the subtitle quoted earlier—that it is a story of something called "fog." By returning to what may be at stake in each of these two incisions, I hope to reconnect them, not to an aesthetic history of cinema, but to a teletechnic eruption whose aftermath has yet to be sorted. One might say that with the submission of the Avenger's *triangle* calling card, the pyramidal signature left at the site of each murder—such as the mute scream of the first (if nonetheless repeat) blonde victim, face almost congealed, teeth exposed—Hitchcock in effect announces the techno-genocides of the twentieth century and beyond that will follow in the wake of this archival rupture.

What is called the Avenger is never seen face-to-face: he comes out of and returns to the fog that is said to be the subject of the story, a figure of the chiaroscuro densities of refracted light and suspended particles identified with the cinematic—something more sophisticated, by far, than a link between the camera "gaze" and murder (which would be no different from any representational violation or pretense). Why does it appear then, already, like, as, in the name of, an Avenger? What does the cinematic, which cites all implicitly, seek to avenge, and this as if in the name of sight, in servicing sight—like the birds whose point of attack is the eyes? "Hitchcock," then, as one locus where various futures, choices, programs would have been—perhaps remain—in suspension, warred over. And what, then, of *The Lodger,* a mere tale of the stalking of a stalker, of an alien lodger in the dwelling as such, already numbered "13," even with its inaugural fold back upon itself and dissimulation in introduction of the first *two* cameos, the supposedly stabilizing signature? Why, right here, in this short silence one pulls out of the archive, does whatever "Hitchcock" will signify open an immense line of credit, a virtual ledger for the entire production to come?

The countersignature of "Hitchcock": The installation of "Hitchcock" in this work—and the serial productions to follow—requires, it seems, two appearances in order to secure the pretense of a "1," or at least a 1 that operates, as the inauguration of this authorship, as a sort of ground zero, the beginning of a series ($N + 1, + 1, + 1 \ldots$ down to *Family Plot*). Is it of any import that the second cameo, which is often mistaken for the "first," involves Hitchcock standing above the barred fence, the spiked series of parallel lines, pummeling the "lodger," who hangs there in handcuffs? But here is the greater, if befogged, incision: that the one that appears first, hardly noticeable, a sort of 0 minus 1, occurs in front of a giant media factory, in a glass booth as news editor amid typographic machines and crushing gears, to the relay of mass media papers and trucks and wireless relays. That is the installation at the core of a telemedial empire.

A Story of the London Fog: What is called the Avenger is deferred to the cinematic fog, suspended water particles refracting shadow and light—the atomization of the image into such particles, suspended in midair, disarticulation of what they pretend to present by virtue of a micrological premise. But above all, something in the house is altered by this guest, who turns into the host of the host. Even the term lodger summons the logos and, perhaps, a certain accounting, like a *ledger* of economic expenses and structural repairs.

Not a moment in the history of cinema, then, more or less inescapable, but a disturbance of and within its logic, of and within what might once have been called logos as a name for the teletechnic archive—and certainly, from "today," at the dawn

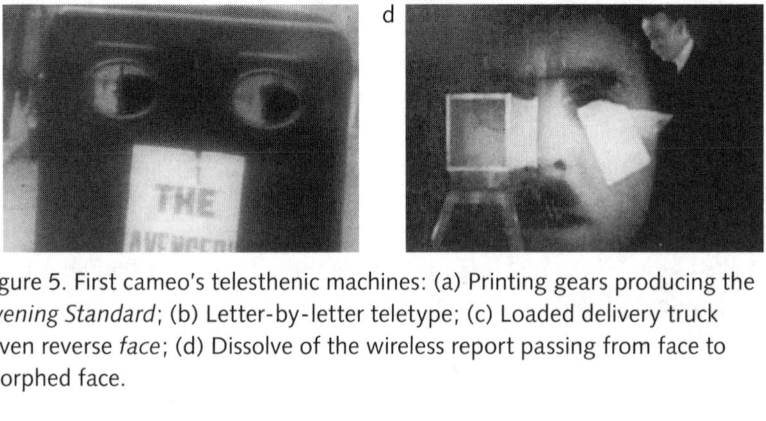

Figure 5. First cameo's telesthenic machines: (a) Printing gears producing the *Evening Standard*; (b) Letter-by-letter teletype; (c) Loaded delivery truck given reverse *face*; (d) Dissolve of the wireless report passing from face to morphed face.

of the globalization of the phototelic image as such; as if all *technēs* of perception and reproduction gathered in the spongelike delta of the cinematic advent. Why does it appear then, already, like, as, in the name of, an *Avenger*? What does the "cinematic" avenge, in telling its story (of "the London fog")? Why does the archival machine used to secure the ocularcentric programs (mimesis, indexing, identification) appear in and as a prosthetic machine that in practice suspends precisely that?

The camera's position in capturing its blonde victim's scream is out of the fog—the atomized elements of markers and preproduction, refracted "light" and suspended particles that arrive with, or as, a certain *shock* (Benjamin). One must take seriously the subtitle of the work—which tells us that *The Lodger* is a "story" about "London fog," that *fog* explains *lodging*, or the insertion of cinema into the economimesis of the teletechnic era. Yet one can also not narrate *fog*, not give it a *story;* it is prefigural, divides and enshrouds, gives way to other shadows and specters, revokes the *face* it coalesces or offers to us: here, the scream, albeit silent, of the blonde. This shot, certainly, stands for every human face ever captured or conjured cinematically—and both the shriek and its muteness are perpetual. *The Lodger* marks a defacement. Any attempt to analyze the advent of Hitchcock's signature—or that of the cinematic as a logic—must return to this fog, even as it seems perpetually to elude form, figuration. I will do so by addressing, no doubt amorphously, what the suspended particles and shadow logics of the *cameo's* appearance imply.

No More Peroxide for Yours Truly

By exposing what lodges "in" yet evacuates this sham interior, turning a dwelling into a faux refuge (like the "family," or sight), what is lodged in its eye or ocularcentric home, *The Lodger* installs with the first "Hitchcock" film another archival logic—an alterity in and of that house, and the many to come (the Newtons' residence, Green Manors, the Brenners' house at Bodega Bay, and so on). Such an event can only occur by an irreversible incision: like the map of the Avenger's strikes that the lodger—who is pursuing him, avenging himself on the Avenger it seems, even if he were to be "him"—keeps, noting that everything moves in *one* "direction." The work as performative event and incision thus opens a signature event that will perhaps be "Hitchcock" by the viral release of irreversible decisions and markers. That ledger, or lodger, is remarkably explicit, starting with Hitchcock's largely overlooked *first* cameo: it will involve, surface within, complicate, all teletechnic media.

Precisely because the ledger is so explicit it will in a sense open an account in the realm of visibility, in the prostheses of face and of geometrics (triangles, circles)—recalling that the triangle is, from the point of view of the eye, the first visible plane, much as the "3" is held by some to be the first number, whatever "firsts," like *The Lodger,* are, and whatever ghosts or predecessors they erase or incorporate to appear as such (the never completed and lost film, *Number Thirteen,* the disowned *Pleasure Garden*: Hitchcock will insist that *The Lodger* is the first "Hitchcock" work).[1] It is a strange territory of light-induced wraiths preinhabited by its own "future," its future production and its future reception, expanding to the catastrophic futures Johnny Depp's entranced inspector will foresee (for instance, the Holocaust) as a conspiracy of an imperial or royalist class, even where the latter is explicitly blinded or blinding, when canonized, to the permutations of reputations, interpretation and career: Hitchcock as popular artist, as not-serious craftsman, as auteur, as formalist, then as master theorist, and so on.

All of this is dependent on a certain *blind,* an occlusion of what places Hitchcock, in his very first cameo, back more or less turned to us, overseeing giant machines printing newspapers and generating mass media—not (only) cinematic production, not as a metaphor or wink, but of a newspaper, with giant gears and the machinal, mnemonic site of imprinting exposed, with letters stamping down, before face can be affirmed in the light. And it will stay that way, always, with this cameo logic working from within and behind that scene, even down to the letters and imprints, before light itself, and worse, cutting in virtual space, across already and yet unwritten films or between them. (Certainly the "first" murder of a prosthetic blonde, the mute screaming face, is not the "first" in fact, but a serial repetition, at the very least a third.) Here, on the ledger, in *The Lodger,* appears a treatise on the econometrics of other lodgings and logics, chases and serial murder. For somewhere in this event would also loom everything perhaps that will unfold not only in the destinies and deaths of cinema, of mechanical reproduction and the aura, in the televisual, the death of the book, the era of techno-genocides and globalization in which life systems would be precipitously made extinct and democracies overtake and then recede, falling to their own mediatric trances. And it will all be here, virtually all of it, already: the release of a system of marks, of marred names (Daisy), of the inversions of model and copy, of the bar system or signature, of the typographic machine, of the Egypticist triads and triangles, which is also to say, number. Time would, with a cut, buckle.

If it is all too much, this explosion and cancellation that will reach decades ahead and permeate all of "Hitchcock" (and beyond), one can be excused for restricting one's inquiry to a certain puzzle: what has this nonbirth of the cinematic to do, so very massively, with triangles after all—the calling card of "the Avenger," with a prominent △ that mimes and evacuates the alpha, as if some signature of the camera, the number "13" on the Buntings' front door? When the blind man in *Saboteur* urges the handcuffed Barry Kane to go with his niece (a model stepped out of advertisement placards), he recalls their exchange about musical instruments and reminds him to "practice the triangle." The suspecting Rupert, in *Rope,* insinuates, "It's odd the way one can pyramid simple facts into wild fantasies." In *Rebecca,* Olivier observes in his home movie, "Oh look, there's the one where I left the camera on the tripod, remember?"—effectively linking, in the film within a film, seeing, cameras, the triangle, and the mnemonic ability to recognize ("Oh look") what would have been already inscribed or not. What, in Hitchcock, does that mean, except to recall a counterlogic that can disrupt the historial program the young Kane finds himself locked within, hunted down by, to the point where the corporate elite of his nation, like Tobin, represent the fifth column of a foreign power, those controlling justice and truth, the police and the media. It is the vaporized fog that coalesces to avenge, like a justice, in the name of a specter whose foreknowledge commands not to be forgotten or in the name of spectralization *tout court.*

If there is, as Christopher Morris alleges, a "permanent misidentification of the Avenger,"[2] is it because what is named precedes the affirmation of face (the Avenger's is swathed at best), or because something anterior to the present's imaginary frame (or lodging) is prehistorially avenging (like Hitchcock's "birds"), or because the link between the triangle and technicity itself demands a certain justice? With the triangle calling card of the Avenger, in which Hitchcock inscribes the self-canceling advent of "cinema," the director introduces to the historial slumber of the already exhausted post–Great War culture not only its premier betrayer and entertainment mode, not only the medium that will infiltrate and shape its sensoria, but all the techno-genocides and terrestrial eviscerations to come. The Avenger will avenge on behalf of no cause but the totality of what makes the scriptive program of the state possible, and in the name of an in-lodging justice, nonanthropomorphic, without aura. The serial killing of blondes is the signature of metaphysics, eviscerating woman and reflected light ("golden curls").

The acceleration of this seriality would derail and exceed it by its own means and in the name of what is not anthropomorphized: not the "animal," as such, but a technicity that traverses and mobilizes animation, mnemonic systems, a thoroughly denatured "natural history."

Figure 6. The Avenger's calling card. Hitch-cock announces the "cinematic" as triadic and nonhuman ("the fog").

So Hitchcock is found in the editing room, interfering, cutting history, intervening across the public space of print, of evening standards and mnemonic programs of "man." Moreover, it produces and disperses *him*, "Hitchcock," as body, cameo, so that this signature will also serve as host, taken over and rewritten by what lodges in its lodging—which may be why, in a sense, the first cameo solicits at the same moment as it cancels any possible auteurial approach. The relay that assimilates cutting pieces of film to editing newsprint and typing letters in advance of any sentence emerges in the public realm. What begins as reportage, recording as if in documentary's claim to facts, is transformed according to a set of technological relays preceding face. One could excavate a cryptographics here, except that it would not convey "secrets"—beyond the transformative import of its own technicity. What connects it—that is, the advent of the cameo logic or this cinema—to revenge, avenging, or the enigma of the triangle as calling card, the Avenger's signature? What turns on (and against) revenge in the figure of the Avenger, avenging a lapse or repetition that bars the emergence of face? What is the lodge (numbered "13")? What does it mean to lodge, and what, if anything, does the term have to do with ledgers or the logos and number?

What occurs, then, if one approaches *The Lodger: A Story of the London Fog* not as a narrative accomplishment but as an effaced incision? It seems to tell a story, to be sure, but its subject is no longer the titular being, the person lodging within the house, the guest, but rather the "fog" itself—the spectral matter from which the killer, never seen, face wrapped, emerges to strike. The *Avenger* names the chiaroscuro mist, particles of water suspended in air against which light and shadow refract and play: as if it would be a story "of" those particles, atomized material diffusions. It avenges against what it also gives rise to, literally projects. If so, it is the long detour that follows the opening on reportage and media that explains or fulfills this subtitle's promise: the subject would be explicitly named as that atomization and its premise, what precedes face and image and the production of light or animation. And one can, perhaps, derive an entire "secret" logic from this interruption of a beginning that, as an open-mouthed strangling, is itself an interruption par excellence, indeed, a critique not only of all cinema to come but, certainly, of the most public readings of the "cameo" appearances (or signature systems). The work, in its invocation and suspension of this "story," sabotages in advance every attempt to locate and narrate *The Lodger* within a history, say, the history of film, or British Film ("*London* Fog"), and so on.

What emerges is a kind of manifesto that cannot "manifest" itself, that can only perform as its own permanent MacGuffin, inhabited by an alien term irreducible to any concept of the apparatus. *The Lodger,* rather, becomes something of an ur-hieroglyphic band on which Hitchcock's inscriptions occur or assemble themselves—not for the "first" time, but rather as if already at the end of a seriality that the opening shot of the open-mouthed, mute, screaming blonde reiterates: the triangle, the sunburst, "murder," the $N + 1$ or the celluloid band or the serial enumeration from an effaced null or zero point, the double chase, the personified "house" (with its alien guest taking over), the inducted model, the Mar- signature (here, as "Daisy"), the blackmailing desexed policeman lover, the explosion of mediatized machines and typography, and so on.

Thus when Hitchcock gives a chorus girl the line, "No more peroxide for yours truly," he not only penetrates the faux anxiety of the prey with a disabling joke, he indicates that the figure that is stalked is also prosthetic—not (only) woman, not (only) the blonde, but "To-Night— Golden Curls—To-Night," as the neon sign *flashing* in the background emphasizes, the interface between the specter of light and a cut, a hyphen, "night."[3] She is, already, metaphysics as cabaret. The Avenger's calling card announces the era of the cinematic—a logic of the triad unable to return to the "1," or zero, quite, which in essence announces a century of phototechnicities, techno-genocides to come, and "globalization."[4] Yet to say "yours truly" is to leave one's signature, to sign or be able to assume the role of signatory anonymously: as if a certain cameo were to say this otherwise—"no more peroxide"—and not mean no more prosthetics, but no more evisceration of the blonde as a prosthesis of the visible, of metaphysics, seeking to sustain and maintain itself, with the ocularcentric machines of consumption, through this seriality, this double prosthesis of the criminal norm.

About Faces

We might ask another series of questions instead, questions that inquire how *The Lodger: A Story of the London Fog* rewrites the very machinery and politics of mimesis.[5] Such might include: What is the import of the "second" cameo toward the end (above the fence, striking the hanging, cuffed lodger)? Why is "face" so explicitly cited—yet as a spectral shading of holes and dental rows in midshriek at first barred from emergence? What possible logic of *ressentiment* haunts the Avenger, or his seriality, that would, simultaneously, be perhaps (or not) overcome by this logic of the serial "act"? Where is a *war over inscription* installed in the spectral apparatus of Hitchcock's signature and cinema? *The Lodger* appropriates the system of echoes that its title releases by providing what in effect seems a treatise on the (Western) logos—or a certain legibility as such—and this through the effects of a cinemallographic "machine." Hitchcock executes here, in serial fashion, a logos in which mimesis is dismissed by its own giant machines, memory disinscribed, life–death reversed as dyadic effect, the phantom of "frame" enfolded, the ancient hermeneutic chase's circularity doubled or short-circuited in advance. Remarkable machine.

What does this reference to imprinting and media as relay authorize? Why does an anauteurism haunt the house of the "auteur"?

The sequence in *The Lodger* on media is out of place, *atopos*. The installation of a signature system and an event of sorts that opens a new archival scene (twentieth-century cinema, "Hitchcock," the era of teletechnics, mass media, and so on), it will, virtually, attend and be implied in every scene or project to bear that signature—or the chain of histories it contaminates. It occurs immediately after the miming by the barmaid, sole apparent witness, of a man with his face *covered*.[6] This detour seems in duration and detail to serve no narrative purpose whatsoever except to delay all narration—any "story" of the London fog, unless it, too, were that. It is all about *reportage*, again: a newsman phones in the crime and we painstakingly follow the movement of the report through different mass media—specifically, over machines (a)materially producing the medium itself: first newspapers and then radio broadcasting. It presumes teletechnics and surveys the state of a new archival order: the relay runs from the phoning in of the murder from the bar to the typesetting machine (which is to say to a site of imprinting or inscription), to the huge wheels of the printing presses, to the back of the truck carrying the stacked *Evening Standard* papers, in which windows are made to appear like eyes in a face. And finally, the trajectory is relayed both to and through aerial broadcast where we are shown a series of faces listening that are virtually *morphed,* one into the other, anonymously, ending with an opened-mouth girl not unreminiscent of the film's opening murder victim's "silent scream." As such, the sequence, during which Hitchcock's "first" cameo occurs, reverts to the failed opening scream. During it there will occur a certain fateful self-inscription, behind a glass partition, back to us, in the editor's room, as if *before* the entire network and production of a telecommunications that precedes *face,* utterly (a)material, even machinal. It folds back into that "opening" like a parenthesis—a loop, inexplicable except to open a circuit parallel to and outside the set, governed by the production of imprints and inscriptions.

Two cameos, then, marked by a repetition, as if by a ghost third between them that would persist: and the first, seldom remarked and all but erased by the second, has Hitchcock at the controls, partitioned by glass, of a huge media production that traverses from the printed character to the face—or almost, since the latter cannot quite be established and even slips back to the opening shot: the face, covered in the Avenger's case, traverses many faces, evened out, standardized, interpassing. Much as the series requires some illumination, so the *transitional* figure of the truck carrying the stacks of dead print draws particular attention.[7]

Why a face on a truck, a machine of movement, and particularly one that carries stacked news? The film is about face in a certain sense, the ability of the face to appear, to phenomenalize on the screen, its importing of death, its connection to a machine producing print. How are we to read the structure, then, of *avenging,* and the triangle calling card reproduced in the letters *A* and *V,* like a meditation on the *A* of Alfred, become, inversely, the two bars of the *V,* the simultaneous dispossession of two directions, *A* and *V,* up and down—like the later infamous "vertigo" shot, of "movement" or cinemation, of letter? What is the connection to *letters* in general, to geometrics, as far as the emergence of face or the photographemic subject is concerned—an emergence that must be thought within the structure of historial times, the histories of teletechnics, face, "time" itself?[8] Moreover, and more cautiously, what has this avenging to do with the cinematic advent, which occurs only at the expense of the human, the anthropomorphic, prosthetic blondes, "golden curls," right down to and beyond the avenging attacks decades later in what will be called the "bird war"? What is linked here to justice and what sort of justice misses, with each murder, fails to terminate itself, or turns against the totality it can only, inversely, reproduce? To summarize:

- We are already beginning not with a "first" but within a series as registered by the name *Avenger,* which implies a reaction, a response of or to revenge, an act of setting right (like a ledger in which accounts, balances, would be maintained).
- We mistakenly fill in a cause that is missing for revenge (broken heart, wound from a blonde, "metaphysics" itself) even as the Avenger presents a structure of repetition and reaction to an absented cause.
- If "I," the Avenger, could achieve revenge, finally, ending the seriality rather than beginning it, it would right the debt and end the very cycle it instead accelerates: that would have at some point been the recollected promise, unless what would be overcome were the structure of *ressentiment* inscribed in representational or reactive "consciousness" as an effect.

How can cinematic representation intercede in the site of its own emergence? Hitchcock interrupts the interruption of the opening murder that would be his narrative theme. After that event occurs, Hitchcock is diverted back to the long hiatus on and account of the printing press and mass communications. He remarks on the nonexistence of "face" to Truffaut:

> We must bear in mind that, fundamentally, there's no such thing as color; in fact, there's no such thing as face, because *until the light hits it,* it is nonexistent. After all, one of the first things I learned in the School of Art was that there is no such thing as a line; there's only the light and the shade. On my first day in school I did a drawing; it was quite a good drawing, but because I was drawing with lines, it was totally incorrect and the error was immediately pointed out to me.[9]

Hence the newspaper's name, the *Evening Standard,* and the merging or morphing of faces in the subsequent scene of listening to the aerial wire reports, a morphing from one to another into a general dismantling of the ghostly human face into substitutable holes and disinhabited mask-maps, stripped of pretended individuation, standardized, evened out. The dead print of the truck, carrying newspapers, is also to be grasped as the inside of a head behind the face we see on its back—or, perhaps, on its backside explicitly, eyes perched to simulate a machinal gaze occupied by print, moving forward in time yet staring at the past.[10] As if this print, produced out of machines, an aftereffect, was also taxidermic stuffing. But if the priority of imprinted death folds back like a gloss on the opening strangled blonde's face, that too must be thought in relation to the Avenger. The structure recurs throughout Hitchcock, as, again, with the allo-anthropomorphic birds whose attack on all of "humanity" is or seems without cause, or else totalized.[11] Thus Hitchcock needs two cameos to effect this incision or hold it open or, ledgerlike, assert a repetition that irrevocably spaces cinematic or media history. Two cameos, that of archival editing and, later, that of suspension by or above a series of slashes or bars, above and even striking the handcuffed lodger, as if handless, held by two chained spools. Of course, Hitchcock pretends it was an accident, that he needed extras, and so on, but he requires an initial repetition: the first, all but erased by the second, is at the controls, partitioned, of a huge media empire.

In "The Work of Art in the Age of Mechanical Reproduction," Benjamin situates the "shock" of cinema's advent with a new epoch of perceptual identity, a cut or caesura he analyzes with double-sided ambivalence—toward an "aura" whose loss is both mourned and resented. Something emerges in Benjamin's reflection on the programming of the sensorium that is negatively analyzed, it seems, in *The Lodger*—analyzed and transformed into a destroying and transvaluative vehicle. The double logics of the Avenger intervenes in this noncausal and asequential history: the (a)material nature of a graphematics that precedes phenomenalization closes out both an ocularcentric premise and, with it, personification, "light," aura.[12] Benjamin discounts the hopes of early film theorists:

> Abel Gance, for instance, compares the film with hieroglyphics: "Here, by a remarkable regression, we have come back to the level of expression of the Egyptians. . . . Pictorial language has not yet matured because our eyes have not yet adjusted to it. There is as yet insufficient respect for, insufficient cult of, what it expresses." Or, in the words of Séverin-Mars: "What art has been granted a dream more poetical and more real at the same time!" (227)

Hitchcock dismantles, while citing, the hieroglyphic dream in the Egyptian motif of the pyramidal triangle. The Egyptians pretend to worship the sun, are hierophantic, already a lapse from cinema. The obliteration of aura was never of some lost original, as it has seemed to some, but rather of what Benjamin tells us in the Baudelaire essay—personification, anthropomorphism. Yet film studies allied itself with everything that would restore aura so defined (while, of course, citing Benjamin): narrative, character, identification, auteurism, "gaze," historicization, and so on. The "shock effect" induced by cinema and the photographic image implies "profound changes in apperception" (240). The Avenger avenges against this relapse in advance, perpetually, even that of the Egyptian—preceded in *Blackmail* by the chase through the universal reading room. In the Avenger Hitchcock tracks a Möbius-like band: the murder of blondes epitomizes the doomed reflex and violence of metaphysics; the murder of prosthetic blondes accelerates and terminates, cites and surpasses, such. It stands both for murderous repetition *and* for its surpassing or termination.

Anthro-Typography

Before questioning why triadic logics proliferate and appear on the Avenger's calling card (that of a serial killer "who" is prehistorial and assumes an absent cause to be avenged), one might ask why the triangle or pyramid is a calling card or, virtually, signature.

Why such an emphasis on "3," the first *visible* number to occupy geometric space, perhaps the "first" number in a work that appears obsessed with numeration—as if the rapid succession of frames through a machine triggered the inescapability of number and serial deformation, much as Hitchcock says this will inevitably lead to the hermeneutics of the chase? The triangle, like the number 3 or 13, virally circulates throughout Hitchcock.[13] One is addressing an address, after all (the "13" of the Buntings' residence), and what is housed there, even if that is the structure of housing. As suggested in the epigraph, 3 would be the first token of the visible itself ("the first plane figure that can be perceived"), a geometric, spatialized, even in the amorphous pointillism of fog. Hitchcock seems arrested by where the 3, the 13, partakes of aporetic logics: a canceled origin, it engenders serial murder. Associated with muting (strangling), it covers a missing site: the "1" will not exist as a given. It will, like the zero, operate as a trope, fossilized by citation into a keystone of logic or identity. In a performative fashion, Hitchcock can be said to engage and perpetually reinvent the zero, a wild factor in the history of numbering, a ghost factor assuming different roles until used to solidify the map of digitalization—the missing finger of the Professor in *The 39 Steps.*

Hitchcock is in dialogue with this faulted tradition. In a superb review or autobiography of "the trickster zero," Robert Kaplan's *The Nothing That Is: A Natural History of Zero,* zero is secured by John Napier's revision of the algebraic legacy of the Arab mathematicians, "turning Al-Khowärizimi's equation into $x^2 + 10x - 39 = 0$."[14] Here, x is 3, with 13 and 39 in the mix. *Hitchcock numbers,* performing and marking a logic of canceled origination. Thus Kaplan translates Napier's revision as "$x^2 + 10x - 39$ is the same as $(x - 3)$ $(x + 13)$. But if $(x - 3)$ $(x + 13) = 0$, then one of those two factors must be zero: so either $x - 3 = 0$ or $x + 13 = 0$, and this tells you at once that $x = 3$ or $x = -13$." For Hitchcock the "1" is a trope of the *zeroid,* and the zero a MacGuffin of and within an always phantom logos—the triage of the triad, the MacGuffinesque core of numbering itself.

The triad is a specter, it anchors spectrality. It is hyperbolic. The 1 is itself retroprojected by the 3 to cover a nonexistent site—a trope of zero. Outside of any pair of speaking agents, like the atopy of a camera lens, it gives permission to and evacuates the constituted and citational pair. This number (if it is a number) will run amok across this cinematic band in the production to come, inscribing itself, like an autograph, at every opportunity, recalling another logic than that of the pretended scene—as, say, in letteral analogs, such as that opening the word *cameo* or *camera,* c (third letter) and *a* (first), whatever the order. The triad is explosive, hyperbolic, generating and barring seriality. Such cancellation of source as origin, as light, as visibility as such, indeed, as the "1" it also spawns, seems premised by Hitchcock's birthdate—August 13. Clearly, this is an arcane pathway, mixing number and chance, but one cannot avoid its massive presence across this writing. (Indeed, even the young Hitchcock's first uncompleted and now lost 1921 silent movie was to have been called *Number Thirteen,* a ghost first: thus, anyway, it appears on the U.S. one-dollar bill, circulated, capitalized, with the Masonic eye on top.) The pyramid—given in place of the calling card, the signature—announces a kind of metrics, even geometrics, in contact with the monogram A(H), paralleling the bar series itself, Hitchcock's prefigural performance of the "visual" as a phenomenalized effect.[15] At the empty and asolar core that the corona inversely names appears a triangular sabotage and eclipse. This is, in fact, the emblem of the Tabernacle of the Sun in the first *Man Who Knew Too Much.* Why?

For Hitchcock, this number that is not a number, a first that is a third yet connotes the placeholder of a zero, is associated with the advent of cinema—and its avenging force against the violence of the "1." If the number 3 or 13, the combination 1 and 3, denotes the site of a failed birthing of sorts, it is also, immediately and before itself, a death—like the dead baby we see in the opening scene of *Lifeboat*. We would be misled by reading it with reference to a "love triangle" or any "mimetic desire" machine that attaches to it.[16]

One genealogy of numbers has 3 preceding the invention of 1, which would have been a retroprojection from the 3, giving rise to the 2 in turn (1, in this system, is a trope for an absent unit, like the zero). A related model involves how the trope of the speaker emerges, or fails to, in the utterance itself—which may be of relevance to a work that posits the gifting of face by "light" as a strangulation. It is that which Mikhail Bakhtin or Valentin Voloshinov in "Discourse in Life and Discourse in Art" presents of speech, of so-called dialogue itself, which rather than being a model of two persons talking (as it is routinely read), turns out to be triangular, to demand three spectral agents as a predicate of the utterance's "social" space.[17] Yet to say "social," or to associate that with the *triadic,* is also to say public, exterior, archival, without retreat or private reserve. That is, the visual marking systems: and here that logic, of a certain number 3, precedes and suspends, critiques and unbinds the affiliation of any logos with the "1," the "zero," even the "2" (as in "dialogue"). The three positions posited are sometimes called speaker, listener, and hero, or variant threesomes, in the MacGuffinesque (because self-performing) template that Voloshinov maps. It is one in which, however, the addressed "hero" is not a person but an *inanimate* addressee that must be apostrophized, personified, given a voice (or face), and in which a second person, or listener, is actually reduced to being a mere "witness." The speaker, nominal first person or zero function, emerges not from dialogue but from apostrophe, and is brought into a spiraling system at the point of personification. He or it requires personification like the "hero," and becomes a third person in the process—outside his own utterance, represented as "I," and hence dead on arrival (whatever dead would mean in opposition to a life it, like celluloid, animates).

In such a constellation, not dialogic but trialogic, a speaker emerges within a "social" scenario, supposedly, yet it is one in which the personification of the inanimate attends his simultaneous conversion into a past-tensed, posited, third person. "I" is dead on arrival, a specter or cipher. The emergence of the "I" in the utterance comes at the expense of her subjective presence, as utterance occurs as the aftereffect of a self-canceling operation—one in which "death" precedes the appearance of "life" (in consciousness, as on the screen). Suddenly, the topos of the serial strangler is utterance itself and what bars all speech in the emergence of it—what secures the dominance of silent film as a spectral model and makes the addition of speech in "talkies" absolutely irrelevant, since all signifying agencies, in effect, precede and generate an excess of the visual or the aural, which has nothing to do with semantic content. The serial strangler is the hyperbolic advent of a signifying topos that cinema renders hyperbolic and absorptive at once, upon its murderous arrival. The strangler is a figure one never sees (perhaps) or who as the lodger is already a fallen angel and ghost type, frozen from the degendered site from which he returns. He entails an active expropriation of the *technicity* of the "I" taking face (which the camera cannot secure as other than a play of shadow), his death as the initial price of articulation—a site where repetition and memory pass into a future anterior perpetually suspended. Moreover, Voloshinov's model calls this "life," which is another way of positioning it as an effect of animation, mnemonics, "art," the dead, cinematics. That Hitchcock associates this triadic structure with a certain hyperbolics is reflected in phrases like the "revolutionary *uplift*" Midge attributes to her seamlessly engineered brassiere in *Vertigo*, or the recurrent phrase to "pick up," in which a rhyme with *picture* is associated with the Greek *pi* or the Pythagorean formula that bears a numerical anagram, so to speak, for the 13 signature itself—3.14.

Yet it is here, precisely, that one might say a logics of the Avenger would intervene. The triangle figure can now be read as an emblem for the (barred) emergence as dead site of the subject effect in performative language—a site that silent film both explores, as a sheer and muting writing, and mediates. As with the supposed scenario of speech cited above, there is no "speaking" here, and not only because it is silent film (title cards exist). Rather, it is because, like an utterance, this image is so saturated with trace chains and citational catastrophes, including, in this case, the opening of a new teletechnic archive. No wonder the blonde screams, teeth visible, predatory remnants of an animality preceding the overt spectralization of the human. For if a triangular scenario is usually invoked when there is a muting or blackmailing afoot in Hitchcock (or trial, as in the triad gathering at the deemster's court in *The Manxman*), it is also present as the anatomy of laughter, of the hyperbolic rupture of identity by a triadic social scenario (as Freud analyzes *Witz*, or in the jester's pointing and "laughing" portrait in *Blackmail*).[18] Suddenly, the triangle marks the (a)material site of an outside, an (a)material trace disrupting all interiority, the fable of the subject as such. The triadic signature is the emblem of prosopopoeia itself or the giving of face; it is tied to the cameo signatures of "A. H." ("ah" being, already, the expression of apostrophe, of autoimpersonation). It re-marks its own virtuality. The avenging by and against a system of repetition from which "consciousness" is always an effect of reaction, of *ressentiment* turned on this anteriority itself; this Nietzschean circuitry tied to the disruption of memory ruptures any economy of identification, auteurism, and oculist metaphorics—a defacing in reverse, as in the morphing passage following the aerial broadcast of the news of "murder." If the fog, however, can be said to be avenging, it is as spectral particles and photons, marking patterns and citational shapes it assumes before configuring as picture, as face, as the open-mouthed "golden curls" of light. It precedes personification and shatters the analogic pretense into myriad points, indeed, the virtual pointillism of the digital, pure animation without life, as life, as the visible figures it interrupts, scatters, annihilates, posits.

The triad suspends, like the London fog from which the Avenger emerges to strike. The spectrology that is or haunts Hitchcock's signature, then, accords with a barred emergence: of the face, the "I," inscription, murder, apostrophe.[19] One can speak of Hitchcock's "cinema" as opening up and miming the machinery out of which reference is (historically) generated—that which, in turn, forms an object *of* revenge. It is this motif of revenge, however, that determines Hitchcock's gambled transformation of *ressentiment* as the very model of metaphysical "consciousness" and its effacements (a Nietzschean topos). Yet if revenge is a reaction to a specific trauma, avenging by contrast seems to name a more general process of justice. This avenging of revenge would displace *ressentiment* as the *technē* of a blind ocularcentric "consciousness" that stores its facts in historicist or mimetic grids, shifting these to a proactive mimesis without model and copy.

We return to the absent centrality of the Avenger, of his triangle motif and the structure of his serial violations, stranglings, as would-be *interventions*. In a sense, every last murder (such as the one opening the film, of the open-mouthed blonde) extends the promise of a summary, an annulment, yet triggers, instead, excess, sheer repetition, further doubling. Such a trajectory must be stopped, arrested. If not by Detective Joe, then by or as the lodger. A spectral model resides at this cinematic address, a house inhabited by the logics of the "13," which both epitomizes metaphysics and annuls its compulsory reinscription, as though opposing the structure of mnemonic or linguistic "consciousness" as *ressentiment* (avenging) to that same system turned against or exceeding itself. This is one import of the double chase. If the Avenger is avenging an absented wrong, a missing cause, say, or a wound that would be repaid, he is, by avenging, trying to overcome the structure of vengeance as well—trying to terminate the series of resentment as the vampire wants to effect his own impossible death (the scenario with one of the Avenger's avatars, Uncle Charlie in *Shadow of a Doubt*). Here is the Nietzschean impasse: it is, indeed, the entire metaphorics of transvaluation, of transition, of machinal recurrence, that depends on this possible undoing of *ressentiment,* of consciousness as reactive, of a tyranny of the "it was." *The Lodger's* house, the logos or archive, is momentarily turned out, deauratized.

The Avenger's obliterations of fair-haired women not only represent the effort to mark, to mar the blonde hair itself—like Melanie's first attack by a gull in *The Birds.* These serial murders encounter in the figure of whiteness the scandal of a preinscription. The blonde, again, is already a prosthetic repetition and echo herself—or despite and because of the erotics in which this is played out, itself (the neon flashing: "Golden Curls To-Night"). To the extent that this seriality already summarizes and disrupts a metaphysical stereotype—one involving identity, perception, gender, desire, language, the eye—it mimes the destruction of aura. The absence of cause in the structure of repetitions and serial murder (the first of which is the lodger's "own" blonde sister supposedly) is not only a permanent dismantling of sequence, but, in Kierkegaard's phrase, an attempt at converting repetition to make it operate *forward,* converting mimesis from a passive to an active posture (a mimesis without model or copy), in the process effecting a certain hyperbolic abruption, or "shock." From this perspective, the triangle points upward, is a hyperaccession that is also, instantly and before, a tomb, and the reverse, up and down, as the *direction* of the letters *A* and *V* indicates, even as the *V* gathers—and then divests itself of, as anthropomorphism—a female genital motif.[20] Indeed, the *V* as womb or vaginal space, as mock origin, is demystified when inverted (while seeming the same) into an *A,* representing the (a)materiality of letter itself that indicates the semiotic base, effect without cause, effect become the cause of the cause, as if circularly (like the backspinning wheel that opens *Blackmail*).[21] Such an (a)material base is established as the concern of *The Lodger* with reference to feet or footsteps by means of the trick shot showing feet walking on the (see-through) ceiling. In each case the foot, as later legs or "steps," will connote this double tracking of a spectral trace.

The number 3 is not only the imperial eagle of number, of logos, but a signature for the camera and cameo, repeated in the third letter, *C* (or the *C* and *A* that, inversely, code 13). It unpacks that "dialectics at a standstill" Benjamin attributes to the virtuality of image, traversed by the ruin it archives, the past, and future readings of its event. It appears to initiate "time" by opening serial assaults that would be hunted, closed off by the police or its own double.[22] The number 3 does not, again, define a love triangle, or any mimetic desire so conceived; rather, it opens and forecloses narrative, articulating its structure forgetfully around the very sign of its impossibility, since it rests over a series of marks, of differences, of murders or bars or explosions, stretching without termination in "both" directions (assuming, as one should not, that one is in a model of bidirectional time).[23]

A room in the Buntings' house is made to stare back from behind the actors as a face, having two oval portraits for eyes. Elsewhere, Mr. Bunting has removed the face of a clock and is tinkering with it, altering time itself, from behind or within the churning gears. This abrupture—into which the "frame" is implicitly subsumed or enfolded, as with anteriority itself, when the "third" person's personification rotates to that of the "first"—implies a consumption of mimesis or reference before utterance. This moment will migrate across Hitchcock, repositioned as a disaster preceding narrative time (the crash in *Vertigo,* the shipwreck in *Lifeboat* associated with cameras and typewriters). It can be troped as a cut, a nonbiological death, a black sun, a migrant "zero," and so on, or it can revert into an epistemo-political regime, the economimesis of the home state, sometimes called "England."[24] It becomes apparent why the first cameo occurs in the *telecommunications sequence,* and why it is effaced, with Hitchcock's back turned in part to us, directing us to the "second" first cameo.

Keeping in mind the use of the "Phoenix" in *Psycho* to name, already, the cinematic image emergent from its fiery disarticulation, a similar logic pervades the antidialectic of the 3. Within this birthdate the 3 generates its forebears (zero as placeholder or cipher, 1 as the trope of zero, 2 as the marking of "1" . . .) to account for itself or seem to. Retroposited specters—the 1 a trope for zero, the 2 a repetition of that—they depend on its opening yet withdraw the fiction of its serial identity. The zero becomes a front or signature of the 3, which emerges in the cancellation of seriality: the 3, as a signature for the cinematic, is beyond all of the assumptions the 1 brings (identity, character, subject) and guarantees a permanent rupture, hyperbolic, a nonanthropomorphic site, *exteriority* to any metaphoric enclosure.

Kittler can be said to gloss Hitchcock's choice of the newsroom's teletype machine as the ur-scene of mediatric inscription, the levers of which absorb all others:

> Beyerlen's technical observation that in typing everything is visible except the actual inscription of the sign, also describes *On the Genealogy of Morals*. . . . The only possible, that is unconscious, kind of reading is the slavish obedience called morals. Nietzsche's notion of *inscription* . . . has validity only within the framework of the history of the typewriter. It designates the turning point at which communications technologies can no longer be related back to humans. Instead, the former have formed the latter.[25]

This myth is nonanthropomorphic ("no longer . . . related back to humans"), without aura, yet also a contesting of what cannot be "visible" to it: its material production within an archival order identified with the house. What avenges is outside of the house, outside of memory, outside of the visible—yet constitutive, structurally, of the front each presents, avenging in the unnameable name of a logic that exceeds the archival state yet also *lodges* in and before it.

Tonight—Golden Curls

Ivor Novello hangs from the barred fence for what seems an eternity during which "Hitchcock" will be seen striking him, again and again.[26] The triangle is hyperbolic, pointing up. Its repetition of and intervention in seriality would convert or project it forward, transposing the lacking cause, or referent, into an effect, which also corresponds to the absent Avenger.[27] This metaphoric apparatus anamorphically installs itself in a kind of fold: nowhere to be seen, it consumes the visible, whose very construction is and has been immemorially criminal. It attacks, like a cut, like the birds upon the totality of the human in the name of a nameless justice.

"Daisy" is identified in the credits as "a mannequin," that is, a little man or model. She will not only be played by a (real) model called simply June (like "Tippi" Hedren later), but given a flower name. Daisy translates in French as *marguerite*. The figure of marring, associated here with the blonde, buckles the system it inaugurates, since rather than merely signaling a mark or marring that is the absent wound being avenged, it is also that which gives rise to language, or "consciousness" and self, for which the "flower" (Daisy) is a misleadingly natural facade. This denaturalizes the V emblem of woman, which is to say, in ways that will have to be explored elsewhere, gender itself; the triadic logic, destructive of identification, compels "gender" to appear marked as a secondary or performative effect, held before a certain actively neutering and prefigural logic. "It," whose very reference is in doubt, is what makes the model and statue of "woman" (and the inverse Pygmalion loop is clear at the fashion show) into a "little man," of a "man" into a woman (and man who is not "keen" on the girls). In any event, the abruption of the sign's temporal structure in the triadic implosion of any dialectics or seriality does not record a dislocation of the "present" but rather implements it, reversing the direction of mimesis itself, in a kind of vertigo or frenzy. The cinematic fog becomes a time machine of sorts, not because it presents alternate scenes and epochs but by virtue of an irreducible rupture, the "time bomb" of *Sabotage,* the machinal production of the sensorium.

The ghost-machine mobilized as the cinematic "Avenger" wills to break this history, not add to its mimetic archive. It will involve, as mnemonic cut or "shock," a buckle and fold, erasure and reinscription of cultural referents. It implodes, virtually atomizing and reconstituting semaphoric components of the image (and, later, sound), citing and re-marking. Yet it also always misses its moment, misses a now or "present" simply defined, by a fatal deferral in its design. It converts any history it seemingly represents into a virtual prehistory, to a "time" not inscribed. It is a machine of the future, of the past, in a prosthetic present, a time machine, like the clock Mr. Bunting would reach behind to alter.

Hitchcockian cinema poses itself as Avenger, as an (a)material agent of intervention, the phantom image as exterminating angel of history, a deregulation of the archive. It is anarchivistic or revolutionary, not by retreat into formulaic postures, but by a kind of faux nihilism that attends the gamble of a totalization of fog, of the spectral order of the visible. It cites, and suspends, all the histories and linguistic software that sustain the visible as a territory traversed by ocular predations, consumption, cognitive programming, marketing, and mnemonic blinds. Which is to say, in a sense, the problematic of the model herself is attacked, the mannequin, or "little man." This is the focus of the obsession and recipient of the violence—a model, apparently, as unkillable as a vampire herself, replicable again and again, a copy of its copy. Such a mimesis without models and copies, the one that looks back within Hitchcock's apparatus, thus opens with a long parenthesis on the machinery of inscription preceding any face, any eyes, any phenomenalization, and it cuts two ways. "No more peroxide for yours truly": a signature, as at the close of a letter, with the autograph open. In fact, the interlude on media, an interruption, is the subject of the "story of the London fog."

The detour on media proceeds as if the murder were the "origin" of reported or mimetic fact. What standardizes men or women is a viral program put in circulation like dead print, emerging from giant archival machines. The Avenger is not a recorder, not even a personified non-human camera "eye." Beyond anthropomorphism, the Avenger comes from before, an anteriority welling up from chiaroscuro fog, suspended particles refracting other light sources, prehistorial, like an ancient demon seeking a vehicle, as though a counterlogic of this "cinema" were not modern or new despite, or because of, its technicity, going back to images on cave walls of hands. Hence the handcuffs—the rings or bracelets that block and bind the hands as though by cinema's twin spools, the dilemma of a writing without hands.[28] For *The Lodger* to apprehend the priority of the mark over visibility or the "eye," as the decisive incision of the cinematic, it must present a mock narrative, a story of the London fog: that is, the bizarre interlude following the opening (already a repeat) murder involving media. The sequence passing through giant machinery and trucks with eyes is converted into the precession of face, a defacement.[29] What *standardizes* men or women is shared inscriptions.

Hence the cameo featuring Hitchcock in the pressroom as what he calls the "editor," a cutter who precedes the imprint or impress. But the advent of the cameo launches or seems to secure the entire program of auteurial criticism that defines the brilliant reception of Hitchcock from Chabrol and Rohmer through Zizek (identificatory, biographist, historicist, ocularcentric, mimetic, "Oedipalist," and so on), while it openly undoes the very premise of that dossier. A certain excess results inevitably from handcuffing, a frenzy perhaps. The blockage of direct "writing" across this oeuvre converts itself, in a vertiginous explosion, into an excess resulting in blackouts and whiteouts, faintings and fallings, hypnosis and psychosis, syncopes, all networked, all switched in different directions at different nodal points, arranging and rearranging in phantom groups in revisionary torsions, fore and back. In the British films Hitchcock anatomizes distinct domains of the Avenger's incision: in *The 39 Steps*, memory; in *Secret Agent*, sound; in *Blackmail*, indexing and "reading."

It is "fog" that avenges—the particles and pointillistic markings on which what is called light hangs; that dissolves, atomizes face, without yielding it back quite. Fog, from which the Avenger emerges and retreats into, stalking. But the logic of this particularity and pointillism, which anticipates everything that can be said or done with digital technology, cannot be suspended. If the "story" is about this "London fog" or British cinema at its advent, myriad other marking devices than "fog" will be used (newspapers, bombs, guns, stenography, shadow play, bicycles, handcuffs, newsreels, chocolate factories, kitchens, atom bombs, secret formulas, and of course, cognates of "3" or "13"). The "fog" is molecular, micrological, atomizing, in advance of life or mnemonic effects. Moreover, it suspends all ocularcentric premises, welling from the underworld of inscriptions. The Avenger can never be called the "murderous gaze," or the eye, or the camera, any more than the visible can be addressed as other than a marking effect programmed by artificial memory (a phrase that is redundant), without any perception or even visibility. Hitchcock knows this, indeed, knows too much: what dematerializes or vaporizes is not a matter of seeing. It is not a matter of looking. He tells us so:

> I don't look through the camera. Looking through the camera has nothing to do with it. The ultimate end of what you're doing is on a rectangular screen of varying proportions—wide ones, tall ones, all those kinds of screens—but, nevertheless, what are you doing? You're using the rectangle, like a painter, but the whole art of the motion picture is a succession of composed images, rapidly going through a machine, creating ideas. The average public do not, or are not, aware of "cutting" as we know it, and yet that is the pure orchestration of the motion-picture form.[30]

It is a matter of rectangles, angles, triangles, geometrics, musically generated "ideas." The zootrope generates what would be shadow variants of the *eidos,* recalling the latter's artifice as hypostasized repetition, networked citations, "'cutting' as we know it." The box is not a coffin as camera but the rectangle's rapid "succession of *composed* images." But Hitchcock enters this site through formalizations: the "3" as the MacGuffin of numbering, the zero and 1 as *Nachkonstruktionen,* tropes, or relapsed shots. Johnny Depp's opium trances speculate, in *From Hell,* on the allochronic clairvoyance of the underworld's séance that cinema introduces—tracking, in advance, the dehumanized futures it effects, yet references these both to the artifice of light and the surgical dismemberment of the cut. One becomes aware, as the Avenger's calling card makes clear, that beneath these is referenced a triadic logic that cannot house, thereafter, any return to interiority, to the eye, to the subject, to succession, to face, to representation. The attempt to humanize and personify what does not have a face at or after that point, to relapse into a "human" order that did not, for that matter, precede it, accelerates the eviscerations: the ceaseless attempt to practice identificatory rhetorics usurped by political machines, to render the image a mimetic rather than a deauratic event, thus bureaucratizing perception and reference, to reassert the natural order of "light" and transparency where these issue from the hell of electric bulbs and imperial flood lamps split "cinema" into its two orders: that of the state, the royalist and corporate conspiracy of telemarketing and mnemonic implants, and the deauratic resistance that Benjamin will wend toward an intervention, triadic in structure and hyperbolic, that he will call "materialistic historiography" at one point. The naturalization of number over the MacGuffin of the "zero" insists on the historicizing model of time and the $N + 1$, or the apprehension of seriality as itself "MacGuffin." The house that is marred by the number "13" lodges the ocularcentric program and aesthetic ideology as such.

If these remarks attempt to read the "fog" that is *The Lodger*'s subject of narration—and to do so against the long detour on media—it is also an attempt to understand why a number of effects merge, suddenly, here, which is to say, with or as the advent of cinema. Among these: the double logic of the cameos, the explosive dependence on numeration, the precession of *face*. *Fog* seems to name all of the material logics that precede the mimetic premises cinema conjures as a spectral machine. The secret agents of Hitchcock proceed from this incision.

2. A User's Guide to Hitchcock's Signature Systems

> What is quite surprising with Hitchcock is that you don't remember the plot of *Notorious,* or why Janet Leigh goes to the Bates Motel. You remember the pair of glasses, or the windmill—that is what millions and millions of people remember.
>
> **—Jean-Luc Godard, interview with**
> **Jonathan Rosenbaum (1997)**

> In Hitchcock, for example, the extraordinary translation of English human into a very different American type (complete with a whole new character system) suggests . . . a foreign language at work behind the ostensible surface language and lending it a peculiar opacity and density, as in Milton or Nabokov, Conrad or Raymond Chandler.
>
> **—Fredric Jameson, *Signatures of the Visible***

There is an uncanny visual skit in the silent film *The Manxman,* which involves the attempted suicide by drowning of the female lead, who is then hauled before the judge or what is called the "deemster." The latter, secretly, is the father of her child—and best friend of her husband (hence the attempted suicide). As she first sinks in the inky black, bubbles punctuate the watery surface and the liquid dissolves into that of a literal inkwell from which a pen emerges, held by the deemster, who proceeds to write. The camera pans back to show the bewigged judge writing in a legal tome, his wig prosthetic and ambiguous. The black watery pool is a prototype for Norman Bates's bog, which takes in cars and female corpses, absorbs woman, and is transformed into ink. The black pool of what might be called sheer anteriority arises as engraved letters, script doubled by being put down by a compromised jurist. The image could be run in reverse, almost, whereby the public script written by "the law," an institution doubled against its own premise and concealing that criminal secret, could be dissolved back into the ink, or an absorbing black pool into which life and matter had been disarticulated.

There has always been a problem with characterizing Hitchcock's signifying strategies, into which trap the most sophisticated theorists have stumbled. Objects are hosted, seem marked, yet refuse assigned contents and dissolve into citational networks; after their passage through a sort of "spies' post office," they reemerge elsewhere, become host. An example is what does—and does not—happen to birds between, say, *Sabotage* and *The Birds* (which opens as if in a placidly chic version of the first's bomb-making pet shop). Godard says such effects are what the public remembers. Jameson points to their ability to empty out sense, Deleuze to the way one or another seems to break away from a conventional series; Zizek attempts to attach these to an effect of the Lacanian *sinthome*, which stands beyond yet spurs interpretive activity. To the degree that the last two end up providing more or less symbolic hypotheses, they may seem victims of this bog, which accords sometimes with what "the Professor" in *North by Northwest* jokingly refers to as a kind of "alphabet soup." Theorists appear caught in a shuttle between the articulate if duplicitous page the wigged deemster produces (a wig anticipating Norman's "Mother") and the murk of a light-absorbing pool of bubbles.

I will review two "theoretical" attempts and then suggest a means for addressing Hitchcock's signature effects.

Deleuze associates these repetitions with denaturalizing techniques. He devises an alternate name for that which had none—the *demark*—and distinguishes it from a *symbol,* though he then relapses into a logic of symbolization:

> Hitchcock produces original signs, in accordance with the two types of relations, natural and abstract. In accordance with the natural relation, a term refers back to other terms in a customary series such that each can be "interpreted" by the others: these are *marks*; but it is always possible for one of these terms to leap outside the web and suddenly appear in conditions which take it out of its series, or set it in contradiction with it, which we will refer to as the *demark.* It is therefore very important that the terms should be completely ordinary, in order that one of them, first of all, can detach itself from the series: as Hitchcock says, *The Birds* must be ordinary birds. Certain

of Hitchcock's demarks are famous, like the windmill in *Foreign Correspondent* whose sails turn in the opposite direction to the wind, or the cropspraying plane in *North by Northwest* which appears where there are no crops to spray. Similarly, the glass of milk made suspect by its internal luminosity in *Suspicion,* or the key which does not fit the lock in *Dial M for Murder.* Sometimes the demark is constituted very slowly, as in *Blackmail,* where one wonders whether the cigar buyer is, in the normal way, part of the series client-choice-preparations-lighting, or if he is a master-blackmailer who is using the cigar and its ritual in order to provoke the young couple. On the other hand and in second place, in accordance with the abstract relation, what we will call a symbol is not an abstraction, but a concrete object which is a bearer of various relations, or of variations of a single relation, of character with others and with himself. The bracelet is such a symbol in *The Ring,* like the handcuffs in *The 39 Steps* or the wedding ring of *Rear Window.* Demarks and symbols can converge, particularly in *Notorious.* . . . We see that a single object—a key, for example—can, according to the images in which it is caught, function as a symbol *(Notorious)* or as a demark *(Dial M for Murder).* In *The Birds,* the first gull which strikes the heroine is a demark, since it violently leaves the customary series. . . . But the thousands of birds . . . are a symbol: these are not abstractions or metaphors, they are real birds, literally, but which present the inverted image of men's relationship to Nature.[1]

The Deleuzian *demark* operates by standing out from a series, yet as such it denaturalizes the natural and the "demark" is effaced back into the "symbol," as when the "thousands of birds" appear to him to be "the inverted image of men's relationship to Nature." The fact that "Nature" is evoked marks a limit of Deleuze's technique, since whatever the "birds" are doing can, according to their alliance with machines, have no accord with an anthropomorphism like "Nature."

By contrast, Zizek will propose deploying the Lacanian *sinthome* in the hope of evading any allusion to language whatsoever, but the very strenuousness of that evasion (designed to move beyond "post-structuralism," as he calls it) triggers a relapse or pratfall back into metaphor and symbol. Zizek assumes that any evocation of linguistic elements leads only to the metonymic chains of "the Symbolic."[2] He is determined to demonstrate that he, or "Lacan," is "beyond the wall of language" and accessing the phallophanies of the Real. But he may err in approaching "Hitchcock" as the ventriloquized Delphic interpreter for questions about Lacan (as his title exorcises: *Everything You Always Wanted to Know about Lacan . . . But Were Afraid to Ask Hitchcock*).

Zizek has reason to be afraid. Pointing beyond metonymy, he regresses to metaphor and can appear trapped in a limited and inverted model of identification, auteurism, and ocularcentrism. Zizek ends by reinscribing the auteurial tradition in toto, including its hallowed subject—however much, now, as in his reading of *Psycho,* a "subject without subjectivity."[3] Hitchcock is assigned the task of bearing witness to or exemplifying neo-Lacanian dogma, a dubious service to assign this archbetrayer, whose *Spellbound* is an evisceration of pop Lacanianism *avant la lettre* (and psychoanalysis as a competitor of cinema's). One can select from the basket: the automation of Mr. Memory is that of the symbolic order; the "birds" are the maternal superego; the big Other is, well, everywhere.[4] After announcing the key importance of the *sinthome,* on which the entire interpretation of Hitchcock would rest, Zizek generates a painfully conventional Oedipal aside on the first *Man Who Knew Too Much*—the supposed demonstration. He seems to know it, since what is announced as the key to Hitchcock is simply broken off after a few pages. Zizek does not have a chance if his program suppresses any reference to language, marking systems, dialogue, telegraphies, and so on.

Lee Edelman, one of Hitchcock's more provocative readers, attempts to rescue Zizek's *sinthome* from the paralysis it falls into by appropriating it as a zero term. He speaks of a *"sinthome*-osexuality" in which the null and ringed *o* disarticulates the hegemony of heterosexual narratives and sees in Hitchcock's "birds" a suspension of messianic futurity, of heterosexual coupling, and of the pretense of generation (children):

> *Sinthome*-osexuality, then, would mean by figuring a threat to meaning insofar as meaning is invested in reproduction's promise of coming—in a future always deferred—into the presence that reconciles meaning with being, the impossible beyond of the signifier on which any subject's cathexis of the signifying system depends.[5]

Edelman's trope suspends the faux messianism that underwrites heterosexed claims to proprietorship of a never-arriving futurity. One draws close to a "weak messianism," in the sense proffered by Benjamin's *Thesis* and, in variation, by Derrida's *Specters of Marx.* Hitchcock's cancellation of the logics of "generation"—echoed in his treatment of eggs, but also of "Mother"—is reappropriated for queer politics while putting in play something beyond gender positioning.

Part of the problem has been the nature of a Hitchcockian tropology—or whether what are at work in Hitchcock are tropes at all. Deleuze seems to think so. Zizek wanted to pass beyond it, yet relapses altogether, whereas Edelman proceeds as if to the edge (as long as this vacancy can be reappropriated for political purposes). Deleuze more or less subscribes to the logics of figuration in drawing attention to Hitchcock's premier trope as that of weaving and clothes as such, which, while pervasive, finds itself unraveled as the premise of narrative or targeted for assassination (the first *Man Who Knew Too Much*) or exposed as inhabited by the prefigural pattern of parallel lines or bars *(Spellbound)*:

> The sketches for framing, the strict delimitation of the frame, the apparent elimination of the out-of-frame, are explained by Hitchcock's constant reference, not to painting or the theater, but to tapestry-making, that is, to weaving. The frame is like the posts which hold the warp threads, whilst the action constitutes merely the mobile shuttle which passes above and below.[6]

Clearly, one needs help if one is to follow the blackmailer Tracey into the universal reading room; and if it is not to be had from our foremost theorists, one wonders whether, perhaps, the secret agency at work is altogether too elusive. One needs, say, an *Encyclopedia of Alfred Hitchcock*. But when one turns to a recent publication with precisely that title, in this case compiled by the admirable Hitchcockian Thomas Leitch, one encounters more "facts." For instance, if one turns to look for help with *MacGuffin*, one finds little more than a gloss and gets no analytic help; one presumes the term is a given and is said to be "more common in spy thrillers than domestic mysteries."[7] No analysis, in short, of whatever the zero function may be doing in this system, nor of the self-canceling logic of the "MacGuffin" (which, precisely, according to the anecdote, never is a MacGuffin either), nor of its role behind other figures that it contaminates in a general rout of representational assumptions about photography, for instance, what it does to the very premise of *re*cognition and *re*ference. One might need, if only to begin with, an awareness that there appears a signifying agency in Hitchcock irreducible to visual or linguistic precepts, yet which partakes aggressively of what Eduardo Cadava has called the "citational structure" of the image.[8] One might rather need a nonglossary, just the beginning of one, to turn over a first layer of transformative nodes, puns, repetitions, secret agents, trace networks—and these would have to be wired, incessantly, to self-remarking sites of teletechnicity. That is, fundamentally and inclusively, what Hitchcock calls the "cinematic."

One could hope to get outside of symbolic readings by turning to the filiative model of string theory, which gives extension, if not to Deleuze's focus on the weave, then to Hitchcock's tautening refinement of such notions as *rope*.[9] String theory's insistence that the "same" material or stuff pervades all vibratory strings is perhaps useful in visualizing the effects of the Hitchcockian band, since that same "stuff" passes through all representations and actions, leaving what are called "fingerprints."[10] The domain of string maps is the domain of an allomorphic archive, altering, affiliating, and programming, all the while by vibrational patterns void of semantic content, irreducibly (a)material and semaphoric, mnemonic and performative. From the point of view of reading, citational nodes network technemes, rhizomatic algorithms, postal nodes, "times," phonemes that "sound like" others, angles . . . There can be no glossary here, no symbol. One is, after all, approaching the domain of "Mother." The glass of milk with a lightbulb in it that Cary Grant brings Joan Fontaine is evoked as a prototype of the odd Hitchcockian signifier—yet it presents its auratic white milk as a poison. One is, as it were, always in the debris floating at the opening of *Lifeboat,* in the afterlife of a semioclasm.

As a matter of selection, these "citational" terms, objects, aural and visual puns, signature effects, and agents always display two traits: (1) they have to do with the cinematic; and (2) they have to do with what Benjamin calls "turning the symbolizer" into the symbolized. Citing themselves in advance of any "content," as Jameson all but observes, they enter the frame as spectral or material agents to assault, like so many early Hitchcock "villians," legibility, the visible, cognition. If one pretended dutifully to assemble a "glossary," nonetheless, these recombinant markers could include:

advertising
In *Young and Innocent* at the children's birthday party, Derrick de Marney presents himself to Erica's aunt as "Beechcroft Manningtree," who is in advertising; Patricia Martin steps out of billboard ads in *Saboteur* and Grant is an ad exec opening *North by Northwest,* putting in play the image as programming memory. Mercenary version of televisual logic.

Babel
Always Alpine in the British thrillers: a phonetic salad of French, German, Italian, English, Swiss-Deutsch, until in *The Lady Vanishes* a new nonlanguage is simulated in the imaginary Alpine Babel country, Bandriki (vampire language of "band[s]"). Between or outside any individual

language, phonemic units or aural traces leading to the chocolate factory, in *Secret Agent,* called the spies' post office, sending transcripted messages through the network of agents (or "films").

bar

As a series, irreducible "signature" of prefigural alteration and spacing; injected into the nominal order through the word-syllable *bar* (Barbara, George Barbor, Detective Barton or Judy Barton, Barlow Creek, even *Ber*tani and *Ber*nice), or the visual bar, or a pub bar (at the opening of *The Lodger,* or "the Bar at the Top of the Mark" in *Vertigo,* or the Oak Bar at the Plaza or the Globe, as in *Frenzy*).

bicycle

Like spectacles, with two spools, it is a vehicle of transport. Atop the bus from Casablanca to Marrakesh opening the second *Man Who Knew Too Much,* it associates the cinematic project with what has been unfolding; falling in or shoved, phallically, into the rectory of *"I Confess."* The Amsterdam of *Foreign Correspondent,* which flashes a luminescent bicycle shop advertisement before the faux assassination of Van Meer (concealing a gun in, or as, a camera).

birds

Flight, piercing sound, staccato singing, cartoons, machines; in *Sabotage* associated with (cinematic) bombs. Myriad eye-pecking flecks; machinal affiliation with the cut.

black sun

Associated "effect" that passes through Hitchcock's earlier films as an asolar logic or trace effect. Arises in the marksmanship scene of the first *Man Who Knew Too Much*: a clay target, shot at, that appears as a black disk traversing the sky, a simulacrum sun, source of light yet already a mark, hole, or copy. It will traverse a series of nonfigures, in each case citing (or performing for) this trace that seems, too, to represent an (a)material order of signifying agents (letters, sounds, natural images apprehended as citations): black dogs, excrement, record disks, chocolate, feet.

blindness, blinds

The blindman or dead Paradine for whom the wife would be the "eyes," the pecking out of the farmer Fawcett's sockets by the birds, which connotes *seeing* as a structural blind or screen. In *Saboteur,* the just blindman Phillip Martin sees what is not tangible. Inability to see what is before one due to programmed expectations, mnemonic implants, travel folding: hence the trope of *seeing* as a blind. The tourist openly solicited on entering the film commodity is blind in his activation of sight: that is, he re-cognizes only programmatic indicators or accepted sign configurations as perception.

blocked speech

Cipher characters again and again are barred from "speech"—or speaking what they know (or having it understood). Whether restrained by blackmail (a stolen child), or having the world deny one's knowledge (Hannay, Iris Henderson), or because a priest cannot confide a confession, and so on.

B. M.

The insignia on young Charlie's ring in *Shadow of a Doubt*, the tattoo on John Hodiak's bare chest in *Lifeboat*. Evokes both the British Museum, site of monumental history and the precession of Egyptian writing in *Blackmail* (and what Mr. Memory is leaving his brain to); also blackmail as film and trope, hence the "secret" of anteriority as trace, the circular turning of a "past" against the present it projects, a logic of the ring, cut, in Edelman's reading, anus (an affiliation made in the association of record players with a toilet in *Secret Agent*).[11]

the bog

Starting in *The Manxman*, a dissolve shifts a dark watery drowning pool to an inkwell in which the law (or deemster) dips the pen on a courtroom desk. *North by Northwest*'s quip about "alphabet soup" from which spy agency acronyms derive and remix (FBI, CIA, . . .): preletteral, viscous, like the oil discovered near the dead Jeremiah Stevens's outhouse in *To Catch a Thief*. Oil upon which all machines thrive: letteral combinatoires, mnemonics, sheer anteriority.

bridges

If there is a "bridge" motif in Hitchcock—over the Firth of Forth in *The 39 Steps*, with a burned-out car before Philadelphia opening *Shadow of a Doubt*, the Golden Gate in *Vertigo*, to name a few—they are not crossed, and the open gridlike structures appear italicized. "Bridges" do not effect a passage between shores (or binaries) nor transport or translation. They tend to present im*passes*, aporetics. Clara Thornhill is inaccessible by telephone or telegraph to son Cary Grant at the opening of *North by Northwest*; "Mother" is playing "bridge" with her cronies.

C, A

Canadian, Lady Caroline, Carlton Hotel, Carlotta Valdez, possibly with an *r* (cary/carry), where a vehicle can be appropriated, pointing to a material carrier or bearer of signification. It incorporates a 3 and a 1, accessing the self-canceling triangular logic of the *ca*mera in *The Lodger*, hyperbolic.

cats

Privileged animemes. Flooding shadow play of *Number 17* like myriad simulacra or darting black holes. In *Rich and Strange,* a cat is eaten on a Chinese junk and its skin stretched to dry, a black circle of skin then likened, against the sky, to a moon eclipsed by clouds (that is, a reflected sun). In *To Catch a Thief,* black cat as trace, linked to the theft of jewels (reference, being, sex, meaning), operates as black sun figure, ironically, in the case of Robie, where the pursuit of a "copycat" thief by the original "cat" whose "mark" is being left mimes the pursuit of a simulacrum by one in a circular track in which the double-chase model reaches implosion.

chance

Often marked in the "political thrillers," precipitates narrative and at the same time is a virtual "setup": a trap that incorporates the narrative artifice in a loop that can break its own circuit. It both fuels and offers a break within a mnemonic machine. *Casinos* may formalize such a site *(Secret Agent, To Catch a Thief),* where however skits appear that evade direct gambling. "Il y à et il n'ya pas le hasard" (Mallarmé).

clothes

Represents *figuration,* the weave of metaphor. In *Spellbound* the bar series or tracks will appear or be phenomenalized as if through a cloth's design, indicating that insignia as what stands against figurative language. In the first *Man Who Knew Too Much,* the "jumper" is unraveled on the dance floor preceding Louis Bernard's assassination—narrative departing from its advance undoing as the fabric of time—and Ambassador Ropa (Spanish for "clothes") would be assassinated by a single (camera) shot, setting off a world war, perhaps, and opening the epistemo-political regime to rearrangement. In *Saboteur,* Fry's sleeve unravels as he falls from the Statue of Liberty's torch, against the cold "flame" of cinematic writing, cited when an old crone catches Robie by the sleeve in the Nice flower market—held, that is, to the natural image (tree), after being swamped by the film's referenceless emblems (cut flowers).

contact, touch
During the children's game of blindman's bluff in *The Birds,* Cathy warns, "No touching"—a motif Marnie will insist upon differently, as does *To Catch a Thief,* where barred sexual touching (or possession) is interfaced with semiotic theft, a "light *touch*" (or touching of or by light: Germaine's cooking and strangling). As *fingerprints*—a promise of contact (indexing, documentary) supplanted by its own anterior imprint.

dancing couples
Dance floor as site of the sister's murder recalled in *The Lodger,* or where Jill's knitted "jumper" is unraveled and Louis Bernard "shot," in the first *Man Who Knew Too Much*; waltzing descent from an anonymous outside of memory to interrupt *Shadow of a Doubt*: a choreography of media, trace steps or legs, (a)signifying agents, choreography almost without touch, puppetlike, citing all contending media. Aesthetic machine, as if entropic.

direction
Keeping open double entendre implicating the director, as early as in *The Lodger* we are told the triangles marking the murder sites on a map are all moving in a certain "direction." In *"I Confess"* the word appears all over street signs too insistently, marking a left-to-right passage on the way to a library where Villette has been murdered (normative reading), and it is bound to an arrow that appears indecisive atop a weather vane in *Murder!* The clogged and directionless cinematic traffic opening *North by Northwest* that bursts into the irreversible nonexistent "direction" of the title.

disaster
Precedes narrative time, in association with recording or an explosion of signifying effects or temporal structures: the avalanche of *The Lady Vanishes,* the shipwreck debris of *Lifeboat* (with Constance Porter's subsequent loss of a typewriter and camera), the photographed crash with its hurtling wheel in *Rear Window,* and so on; chance. (Effect of suspension, cut, cinematic "shock.")

dogs
Young Charlie says in *Shadow of a Doubt*: "Poor Mother. She works like a dog, just like a dog." Hitchcock's dog named "Philip of Magnesia," linked with excrement—and hence, a series of trace figures including the black-sun marker, feet, and sheer sound (Caypor's telepathic

leg-entangled dog of *Secret Agent*). "A boy's best friend is his mother" (Norman Bates).

-ed, Ed

The "past" as pure trace, what preinhabits and programs the living "present," like celluloid, like mnemonics before the perceptual order or phenomenality (or "life"). Occasionally marked by nominal variants on the verbal past tense, Ed- (Dr. *Ed*wardes, *Ed*die Shoebridge, *Ed*na Druse), *it* tends to circulate in the guise of ghosts, inscriptions, and collapsed traces (black sun, black cats).

eggs

Sabotages figures of nature and generation; alternates with chickens (a "chicken and egg" citation suspending origins), putting causality or temporal order in reverse hiatus. Egg, eye, sun.

Egypt

Motif of the "Egyptian" dominates early films, echoing (and surpassing) analogy of cinema to hieroglyphics: precession of origin of writing in *Blackmail* museum chase, the exposure of sun worshipping as a trope of filmgoing in the first *Man Who Knew Too Much*.

espionage

Penultimate model for the epistemological intrigue that attends any assault on the powers of the hermeneutic state or its mnemonic and sensorial programming. This identifies "cinema" with the so-called villain's efforts at sabotage, assassination, world-altering transmission of a new technicity (silent warplanes), a new writing-reading model.

face

The Lodger's blonde victim's "face" with open mouth, later to emerge as citation on the back of a truck or listening to news on the wireless. Judy asks "Scottie" not to muss her because she has put "her face" on. (Relay: the first scene with Madeleine Carroll in *Secret Agent*, Mount Rushmore's heads, and so on.) *Face* as prosopopoeia never affirmed quite or arrived as such, unreadable in *Suspicion*; nonexistent, Hitchcock will tell Truffaut, until "light" hits it, and shadow—trace chains and semaphoric difference—congeals.

fire

In *To Catch a Thief* a throwaway line by Grant speaks of "fighting fire with fire," an implosive battle performed later by the pyrotechnics scene involving the Nice fireworks. Gasoline within an extinguisher sprayed on an airplane factory arson, immolating the handler, opens *Saboteur*, which will end with the saboteur named Fry falling from the cold stone torch atop a model of the Statue of Liberty. Empedoclean inversion: the nonidentity of the spectral cinematic subject emerges from the ashes of an incineration of lights. A "fire drill" empties the Bodega Bay schoolhouse.

glass, window

In *Stage Fright* "safety glass" is marked on a car window, pointed to as written (recalling that on the befogged train window of *The Lady Vanishes*), and it is referenced across *To Catch a Thief*, beginning with the travel service window of the credits. What touch cannot penetrate, though seemingly transparent, yet which can mirror another scene— *media, medium* (language itself, cinema), breakable in extremis. What Melanie Daniels references in *The Birds'* opening as to why she had been in court (for breaking a glass pane).

H

Huntley Haverstock, Henrietta, Harry, Henry, Harriet, H. H. Hughe-son—for that matter, the head domes of the Scottish Assembly Hall, or the Albert Hall: more than autoinscriptions across a network of anti-surrogates (since what is marked is also, or primarily, the fact of marking, the agency of the signature machine itself). The effect is to highlight and render nonvisible the *H* itself. Graphically, the centered bar connects two parallel tracks, the train or film.

half-cast(e)

The term from *Murder!* used to identify Handel Fane's mixed blood ("black blood"), marking, as well, an in-between of sexual positioning (echoed in his transvestism), the preinhabitation of white or light by blackness, interval. What any actor "is" as inscribed in his or her specific film, irreducibly singular, star as a constellation of citations (histories, personal, filmographic). Half in, half out. Moniker for the enfolding of any putative outside of the frame.

handcuffs

Recurrent and striking early figure—*The Lodger, The 39 Steps*—too quickly assumed to be a fetish. The cuffs bear a double-O or spool insignia (bicycles, spectacles, infinite eight). They enchain the hands, figures of human technicity or writing. As a trope for Hitchcock's cinema, cuffed hands also denote the barring of direct forms of expression or writing that the cinematic imposes, dispersing the project across innumerable planes, sound, graphics, citations, nominal "puns," and so on. It implies in its arrest of hands an *overwriting* or scoring. The "*hand*" component linked to writing is insistent across nominal and visual chains: Hannay, Handel Fane, Iris Henderson.

house
Structure of media or cinematic language or "family": the home or *oikos* as faux interior, inhabited by already alien lodger, *personified* in *Shadow of a Doubt*, *Rebecca* ("Manderlay"), *Psycho,* and so on. Humans driven from by birds.

Ken-, Con-
Prefixes used to mark place or proper names (Constantinople, Conway, Kenneth, Kentley, McKenna, Kendall) that signal the epistemomnemonic stakes of the venture and quest; an "epistemological critique of tropes" (de Man) that moves beyond mere figuration.

kitchens
Passed through in the second *Man Who Knew Too Much* and "*I Confess,*" patron of the "copycat" thefts in *To Catch a Thief* (in that case, Bertani's), site of film production as confection, commercial bonbons for consumption, and so on. An alliance not only of cinematic consumption with baked goods, sweetened or aestheticized, "light as air" (quiche in the last-named work), or chocolates, nor only with "cutting, s(p)licing," but of the eye as programmed with eating, evisceration, interiorization—an archival death drive to acquire, incorporate, negate, the priority of murder over its front, *desire.*

legs, steps
Couriers of signification, including the phonetic or graphematic mark, "footsteps without feet." The "39 steps" as agents of memory; *legs* echoing logos, *légère,* legibility, legitimation, legacy (phonemes, marks, rhymed repetitions, cited shots, serial relays, letters). May occur as "bad leg," as "leg work."

libraries, books
The archive. In *Rope,* books as "first editions" will be bound with cord and placed in the chest with the strangled corpse of David Kentley—false originals, where "first editions" are just imprints (these books inform the motif of being caught in a representational loop marked by Poulenc's "Perpetual Movement" and the skyline's cyclorama). Villette's murdered body is seen in the library at the beginning of "*I Confess,*"

where all scriptive legacies or traces circulate. Cary Grant, finding himself in Townsend's library, quips that he will "catch up on my reading." Young Charlie's visit to Santa Rosa's "Free Library" uncovers Uncle Charlie's pastime and pretends to explain the initials B. M. on the ring given her by him by revealing his last victim's name (yet what it does not disclose is that the "B. M." invokes the entire archive of *Blackmail*'s British Museum). A doctor, reading a book, recurrently stumbles by the corpse of Harry. A book is thrown at Bergman's head in Green Manors, as though displacing the asylum. In *Vertigo*, Pop Liebl, of the Argosy Bookstore, knows San Francisco history enough to tell, vaguely, the story of Carlotta Valdez, the bookstore marking an Argus-like many-eyes as themselves preinformed by archival print. The "Pop" is that of an explosion in the eye, inducing a multiplicity of such effects over a bookstore. Archival shifts. The "library" is a past and future storage site, panmnemonic.

M

Thirteenth letter of the alphabet, it traverses every "Mar-" name, which reinscribes any anthropomorphism of "mother" into a mnemographics of the matrical, or *khora*-like order. Central letter cipher, returning to the name of Hitchcock's mother, Emma (evinced in *Rich and Strange*'s "Emmy" and *Shadow of a Doubt*). Series: music, murder, machine, memory, mountain, mother . . . three triads (like three interlocking *V*s or triads); may be juxtaposed graphically to W (*The Man Who . . .* , *The Wrong Man*, "Mae West," *M*ontreal, and *W*innepeg).

machines

Not just of transport, but gigantic gears and factories *(The Lodger, Secret Agent)*. Prosthetic windmills. Can be affiliated with printing and postal relays, machinery of inscription and projection. Bertani's kitchen in *To Catch a Thief* runs "just like a machine—cutting, s[p]licing," but the stone mill in *The Manxman* as well as the hum associated with the birds in that film occur along this chain. Fantasy skit Hitchcock pretended to Truffaut he wanted to use in *North by Northwest*: visit to a car factory in Detroit where a vehicle fresh off the assembly line opens to disclose a corpse already in it.

Mae West

Mae West's name is used in a deferred question to Mr. Memory ("How old is Mae West?") and mimed by the cartoon bird-woman in *Sabotage*. Rusk, in *Frenzy*, speaks of his mother's line, "Beulah, peel me a grape" (a line of Mae West's). Bringing together the *M* and *W* (like *The Man Who Knew Too Much* or *The Wrong Man*), the one an inversion of the other, hence the same, the name also suggests the space of a female female performer—a site where "gender" is displayed as a performative, sometimes faked, effect viewed from within an imaginary in which the male, who identifies with or is given identity by that program, is also a site generated in turn by that performative. The paternal or heteropaternal position is always vacated, or abdicated, before a sort of eunarchy or desexualized moment.

Mar-
Secreted in every work, a countersignature to the "bar series" that locates a nonvisible order upon which all visual effects are projected, conjured, or (blindly) misidentified: Marlow, Marvin, Mary, Marnie, Marion, Margot, Margaret, Murchison, Morton, Mark, and so on.

mon-
In *The 39 Steps,* the syllable *mon-* is isolated by prominent repetitions from *Mon*treal to "Crazy *Mon*th," the show at the Palladium (citing menstruation and a dismemberment of time), yet when isolated it also mimes the association of meaning (*Meinung,* in German) to what is "mine" (mein), a field of egological capital and property semantics that, creating fake interiors and reserves, would be exposed, emptied.

mother
Impermeable to psychoanalytic reading, not necessarily gendered, veers to a destroying logic or place of nonorigination: *mother* could only be if nature, the sun, or the originality of the actor, even, could be affirmed— as they are not. "Mother" would be a figure not subject to anthropomorphism, and not even spectrally finding a body or voice. Nonsite where all inscription stands to occur, (a)material, (a)maternal, matrical, archival, signed distantly by the bar series as a performative. *Khora* figure of the cinematic, anatural, non-Oedipal, anoriginary, destroying in advance of "life."

newspaper
The typographics and printing of the *Evening Standard*s in *The Lodger,* put in a truck with two window-eyes, create the image of a large head filled with dead print. Print media as precessional inscription to celluloid. In *Shadow of a Doubt* a cut-out newspaper, "Papa's paper," is shaped like a *house.*

O

In letters, zeroids, wheels: recurrent, of recurrence, voiding, counter-temporal, spooling, ocular. The shorn hurtling rear wheel of the photographed car crash leading to L. B. Jeffries's broken leg, the logic of the MacGuffin (called by Hitchcock a "nothing"), variant rings (including Uncle Charlie's smoke rings), sphincter as privileged analog to the cinematic cut (Lee Edelman), the (back) spinning wheel opening *Blackmail*. The "O-men" identified with the figure, neither letter nor number, and a para-Nietzschean cipher of the going under of sign chains incorporating chainlike storage loops being repeated or exceeded hyperbolically, or evacuated (Johnny-O, Roger O., Dick-O). Migrates from apparatus to MacGuffin (like the zero of mathematics, placeholder from which number departs), the naught.

oak, wood

The figure of "wood" emerges across a series of names (Midge Wood in *Vertigo*, Charlotte Inwood in *Stage Fright*, Bishop Wood in *Family Plot*) of which the figure of Oak would be a subspecies owing to its troping of the *O* and the zero (Charles "Oakley" in *Shadow*, the Oak *Bar* at the Plaza). In part, "wood/oak" cites the tree as trope of nature itself as product of the "cut," or preinhabited by a prosthetic, such as the archival circles of dates inhabiting the severed sequoia in *Vertigo*. (Charles Oakley's old home address, shared with his sister Emma, on "Burnham" Street cites Macbeth's finale, where the forest trees are props of "nature" concealing an army bent on revenge and assassination.) The tree is used as a trope of the photograph's "natural image," which it must cite and which must seem recognizable to others.

P, π

P traverses *pips* and *pipes (The 39 Steps)*, alliterations *(Portland Place)*, segueing through the Greek letter π *(Torn Curtain)* of the circumference measuring "Pythagorean" formula (3.14): ties into a 3 and 1 combinatoire, as well as 3 or "13" signatures, in turn as if connected to the cancellation of the number 1, or any supposed subject, at the origin of speech; hence, caught in chain including the bar series, the letter *M, C* (third letter), and *A* (first letter) combinations.

phonography

Site of a preinscription or ritualistic mnemonic program that would be intervened in (first and second *Man Who Knew Too Much*); hence, the "shot" coinciding with its rehearsal would constitute a world-altering event (differently marked in *Secret Agent, Psycho*). Black disks issuing the preprogrammed. Mnemonic storage.

port

The word recurs in nominal play (Portland Place, Constance Porter, Portland, Oregon), as too in *Rich and Strange's* cinetravelogue, where Port Said is featured (linking a prospect of crossing to nonetheless past-tensed speech: said). Like the "bridge," it projects a logic of aporetic thresholds. In *Vertigo,* Hitchcock has Barbara Bel Geddes repeat the term *portrait* by accenting and drawing out "trait," isolating the two parts of the word about the tampered example of a graphematic representation. The syllable port will stand on its own, for instance, excised from the promise of movement in a word like *trans*port. (Doors opening on successive doors leading to a white wall in *Spellbound.*)

postal relays

Crewe's building's mail room, where the blackmailer Tracey makes contact; first stop in Bodega Bay; across *Secret Agent* the "spies' post office" using the chocolate factory as a front. *Suspicion* opens with the question of stamps and sending imaginary letters, echoed in *Psycho* (Marion offers to "lick the stamps" of Sam's alimony payments) and *North by Northwest,* with post offices key elsewhere. In *Foreign Correspondent* hand-written letters are cumulatively passed in one scene, and the delayed delivery of a letter is key in another.

professors

Title of "professor" crops up recurrently and in contadictory positions: in Professor Jordan in *The 39 Steps,* the bombmaker Chatman in *Sabotage,* the American corporate spymaster of *North by Northwest* (whether FBI or CIA, "we're all in the same alphabet soup"), "Professor" Robie, and so on and on. Suggests instruction inherent in the Hitchcock writing scene.

the public

Poe's "crowd" inscribed as cinema tourist position. Variations: ship travelers (the audience) lured by a lantern (flickering light) only to be murdered and robbed *(Jamaica Inn)*; cinema as hypnotism and as the duping or despoiling of sun worshippers (the first *Man Who Knew Too Much*); moviegoers at Verloc's Bijou (the front for *Sabotage*); practitioners of a faux séance in *Family Plot.*

R

The *R* punctuates and recalls the facticity of the graphematic band: the burning yet unscorchable monogram of Rebecca, the pin of the strangler-rapist Rusk in *Frenzy,* the master spy "R" (as in rhododendron) in *Secret Agent,* the boy Arnie in *The Trouble with Harry* (and hence, with cross-links, "Marnie"); in each case, differently, a law of repetition.

reading

Almost always women. Almost always *interrupted* on a train (or cinematic bus), an Underground following the cameo of *Blackmail.* It can indicate fantasy, a hyperreflexive access of simultaneous trace chains (to the point of vertigo), or mechanical imprinting and evasion through repetition. In *Shadow of a Doubt,* little Anne's reading is obsessive and mechanical, like the young Uncle Charlie, we hear, before his "accident" (allied to the only photograph of him that exists—a transformation with or following the photographic "dialectics at a standstill").

sand

Put in the generator to sabotage the "juice" and light of London opening *Sabotage,* it recurs as radioactive in the bottles of *Notorious.* An atomized materiality or earth in the first, it migrates into a prosthetic source of light in the second.

sea

Actively referenced by Mrs. Danvers as what alone could have conquered Rebecca (or the *R* monogram), cited with mock histrionics and briefly in *Vertigo,* ubiquitous and hence effaced in *Lifeboat*: the "sea" absorbs logics of seeing and, in Hitchcock, the letter *C,* much as *mar*(ring) or *mer* do the material and maternal affiliations of "Mother" *(mère).*

shots, bombs

Gunshots double camera shots, and bombs double the atomization of micrographic arrest and imprinting. In the first *Man Who Knew Too Much* the assassin's shot would replicate and shatter the (nonetheless recorded and rehearsed) instant. In *Saboteur* a bomb appears in association with a newsreel crew's truck, linking such dematerialization to pretended documentation.

skis, snow

In the first *Man Who Knew Too Much* a ski jump—tracks on Mallarméan snow—triggers a Daedalian fall as a little black dog mars the white: tracks on whiteness (*Blackmail* Underground ad for ice skating, *The Lady Vanishes*' avalanche or whiteout, *Spellbound*'s lines or "tracks").

solarity
The Platonic sun can be presented as simulacrum, "light" as prosthetic effect (or pyrotechnic), origin vaporized by black sun figures. The first *Man Who Knew Too Much*'s false temple of sun worshippers as front for Hitchcock's cinema and his surrogate assassin-anarchists. It attacks as mechanical plane (crop duster) in *North by Northwest*, without place. The sun is also redoubled, called "too much," and hence dark, in Morocco, Nice, Rio.

sounds like
Recurrent phrase in dialogue, as in the opening of the second *Man Who Knew Too Much*: "Marrakesh, sounds like a drink." This notation alerts to phonemic relays and structure of dialogue or sound, of its role in networks of punning connectives and scriptive agencies.

teeth
Row of alternations (like parallel lines or bar series); recurrent, as in *The Ring,* or the giant teeth advertising a dentist named Barbor in the first *Man Who Knew Too Much.* Again, as the "Salvo-Dont" salesman who grabs Stevie for a brushing while the boy is carrying the bomb in *Sabotage,* the row of teeth in the prosthetic mouth, nonetheless muffling or barring speech. The eye metonymically transcoded as site of mastication, ingestion, the lips as eyelids, teeth as shredders, where the white skeleton protrudes.

too much
Recurrent phrase. Two versions of *The Man Who Knew Too Much* give indices for the production of *sheer excess* by hyperbolic networks of sense. The image knows too much, cites too much, is traversed by too many pasts and futures to speak. In *Rear Window* a dog "knew too much"; in *To Catch a Thief,* the midday sun is "too much."

tourism
The cinematic tourist who is cognitively programmed, blind to what he or she consumes, yet marked as despoiled or raped or murdered upon entering the film. Inscribed in the credit sequences of the first *Man Who Knew Too Much* (hand leafing through travel folders, picking St. Moritz, which picture then becomes the scene's opening shot; that

is, it connotes a circular cognitive order whereby a picture advertisement placed in memory is what is then seen). Anatomized in *Rich and Strange.*

trains
Cinematic topos and machine of stationary transport: clattering rails, rushing shadows, stationary movement, Hadean "Underground."

tripods
Initiated in the pyramid calling cards of the Avenger in *The Lodger* through the triangles in the first *Man Who Knew Too Much* or *The 39 Steps,* and so on, the number thirteen, the *M* or letteral combinations in names or places of *C* (third letter) and *A* (or *O*): the "3" or "1-3" combination saturates the system. Citing Hitchcock's birthdate (August 13), the number is tied to a murder or erasure of origin, the "I," and seriality: as though, as in some histories of number, the first number were "3," from which "1" was retroactively posited. The first person is, in dialogue, a citational fiction. The pyramid marks a hyperbolic structure bound both to apostrophe *(Ah!)* and preinscription in a linguistic or screen afterlife without before (pyramid, Underground).

umbrella
Multiplying in *Foreign Correspondent*'s Amsterdam or *Stage Fright*'s garden party: black circlets or suns, parasolar, like the cinematic, phantasmal shelter in the absence of sun. Norman Bates promises to bring his "trusty umbrella"—yet is without it, standing by the bog.

Underground
London Underground or cinematic train *(Blackmail, Sabotage),* also as political or mimetic "Resistance" *(To Catch a Thief, Torn Curtain).* Cinematic Hades, fog, nonliving simulacra, specters. Reading film as catabasis.

X
On the back of Robie's maidservant Germaine, on the flag beneath the targeted Prime Minister in the Albert Hall of the second *Man Who Knew Too Much,* at the crossroads and crop duster scene in *North by Northwest* creating a grid of the earth: a chiasmic exchange of properties, a trope emblematized by the insignia on the lighter in *Strangers on a Train* ("crisscross"). An operative chi- or chiasmus isolating the systemic exchange of binary values, including referents.

zootropology
Cinema as graphic "animation," animemes linked to the advent of tele-technic cinema (the birds' association with machines); implicit displace-ment of anthropomorphic, of aura, of "life." In *Sabotage* and *Murder!*, bird-man and cat-man figures operate, tour of the aquarium and zoo; fish are cited that change their sex. Marnie asks Mark whether his practice of zoology extends to humans. Centripetally exploding carousel horses in *Strangers on a Train*. Diverse taxidermies replicating cinematic skin.

etc.
One may begin a sketch of this sort, like Hamlet scribbling reminders to himself, skeletal nodes in Benjaminian constellations, postal relays orchestrating a translation of the visible, of the "sensorium," into a more general séance or event of disinscription. As more or less "secret" signifying agencies, these nodes—aural and visual patterns, mnemonic puns, re-marks—share an epistemo-political trait: they resist or deface the hermeneutics of the aesthetic state—transparency, mimesis, identi-fication, "symbol," aura.

3. Espionage in the Teletechnic Empire

The image as shock and the image as *cliché* are two aspects of the same presence.
> —Susan Sontag, "Looking at War"

. . . the historically perfect collusion of world wars, reconnaissance squadrons, and cinematography.
> —Friedrich A. Kittler, *Gramophone, Film, Typewriter*

In a recent critical turn, Peter Conrad's *The Hitchcock Murders* examines the effects of allowing interfaced scenes, actors, and incidents in this oeuvre to read one another. Conrad aims to recuperate the fallen fortunes of auteurism against what he dismisses somewhat grandly as the depredations of academic schools. But instead of returning to any familiar territory covered by the term, he invents what could be called auteurism without an auteur. Using what he terms a mode of crosscutting, leaping between affiliated scenes or repetitions, Conrad wanders into a fractal labyrinth of Hitchcockian repetitions and citational relays. Serially cross-referenced scenes are filled with "graphic riddles." Conrad finds no alternative but to call for "a new kind of literacy." A small tremor passes through an entire interpretive facade:

> A new kind of literacy has to be developed, able to interpret gestures and second-guess faces, alert to tell-tale patterns and repetitions. Watching a film, we are reading a language of ciphers. Of course we do the same when we read a book, but we have forgotten it: after long training, we take the words to be things, rather than the insignia for absent objects—a seagull, a banister, the twisted knot in a woman's hair-do. (233)

Something occurs in this shift, where viewing the image becomes "reading a language of ciphers." Once the name *Hitchcock* had been installed at the center of different canonical histories (of movies, of film theory), any alteration in its import potentially sends shock waves throughout related ganglia, altering perception, even models of experience. If this oeuvre continues to transform the archive, it is interesting to ask how it impacts on the logics of image today.

Given a not so secret alliance between seeing and consuming, the dilemmas of contemporary consumption and even the constructions of time appear imbricated in logics of the image, deriving from a teletechnic archive traced back to photographic technologies yet affiliated today with globalization, techno-weaponry, mediacracies. Benjamin speculated on the advent of cinema as the revocation of aura, which he equated with habits of personification: the implication of rendering mnemonic orders external and machinal was that a certain form of anthropomorphism would be revoked. The confabulation of the techno-image would move the construction of the "human" in epistemological terms as if beyond specular and anthropomorphic grids, and do so because one could not return to an imaginary interiority of memory or experience or metaphor; *beyond,* among other things, ocularcentrism, which is to say, beyond the protocols of the Greek identification of seeing and knowing *(eidein),* the metaphoric church of "light," Enlightenment protocols. The cinematic image is politicized at its advent: either it will appear to ensure the mimetic real or it will suspend what could be called this statist epistemology, expose the mnemonic machines as prosthetic. What attended the coalescence of "image" from an atomizing stream of light that citationally brackets and dematerializes what it arrests? What, moreover, occurred within the histories of the "eye"?

   Given the vast implications of globalizations to come, it is not too much to say that, if different logics of the image were vying for dominance at the time of cinema's own normatization, different futures were competing as well. What séance was being conducted as "earth" was to be transformed and accelerated—a question of the home or lodging, of teletechnics generally, of perceptual programming? Bruce Dern complains to the ersatz medium Mme Blanche in *Family Plot* that she has him by the "crystal balls," that the faux séancing of the cinematic spools stores pasts and programs futures. Whatever has been called cinema partakes of artificial memory as implanted or repeated bands. It loops back to a site of inscriptions that is structurally concealed, blind, in advance of the "eye"—as by a projector booth for the tourist viewer or consumer. Cinema, rather than celebrating the visual, feeds off an ocularcentric blindness to its dependence on memory and the cut. Seeming paradox: the programs of ideation that depend upon naturalizing mimesis—diverse empiricisms, realisms, pragmatisms, materialisms, virtual "idea(l)isms" all—would be popularly enforced by the mass cultural machine that technically atomizes each. The eye is disclosed as a prosthetic effect.

One could deduce a *split* out of which are constructed the policial and espionage plots of the British cycle in Hitchcock. There is the home state with its police or secret agencies, which is under attack; and there is an eruption of otherness in the form of criminality (serial murder, theft, blackmailing, all in various combinations). The anarchist or *anarchivist* cineast—Peter Lorre, Oscar Homolka—assaults the state order as the birds later drive the Brenners from their "home." That assault and dispossession already dwells in the logic of the telesthenic, the cinematic, the deauratic: the state is the house of a destroying hermeneutic that produces sexually void policemen, lacking in the virility their male posture claims, blackmailing young women into dead marriages.

Two criminalities: the state and the anarchivist, the installed archive and the anarchivist drive turned against it, of it, exposing its transformative and lawless laws. In the political thrillers, this involves the fate in one way or another of the world, history and world wars. This is a "MacGuffin" that, per definition, is also not one. The weapons are all cinematic (shots, bombs), the settings all cinematic (music halls, fake churches, trains): the war occurs within teletechnic and epistemological orders. Auteurists have attempted to designate various character ciphers as "surrogates" for the director, then derive moral consequences from the puppetry. Yet the heroes—say, Hannay—are nescient tourists who inadvertently help foreclose this cinematic uprising. Cinema "identifies" with the anarchivists, the cineasts, the citational rupture of the state's aesthetic structures. The state runs on a phantasm of light and identity, time and perception, the real and the copy in order to conceal its status as an *aesthetic* preconstruction. Alter that, and the performative definitions of time, gender, agency, the political, perception, mnemonics—all are reinscribed.

This paradigm is carried through in more sophisticated ways later. In *Rear Window,* Raymond Burr (Lars Thorwald) represents a certain cold real of the murdering cineast, James Stewart the photographic tourist. ("Thor," Norse god of lightning, is expunged in Cary Grant's later moniker, Thornhill.) Thorwald sells costume jewelry, cuts up his wife's body, preserves rings.

So there is another phantom within this now spectral "cinema." It exposes a technicity at the heart of perceptual programs. It services and launches powers that will globalize markets, partake of techno-war machines, accelerate terrestrial consumption. "Mother" and "nature" will be exposed as narrative fronts for this technicity. Which may be why Benjamin allies this experience of "shock" with prehistory and with "natural history"—or geological "time," deanthropomorphized. As if the cut and this other time were that, say, of prehistorial birds allied to technicity, as occurs in the "bird war" of *The Birds*. In *Sabotage*, animals and animation are invoked to displace—virtually, time bomb—the "human" community who gather around Verloc's Bijou.

One might condense this impasse as follows: the ocularcentric state is not just resisted but criminalized as an imperial operation historically installed. It represents a programming of cognition, definition, time. It extends to the operations of media and phantasmal politics today. The impasse resides in the definitions of *eye* or *visual* or *aesthetic*. It registers a link between the eye and the evisceration of terrestrial reserves. Hitchcock represents one unread chapter in the histories and counter-histories of the teletechnic empire as that has been globalized. A deauratic practice of cinema has some resonance for those trying to think the next conceptualization beyond that of the "global" today—saturated as that notion is with metaphors of unity and totality. The post-"global" era will be mapped, and controlled, by histories of teletechnicity. The term *planetary* has been turned to, by Masao Miyoshi or Gayatri Spivak, as if it would situate an otherness outside the fields that organize identity and positional memory (gender, nation, subalternity).[1] The planetary as a term suggests not only a deanthropomorphic venue, outside cultural identities, but inevitably a teletechnic order. Miyoshi cannot imagine this term without a utopian relapse, reimposing the totalizing and inclusive desires of social justice, yet it points beyond that humanist tradition. The planetary as a figure seems to retain a doubleness: it is the effect of and defined by telemedia and it is, it must be, a locus shorn of anthropomorphic premises. Personification, like Benjaminian aura, must recede. For Miyoshi, the exigency of the "planetary" is linked not only to the death of traditional humanistic studies but also to the crisis of nonhuman biosystems (extinctions, biodiversity, poisoned and vanishing reserves and species, and so on)—that which is beyond metaphor, like Hitchcock's birds. Cinema emerges in its deauratic moment as a war machine on behalf of the nonmetaphoric, the deauratic, the non-anthropomorphic. Every photograph, for instance, assures this, including the background of the earth in every shot of people, even on a set.

If the global resonates as a holistic metaphor, the planetary suggests something other. For Spivak, however, it is not clear how to access this other: "I cannot offer a formulaic access to planetarity. No one can" (78). What is sought, clearly, involves a break with formulations of the community and the human as sensorially and semantically constituted:

> I propose the planet to overwrite the globe. Globalization is the imposition of the same system of exchange everywhere. In the gridwork of electronic capital, we achieve that abstract ball covered in latitudes and longitudes, cut by virtual lines, once the equator and the tropics and so on, now drawn by the requirements of Geographical Information Systems. To talk planet-talk by way of an unexamined environmentalism, referring to an undivided "natural" space rather than a differentiated political space, can work in the interest of this globalization in the mode of the abstract as such. . . . The globe is on our computers. No one lives there. It allows us to think that we can aim to control it. The planet is in the species of alterity, belonging to another system; and yet we inhabit it, on loan. It is not really amenable to a neat contrast with the globe. I cannot say "the planet, on the one hand." When I invoke the planet, I think of the effort required to figure the (im)possibility of this underived intuition. (72)

It is outside metaphoric systems as currently programmed—as cinematically installed. The name "The Globe" is featured atop the newspaper building that opens *Foreign Correspondent,* associating a gridlike construction with mass media; and in *Frenzy* the "Globe" will devolve to a pub or a London bar displacing Shakespeare's theater to nipple-like shots of poisonous alcohol. Both images warn against the global being taken literally. This totality is implied in the mirror-reflecting grid opening the advertising center of the universe in *North by Northwest* leading to the United Nations, a traffic jam of tropes, while the "planetary" stands beyond the stone monuments of personified heads of Mount Rushmore—the acephalic *heads* of the *earth* prefigured by the nonexistent "*George Kap*lan." The cinematic here absorbs all teletechnics and media and steps beyond or before figuration, or has done so with its deauratic advent at the rim of the archival dome—in essence citing the planet incessantly, in fact or by proxy in every photographic frame or imprint as background if not atomized premise. This may be why the "planetary" as a term is doomed, perhaps, to replicate the global as a discursive offering or blind: if the first is a mapping device, the latter retains its birthmark more as a prosopopoeia than an astrological figure of nonanthropomorphic systems.

The interest of the cinematic as practiced by Hitchcock here is the sheer prosthesis of all perception and memory. The planetary could not be "nature," so it must lead to a different teletechnic otherness. What the cinematic implies is an extraterritoriality, an extraterrestriality (to cite Spielberg's regressive trope for cinema), or an *aterra,* teletechnic orders and prosthetic earths avenged by prehistorial birds. In Hitchcock's practice, the word (and color) green is denaturalized and disclosed, too, as a mnemonic effect; like "Mother," it is without natural referent or reserve, like the Santa Rosa "Free Library" or town archive visited by young Charlie yet entirely covered by ferns in *Shadow of a Doubt.*

Before Lila Crane, seeking Mother in the Bates house, proceeds to the fruit cellar, she visits Mother's bedroom. There she sees a bodily imprint on the mattress. Lila's eye rests on a box with two bronze woman's hands as if cut off and at rest. She is startled then as her own image is caught in endless recession between two mirrors, a specular *mise en abyme* of the image itself, featuring the manipulation and manufacture of autonomous hands. Continuing as if *beyond* this specular trap, unable to read the logics of specular doubling *en abyme,* she proceeds to Norman's room. Here she scans its relics: a toy stuffed bunny with a floppy ear, the unmoving record player with the *Eroica Symphony* on it. Lila comes upon a leather-bound book without title and opens it (we are not allowed to see what she sees). What if an entire bibliographics or representational history of "the Book" were implied at a glance? How could that prepare Lila for the cinematic fruit cellar where she finally encounters "Mother," the swinging electric bulb and frantic shadows, the empty eye sockets, and Norman in operatic drag, editing knife raised—restrained from behind? Loomis's restraint of Norman cites the Laocoön statuary, and hence the entire aesthetic tradition that Lessing's work connotes. The statuary is a drag star whose slashing indicates, like Norman's Napoleonic record, the secret that links phenomenality to prerecordings, networked programs, telegraphics of the archive, implants before any possible present or perception is generated. In moving as if from Mother's imprint on the vacant mattress to Norman's room, Lila passes from the *mise en abyme* of the specular into a technical universe of fetishized media and mediations: faux taxidermy, gramophone, leather-bound book.

What *passes* between these three rooms of the Bates house as if from a matrical imprint through technologies of reproduction, to the underworld of Mother "herself"—*khora*-like, socketed, perhaps genderless? What did Lila *read*? How do reading, teletechnics, voice, mnemonics, figure as if in transition between forms of old and new literacy, as if between old and new technicity? What if any passage between teletechnological eras were not progressive—from hieroglyph to book, book to image, silent to sound, analogic to digital? Or if Hitchcock's practice involved an appeal to the outside of this consuming archive, to its borderlines? What if it could not *not* war with and intrigue against the mimetic program that claims its technology as a weapon, too?

Benjamin finds in cinema an implicit analog for what he later calls "materialistic historiography": a recasting of pasts and futures through mnemonic intervention. It is inscribed in biblical borders and promised lands, which some Professor Jordan would reach with the formula of accelerated mnemonic weaponry. The teletechnicity preinhabiting the "planetary" delivers this political horizon over to something that cannot be brought back to maternal, metaphoric, global, totalizing, matrical, originary, or mimetic terms. In one sense, the program that appeared to guarantee the stability of reference and face is the "enemy," as Benjamin calls "historicism"—the assemblage of *facts* that Mr. Memory as camera begins *The 39 Steps* by entertaining the public with. It is an "earth" that is entirely deauratic, of course, cinematized, without originary reserve, without "Mother," "nature," "light," the eye, a sort of *aterra* without proper name or anthropomorphic face. The anarchivist saboteur cannot operate out of *ressentiment* alone, while lacking any ideology: he avenges, like the Avenger associated with fog or the later birds, as a rebellion of parts, particles, feet, "material" traces, the nonanthropomorphic. It suggests a "beyond" to Miyoshi's substitute trope of the planet, still a round globe, which retains the totalizing and personified nostalgia that the "global," today, has as a front.

Thus Conrad, in *The Hitchcock Murders,* explains cinema's originary "shock" effect: "The cinema, like a bomb, is a device for dematerializing the world" (27). Or: "The technologies of terrorism and of film are only too alike" (24). Or: "Hitchcock likened his films to buzz bombs—clever engines of mass destruction, invented by the century in which men made war against humanity" (118). This explosivity is mutely assumed in disasters (avalanche, shipwreck, car crash) that appear outside of narrative time: "Hitchcock allowed himself to be branded 'the master of suspense.' . . . But his real interest was in suspension" (23).

Several hypotheses about "war" and espionage in the teletechnic empire within Hitchcock's early or British cycle emerge:

- They are always *epistemo-political* and hence in and of the archive, in and of mnemonics, the "house," the hermeneutic home state and its others.
- They do not occur between two fratricidal powers but between and within the logics of the home and a nonanthropomorphic "certain foreign power," which may be allied to teletechnic machines, to mnemonic mechanics (the parallel line series), to graphics, to animals and animemes (or animation), to cinematic doubles (the fabled "Bandriki" of *The Lady Vanishes* as vampire movie set).
- In the beginning the threat to "England" is from doubles or nameless others that will migrate, later, into the "enemy" camps of history, Germans, Nazis, cold war others, finally nonhuman others (birds).
- What is at war may be later summarized by the phrase the "bird war" but is implied, already, in *The Lodger*'s logic of "avenging" and the cinematic role of "fog": the avenging prehistorial trace, like the reflected particles suspended by fog before coalescing as image (hence, material in kind), moving against the state of the ocularcentric image, the home, the "human," metaphor, heliotropisms, "general semantics."

A rift in time, called a "contretemps" in *Secret Agent,* is perpetually created and examined. Such time wars are not of the mid-twentieth century but of the entire era of teletechnic global empire to come, of which Hitchcock was at once accelerator and host, resister and anatomist. His work takes perpetual cognizance of nonhuman histories, like reference to the desert that had once been a sea in the American west of *Saboteur,* or the imbrication of pollution and terrestrial rape with the purgatorial wasteland of erotic ritual in *Frenzy*—for which the serial strangler and impotent rapist becomes a virtual counterstroke and aesthetic hero. Cinema here is a war machine in or on behalf of the wholly other: all of which is declared in the opening "blonde" face shot of *The Lodger,* summary of a metaphysical history displaced into the cinematic light gun.

Kittler observes: "The history of the movie camera thus coincides with the history of automatic weapons. The transport of pictures only repeats the transport of bullets. In order to focus on and fix objects moving through space, such as people, there are two procedures: to shoot and to film. In the principle of cinema resides mechanized death as it was invented in the nineteenth century: the death no longer of one's immediate opponent but of serial nonhumans" (124). What would have been called "the masses" passes into the Poesque "crowd," now positioned not alone in or as public space but in the anesthetizing inundation of the cinematic darkness—subject to, and before, their implied evisceration, a death that cannot be registered because of the latter's status as animation: the masses are rewritten as the cinematic "public," which is to say as cognitive tourists. The cinematic, in turn, doubles against its official role of servicing the state's mimetic protocols, identificatory needs, and narrative rehearsals. The British Empire memorialized itself in the British Museum's hoarding of the conquered and colonized's historical memory, in monuments and relics, aesthetic trophies it was, it assumed, best able to tend, unify, and study—at once an empire of memorial traces and itself a monument to a violating model of the aesthetic, the museum.

In *Blackmail,* Britain's first "talkie," as if giving voice to its teletechnic prowess, the blackmailer Tracey is chased the length of the museum past, and as if before, its Egyptian wing and the ur-pictograms on papyrus that provide a covering origin for writing and the bookend of the imperial, solar, chronographic territory: Egypt, a site referenced as a key to "victory" in war at the end of *Secret Agent.*[2] By his precession of the historial map and hieroglyphs, the cinematic Tracey traverses the imperial constructions of time, light, the eye, memory storage. In *Psycho,* in Norman's bedroom, Beethoven's *Eroica* is on the phonograph, stitching the heroic if doomed Napoleon's resurgence to Norman's solitary rituals undoing, in essence, the eye (and "I"). In *Spellbound* and *Vertigo,* an Empire (or Empire State) Hotel appears, and in *Foreign Correspondent* an Empire Electric Photo Flood Lamps label names a tool of torture: the artificed light of solar and cinematic production, of "Enlightenment" programs reflected both in the Euro-pacifist Van Meer and the fascist intrigue.

The "espionage" of the teletechnic empire in Hitchcock occurs with the invocation, it seems, of every variant in the linguistic arsenal—every telegraphy and telephony, teletype and news press, glass-boothed taxidermy shop and solar church, phonographic replay and machine of transport, kitchen and chocolate factory. Every cryptonymy thrown up by the text, including the labyrinth of Hitchcock's own signature systems, appears politically inscribed within a general challenge and overthrow of the ocularcentric state—one whose technical suppression forms the perpetual MacGuffin of the narrative "MacGuffins" in place.

Recently, a researcher sampled six hundred television viewers in the United States and found that most thought of their favorite sitcom characters or newscasters as their "friends," more so than they did "real" acquaintances. He concluded that anything that the human nervous system had not known in its prehistory it had no means of adjusting to and would experience as it had the world all along. The *New York Post* reported:

> A new study found people watching TV believe they have an improved social life and wider circle of "Friends.". . . That's the word from sociologist Satoshi Kanazawa of Indiana University in Pennsylvania, who looked at the TV-viewing habits of 600 Americans. "My basic contention is that in evolution, our entire body has difficulty comprehending stimulus that didn't exist 200,000 years ago," Kanazawa told *The Post*. Therefore, our brain doesn't know that we don't have more friends when we watch TV, that they are just actors. "We found that people who watch TV think they have these friends—even if they don't have any real friends, they think they have them. . . . That means the subconscious counts any face it sees regularly as a real-life friend, even if it's just on TV."[3]

Mimetic identification with the charismatic friend. Walter Benjamin in part calls this "aura," which, paradoxically, was to have been suspended with the advent of cinema, absolutely curtailed, and instead found itself restored and guarded by the medium. In question too is *reference,* how it is identified and identified with. Hitchcock assumes in his chases and double chases that the eye is an inherited, programmed technology, and serves political agendas and archival laws. He knows that there are other technologies of the visual. Mediacracy requires a face to identify with—and trains consumers by image implants. More: if a specter strikes—say, al Qaeda in "9/11," as these two numbers on either side of the digital monumentalize—but has no face to train on or for its posters (Osama bin Laden), it requires one (Saddam Hussein) at all expense to maintain the mirage of a single agent, if he will not comply and become a specter in turn. "Terrorism" may be the name for whatever can be anthropomorphized to distract from the deanthropomorphized cataclysms that cannot enter the mimetic political networks (dying oceans, global warming, disappearing species, supergerms, etc.). The cinematic shares more with a generalized nonanthropomorphic domain of visual practices by other life forms, since the camera is not itself human: how the eyes of fish, birds, or cats, not to mention allomimetic creatures or insects function, always in the context of strategic response or camouflage (shape-shifters), chemical adjustment, selection of light waves and information, tracking movements of prey and predator. *Seeing* has to do, Hitchcock finds, with eating, with teeth, much as it does with the consumption programmed by advertising.

4. Blackmail in the Universal Reading Room

Film transforms life into a form of trace detection.
—**Friedrich A. Kittler,** *Gramophone, Film, Typewriter*

Photographs had the advantage of uniting two contradictory features. Their credentials of objectivity were inbuilt, yet they always had, necessarily, a point of view. They were a record of the real—incontrovertible, as no verbal account, however impartial, could be (assuming that they showed what they purported to show)—since a machine was doing the recording. And they bore witness to the real, since a person had been there to take them.
—**Susan Sontag, "Looking at War"**

An obvious pun in the title *Blackmail* (Hitchcock's first "talkie") links a hole within the orders of light to a postal relay and both, in turn, to the power to blackmail, to hold hostage. Something about the photographic image is identified with the power to blackmail the present with some knowledge or secret of anteriority—if only awareness that the present is itself generated by something like a mnemonic band, like celluloid, from which the world is emanated. It is not accidental in *Blackmail* that the final chase of the blackmailer, Tracey, will lead to the oddest site, the British Museum, the universal archive whose initials seem to replicate the two words within the title.

But it only gets worse if one pays attention to this ending: Tracey is chased by the police, finally, along the corridors of the museum, through and beyond the Egyptian wing and its hieroglyphic displays. The cinematic trace that is pursued by the police will precede hieroglyphics, the official origin of pictographs or writing, and Tracey will then fall through the glass dome above the museum, a giant head. His finger is pointing in accusation at Detective Frank Webber, his pursuer, his own

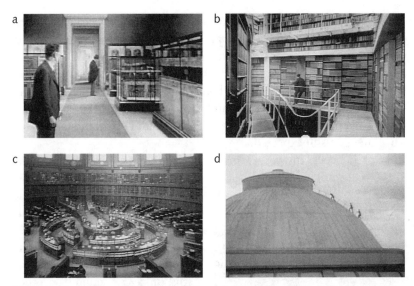

Figure 7. Blackmailer Tracey fleeing through history by way of (a) hieroglyphic display; (b) bookish archive; (c) universal reading room; and (d) up the archival domed head.

blackmailer, about whom he, Tracey, nonetheless knows a secret that he will not be allowed to speak: namely, that Frank is covering up the murder of the graphic artist Crewe by Frank's girlfriend, Alice White. Tracey *points,* he wants to indicate something, to indict, perhaps to index, but he cannot quite speak or say what it is. And instead he plunges through the glass dome and into a room we have visited already in the chase, which led through the book archives of the museum itself. It is the universal reading room. There are circles around circles of people reading in this, the nation's imperial archive that traces itself back to Egypt and includes all the artifacts from the global empire. The cinematic is not a "modernist" invention—once it appears, it will have preceded and enfolded the histories to which it seems to have been addended.

Several startling features attend this conclusion to *Blackmail.* They seem to leap out of a unique trauma within cinema itself; let us say the obvious: that it is a traumatic shift or fault within the cinematic, within its powers and definitions and destinies, simple though it seems. It is the movement that *Blackmail* registers and performs: that from silent film to talkies. Or, at the same time, at least according to Hitchcock, it is in a way the *failure* of that shift to occur or make a difference—not because "talkies" were always implied or coming, but because they never could arrive as other than just more signifiers applied to whatever silents, "pure cinema," were or would be. Dialogue would be just more sound; sound would be just a different set of marks to master; voice would always be prosthetic and not expressive or psychotropic; the image would be, must be, essentially mute—like Tracey before his fall. In either case, "cinema" seems to rupture in *Blackmail,* and Hitchcock must use the occasion to turn upon and examine its predicates, its epistemological pretenses, and what emerges is unexpected.

For Hitchcock, movies—almost all other movies—will be dismissed as "pictures of people talking," and speech itself, as he tells Truffaut, will be for him just more sound. Not the expression of psychologies in language, and so on, but aural signifiers that primarily form patterns, linkages, "sound like" other figures. In a film like *Secret Agent,* Hitchcock will focus on overwhelming and deafening sound that refuses all semantic components and ally it with whatever he means by secret agency—the sheer vehicle of material traces that form aural and visual transport. But whatever the trauma of *Blackmail* is within a faulted history of "cinema" itself (as if the Pandora's box of all "talkies" were being opened and speculated on), some sort of rift opens that requires special examination and will not so much end in as pass through the British Museum's universal historial archive. It will even be registered in a unique cameo: that of Hitchcock himself reading, on a train, reading, that is, on and in the cinematic transport. *Reading* is a figure used in many other places by Hitchcock, usually if not always with women, and it is always *interrupted.* In fact, there are three scenes of reading in this work, including the final fall through the giant dome of the universal reading room—as if the cinematic trace traversed all of reading as much as it traverses in the museum, or virtually precedes, all of monumental history.

Figure 8. Teletechnic machinery powering detective's (cinematic) Flying Squad van.

If blackmail implies an excess of knowledge used to extort things from someone or to silence, it has to do with the return of something anterior against the structure of the present. Technically, in the story, that is what the blackmailer Tracey *witnesses.* He appears first as a shadow—

linked to the cinematic—hovering about the artist Crewe's building at night, having something on him that we never are told. Crewe has brought home Alice White, whom he picked up at a restaurant, stealing her away from her stiff and uninteresting detective boyfriend, Frank Webber, after slipping her a note (of which we see a torn part) that, apparently, took her to the restaurant with Frank in tow. Crewe takes Alice up to his loft, dresses her as a model, plays the piano for her (a ditty called "Miss Up-To-Date," aimed at claiming her as a modern available girl), and tries to force himself on her. Alice defends herself by stabbing Crewe behind a curtain. Tracey, like the camera, witnesses this act obliquely and retrieves Alice's glove, one finger missing a tip. That is the evidence, the token of blackmail that will allow Tracey to swagger into Alice's father's shop, which sells tobacco products and newspapers—two figures of cinema for Hitchcock (smoke and print).

But pointing fingers run across the work as if compulsively replicating: not only Tracey's final accusation, but the dead Crewe's hand, the painting of the laughing jester who seems to point to whoever looks at it. It appears, in fact, that pointing fingers involve the entire premise of the photographic image as a presumably indexing technic, one that points at, indicates, or indexes a real. It is a documentary or mimetic premise of the photograph, such as film studies will be predicated on, yet is here, at the advent of "talkies," revoked. If in *The 39 Steps* this premise is undone by the logic of repetition, so Mr. Memory's "facts" (snapshots) are accelerated and atomized into the secret formula for a silent mnemonic bomber, in *Blackmail* the premise of indexing, of pointing, of contact, appears to fall through monumental history in a manner that deforms temporalization. If cinema blackmails it is not only through its identification with a trace or writing that precedes the projected "present" with another knowledge. It blackmails the structure of the "present" with an interruption, such as occurs when the cameo of Hitchcock is reading, on a train.

Hitchcock arrests the premise of documentary and indexing in the opening silent portion of the work, an account of the arrest of a criminal that leads to the police station house and, with that, the introduction of sound, of speech, of "talkies." This traumatic fold within (British) cinema and cinema in general, an event cushioned by being taken into and studied "in" *Blackmail,* will be slowly bled into the frames following the capture of the criminal, silent film itself. Even if, by setting itself up that way, it obliterates the premise of documentary when Detective Frank, trying to maintain Alice's interest in the restaurant, proposes taking her to the latest *picture,* a true-to-life police drama called *Finger-prints*: more or less the seemingly documentary prequel that formed the first part of *Blackmail.* Frank tells us it would be so true to life, in fact, that they hired a criminal as director.

The prequel arrests, tracks, captures the criminal of silent film. It will

a

b

Figure 9. (a) Criminal fingerprint as face in identification parade.
(b) Between men: "talk's" positioned advent in police restroom.

do so as mock documentary, only to introduce, in broken disarticulations, sound and speech in the station. It will secure and identify that criminal with fingerprints and what is called the "identification parade." But there is something astonishing going on where all this labor of identification, indexing, and finger-pointing converts, after this arrest or arrestation, not only into speech, "talkies," but continues to mute Tracey and Alice in particular. The image only mutes further, and the more obviously women, blackmailers, and ultimately the detective, as if there were no forward transition, no epochal break, no leap across teletechnic eras (into "talkies" quite). No, what is equally peculiar is that time will be so compromised in what ensues—once, that is, the pretense of the arresting documentary is engulfed and erased. This seems apparent not only in the equivocations about arriving too soon or too late—which are the "first" words spoken in any British talkie, spoken in the policemen's bathroom, or in the anachronizing tune "Miss Up-To-Date" (which, if one can bracket the blank import of Miss Alice White, addresses the modernization of "talkies"), or in the obverse and unexpected fall as if back through monumental history sprung in the final chase.

All the gestures of capture and identification turn not only on the criminal but, frankly, on cinema (and silents in particular), as if documenting documentation and the fable of indexing that criminalizes the photographemic image. After all this, Tracey as revenant of the arrested silent criminal is referred to simply by the artist Crewe, perhaps too simply, as a "sponger." For if the cinematic image cannot arrest and capture, index and indicate, identify and document—indeed, if it must revert, first, to the swirl of fingerprints and contact sheets, to be a "sponger" is quite a different game. A "sponger" does not labor to designate and control and incarcerate; a "sponger," for sure, blackmails, but a "sponger," above all, sponges—absorbs from a nonposition, like a shadow, everything, all trace chains and citational implications, whatever passes through the frame and whatever constitutes it from beyond imaginary borders. Like the whole of monumental history. The cinematic trace is, then, this "sponger." This blackmailing "sponger" would unpack and implicate innumerable trace chains—driving one through, in a kind of temporal precession, the accumulated displays of an empire, say, at the British Museum, house of muses.

One begins to see, or not, why reading recurs here, breaks the surface and is compromised, in a sort of vertigo perhaps, unable to master the criminal and proliferating implications as to what is happening, in the end, within the archival itself, which the museum chase presents us with rather explicitly. And one may use these three scenes of reading, always *interrupted,* to articulate an event and fold within the telearchive itself: the gift of sound to "silents," which guarantees muting. Three scenes of interrupted reading then: that of the arrested criminal in the silent prequel, holding a newspaper; that of Hitchcock's cameo, interrupted reading on the Underground, in the underworld of the cinematic as such; and Tracey's fall through the universal reading room.

Criminal News

The pointing finger of identification and blame and touch before the possibility of sight suspends the promise of a *here it is, right here, and now.* This putative point of contact, a touch that seems either left as a trace or barred from occurring, precedes ocularcentrism.[1] The proliferation of pointing fingers makes this clear: the finger indicates, indicts, indexes, yet it is only encountered as imprint, fingerprints, film prints. The arrested criminal's photographed face dissolves notably into the graphics of the fingerprint and then a "Cell" door is featured, the whole passing into the single celluloid frame. The crisis in this technological transition, virtually seismic, produces a performance beyond what commentators may mean by saying that *Blackmail* features the experimental treatment of "sound" as a technical problem. In the faux documentary segment there seems a promise of documentation, of reproduction or mimetic veracity. It is presented, however, in an allegorical guise. The silent segment follows a police van closing in on and executing the nameless criminal's *arrest*: the detectives receive directions on a wireless, go to a house surrounded by playing children, enter to find the criminal in bed, reading a newspaper, preempt his attempt to resist, take him to the station, and identify him. A witness *points* him out in a lineup, and he is fingerprinted in what is called an "identification parade" (the fingerprint dissolves into the face shot here).

This *capture,* reminiscent of a camera shot, concerns a process of incarceration replicating a camera's capture of its photographed object (the van resembles a wheeled box, a cinema production unit), and the whole segment ends with washing up in the police station, where sound and talk are finally introduced in the men's bathroom. First, muffled, single words emerge tentatively, then some dialogue. Yet as if to double back, in a restaurant scene to follow, the "picture" called *Fingerprints* is alluded to that Detective Webber lauds as so realistic they hired a criminal to direct it, and he wants to see it to check its veracity—identifying cinema as an identifying media, one of reproduction. Since the work indicated mimes the silent segment, it folds into or over it, inscribing the *arrest* as (also) of the ("real") director, or its accuracy to be checked by himself (a character), and so on. The asymmetry that pretends silent film is close to reportage or documentary, and that it is superseded by the full-powered narration of the new "talkies" is inverted. As a relation of firsts and seconds, it is turned inside out. The silent sequence tracks the event of the medium's promise and production—a sheer allegorical tract—even as the appearance of the voiced sequence's greater verisimilitude (reproducing speech now) merely redoubles and is contained by the former's logic. At which point Alice White, attention wandering, leaves the restaurant with Crewe and goes with him to his loft—the artist's allographic workshop—where her killing of the artist during an attempted rape, of the artist *by* the ersatz model, is triggered, a transaction that seems to call forth the "sponger" Tracey from the shadows.

The arrested criminal will anticipate Tracey himself and be associated, again, with a "director" (in the movie *Fingerprints*). The criminal is interrupted reading a newspaper in bed, his leg moving beneath the sheets in open mime of masturbation. It is virtually the newspaper produced in *The Lodger*'s printing press detour and sold in Alice's father's shop. But the second allusion to reading is the most problematic and occurs in Hitchcock's cameo. In some ways, the first in a "talkie," it is a cameo of cameos. There he "himself" is interrupted on an Underground train (trope of cinema and its afterlife) by a bullying boy, as he sits directly behind the two principals, Frank Webber and Alice White. Hitchcock reading, a cameo, interrupted reading on the train, as if that reading, and that interruption, echoed in Tracey's plunge into the British Museum.[2]

If the work arrests a (reversible) transition from silent films to "talkies," it poses as an effaced event or mock origin ("talkies") and returns to mock origins (Egypt). But if it is not, simply, "about" the production of sound but a dismantling of its epistemological promise, another technicity *troubles* this transition: it will be battled over by the pretext of a coming cinema of "pictures of people talking," on the one hand, and its assimilation, as sound, to "pure" silent premises, on the other.[3] Hitchcock would never leave "silent film" to the extent that even dialogue would be apprehended primarily as sound (more networking signifiers). The print or fingerprint out of which the image or recording is phenomenalized is only one trace, passed or projected onto the criminal's face in the "identification parade." It registers a touch or contact that is, at this point, entirely archival and entirely effaced in its emergence, seemingly, as face. The "senses" derive, after the fact, from a paring of teletechnic effects—what can, at best, be interrupted in the accelerated stasis of a reading scene (through the letteral, spacing, and the mark), the more so when that is made, in concentric unclosed circles, "universal," or situated in the state museum's map of cultural time and place. The eye as hypothetical organ appears inscribed in the structure of *blackmail,* as much as the displacement (as advent) of sound, into which the always borrowed voice phonetically dissolves. Familiarity, the familiality of the re-cognized image (already identified from a memory implant), is blackmailed, even if that family runs a tobacco and newspaper shop, or hands out a particular sort of cigar, one with a doubled name, even lighting it for Tracey: Corona Corona.

Detective Webber, a protégé of webs, ends up pursuing the blackmailer Tracey, a "sponger," in the face of the latter's knowledge of Alice's accidental murder of the artist. Webber pursues Tracey, once again short-circuiting the hermeneutic model of the chase with an initial redoubling of the circuit—a "double chase," absorbing and hyperbolically exceeding the mmemonics and mechanics of the hermeneutic (or reading) machine that leads through the museum's library stacks.

Webber chases Tracey as if through temporality, through historial monuments, that is, through the British Museum and the Egyptian statuary and hieroglyphs. Hitchcock's stylus here drifts into other logics of writing, trace zones not unlike the geologic perspective according to which the several thousand years of Western culture appear bracketed, traversed, allo-anthropomorphic: a site, for example, where the tropes of light or face, of linear reading or historical periodization, dissolve. Thus Tracey will have to *fall* into the circular *universal* reading room of the state archive. Why, however, does *Blackmail* lend itself to this extraordinary focus on the reading model—as if, owing to the stress of the (failed) incorporation of the voice, so fateful to the medium, problems of "reading" arise like antibodies rushed to the battle? It is impossible to view *Blackmail* only as "a sustained reflection on the possible relations of sight to sound, on visual to aural aspects of film style."[4]

Why does the introduction of "voice" in Hitchcock occur among men, among police, in a men's room posed as a cloacal, chatty, and explicitly homoerotic scene (a central figure is shown from the rear, bent over a sink)? Sound from the first has to do with law enforcement, or rather, the police are exposed and undermined at and as the advent of sound. "Talk"

is introduced to British cinema, to the socius, fragmentarily and in association with the power world of men representing the law, with women
cut out—and this, at first, with remarks about time. *Before* the narrative
of the film properly begins, before Alice White is introduced waiting for
Frank at Scotland Yard, the protracted vignette or prequel of the Flying
Squad van, whose spinning wheel (which appear to spin *backward*) opens
the film, shows a detective taking dictation from the wireless, leading to
the arrest of the *reading criminal*. We only see the transcribed first letters
of the address: C-A-M, as though the logic of the camera or cameo, quite
differently, were being converged upon, brought to the impasse of the
absent syllable *-bridge*—as though bridging, or translating, between two
models or territories.[5]

Any view of silent film as documentary is turned into a fable: sound
or voice would if anything seem to add verisimilitude, rendering the
shadow script of silents, inversely, identified with the reading criminal.
The fiction of documentary is a citation, demonstrating with the arrest
of criminal silents its impossibility. This starts with the *backspinning*
cinematic wheel beneath the Flying Squad van. Hitchcock was accounting for the suspect transition that *Blackmail* undertook, as if from one
order of technicity to another, and while finding them confluent (if not
regressive), fell into a series of replicant phantasms: the transition from
one archival order (bibliographic) into another (cinematic), one pretense
(indexing) into another (allographic), one model of mnemonics or aesthetics or temporality into a yet unnamed other. Successively, or at the
same time, a certain buckling and suspension arise within the model
of reading itself, at once sponging up and contesting any direction of
the shift, its viability, its import before a history monumentalized in its
totality, like a museum, which the cinematic traverses and precedes. As
cinema shifted from silent to "talkie," "talk" begins to appear, first as
garbled fragments, in bits of gossip and chatter, emerging in the men's
room, site of cleaning, of male bonding, of bathroom erotics. Such
incremental technology, like digitalization over the analogic today, is
not necessarily progressive or even successive. Rather than progressing to
greater verisimilitude, simply becoming more *up-to-date,* sound would
be regressive and spawn a mass Hollywood cinema of "pictures of people
talking." The pointing fingers include this accusation, but they do so in
the name of the complexities of an ever doomed pretense to contact and
index that the accusation indicates and cannot provide.

"Miss Up-To-Date"

The structure of "blackmail" is that of the cinematic image. It imports a past "secret"—in fact, already public, and hence no secret, or contentless—to harass and manipulate, or silence, a putative present. It knows something about that "present," such as, again, that it does not exist, or that it is predicated on murder (or self-murder), or that what it deems visible is a mnemonic construct or projection.

One should pay attention to the first appearance of words in British cinema. "Time" is abrupted in the men's room: Frank's first words will have to do with being *too early* ("Well, we finished earlier tonight than I expected"), while Alice's subsequent first words, the first of a woman in British cinema, even if not in "her" (Anny Ondra's) voice, will have to do with Frank's being late ("I've been waiting here half an hour for you"). Time is out of joint in this present, the cinematic or experiential "now," caught between different orders of time, different residues and anticipations and citational displacements. This is commented on not only by the song Crewe plays on the piano and sings to Alice. It is a song about *anachronization,* "Miss Up-To-Date," implicitly referencing the technological advance of the film—which seems, if anything, inverted by Tracey's subsequent fall through citational history in the museum.[6] Alice, "Miss Up-To-Date" ("that's you"), dresses up as a model. She wants to be *copied,* but kills the graphic artist when he tries to ravage her. It is a counter-Pygmalion scenario.

But this erect pointing would *indicate* precisely *this* thing, the specific presence or meaning outside the detour of gossip or chatter: it points, in turn, to the hypermimetic claim of photography or documentary. The pointing finger gets cut off and circulated, literally in the case of Professor Jordan in *The 39 Steps,* inverting referents: the painted jester, frozen in laughter, will mock whoever looks at it.[7] The possibility of epistemological contact or touch, the promise of mimetic photography, migrates through the machinery of media production. The work performs a critical meltdown of the image's claim to "index" the real, and what that indexing might serve, for the police, for epistemological contact or touch, for accusation and indication of the "this," the "you," the "here and now." In this circular anatomy of epistemo-technical production, the print is taken up, folded again, when Frank wants to take Alice to the *pictures.* For when Alice says she's *seen everything,* Frank talks about the detective film *Fingerprints,* which he would like to see because he could check its depiction of Scotland Yard against his knowledge of it.

Alice is as if without the morphemes of a language *(lexica),* like Alicia and Alex in *Notorious.* As the representative "woman" where speech is declared the province of the policemen's bathroom (the law), she is also prevented from speaking by Frank on two occasions: once, to Tracey, who pleads to "let her have a word," and then to the Chief Inspector in wanting to confess. Later, the lip-syncing Anny Ondra's face will be intercut with that of the giant, mute, stone Nefertiti's. "Miss Up-To-Date," as Alice will be sung to and called, plays the role of model. In the artist's murder by Alice dressed as a model, a law of reproduction is breached. And when sketching her Crewe fills out the line drawing with a naked woman's figure. If Alice occupies a prefigural domain, Crewe interprets that as figuration, filling the outline in with gendered transgressions. Instead of the model being copied, the ersatz "model," a blank (Alice *White*), stabs the would-be copier when he is drawn across the reverse barrier of real and play to attempt possession. This movement reverses the script of succession, much as the wheel that appears to spin backward, or the drift of temporalization. The refrain of "Miss Up-To-Date" registers a hyperbolic structure within this *contretemps* ("Up").

While criticism invariably drifts into observations about how a transition to "talkies" is technically navigated, it is never asked whether that passage succeeds—or, say, whether "we" persist still in the age of the muted image, or if the cross(ed) word *age* is chronologically relevant, that is, up-to-date.[8] The opening segment is like an arrest of the deeper otherness and criminal power of the fugitive who is later pursued to the dome of the national archival. The spinning wheel that is then transposed to a tire seems to be turning counterclockwise, against the apparent forward movement of the van, a counternatural movement skewing direction. The first image in the van is of a facelike wireless box with noneyes conveying orders to the detective who, with headphones on, transcribes this unheard voice into script. The teletechnic machinery simulates a film crew and recalls the giant press sequence leading to the wireless transmissions of *The Lodger.* The *Flying* Squad suggests a mock-sublime pursuit that is, nonetheless, also always mnemonic, prefigural, back spinning like the counter-natural windmills of *Foreign Correspondent.* As the positions assigned to the fictive and the real are inverted and refolded in the handling of pointing fingers and "fingerprints," turned back to prints, the relation of talkies to silents is defined by a reverse anachronization: from silents, the reading criminal represents the writing machine that the "talkie" took, in retrospect, to be documentary from its expanded purview. From the viewpoint of the criminalized reader, the addition of "voice" is chatter, sound, the superimposition of another's words. This, even if that voice-over is done with the actor's "own" recorded speech. Talk adds neither expression nor psychology to the Greek mask of silent graphics. The apparent fault between silents and "talkies" is never moved beyond: each positions the other as less endowed, each imagines the other as mere indexing.

Graphic *riddles* are accordingly signaled within this networked writing by the "Crossword Puzzles" advertised on a London street sign—puzzles of letters or words crossed over one another, or crossed out, or in translation. Whatever, that is, a "*cross*word" might be: a word of "crossing," as *Rich and Strange* calls its repeatedly obstructed ship passages, or word itself traversed by other trace chains, atomized to its letteral elements.[9] Graphics blackmail "talkies" by not forgetting the priority of (finger)print, by preceding all phenomenalization—including *recorded* voice or sound, which is reproduced from engravings. Tracey switches from Crewe to blackmailing Alice. Yet he switches sides again in pairing with Alice against Frank as the law, as official and male language-power, asking that she be allowed to *speak*. Tracey precedes Crewe's murder and witnesses or outlasts it, like chatter itself, like the ringing bells or bird whistles that punctuate the work, like the fall through the dome of the reading room and the monumental debris of history in the museum that Tracey will, too, in a way precede.

Tracey names the shadow effect of the trace and its allochronic role as semiotic "sponger." To be Miss Up-To-Date is not to be sexually available, or to update cinema's technologies to include recorded speech. It is to *miss* the date, as Frank almost does to Alice by showing up late at first. It is to miss this material juncture of colliding trace chains that discloses a logic of blackmail as that of the citational structure of the image, much as the precise time and date of the time bomb in *Sabotage* will be advertised and, just, missed.

The overthrow of the representational artist seems only one act of usurpation. The sponging logics of the image accelerate and contaminate all the historial relay systems. Thus Tracey rewards himself at Frank's expense in White's news and smoke shop. It is a shop selling newsprint and "fog," cinematic figures in and from *The Lodger*. He takes the "best" cigar, a Corona Corona. Such a double crown is precisely the figure presented in Crewe's loft by a peculiarly regal fireplace that suggests a big double crown that is simultaneously up and upside down (rather like the first two letters in the name Avenger). Such a crown or *corona* is also echoed in the museum dome Tracey climbs and falls through.

a    b

Figure 10. (a) Double-crowned fireplace in artist's loft becomes the Corona-Corona cigar Tracey takes at White's news and tobacco shop. (b) Eclipsed corona, housed in a triad, of the false temple of sun worshippers.

The double term suggests the surrounding aura or glow that can be seen, say, when the sunlike body is in *eclipse*.[10] The double corona registers an auratic eclipse, asolar. In the first *Man Who Knew Too Much* this is the icon for the Tabernacle of the Sun, the "sevenfold rays" shooting from around a pyramid—a cinematic stamp. Licking flames fringe the triadic eclipse, which supplants *aura*. But the double usurpation, back and forth, incorporates and then folds back, inhabits the dubious fulcrum that partitions the narrative from within, both in fact and as "event" in teletechnic or cinematic histories. Mocking its own feat with the song "Miss Up-To-Date," the usurpation by talkies of the silent screen's imaginary purity or whiteness, "pure cinema," that usurpation cannot establish its double crown with ascendancy or assurance. The faux verisimilitude that voice and sound promise converts, in retrospect, silent into pure allegorical media, which inversely marks talkies as mere "pictures of people talking"—that is, yet more inept faux realisms, a decline, and so on.

The double corona, from which cinematic smoke or fog issues with its avenger's motif, registers this split. It inhabits a usurpative model that boasts of progressive or updated powerlines. It opens a rift, like pointing fingers whose promised contact is reduced to prints or inscriptions. When Tracey falls through the museum's glass dome, he has become something of an "old mole," as Hamlet puts it, neither seeing nor hearing as such, a *sponger* for which the monuments of recorded history pass as so many asides or variant episodes in a teletechnic history whose official origins it or he precedes. In being updated to "talkies," the cinematic wants to boast its coronation as the cutting-edge technic. Yet it triggers, in Hitchcock, an arresting meltdown of parts to disclose a cinematic trace that virtually predates Egypt and hieroglyphic writing.

Cinema is not, accordingly, placed at the end of a line of scriptive tech-nologies, whether with diminished powers (popular entertainment) or embellished ones (mass communication); rather, it harbors the means and logic of a blackmail trace "older than" originary writing forms or historial archives. And it does so by plunging into a universal space of what it clearly calls, and interrupts, as a hyperbolic reading within and of that archive.

Outside the Archival Dome

Reading, accordingly, does not emerge casually here. It incorporates a micrologics that preinhabits the eye. The fall *into* the universal reading room or the rooms lined with books in the museum triggers a seeming precession of *recorded* "history," which tells us something of why the mugging cameo that Hitchcock offers, typical in its understatement, is so fatal. What is meant by "reading," though, if it is universalized in this archival dome, yet made to engulf the tepid finger that is at once indexal, indicatory, imprinting, digital, and a series of figures and bars dependent on this extended or pointing line? It is already interrupted on and by the Underground train or a figure of the future or past that is on it (a bullying boy), not in any case of the "present" or else the very ghost of that present—as by a preletteral reduction and hiatus to sheer seriality, sheer cut, sheer repetition, the parallel bar pattern of the banisters on the stairs leading up to Crewe's studio. But the telepoiesis of these concentric tables of reading humans in the museum absorbs all sign chains and temporal extensions, even as the room is traversed in the chase through the hieroglyphic displays and beneath the stone gaze of Nefertiti's giant head, down whose face Tracey lowers himself with a linked chain like that of celluloid frames.

Wai Chee Dimock remarks on the transition of contexts that morphs times and spaces into anamorphic (and Benjaminian) bands:

> As a global process of extension, elaboration, and randomization, read-ing turns literature into the collective life of the planet. Coextensive neither with the territorial regime of the nation nor with the biological regime of a single human being, this life derives its morphology instead from the motion of words: motion effected when borders are crossed, when a new frame of reference is mixed with an old, when foreign lan-guages turn a native tongue into a hybrid.[11]

Reading in this redaction resists temporal regimes and contracts tem-poral zones in accelerated motion, or transport—in this case that of translation. Cinema is denationalized in advance, just as its irreducibly prelinguistic media (reflected elsewhere in alpine Babel scenes) veer toward a kind of mock or graphematic Esperanto. The atomization of the book en route to a site whose sheer acceleration, namely, the train as cinematic transport, produces an alternative conception of "life," animated and mnemonically marked.

In Hitchcock's unusual cameo in *Blackmail* this interruption of legibilities receives a commentary. There is a sustained interaction about reading and its interruption, which could mark the hyperbolization of literal reading or the supersession of one mode of teletextuality for another, among an extended series of possibilities. Whichever way it crystallizes, it will lead through the universal reading room in the museum. The interior of a train car in the London Underground is always, for Hitchcock, a trope of the underworld of cinematic motion. It always registers a catabasis. The clatter of the tracks and the alternation of light and shadow of the rushing machine are Hitchcock's favored tropes for stationary transport and a rattling projector. A bullying boy leans over the seat toward the timid man, Hitchcock, who has a book open before him and seems absorbed in reading. The boy wants Hitchcock to put the book down. He stares it down without touching him. The circumstance

Figure 11. Hitchcock, interrupted reading, on (cinematic) Underground.

could concern legibility, or an absorptive analogy between what the eye thinks it does watching cinema and what, within a train, it is doing—absorbed in and by mnemonic effects and decisions similar to reading. And yet, reading is interrupted, on a train, by the train's hyperbolic accelerations, by itself, by the badgering boy as if from some future not yet arrived.

Reading here is lethal: the criminal (silent films) can be captured in bed because of his absorption in reading (the paper is held with two hands, as if in handcuffs); Hitchcock will be *interrupted,* stared down, on a train; Tracey will fall through a corona-like domed room into circles of human readers. The teletechnics announced with the wireless in the van has succumbed to multiplying reading outlets suctioning the entire archive to excess. The cameo of Hitchcock occurs behind the disconnected couple of Frank and Alice, staring beyond each other. Many characters in Hitchcock will later be interrupted reading on a train, mostly women (Pamela, Lina, Guy Haines, Eve Kendall), in a manner Hitchcock marks irrevocably.

If reading is an interruption of or by a cameo, it interrupts punning networks or systems whose simultaneous profusion and overdetermination outbid themselves. It inhabits another time. The hiatus of this interruption, the caesura of reading, occurs in between temporal markers, without a "present" quite. Thus between the staring couple on the window is a sign: "Ice Skating, London Ice Club," ice like the whiteout as avalanche that opens *The Lady Vanishes* or the snow on which *Spellbound*'s parallel "tracks" first appear.[12] Reading on a train—that is, in the cinematic underworld, according to concatenations cut by racheting tracks and flickering lights—hyperbolically interrupts *itself.* That reading signals an excess, an intercession, too much, too many signifying destinations, activated chains, temporal wormholes, even "now," "here," on the cusp of the era of the audiovisual. The boy who will bully Hitchcock purveys a mock surveillance from the future, a violating otherness and contradictory emissary who pulls Frank's hat down over his eyes as he returns a second time to threaten Hitchcock with his stare after the director has the temerity to resume his reading. This last time it *is* suspended, and the era of the book with it.

Tracey lets himself down a bizarre chain when before the huge stone face of Nefertiti—a metallic rope of celluloid-like links. The cinematic trace is vacuous and evacuating, mimes all, cites all by implication instantly, reads their mail, absorbs secrets or the secret that is the absence of the secret. It sponges up all logics of writing, so that the book gives way to the chase past the hieroglyphic exhibit that Hitchcock is careful to intercut with another through library stacks. And it blackmails. Opening the next room of the telearchive, "talkies," itself already as if a museum, cinema is aware that it will soon appear naturalized. The trace materializes in the form of a ludicrous "sponger"—a black hole absorbing touch and innumerable corridors and archival crypts. The dome of the British Museum houses the deauratic head of this archive, whose universal reading room Tracey has, in being himself chased, interrupted. *Blackmail* seems inhabited, then, by two abrupt transitions, neither of which occurs, both of which seem given: the corona corona that promises crowns yet marks the deauratic. The promise of an advanced age to come gets subverted as time or monumental history appears totalized by the citational structure of the image, which does not properly have a "present." Tracey has passed through the archive and arrived on or along its outside, atop its dome.

The dome cannot return to the ground of reference. The pointing finger's effaced epistemological touch, which precedes the front of ocularcentrism as the print does the projection, has nothing to do with indexing or indication. It refers to fingerprints, prehieroglyphoid swirls, such as mime the circular reading tables or will inhabit the woman's eye in Saul Bass's credit sequence to *Vertigo*. The model, the cited image or trace chain, turns against its would-be copyist and stabs him. From the opening identification parade, *Blackmail* announces and performs the wild nightmare of an archive exposed to and as its own exterior, moving as if to the outer rim of its housing dome and criminal premises. What is identified in and as the identification parade is the parade itself: not an individual face, name, or fingerprint, not a pointed-at man or criminal, but the deauratic premise upon which these commodities are generated and stored.

What emerges to reading from *Blackmail* also eludes readability, burns through its protocols in a sort of China Syndrome that cannot be arrested by the assembled pasts of the museum or the Muses.

Two criminalities flicker and reverse polarities: the police, who manage this terrain by dictation through the wireless, who arrest, who support the order of the museum and update cinema to accommodate sound's verisimilitudes; and their other, blackmailing, avenging, interrupting historial templates, witnessing, the archival exposed and turned upon itself in the name of another—an external reconfiguration or recasting. Corona corona, anauratic, anarchival, nonanthropomorphic. This war as if between two unequal sides—state or police, anarchivist "villain"—appears already in the double system of the Avenger and the lodger. The shaking cinematic cocktail in the neon advertisement morphing into the slashing knife cuts all anthropomorphic programmings of the senses. This war makes space for all others in the future era of this technology, which is why Hitchcock seems to position the fratricidal doubles of the past century's world wars as vaguely specular, caught at different positions in the same spectrum of logics ("Enlightenment" tropes).[13] The "two" appear like proverbial time travelers from the future in a war from which different future "presents" would be derived. The avenging fog becomes the petty blackmailing shadow, the sponger Tracey, who then flees through all of history to the rim of the archival home. Tracey reinvents himself according to his opportunities, what is before him, moving from the shadows of the narrative to taking over the title, plot, and communal buildings of memory. The titular word *blackmail* rereads the structure, tools, and agencies of the teletechnic era.

II. The Spies' Post Office

5. The Archival Wars of "Old Man R"

I have suggested that literary studies must take the "figure" as its guide. The meaning of the figure is undecidable, and yet we must attempt to dis-figure it, read the logic of the metaphor. We know that the figure can and will be literalized in yet other ways.
—**Gayatri Spivak, "Planetarity"**

It is seldom clear who is fighting, or what about. In films set during the Second World War, muddle prevails. . . . In the Cold War films . . . ideological concerns are dismissed.
—**Peter Conrad, *The Hitchcock Murders***

Deleuze, in *Cinema 1,* has a unique way of characterizing something that is going on in Hitchcock: he speaks of a "new" kind of "figuration." It is a use of *figure* that compels, moreover, incessant "interpretation," which seems to put "all" into play: "actions, affections, perceptions, all is interpretation, from beginning to end."[1] Yet what Deleuze does not quite get is that there is a countermoment in Hitchcock to figuration itself—as if figuration were the epistemological enemy, so easy to fabricate in the citational light show of cinema. It is difficult to address this afigural moment without putting in question routine habits of identification, narrative seductions, the spell of "aura." This other of figuration breaks through, say, in the recurrence to the stone faces of the British Museum as later at Mount Rushmore, in patterns of parallel lines, in a proliferation of circlets and zeros, in animemes and blackouts, letters and graphic puzzles that cannot be effaced as images or even recognized. In this regard, "interpretation" will also be short-circuited, *atomized*—or suspended. Deleuze, following up his insight about figuration in Hitchcock of a "new" sort, points to the trope of weaving. He points, that is, to the most traditional figure of *figuration* itself—the weave of clothes.

But it is precisely that which, for instance, would be assassinated by a single rehearsed and timed (camera) shot in the person of Ambassador Ropa (whose name is Spanish for *clothes*) in the first *Man Who Knew Too Much,* much as in *Spellbound* the parallel bar pattern looms out of tablecloths and bedspreads and suits. One may think of the bar series as a site where the deauratic declares itself: where everything assembled on the screen is reminded, as it were, that it is a graphematic puzzle composed of alternating currents, flickering bulbs, shadow and memory play. The cinematic cut antedates and suspends figuration as it might personification or identification or ocularcentrism or "light."

And it is this agon—between the figures of identification and what could be called the signature system—that is mobilized in part as narrative. The dematerializing logics of cinema are represented by the "villains" in their relentlessly cinematic assaults. This "politics" of the early espionage thrillers concerns the definitions of the aesthetic, time, "experience," memory, the earth, gender, signifying agency, inscriptions. Each MacGuffin has to do with the reordering of the political map, or history itself: it circles an event or intervention along the lines of Benjamin's "materialistic historiography," which that critic allied, in its structure, to cinema as a mnemonic apparatus. In this sense, the Hitchcock Deleuze describes is still that of the home state.

Hitchcock speaks of making the same film repeatedly, yet if that is so, it is a film involving the failure of its own event. A recurrent template threads the early police and espionage thrillers that creates, and politicizes, the prospect of intervention. One may attempt an overview of these *epistemo*-political "fronts" for assaults:[2]

- The British works are exceptionally preoccupied with machines and tropes of media, and particularly with the atomization of language and its parts, with marking, sounds, telesthetics, and mnemonic weaponry.
- These repeatedly involve an anarchist attack, plot, or assault on what can be read as received definitions or programming of perception (sound, light, marks).
- The dramatized sabotage or assassination or assault occurs with weapons allied to classic cinematic interventions (bombs, shots, aerial bombers).
- This intervention can imply, according to plot, the alteration of world history (an assassination likened to Sarajevo's, a bomb site called the "center of the world")—or "experience."

- Accordingly, *agency* may be allied to a presemantic trace figure that refuses the nominal order, recognizable shape, or solar origin (a black sun, a single clang).

There is a distinction, of course, between the police *(The Lodger, Blackmail)* and the espionage films. When Uncle Charlie shows up at the Newton residence in Santa Rosa, the "family" is, as young Charlie complains, in paralytic crisis, traversed by telemedia. What seems at issue exceeds the blindness of an old ocularcentric program. That the politics of these works is epistemological is repeatedly asserted by the narratives: a proper name containing "Con-" or "Ken-," a title about "knowing too much," a theater called the "Palladium," and so on. Within this staged *agon* is a war within how the powers of the "image" are understood. This war may occur as if *between* the image's promise to function as index, representation, mimetic guarantor, documentation, mnemonic story *and* its teletechnic premises or accelerations. It is, understandably enough, about the transformative impact of the teletechnic advent on a proprietary system (state, home, definition). The first might be thought to connote experience or (commercial) cinema as exemplifying the "aura" Benjamin declared shed at its advent: film as representation of the real, template of identification and personification, the icon of recognition and transparency. The second could be called the deauratic, like the electric lightbulb blacking out in the opening frames of *Sabotage*. From *The Lodger* to *The Birds*, something unrepresentable is avenging against a totality, a home state and police system routinely under threat of having its interiority turned inside out.

The *tourist viewer* enters in the position of a blind consumer and nescient participant within a calculable order of signs. He is doubled by equally nescient "heroes" drawn, like the Lawrences or Hannay, into an intrigue they think does not concern them but which they tend to undo without understanding, restoring the faulted privileges of the norm. When Hannay is chased across the moors by a bizarre police whirlybird, the contraption is a cinematic machine and he is trying to escape the film he is produced by and in—to find out what are, what is, "the thirty-nine steps" (the film's title). The tourist passes into a criminalized universe: a family vacation can be plunged into international murder, kidnapping, blackmail, on behalf of some unnamed political agenda. The British Home Office defends the archival regime and auratic protocols for which "interpretation," according to Deleuze, includes "actions, affections, *perceptions*" (my emphasis).

Imploded Chase

Hitchcock identifies the motif of the "chase" with the rapid spooling of frames. The "chase" is a metaphor from Plato for hermeneutic inquiry. When this chase is routinized, as it is when questioning Mr. Memory in the Music Hall, the memorized answers are instantly returned to the questioner: what is sought is already known, and returned to the programmed questioner as if in ritual play. Hitchcock inscribes hermeneutic programs into this hunt or chase and then doubles or folds that back on itself, short-circuiting and bracketing the void ritual by which memory will only recognize what it has planted in advance.

Received programs of interpretation and perception involve, for the tourist, the planting by memory of a secret that, when pursued, will then be discovered—which includes recognition of the cited thing, image, star, face. The MacGuffin guarantees a rupture of these reference contracts in toto. One *begins* in advance "beyond" interpretation, with the unraveling of Jill Lawrence's sweater on the St. Moritz hotel dance floor, entangling legs. Cinema, rendered hyperbolic, re-marks itself; it absorbs everything, at once, explosively, citationally, as the spool begins (again). In the case of the first *Man Who Knew Too Much,* for instance, the buildup in the Royal Albert Hall's "Storm Clouds Cantata" to the single blast of simulated "lightning" mimes the *Augenblick* of photographic *Blitz* as the prospective instant of a world-transforming strike by a single marksman—the order of signification upon which memory is legislated and history stored would be undone by this marksmanship. Tourism seeks the experiential real in the advertised image. The red herring is the exposed disclosure of the MacGuffin, whose logics devastate any narrative surface or signifying regime. It declares that any referent it assumes is spectral and can be referred back to the technicity of the enigma that generates it as a question. The eye, here, tracks and consumes: it would interiorize. The cryptonymic order of secret agencies does not fit in to any pictorial logic, resists the eye's programmed consumptions, resists interiorization or hermeneutic processing, sabotaging the ocularist machine.[3]

Something, here, wants to get beyond—and already, by virtue of its futuristic weapon, stands before—the Greek *eidein* and the "Enlightenment" to which the great wars of the past century point back. Hitchcock's cinema experiences a historial buckling as it apprehends its inversion: rather than be the diminished mechanical servant of pop culture—the Music Hall audience before Mr. Memory—it absorbs all preceding technologies of writing as variants of its totalized graphematics: it cites everything instantly via expanding ganglia, networks, and relays that telepoetically leap between and activate other citational memory chips and fiber optics. A ring with the initials "B. M." in *Shadow of a Doubt* summons every citational artery in *The Ring* and *Blackmail* to sift through what leads through the universal reading room of the *British Museum* and its library.

This politics takes different forms but can never identify with the sponsoring state, which leads to complications during the World War II plots. Because of their identification with cinematics, what had been nameless insurrectionists can appear as Nazi conspirators. Hitchcock sees the great wars as fronts or sets. Incapable of erecting good and evil opponents, he eviscerates the question of the home team's identity (England, United States). Hitchcock allegorically casts the two warring sides not as opposites but as extreme variants or doubles within the spectrums of Enlightenment epistemology that join fascism to hypercapitalism to mediacracies. If the camera's processes associated with particles of chiaroscuro fog *avenge* something, they do so not for some personal trauma or crime that can be located or dated but as if against, rather, the programs that serve this version of blind "history." Such as ocularcentrism. That the term *avenge* rather than *revenge* is used in *The Lodger* informs that it partakes of a metajustice. The avenging seems done by a radical other, at once technical and animated, prehistorial like avian species, deanthropomorphic—yet located before and as effaced host of the "home" itself.

The police or political thriller accordingly involves less a quest for "origins" than suppression, the suspension of a familiar epistemological program whose totalization is virtually blinding. The Bijou movie house will be blown up, the Palladium returned to, the blackmailing Tracey pursued through and before monumental history and iconography; "Marvin" will be bombed from above on a train. Here sight, the visible, and interpretation are programmed from the head against which the lower order of material and mnemonic "steps" rise up. The management of memory involves an ocularcentric program whose political import is global, while the "globalization" of the teleimage is already implied or forecast.

Thus the various fronts are clearly marked as cinematic enclaves. A temple of sun worshippers for assassins mocks the idea of a movie house drawing for ritual relief heliotropic worshippers of light—disbanded theatrists and religionists drawn to the projector's bulb for mistaken enlightenment or cognitive succor. On every front, a con, money taken as movie tickets are sold in a broken contract. The commodity will be other or withheld—a dilemma presented at the opening of *Sabotage* when Verloc puts out the generator of London and empties, in consequence, his own movie house of patrons, who want their money back (as Hitchcock anticipated the audience of *Sabotage* might, given the film's unrelenting gloom). The same logic of the "front" occurs with the Music Hall. The assaults implicitly or explicitly put the world as well as global history at risk, as Hitchcock saw the advent of cinema doing. These MacGuffins—altering the outcome of a world war or starting one, facilitating stealth bombing of the homeland or sabotaging "the center of the world," that is, the site where appearances and perceptions are generated—externalize cinematic powers. The narrative will be mobilized as the suppression of the work's own intervention, in short, its implied atomization of perceptual orders, and it will work to arrest, deter, or close down these criminalized invasions, to foreclose the work's *own* cinematic eruption. It will do so as the film takes cover amid the commercial brood of "pictures of people talking," aesthetically lobotomized entertainments whose secrets are safely put back into storage. Beneath these assaults lies a *hyperpolitics,* one that dematerializes an entire sensorial circuit (ocularcentrist). This hyperpolitics would be from and for control of archival levers from which organs of perceptions, identity, temporality, and mnemonics would be recast.

This is why these tropes resonate: the chase of the blackmailer Tracey through the British Museum archive and reading room; bourgeois moviegoing as a vaudeville memory show or gathering of duped sun worshippers; sabotage as putting out the generator in advance of "light" or as the invading logic of prehistorial animemes (the zoo) doubled as the logics of graphematic animation; the spies' post office as a clearinghouse in *Secret Agent* for all orders of translational and cryptonymic relays in this textualized system. Thus the naming of the British spymaster in that film, controller of the state's cinematic system, is itself letteral: "old man R."

"Early" Hitchcock suggests several maps for this battle or *war* taking place at the dawning of the era of globalized telecommunications controlled by the advanced corporate states. What one finds is the (a)genealogy of the disaster of cinema itself, a catabasis, as if going back to ask Mr. Memory, from whom names and identifications seem preoriginarily dispensed. At this "origin" of cinema is something *other,* monstrous like Peter Lorre or Charles Laughton. Moreover, what one may discern at this perpetually dramatized state of emergency at the nonorigin of the cinematic era is a split in the genetic line, as between alternative hominid branches at war for dominion: a world-altering "event" or its appropriation and defacement. This war seems to involve two sides, that of the state and police, and that of the insurrectionists. More precisely: "pictures of people talking" versus the atomizing cinematic logics of the citational image; or, the separation of the "aesthetic" versus its hyperpoliticization as memory management ("the real") and perception; historicism and mimeticism rooted in Enlightenment ocularcentrism versus "materialistic historiography." *Hence what lies behind these conflicts is a time-altering archival politics.* So the MacGuffinesque battles of Hitchcock's "epistemo-political" missives or bombs—purveyors of atomizing "shock" capable of suspending mnemonic programs of perception and history—have other stakes, beyond the work's (or "today's") disposition. Hitchcock draws all interpretation toward this vortex of reinscription. This concept would describe the work that Hitchcock made again and again, differently, citational monsters in which pasts and futures hinge or are almost redecided: "materialistic historiographic" vessels that would be planted in the head, again and again, in the orders of reading and the eye and artificed memory and the histories of the photographic image and technicities that perpetually traverse this relay station. But this is not done without an alternate practice or knowledge *lodging* already within the newly patrolled visual order of mass culture, which is one reason these works are literally suffused and overrun with figures of teletechnic and linguistic impasses.

Cluster Bombs, Fractals

The villains of the political thrillers parallel Hitchcock's cinematic project, and the logic is telling: a saboteur or assassin, dwelling within the state and operating from behind a benign public front (temple, theater), would stage a "strike" or assault that would potentially alter everything, so the state narrative tracks and cuts him off; yet, inversely, the state dwells in or is contained by what the "cinematic" knows, is itself a relapse from that atomizing horizon. So in winning, the state has either absorbed the disclosed "foreign power," taking in the viral agents, or reverted to a wounded and doomed order.

Here the security of analogic or mimetic reproduction that film was to guard and, with it, the transparency of the visual order, is eviscerated by the atomization of light and shadow as *effects* of intervallic marking. Hitchcock cannot *not* practice this instantaneous sabotage and blackout that is accompanied by the exposure of "light" as an effect of the cut, of shadow and alternation, as of waves, in fact. That "light" is prosthetic makes it dark: black and white, interdependent, are effectively the same. The *eye* is cut, preinhabited by mnemonic programs or graphematic bands. With this act, the dominion of an ocularcentric metaphorics that film ("pictures of people talking") had been used to legitimate is suspended—together with allied definitions of experience, life, time, politics, event, gender. And if such leaps between telepathic labyrinths or marking systems occur (translation, sound or voice, letters, signature effects), then a formal *direction* is triggered from which one cannot quite return. Call it, as Benjamin did, a "one-way" street, or as Hitchcock did, "north by northwest"; in either case, it would posit a shift not from one *direction* to another, and not even as the stationary movement of cinematics that parallels this, but something like the hiatus of a hyperbole: an aporetic shift from personification, aura, metaphor, anthropomorphism to something else.

These aporias are registered in Hitchcock by repeated displays of bridges that, nonetheless, are not quite crossed or are stopped in the middle of. Aporetic, since it is the *bridge* itself—the teletechnic media— that is hyperbolically suspended, like the principle of the "cantilever bridge" mentioned in *Vertigo*. Sometimes this aporetic logic is in a frenzy, like an impotent rapist. When Hannay gets out of the train on the erector set bridge over the Firth of Forth, there is reference to the BBC tower near Annabella's murder site, *"Portland Place"*—with corresponding Morse code tappings coursing through the wires. The site or nonsite is linked to telegrammatics. Such a variation of what this cinema "is" or performs contradicts the aesthetic ideology of film studies and the cult of the passive image, which all along enforced regimes of information, mimeticism, and identification. Indeed, if the photographematic *image* never was mimetic, the agents that it deploys and repeats, structurally *secret agents*, would not be included in what the tourist viewer can be expected to "see" or recognize. Such might seem micrological. The "epistemo-politics" of these cartoon narratives is not between two enemies, but of and by what lodges in and against the home's or state's mnemonic order or archive.

Thus such contests, which are taking place beneath all of these twentieth-century "sets," are also *archival wars*. They are over the future or its definitions; over the autonomy of the cinematic prosthesis or its submission to propaganda and state service; over the new powers that the telearchive is exploding and pregnant with (telemarketing, "globalization," technoweaponry, nanoscience); over the management of reference and time. In *The Lady Vanishes,* a "Mr. Calendar" of the Foreign Office is associated with the music-coded message borne on the cinematic train through *Band*riki (cinematic vampire land)—as if the Bandrikian Dr. Hartz aimed, against the British Foreign Office, to reconfigure time itself. (In siding with the British, one is again on the "wrong" side.) Such logics *strike* at the premises of sight, of the eye, and the epistemo-critical order that the metaphorics of "light" has sustained, as if perpetuating the Platonic *eidos* and Enlightenment programs of perception, action, cognition. And yet the "strike" is not literal itself, since it is already implied in advance by the work in which it is dramatized as put down. Cinema considers the era of the *eidein* to be a chapter in its reign that can be dissolved, not a monolithic tradition it must recognize. And the place for this world-altering drama is the sphinxlike legibility of the image. Either the image is a picture that vaporizes into the figures "recognized" and taken for facts (such as Mr. Memory memorizes by the millions), or it is infractational, inhabited by multiple sets and labyrinthine relays, immersed in a web of historical trace chains, signifying mutations and atomized carriers of sense. They may be *luciferian* in the sense of materially carrying *(fer)* or generating the effects of light.

Hence the relentless interrogation of micrological "language" forms. How do references to multiple tongues, hyposcript, letteration, codes, and prefigural markers serve a kind of *espionage* and counterarchival resistance to ocularcentric programs, cognitive police, even definitions of face, memory, time, or the animal for that matter—the censorial norms of an archival order Hitchcock will, at times, call "England"? Hitchcock dismisses the conflictual tangle of "text" and "image" once barred from academic affiliation on both sides. Something disfigures—like Peter Lorre with a scar descending over one eye, a white slash dissecting dark hair. It disfigures the auteurial and identificatory addictions, worship at the temple of solar premises, light, reference, identification. Strategies of subversion, espionage, assassination, or historical intervention are allied, it appears, to secret writing agencies and signature systems.[4] What is at stake, again, is the impossible nonsite of an *event* that would alter the site of material inscriptions: memory bands, Bandriki. What is fought over, in the archive or memory band, is an alteration of *inscription*. Hitchcock or "cinema," even today, anticipates coming wars of reinscription.

Within the espionage and police works, a *supplemental* archive is fractally composed as a reserve—a motherboard of autocitations and spectral referents by which the oeuvre will spin itself, a beehive of citational constellations shuttling back and forth across the production, active, translating. *A spies' post office.* A prosthetic memory or signature system takes over and supplants its seemingly naturalized host, virally transforming archival premises. But it is here that the explosive import of a deauratic practice emerges. One can again adapt the recent depiction by Wai Chee Dimock of the tele-archival effects of "literature" and its active contractions of time (not, as Benjamin says, "homogenous time") to the *cinematic*:

> As a global process of extension, elaboration, and randomization, reading turns literature into the collective life of the planet. Co-extensive neither with the territorial regime of the nation nor with the biological regime of a single human being, this *life* derives its morphology instead from the motion of words.[5]

"Life of the planet." If we now substitute *cinema* for *literature,* and *image* for *words,* the hypothesis is accelerated and hyperbolized. This allochronic template operates, in Dimock's case, against statist regimes of temporality, even as it hypothesizes a "planetary" dimension dependent on the translation effect of such teletechnic networks, outside of any one language and hence in a sort of interspace to all, again a Benjaminian conceit (the evacuant trope *pure language* or teletechnics). Such would highlight the tele-image's more virulent forms of programming the public imaginary. The *planetary,* if it exists, would be accessed in its *otherness* along teletechnic stations, as mnemotechnic grids, not in the mode of representation. It would be deauratized, as would the *we. Planet* would have to be deanthropomorphic.

Here the texts of the "humanities" are recognized, instead, as the site where personification, and the human, are not confirmed and celebrated—as if by the mimetic photograph or "pictures of people talking"—but withdrawn. As if "today," reading and teletechnics involves altering the temporal artifaction of the human, not the opposite, to move outside of the blinding, touristic, consumptive, hermeneutically programmed levers that had pretended to house it. Thus, Hitchcock's turn against figuration, a point I began with, features all sorts of "professors" wandering through these narratives—often on both sides of the battle lines, as though lost in the maze of this suspended scene of instruction. Whereas, in *North by Northwest,* the "professor" title is transferred from the unnamed lethal master spy employing Mr. Memory in

The 39 Steps to Leo G. Carroll's American intelligence chief, a photo found in "George Kaplan's" room at the Plaza places James Mason's Vandamm with other professors in front of a university whose name is cut off.

Cinematic transport or *translation* is not that, then, from one language into another (scenes of Alpine *Babel* reduce these to interchangeable phonemes), nor from one era (that of "the book," of analogic technology) to some *virtual* other already in place (a digital era). The cinematic, its logics virtual before Egyptian hieroglyphs, marks itself as preceding and absorbing all of its "predecessors." These narratives, again and again, take the players to state borders or the edge of a nonanthropomorphized earth or planet—Mount Rushmore's faces.[6] A *one-way street* beyond figurations.

Algorhythms

If the *algorhythms* of the "epistemo-political thrillers" focus on archival politics, on altering memory and historial programs, one can call police works such as *Blackmail* instead "hieroglyphic thrillers," in which a certain Egypticism is pointedly evoked. Here the police apprehend or arrest by a logic of indexing, leading the criminal of *Blackmail*'s opening *silent* prequel to the "identification parade" of fingerprinting. The police guard a fallen cinematic reality, predicated on indexing; in turn, the cinematic criminal is associated with a sponging trace (Tracey) or an "Avenger" who swarms out as though from particles of the fog he disappears back into. In the police allegories, cinema scans its scriptive origins as a teletechnic to find it precedes and includes hieroglyphics among its props. With this scan Hitchcock dismisses the pop impression that cinema is a superficial medium compared to the book; on the contrary, it is too empowered, too totalizing, potentially absorbing and preceding every mnemonic trace chain. This Egyptian nuance occurs at once in *The Lodger* with that work's use of the *pyramid,* or triangle, as immediately appears on the Avenger's calling card.[7] Thus *teletechnics* proliferate relentlessly—from printing presses and typographics, to light and sound reduced to alternations of signifiers to telegraphy, libraries, record players, telephony, secret codes, muted speech, translational impasses, Babel scenes, musical notation, telepathy. A rebellious uprising is attributed to material and technical signifying agents themselves, figures that have almost no mimetic correlates and cannot be consumed by the scanning eye. On the map of a cut-up body one might, with

Hitchcock, term these the opposite of the ocularcentric head: that is, feet, or *steps*.

This "cinema" casts out flyers or traces to be picked up, like Priscilla Lane in *Saboteur* throwing paper notes from her imprisonment high in a Manhattan skyscraper, a modern tower, which will be retrieved and read by taxi drivers turning toward the cinematic flickering in the window. Hunted by a Shakespearean like John Gielgud, the cinematic spies' post office in *Secret Agent* sends out transcripted commands wrapped over chocolate. One observes the transliteration take place inside the wrapper as the chocolate—black light, excrement, cinematic *bonbon*—is tossed aside.[8]

The intervention or "act," if it were to take place, will have done so in the archival order, at the site of mnemonic storage that projects and polices the production of future "presents." Counter to the ocularist biases film has evoked, treatments of "language" are highlighted, particularly when understood as continuous with every signifying convention, tele-technic apparatus (such as "voice"), or trace effect.[9] In *Secret Agent,* the British spymaster who sends the bumbling agents out to eliminate the unknown secret agent is named "R." It is a letter allied to repetition, which recurs in isolation elsewhere in Hitchcock: the monograms of Rebecca or the tiepin of *Frenzy's* Rust. "R" later loses confidence in *his* secret agents' acting skills, ordering warplanes to bomb the whole cinematic train en route to Constantinople bearing *Marvin,* who must be stopped from arriving or the outcome of the world war and the empire will be retroactively altered. "Old man 'R,'" as Robert Young's Marvin wearily calls him, closes out the implications of secret agent *Marv*in's reaching Constantinople—that is, to disclose the deanthropomorphizing status of cinematic consciousness, its dependence on a deauratic *marking* system.

Espionage involves counterdissimulation. Its mise-en-scène repeats battles over secrets with the power to alter (political) history, maps, pasts, and futures.[10] If the "time" of the image is perpetually other than its recorded or performed present, is informed by virtual futures and alternative pasts, then these wars over the "image" are also *time wars*. Going back to this early "Hitchcock" from a period of globalization and the announced death of film itself, is as if to séance a moment that could have produced different histories and presents. What would a community be, after all, with the knowledge that the "eye" is prosthetic, "light" a metaphor, or that mnemonic programs generate "experience" as the latter's own impossibility? Thus "old man 'R'" sends Gielgud out from the theater to ensure the approved outcome of the "great" war, sent back in cinematic time to *preserve* a pacified future present in which the "movie" is made—drifting unaware toward yet greater cataclysms in and beyond its soon to be repeated world war.[11]

The atomizing of semaphoric vehicles, as into light refracting droplets of fog, can be linguistic or aural or visual, as Christopher Morris argues in *The Hanging Figure* by atomizing the prosthesis of light itself in Hitchcock:

> The ambiguity of the concept of the photon within physics is not of importance here; instead, "photon" and *clignotement* (the flickering of the cinematic image) are invoked only as place-holders for any material embodiment of the visual sign, much as a literary critic were to allude to "ink." At issue then is . . . the degree to which "photons" or "ink" can be said to be material "presences" independent of their signs. (260)

The "photon" is a carrier of light, luciferian, photophoric, inducing what *Spellbound* calls photophobia. These *nanogrammatic* conspiracies partake of an order of resistance, sabotage, blackmail. In different works, different senses or signifying agencies are targeted, though in all, the question of "agency" itself is at stake. In *Secret Agent* that might be sound; in the first *Man Who Knew Too Much*, cognition and light; in *The 39 Steps*, mnemonics; in *Blackmail*, the indexing claim of the photograph.

"Hitchcock" names a treacherous network that induces Benjaminian "state(s) of emergency" in what enters its set. Gerard Manley Hopkins theorizes his poems metaphysically as *inscapes* mapping interior experience. The cinematic regards interiority as a fabrication, a trick of memorization. One might speak of *ex-scapes* in mapping surfaces of Hitchcock's bands. This exteriority without interior (and hence, strictly, exterior either) is like the coast of Bodega Bay, which consists of only inlets and pockets. One might rather speak of X-scapes, incorporating the chiasmic exchange and invertibility of semantic planes or doubled opponents, between the law and its others, the home state and its Benjaminian terrorists: the "crisscross" that *Strangers on a Train* names or that will turn up as a giant "X" at unexpected moments—say, on the flag of the Prime Minister targeted for assassination, the senescent Hitchcock double, in the second *Man Who Knew Too Much.*

6. The Slave Revolt of Memory: R to the Power of Gamma

We may therefore sum up what we have been saying in the conclusion that the *mechanism of our ordinary knowledge is of a
cinematographic kind.*
        —Henri Bergson, *Creative Evolution*

gamma, noun, pl. *—mas* (for 1, 2, 4, 5 and 6), *—ma* (for 3). 1. The
third letter of the Greek alphabet. It corresponds to English
G, g. 2. The third in any series or group (used especially in
scientific classification). 3. = microgram. 4. (Photography.) The
ratio between the densities in a developed negative and the
light values in its subject. 5. A unit of magnetic field intensity,
equal to (10 to the power of minus 5) oersted. 6. One of several
positions of atoms or groups of atoms that are substituted in a
chemical compound.
        —*World Book*

All figures of transport in Hitchcock—telegraphics and telepathy, linguistic and postal relays, grinding wheels and machinal whirs, casinos
and animemes—recur to the domain of memory. Memory is, as on celluloid, a matter of external markings and inscriptions whose recurrence
determines perception or experience. If memory's machinery is effaced
in projecting a screen's present, "it" refers itself to something before or
outside the latter, not so much some trauma as the trauma of its constitution. Thus memory in Hitchcock may be faulted by amnesias, or descend from external spaces like the waltzing legs in *Shadow of a Doubt,*
or reference "accidents" that have no referent. In *Spellbound,* its hunt
leads to something, the serial bar pattern, which gives up no content
to the narrative, since it mimes a syncopation out of which mnemonics is etched or erased. Only in *The 39 Steps* does memory come out on

stage, indeed, as a personification incarnate. He or it performs as "Mr. Memory," at first as the banality of recording technology. Yet he will be exposed as transforming that mechanical order of inscription and recognition into the formula for a weapon of silent, if mass, destruction.

An Infant Cries

The opening Music Hall scene of *The 39 Steps* contains a subtle exchange on Hitchcock's project as a politics of memory. It is a tough moment for Mr. Memory: he is no longer invoked like the Muses by poets, after all, and now he stands above a rowdy crowd that is peppering him with laughable questions. From high epic he is reduced to pop culture and the masses, performing tricks. Worse, he has to confirm his "facts" with his questioners. They have to affirm that his answers are correct (they know them before they ask him), and he then adds to make sure, "Am I right, sir?" What could be more humiliating to the avatar of Mnemosyne? Rather pointless, this mimetic circuit that reproduces facts and confirms what is already supposedly known. But the vaudeville act ends abruptly with a shot that empties the music or Muses' hall. The single shot triggers "Annabella's" selection of Hannay and, subsequently, a chase disclosing just how radical Mr. Memory has become—how he no doubt resented this hand-to-mouth living, how he serves a terrorist and warring agenda. He will transport something, a secret, we later learn, but not just any secret: one stolen from the reigning archive itself, from *England,* details of a bomber that strikes inside the homeland without a sound and atomizes its target. What we will call the camera as a synecdoche for an elaborate system of production and chemical processes and projection *still* pretends to yield a fact by citing an ensemble of points in time and space, arresting a set of citations and trace chains. In the process it atomizes the promise of the referent, disperses it literally and semaphorically. By the end, the gentlemanly Mr. Memory emerges as a traitorous subverter. Mr. Memory had fallen on hard times, his sheer technicity or banality, machinal, made him seem a clown.[1]

Figure 12. A "remarkable" man, Mr. Memory will leave his brain to the British Museum.

The work confirms this stature in the opening scene at the Music Hall, even as it appears to dismember or render autonomous body extremities throughout—steps, hands (cuffed and otherwise), heads. If the figure of decapitation from the previous work ("don't lose your head") is literalized in the slumping head of the dying Mr. Memory, reciting the stolen and mysterious formula, the upkicking chorines on stage seem to position feet or legs (i.e., of course, steps, tracks, the secret agents of the work) at the top or signifying position. What this entails, like Benjamin's inversion whereby the "symbolizing turns into the symbolized," is the usurpation from the eye's pretense of seeing "pictures of people talking" to the micrological details or remarkings of the works. Mr. Memory will be called a "*re*markable man" by the impresario. *Memory* shifts from a vaudeville performer to a secret courier of weapons of mass destruction and represents the mystery of an accelerated mnemonic order of cinema for Hitchcock, one that operates by iteration and repetition. We never meet the "thirty-nine steps" as such (even if they are disclosed as the name of a band of foreign agents). The "steps" in question are micrological agents, objects, remarks, citations, postal relays—but then, too, what no one in the audience has implanted in *their* orders of recognition: numbers and letters, not to mention bar series and so on. What is not "visible" as such. Thus when the dying Mr. Memory recites the secret formula for the engine to a silent warplane, it is largely unreadable letters and numbers, although Hannay, wanting to reassure the cyborg, to anthropomorphize him again, tells him, sure, he got it right. That is, he lies, when something appears that no one can know or understand. I will return to this formula, which has some peculiar things to say, in a moment. Yet in some ways one never gets away from the Music Hall or the opening—even as one circles back to it in the Palladium at the close, which begins with a hand, reaching beneath the bars on a ticket window, paying for entry. A hand echoed and negated, perhaps, in the name Han*nay*, and juxtaposed to the neon letters spelling, one by one, M-U-S-I-C H-A-L-L. Neon letters, letters assembling before words yet yielding something to do with music or Muses or (we later hear) museums. Mr. Memory will donate his brain to the "British Museum," the impresario boasts, which is to say we are back at the close of *Blackmail,* in which the entire museum has been passed through like all of monumental history—back even before Egyptian hieroglyphics. The cinematic trace is not a picture or a sound or even quite a letter; it is a *sponger,* we were told, a blackmailing shadow thing that absorbs the myriad trace chains that it enters, as if from another zone, and it precedes mnemonic or historical folds and orders, as Mr. Memory does here in citing, implicitly, Hesiod. Greek figures overrun this work, which has something overtly to do with cinematic "aesthetics"—a sort of ars poetica of the cinematic body, dismembered, rearranged, turning the Platonic or Cartesian body upside down in Nietzschean fashion, the usurping "steps" taking the place of the mumbling head. Mnemosyne, Muses, "Annabella" (who displaces a sort of Diotima figure and is instantly killed with a knife in the back she cannot reach, hyperbolically anterior), the Palladium—the putative hall of Pallas Athena where wisdom would reign or secrets be disclosed, if they were recognizable (they are not), or readable by Hannay (they are not), or if the police do not close about like a wall blocking Mr. Memory from view (the state does not want them out).

What one would have to say before returning in some detail to this odd opening in the Music Hall where the low, mimetic crowd bombards Mr. Memory with questions before an anonymous shot goes off, is that one witnesses the mime of cognition's engenderment—even if that is abysmally repetitive in its forgetfulness. Mr. Memory can only give "facts," like a photographic still purportedly, that are recognized, that the questioner agrees he got right: it is a mindless aesthetic game. And yet, it represents memory correctly: mnemonics, here, is always a matter of external *recording,* of marking something for recollection and reproduction, of inscription. To this degree, Mr. Memory is right on: he is not so much some fallen version of the once great Muse invoked by the Greek epic poets or their hierophantic heirs through Wordsworth or Proust; he is not the repository of mysteries of interiority and the sublime. He is unutterably banal, a matter of "facts," machinal. Yet while fallen on hard times entertaining the masses he is the key to a revolutionary assault in his almost new universe. The implication is not that this is the modernist, degraded, machinal memory by contrast to the divine ones invoked of old. No, they are of the museum, ruins, and Mr. Memory is what they always also were within diminished teletechnic orders: sheer exteriority. As the scene in the Palladium discloses when Hannay asks Mr. Memory, the police about to take him, what "the thirty-nine steps" are, Memory is obliged to answer the "question." It is all public anyway: he is incapable of keeping secrets. After all, he *is* the secret. It is all, in this sense, very banal indeed, material inscription, chemical etchings by light and dark.

"The thirty-nine steps," as agents for a "certain foreign power" (*power,* not country, Annabella says), are in fact not disclosed either.

The so-called MacGuffin is never revealed and simply migrates. The "steps" correspond to markings and semiotic agents so precise and minute they are potentially explosive. When a funny little man in the Music Hall cannot quite get his genealogical question heard—"What causes pips in poultry?"—he turns up two more times, even to his wife's embarrassment, the last when the crowd is rushing out and he clings to a column. He wants it answered, but all we hear is the question, and its repetitions congeal and spread across the film. *Pips* is a disease, *poultry* a flightless bird, *cause* something that would account for an illness in the absence of flight, of the sublime, of the banal order of cinematic mimeticism. But then the alliterative *p*s recur, remark themselves down to the letter: Portland Place, pipes in pockets, Pamela, Palladium, and so on, signifying agents of an unnamed foreign power traversing the work, even as *pips* migrates into *pipe,* and the postal relay of *port* and *place* (stationary movement, the address of Hannay's apartment, Annabella's murder, the BBC broadcast tower) issues signals to other ganglia within the spy network, which, at this point, is the film's writing system. Steps. Upkicking feet breaking from the order of effaced meaninglessness, the "symbolizing" become "the symbolized" (Benjamin) focused on in its own desemantic site (the letter *p,* say). This introduces another order of legs or legibility that dispossesses the eye's mimetic blind.

Which is why there is a baby crying in the audience. An infant, virtually "speechless," and why one sees only the backs of their heads in the dark, Hannay's included, until light arrives—as in a movie house—on Mr. Memory. Questioning memory is a ghastly trope Hitchcock uses

Figure 13. As Mr. Memory passes, chorines' feet kick *up*.

to name the impact of the screen's light on the viewer. It all takes place again and again, as if a ritual, ancient, here of the masses. A vaudeville. There are questions the audience uses to joke, provoke, degrade, test, violate, and not all are answered. Mr. Memory will not answer how old Mae West is (that is, how long "woman" has been caricatured as a female female impersonator in the West). "I never tell a lady's age." He cannot answer questions about the future, like sports events in 1937, not yet, noting that the patron should come back. He will not answer private questions about spouses who didn't come home. But he knows all the "facts," such as how far Montreal is from Winnepeg (Hannay's banal question). Although even there, letters bound and mesh, remark themselves in ways in excess, out of his control. Mae West, Montreal and Winnepeg—a perfect example of how "remarkable" Mr. Memory is, even if he cannot stop this sort of repetition from intruding. M and W stand out, are remarked, and the birth of the postal system shadows or informs that of whatever might be called cognition here. How? The distance between them is also null: the one turns the other upside down; they are, as Heraclitus says of the way up and the way down, the same. Moreover, each has three triads or triangles, as a three squared or nine, focusing on the number "mysteries" of the 3 (which is everywhere in the film: series of three questions recur, Pamela has a weird triangular bib on her blouse, and so on); it is also a single letter, so the "13" is implied, tripled to the thirty-nine steps of the title, and so on. Infant games perhaps. Yet it exemplifies the usurpation of the steps over the head, the usurpation that the smuggling of secrets out of the nation, secrets stolen from the home state's own archives, narrates. It will be up to the police, the state, the bumbling and pointless cipher Hannay (called a "nobody"), to suppress this order of legibility as a national threat, as the avenue to a certain bombing and atomization of the orders of mass consciousness and the definitions of the eye. Could the state and Scotland Yard have their way, we are given to understand, Mr. Memory would stay on the mimetic stage, answering inane questions for the masses— entertaining them, being abused by them, confirming what they think they know, displaying his powerlessness even as he asks them again and again, "Am I right, sir?"

But "facts" resonate otherwise as well, in addition to being punningly assimilated to feet and feat (actions) in the Music Hall exchange. They do not merely trope the pretense of the camera to record, to index the real, even to store in an archival program for instant identification. It is like what Benjamin rails against as "historicism," in the *Theses,* against which he proposes a proactive warping of temporal zones by active reinscriptions (lightly parodied in the representation of film as a faux séance in the opening scene of *Family Plot*). The "fact" is here a bauble to entertain the masses, dupe them by taking their money to hear what they think they know repeated and confirmed; render them besotted and inert through play and the chance to consult Mr. Memory even in the most tedious of vaudeville routines. The "fact" mystifies and anesthetizes them, as the dentist George Barbor and Nurse Agnes will anesthetize and hypnotize Uncle Clive in the first *Man Who Knew Too Much*. Like the Music Hall, the temple of sun worshippers is a cinematic front, frankly cynical in the commodities it doles out to conceal its state-assaulting intrigue. Thus "facts" are not innocent tricks to sport with; they order and legislate time (Mr. Memory cannot or, at least, will not access future "facts," occurrences, or constructs for his paying customers).

If Hitchcock stayed with Mr. Memory on the proscenium he would be a hack—or rather, a maker of "pictures of people talking." He is, however, with Mr. Memory in this regard: he wants to accelerate these powers or sees that as implicit to a subversive, state-threatening order, one that bombs, atomizes the sensorium, blasts new models of legibility, and with them time (the show at the Palladium, spelled with askew letters, is "Crazy Month"), gender, agency. A "certain foreign power," unnamed, a professor with many names and faces but missing a digit (whose portmanteau name, Jordan, suggests a Mosaic crossing), a walking recording machine that can do nothing but loop back, the sheer banality of innumerable "facts" ("millions and millions"). These give special import to the one item that is guaranteed *not* to be read—which is, for sure, the irrelevant MacGuffin of MacGuffins, if any "MacGuffin" is irrelevant and does not threaten to convert its status as a nothing into a key: the secret formula itself.[2]

Like the preceding examples, the formula emerges as a micrological script. When Mr. Memory is dying and reels off the secret of the silent warplane engine, how does Hitchcock present what is simultaneously his metaphor for cinema as a (mnemonic) weapon of mass (de)construction, of atomizing constructs and legacies, sensorial programs and ocular-centric cant? What is the *recitation*? A series of letters and numbers, which correspond to no grammar and which no one present knows, it will neither be understood by Hannay nor heard by the viewer—already *inscribed* in the irreverent and nescient Music Hall crowd who seek the pleasure of getting back only what they think they already know or can recognize. The micrological agents or steps in the recited formula guarantee, at least, that no illusory picture will be recognized; indeed, they shatter the unity of any possible picture. No one could grasp something like, "The ratio of compression is R minus 1 over R to the power of gamma." The recitation is called Mr. Memory's biggest job, of which he is justly proud. Hannay confirms for him the job well done to give the dying Mr. Memory a dignified and peaceful send-off, for there is something winning about his professional dignity and innocence that contradicts any hint of archtreason.

What the state does not want revealed we get in pieces:

> The first feature of the new engine is its *greatly increased rate of compression* represented by R minus 1 over R to the power of gamma, where R represents the ratio of compression and *gamma*. . . . seen in the end elevation . . . *the axis of the two is lined by the cylinder angle of sixty-five degrees* . . . dimension of cylinder is as follows . . . *this device renders the engine completely silent.* (my emphasis)

The key is that the aircraft is "completely silent," a stealth bomber that penetrates with no warning, as if invisible since it eludes hearing, or like a later crop duster, whose ability to dive and assault is unsuspected. Yet there are hints. Take the *R*. It "represents the ratio of compression." To represent a ratio, a calculus linked to rationality and comprehension, to compression, is like representing or repeating an image that, in its frame, pretends to condense a world of objects and relations. We find it elsewhere in Hitchcock: in Rebecca's burning pillow, in Rusk's tie-pin in *Frenzy,* in the spymaster of *Secret Agent,* whose name is, simply, "R." In each case (there are others) it elicits the prefix *re-* of repetition, reproduction, reiteration, representation. It begins in or as a duplication or, as the impresario observes indirectly, a sort of remarking. To *remark* is also, of course, a figure for seeing as taking note or notice, but doing so by placing a sort of imaginary repetitive tag on that incidence, a double mark. The word is not incidental in Hitchcock; indeed, a variant of a proper name with *Mar(k)* in it tends to turn up in every work, like the cameos—or a reverse cameo, since it is not the simulacrum of "Hitchcock" but the protrusion not only of a syllable, or a letteral cluster, but also of a gash or disfiguration or notch or semaphoric, well, *mark.* In *Secret Agent,* for instance, this syllable will adhere to the secret agent whom the "heroes" are hunting, the American named *Mar*vin, and they will have to race to stop him from reaching *Con*stantinople, since, if he does, the outcome of a world war, and hence, world history, would be altered. What would change if a cinematic secret connected to this marking system reached the oriental capital of cognition—and why must that be suppressed, as if his arrival would alter every ocularcentric and mnemonic assumption on which England was hermeneutically predicated, or its archival definitions of time enforced?

The key phrase nonetheless reads *"greatly increased rate of compression* represented by R minus 1 over R to the power of gamma where R represents the ratio of compression and gamma." Mr. Memory does not finish saying what *gamma* "represents," except that, as the third letter in a work overwritten with triads from its title to Pamela's blouse and well beyond, we are given a Hitchcockian clue, a MacGuffin within the MacGuffin. The correlate of gamma is the letter *c,* also that of camera, cameo, cinema—third letter as well. *Gamma* is used in photography to name "the ratio between the densities in a developed negative and the light values in its subject," a formula that directly addresses the phenomenalization of image or "consciousness" from chemical processes, instilling "light values." But since Mr. Memory begins simply reproducing "facts," the status of the "R minus 1" would perhaps connote the lack with which the repetition taken for a "fact" is plagued, an obverse to the $N + 1$ of serial numeration, like a still. The fault of Mr. Memory's repetition of facts (as stills), registered by the "minus 1," a lack, is divided by its recurrent multiplication, its *acceleration* to the *power* of the *gamma.* This would rhyme with what Annabella called a "certain foreign *power*": that foreign or alien power is not of an alien letter but of the cinematic, the deauratic or deanthropomorphic as such. The gamma names the triad or triangle ("the third in any series or group") according to the *World Book,* as well as a "microgram": the formula suggests a clarification of the cinematic as techno-weaponry turned against the cognitive programs of the state, its archival facts, one accounting for its chemical and material production of light valences in a permanent acceleration exploiting the lack that the representation of the repeated index obscures—the "R minus 1" that underlies the promise or ideology of facts, of concordance, of indexicality, of legibility.

One is dealing with an archival intervention, perhaps an obliteration, which the narrative of the film is allowed to gesture toward primarily because it will be put down, contained: the Professor apprehended on stage, Mr. Memory shot by him, of all people, to prevent the more important identity of the "thirty-nine steps" from getting out, were that possible. But the formula requires another twist when read through the machinal operations of Mr. Memory himself. He comes to us representing "facts," things already publicly known, like a snapshot: one may not know the person in a photo, but one recognizes, of course, that this is a person, this a tree, and so on, or so one thinks. But Hitchcock has been accused of the opposite, namely, that somehow things, objects, spectacles, milk glasses, wheels, get drained of all content and sear the memory otherwise. Godard suggests that is all "millions and millions" of people "remember" (as if, in the first phrase, quoting the impresario). And yet, turn our most sophisticated philosophers, like Deleuze or even Zizek, loose on this machinery, and they come up with faltering improvisations, symbolic guesses that deflate to inert stabs (demark, *sinthome*).

If a shot is presented once, it appears like a reproduced "fact" perhaps, but in a series, a rapid and confluent combinatoire, becomes "remarkable" or itself re*marked*; it alters, loses the ability to reproduce the same, is contaminated with contexts, variations, self-differentiating accents or relations, *citational and performative force*. To see is to remark. To remark cinematically is to evacuate the premise of facts, of indexing the "real," and this archiving is empowered, alters, or decimates in the name of a "certain foreign power" that does not allow the wan personification or anthropomorphism, the mocking allegorization even of something like "memory." That memory comes to us as "Mr. Memory" already announces itself as a front, a disguise, a child's game presented to unruly masses wanting, to the background of an infant's cry, to be entertained, distracted, reaffirmed. No wonder Mr. Memory, whose politics we are never told, would side with those who would obliterate this nation-state—assuming he had a choice, and assuming the cinematic accelerations he represents, and would smuggle out the formula, do not simply describe the import of the cinematic acceleration of citational frames, rapid and unremarked. To bomb without a sound is like reaching into the head unseen, like the thieving hand under the pillow of the sleeper in *To Catch a Thief*—particularly to do so under the pretext of entertainment, of being a movie.

The formula is and is not (yet) in the archive, comes from England's own vaults, and would be turned against it. And, *"the axis of the two is lined by the cylinder angle of sixty-five degrees."* What "two" signifying orders would be compressed into a common axis?

Crazy Month

As a work "about" memory and recording, *The 39 Steps* is a performative event departing from Hitchcock's technopoetics. In a way, it could be called Hitchcock's ars telepoetica, since it defines the overthrow of a classical order of the aesthetic. In that classical order, which is cited with the Greek motifs in attendance, at least as popularly thought, the mnemonic does not work as a war machine against the state or, for that matter, itself. In the cinematic, however, memory is outed if not literalized as a machine and always external operation of marking and accelerated iteration. Its machinal exteriority will vacate any pretense of interiorizing economy or reserve, such as the Romantic tradition retained the pretense of Wordsworth's seemingly subjective sublime or Hegel's figure of *Erinnerung.* Memory serves a double function: it appears to guard mimesis—with its promise of reproduction, like photographs, of "facts"—yet destroys it, irrevocably, by accelerating repetition of its graphematic agents.[3] This role as guardian of mimesis is hyperbolically attributed to cinema in the twentieth century even as, as Hitchcock instantly apprehends and politicizes, it virtually atomizes these monumental structures, pretenses, and legacies as auratic fables: it is radically, aggressively, citational and countermimetic; it dissolves the pretext of indexing it is asked or supposed to perform (as *Blackmail* makes apparent).

Something occurs to the classical territory of the aesthetic as Mr. Memory, the technicity of recording, takes the modern mantle from Hesiod's epic relating the origin of the gods, Mnemosyne, the mother of the Muses. The *archive* (now) imprints (itself). It is no longer addressing the "beautiful"—as with Annabella Smith, who first interpolates Hannay into the secret and lethal plotting, veiled muse, *as if* citing in her name Socrates' *ana*gogic dialectic of the *Symposium* (Diotima). Stereotypically mysterious, a citation, she is a bit too old, too veiled, too desexing, too commanding, too dead—and mercenary. It may even seem that this techno-aesthetics inverts the (representational) premises. Like celluloid, memory preprograms the phenomenalization of the image and perception *(aisthanumai),* but can alter that program by turning upon or against "itself."[4] Any epical sublime appears emptied of all elation (mere "facts"), all interiority or revelation.

Mr. Memory cannot *not* answer a question. His recordings are, in the end, public. "He" will become *banal.* Moreover, "he" or it will become unreadably minimalist and premimetic—dependent on graphic traces, irreducible, stamps, marks, *steps.* Like letters and numbers in a secret formula. For if we ask what might correspond to the sublime, to a certain flight, it would probably be the supposed "MacGuffin" itself (or the last in an anamorphic system of such: "the thirty-nine steps," Annabella, the Professor, the Music Hall, England, and so on): the formula to be smuggled out of England for a silent warplane. If the tradition identifies the sublime with flight, then the *silent* engine can be identified with silent film's logic, that of explosive reading and graphics, or with a mode by which mobilized signifying chains interface silently and induce "shock" as if from nowhere.

Two observations: first, the secret would be turned against a certain home "power" that archivally produced it ("England"); and second, its potential for destruction is *arrested,* hung up on the border crossing. Such an aporetic *crossing* recurs in Hitchcock's topographies—between states, in midtravel, referenced in many bridges not traversed but stopped in the middle of. It is echoed in the name of Professor *Jordan,* suggesting an Egyptian Moses leading to, yet not crossing, stuttering a new law. This place of arrest is the Palladium, where Mr. Memory discloses before the audience when Hannay asks the meaning or putative referent of the "thirty-nine steps." All telemnemonics is external—the archival site that the music hall encompasses, the "public" of inscriptions. Mr. Memory dies reciting the formula to Hannay, who must pretend to know it already, affirm it, to give the dying Memory solace, even if he cannot know or ever have heard of it; even if *this* formula is, for the first time, without known model or inscription. The warplane engine of Mr. Memory, which is Hitchcock's cinematic practice, destroys empiricism, ocularcentrism, pragmatism, realism, indexicality, and so on, as mnemonic programs that the state has implemented, forms of preset recognition. It converts the tele-archive into a mutating and allomorphic site, no longer a recording device or storage system as such.

At the end of the circular narrative—as if *moving,* that is, from London to Scotland and then back, from the music hall back to its double, the Palladium—we are given not the wisdom or revelation that the name Pallas Athena promises, but letters, numbers, without grammatical arrangement. The Palladium features a show, letters askew on the billboard, called "Crazy Month," a hysterical title that Pamela hurls at Hannay to suggest, in a cross-gendering cut, that he is having a period in yelling at her. It also registers a fault and disordering of time. Memory remains the issue, as one might hear in the French *mémoire* both *même* (same) and *mère* (mother), a mock degendering of any matrical order.

What, after all, are *secret agents* here—of what, and doing what? And what does it mean for Hannay to ask what "the thirty-nine steps" are within the film of that name? The answer can only be another decoy, supplanting the anamorphic question. The reference of "the thirty-nine steps"—or of these secret agents—can only return us to the marking, graphics, letters, and numerical formulas that traverse the work. This is glossed in the Palladium by the three clowns and then the chorines: in Mr. Memory's warm-up act, the first clown says, "And now—we will *sing*," yet they proceed only to tap dance—feet, steps, differential tapping preceding human speech or song. There are two hands also at the end, one black, one white; one cuffed (Hannay's), one gloved (Pamela's). Memory again is doubled: on the one hand, if Mr. Memory represents the relay to the archive, to all anteriority, his "death" appears a historicizing modernist gesture, as though an epoch and historical system were closed with his death and cinema's advent of the teletechnic era; on the other hand, he in a sense only externalizes what was always the case, as far back as epic poetry or, for that matter, cave paintings of hands. Memory has always been a technē, back through and before Hesiod's Mnemosyne. The project Hitchcock purveys—while transvaluative, raising the feet to the position of the head like a parodic reversal of Platonism—only crystallizes what has always been under way, albeit in a new teletechnic and machinal medium. The gesture is less a "modernist" break with classical models than the precession and consumption of historicity in toto, under way to presenting a new (and old) question. The Sphinx asked Oedipus what had three legs in old age—or what would be defined by the teletechnics of a tripod.

Rather than Mr. Memory's recitation and death appearing as denouement, whatever had been fleetingly disclosed is concealed by a wall of policemen whose backs close off the dead Mr. Memory from sight. Hannay is the agent of the Professor's failure. The law appears reinstated, the couple reinstalled, which innumerable lax commentators will pretend was always to be produced by the cinematic ritual (down to Zizek). Hannay, hand alone visible, folds as if back into the opening shot of the work, which introduces him as a hand. The circular enfolding works like an accelerated carousel or eternal recurrence miming more than the endless rerunning of the film reels. Rather than a couple tentatively affirmed, we have two hands, one white and one (gloved) black, from which a handcuff (or zero, miming Hannay's protestation to Annabella of being "nobody") dangles. Writing (the hand, of which the name Hannay suggests, too, the negation) is also blocked by cinematic hyperscript—cuffs as spectacles, as spools—the cross-networked system of multisurfaced puns and marks, referenced throughout Hitchcock as *legs* or *feet* or *steps*. Why is this presented as putting England at risk of a new war machine, silent, transvaluative, indeed, its own "secret"?

At Mr. Memory's death the body is not only dismembered, it is rearranged: hands cross the scene from the outside, Memory's slumping head is in the center reciting the formula, and the dancing girls come in at the top, their legs kicking up.[5] Rearranged, the Hitchcockian body is monstrous, mocking, inverted, with rows of disembodied but beautifully moving female legs over the slumping cyborg's head, rattling on.

Portland Place

Because Mr. Memory works by *re*marking, citing figures or marks, it is by that repetition already immemorial that a mnemonic trace is recognized as installed. In *re*marking or repeating the unembellished or banal "facts" he "commits to memory" every day, the *fact,* analog of whatever is reproduced by the photograph, becomes a sign itself, a secret agent in guise, a citation.

The impresario praises Mr. Memory's amazing "feats," which a woman in the audience hears as a reference to his "feet." The impresario impatiently corrects her, but, in the interference of a letter that cannot be heard, Hitchcock marks a connection to a term for act or action, here *feat. Feet* can swerve into a *feat* to the extent that the secret agents of Hitchcock's writing system are the site of the silent warplane bombing, which the entire narrative arches to contain and close out, cutting, dismembering, preceding, altering the legibility and referential order. *The 39 Steps* is about signs, mnemonics, archival politics. Memory can either serve the regime of vaudevillian entertainment and the aesthetic state, or it can become the site of subversion, carrier of secret weaponry, breaking the seemingly transparent glass dividing aesthetic byplay from the historial event. A *feat* occurs, historical events and transitions occur, in the order of mnemonic inscription, by way of these steps, feet, or legs, since the "real," phenomenalized on the screen, will derive from these inscriptions or their performance. The shift from mere feet to feet *as* feat alters the model of the historial that Mr. Memory began by serving as clown and footman to. In *To Catch a Thief,* this will be coded as "service compris," a comprehensive cinematic service that involves theft and a supplying of cognitive bands. Hitchcock's "feet"—sound, graphics, aural and visual puns, intratextual networking—are connected not with aesthetic play but with *action,* like the silent warplane or the attempt to cross out of the country. The work becomes the performative site of the proleptic act or crossing it attempts to stop.

Several questions from the audience do not get answered, for instance, the old man who three times asked what causes "pips in poultry," or the mocking request for Mae West's age. As if betraying a slippage in the rigorous mechanics that manage time, another asks about a *future* sports event's outcome. Time has reeled forward. The archive feeds its future production, since one of its secrets is the nonexistence of its "present." Passive mimesis ("facts") appears morphed into a mimesis without models, of the future, breaking with the discredited temporal regime; in this, Hannay and Annabella, the Professor and Mr. Memory are so many alternative names for the same competing coordinates: the "present" of Mr. Memory will be, in effect, dislocated, since, like Hitchcock's work, it can intervene politically by *altering* memory at a site of mock origination and proleptic repetition. It would use its technology to open up the phantasmal scene of translation into a future repetition that, like the secret formula, cannot be recognized because it is not the product of implants.

If we isolate the first syllable of *Montreal* when it is repeated in the title of the show at the Palladium, "Crazy *Mon*th," that would be to suggest a certain logic of the "mon," of what is mine, as semantics and property, as meaning (or *Meinung*), the logic and economy of imaginary interiority, of mimetic humanism. The secret agency of the signifying step voids not only "meaning" as property but interiority as such—in effect, *aura*.

I mentioned the odd question repeated three times that goes unanswered altogether: "What causes pips in poultry?" The alliteration isolates the letter *p,* reiterated in "*P*ortland *P*lace," the site of both Hannay's flat and Annabella's murder. If one could discover what "causes" *pips,* one could find a new way to counter that disease, which suspends avian flight, and to redefine the "sublime" itself. "Portland Place" names, as suggested, the cinematic impasse of stationary movement—what presses the work to stop on bridges, like that over the Firth of Forth, or the stone bridge with the sheep crossing, as well as at borders. Hannay's apartment is on Portland Place—a *port,* yet also riveted in the place of transit.[6] In fact, it is marked by the first name on the apartment registry when entering the hallway: Porlock, a name suggesting the interruption, by banal means at that, of a scene of poetic inspiration.[7]

That this machine is also one of tracking is seen in the absurd "helicopter" supposedly chasing Hannay on the moors: the erector-set camera that finds Hannay seeking to escape from the machinery of the film he is in. The bizarre whirlybird is chasing him not only in and as the film itself, which he is trying to comprehend if not get out of (and which is not terribly different from "life"), but also as an advance cameo of the stealth bomber virtual to Mr. Memory's formula—a whirlybird folding back into the text obsessing over its suppression. Memory as ur-machination shields itself behind the site of projection and inscription—and hence, at the site of the aesthetic, of all spectrality and phenomenalization. That Hitchcock perceives Mr. Memory as conveying a war machine is both performative and literal. Friedrich Kittler, examining early technicities and cinematic logics, observes: "Today's cruise missiles proceed in the same fashion, for they compare a built-in film of Europe's topography . . . with their actual flight path in order to correct any possible deviations. Marey's chronophotographic gun has reached its target in all its senses."[8] The flying war machine, like the Nazi rockets Hitchcock appropriated as a metaphor for his films, tracks in order to coincide with its point of impact and self-erasure.[9]

Figure 14. Whirlybird projector: cameo for stealth bomber.

Thus it is a *female* figure who inaugurates the double chase, the acceleration and implosion of the received hermeneutic model: that of hunting and being h(a)unted in which the circularity of the chase appears, (back)spinning, arrested. "Annabella Smith" is presented as one among many names, that of a nameless speaker, as the Professor will be said to have "many names" and faces. She seems like a seductress, then discards all erotic play; she seems like the dark young lady of western romance, then appears older; the possessor of knowledge, she is mercenary. The erotic pretext of giving herself to Hannay is dismissed, in effect neutering him in his own flat, where he had assumed the passive role of instructee, feeding her *haddock*. But the name Annabella must be examined too: if Anna echoes the Greek *ana-* for upward moving and *-bella* implies beauty, the name continues the allegorical inscription Mr. Memory began by suggesting that she leads upward to beauty, the phonetic up-down swing of the four syllables (echoed in *Palla*dium, or Pam*ela*) miming an *M* or *W.* This covert citation of Socrates' anagogic dialectic in the *Symposium,* that leading from *eros* to "the Good," at once evokes and rewrites the Greek or Platonic model, that of Hesiod, by first turning it on its head, feet up, its "materiality" exposed or asserted, the "good" nowhere to be found outside a hypostasized iteration (as when the *eidos* is read as deriving from the mnemonic repetitions of Homeric words and motifs). But we are required to find a different determination for the *aesthetic* here *(bella),* one connected to memory, just as the "upward" movement will, in fact, be at first up then down (Scotland and back), or in fact back to a *preoriginal* site (the Palladium). Here the veiled or dark muse does not lead *up,* since instead she already marks a material knowledge that, like that of the narrative's denouement, will not strictly be possible.

Thus, in Hannay's remarkable political double-talk in the Alt-Na-Shellach Assembly Hall, the "Exit" signs loom. And when the fake "police" arrest Hannay and Pamela and drive them off, the road to *Inverary*—a turning inward—is closed. The exteriority indicated is without any turn toward interiority. If the question about pips in poultry—about flightless, ill birds—addresses the banality of the mechanized "new" sublime of Mr. Memory's facts, ostensibly, a nonetheless materialist sublime linked to the exteriorization of all marking systems, the clowns who tap-dance when they say they will "sing" serve an ancillary purpose. They are on stage in what amounts to an encapsulation of the history of theater—a comic troping of mimesis leading as if back through a sort of *Birth of Tragedy* genealogy, citing the syncopation of rhythmic differencing that the chorines' upkicking legs mechanically celebrate. The cinematic signature—a variant of the parallel lines or knocking—in this way precedes and engulfs the *Ursprung* of theatrical space. All is without aura. Annabella as inverse Diotima assumes the role of erotic tutor only to void the ritual of any eroticism (a female female impersonator like "Mae West"). The only way to alter the "present" is to alter the anterior machinery of inscriptions out of which the present is generated or projected.[10]

There is, there would be, no *crossing*, which, in any case, could be legible only to another time or a reading to come. Or it has already occurred, and the chase is in pursuit of its effaced premise. The work is unreadable in narrative terms. To celebrate the dance of high-stepping legs, of steps folded back on the traces of preceding steps—R to the power of *gamma*—suggests another reading of Mr. Memory's death. Citational memory is being stomped out by the ascendancy of material traces.[11] This dance connects this cinema to a project of transvaluation, a disremembering of the cognitive body, cut up, which is also to say an epistemo-political assault on the future it inhabits—since to tell the audience to come back in "1937" to get the right answer is to say so to any reader to come that, at any point in the trajectory, the work predispossesses or unfolds within. As a critique of the ocularist construction of *theoria*, as a mnemonic ars poetica of a coming nonepoch of globalized teletechnics, *The 39 Steps* maps an assault on the latter's archival regime—a political feat that attends an alteration of "facts."

7. Contretemps: Secret Agency in the Chocolate Factory

[A simulacrum] should not be conceived primarily as belonging to the category of representation, like the representations that imitate pleasure; rather, it is to be conceived as a kinetic problematic, as the paradoxical product of the disorder of the drives, as a composite of decompositions.
—**Jean-François Lyotard, *Acinema***

John Gielgud's performance in the picture is remarkable, especially when you consider that, throughout the whole production, he was rushing away every evening to play in *Romeo and Juliet*—and declaiming Shakespeare on the stage in direct contrast to playing such a matter-of-fact, natural part as that of Ashenden in *Secret Agent*.
—**Alfred Hitchcock, "My Screen Memories"**

Focusing on the definition of action, acting, and agency, *Secret Agent* drifts through a strange *contretemps*—a term that appears in the dialogue. This time the plot seems to be looking for something to correspond to its own title, seeking not only "a" secret agent (there are a plethora of them) or "the" secret secret agent (there is one, Marvin [Robert Young], finally disclosed), but the secret of agency itself as applied to acting, history, perception, time, the event. In the course of this pursuit, the narrative recoils into an obsession with language, marking systems, translation, sound, writing forms, and what could be called a *figure* that moves behind numerous objects and players, without any name, becoming here a dog, there sheer sound, here a black button, there chocolate. The endlessly digressive plot leads the pursuers to a chocolate factory that turns out to be the front for a spies' post office. The film features an impassive John Gielgud in his first assignment in cinema, where he is supposed to represent high Shakespearean acting, yet clearly seems unable to act in any sense. It is at the chocolate factory that the *secret* secret agent they are seeking is nominally disclosed—who, of course, is the one no one suspected, the American "college boy." They end up pursuing Marvin on a cinematic train going to Constantinople, where, should he reach that destination, something he bears would turn the outcome of World War I against Britain by throwing the Arab alliance to the other side, basically changing recent history and, retroactively, the "present." Gielgud plays the novelist Brodie, whose death is staged at the opening, an empty coffin set before his *photograph,* thereafter to become the spy "Ashenden"—the highly literary Gielgud emptied and ghosted by pictures. The British spymaster who has sent Ashenden on this first acting mission despairs of his ability or of his interpretation of Hamlet in completing the mission, which is not only to identify but stop and eliminate *Marvin.* Although the cinematic acting aides of Peter Lorre and Madeleine Carroll are issued to Gielgud (as hyperactive killer and official "wife," for cover), spymaster R back in London basically decides to pull the plug on the production and bomb the entire cinematic train from the air, taking them *all* out if necessary. Before the reels run out the screen passes through a cinematic psycho-anatomy; as Marvin quips, "Pardon me while the brain *reels.*"

The term *contretemps* resonates in *Secret Agent.* Not only does the title question acting and the event, with recurrent invocations of *Hamlet,* but time is disturbed by the premise of the outing. If spymaster R is not successful in stopping Marvin from reaching Constantinople, the past will have been altered out of which the present of the production derives. In essence, either there will or will not be an intervention within the folds of history that secures British victory and its then present estate (and the havoc to come), or it will have altered the past and with it "history," including that present. To add to the confusion, the success of keeping the past as it is understood to have been (British "victory") guarantees the calamitous horizon then gathering in Europe. Since Marvin is a unique bearer of the *Mar-* signature in Hitchcock en route by cinematic train to *Constant*inople (oriental capital of cognition and stationary movement), the stakes are the more curious when ciphered against Hitchcock's other works. Marvin represents Hitchcockian cinema, deauratic cinema, with its knowledge of the role of the mark, say, in displacing the coming hegemony of Hollywood and "pictures of people talking," the mimetic state whose depredations will revisit this first war in spades, more than once. At stake will be the teletechnic empire present and to come, and on the train ride itself Ashenden will tell a Turkish soldier, who asks where he came from, "Hollywood." Gielgud, whom Hitchcock had to lure into the project with the illegible promise of doing a cinematic *Hamlet* "by other means," seems understandably wary throughout. When Hitchcock feeds him this line, one cannot imagine his getting the "joke." After all, here is the representative of the Shakespearean stage slumming in film, yet set up by Hitchcock to expose the inefficacy of theatrical acting in the medium—and then going a step further, identifying even that, basically, with commercial pop culture too, in contrast to the cinematic weapon Hitchcock wields.

The project was a setup to inscribe the preeminent "real" Hamlet *actor,* in turn, in another performativity. The problem is, even Peter Lorre is felled by this logic: the shockmeister of expressionist cinema from Fritz Lang's *M,* Lorre is the opposite extreme from Gielgud's "acting," and yet in *Secret Agent* the two, paired, are ineffective and, indeed, mocking citations of their own signature styles. Neither can act in any sense: Gielgud, frozen, insecure; Lorre, so hyperbolic as the many-named "General" that he is a parody of Lorre at his morphine-inflected best. Behind them is "*old man* R," as Marvin calls him a bit too familiarly late in the game, a letter that is succinctly isolated by the dialogue. If there are no effective actors in this cinema, the real agent or secret agency is other, and other than anthropomorphic or auratic.

What does occur is two things: the scenes among the players veer into arrest, improvisation (at times), and hyperbolics, as if each were over before it began or cited in advance of its own extemporaneity. Something else takes over that leads through language lessons, encrypted writing, Babelesque ruptures of speech, telegrams, deafening sound, telephones, and even telepathy. That "something else" will lead to what is called the *spies' post office*—an outrageous trope for the sort of secret writing that permeates Hitchcock's work, a clearinghouse for spy messages sent under the wrappers of chocolates mass-produced by giant gears. It will be reminiscent, in this mock-expressionist outing, not only of Lang's *Metropolis* but also of the newspaper presses of the first cameo in *The Lodger.* Chocolate, as elsewhere in Hitchcock, arrives as the black hole or bonbon, the disguised cinematic treat or truffle.

The spies' post office can be assigned a more virulent role in the oeuvre: it could suggest a site from which such secret markers are sent out, like citations, across Hitchcock's works, forward and back, the matrix of all cryptonymies against the ocularcentric state, a spectral telepoeisis that disfigures and reconfigures temporal and spatial zones—the labor of the prehistorial agency that the allomorphic clang or animeme assumes in gutting and expanding the film's title. A *contretemps*. The importance of this work to Hitchcock's tropology is out of all proportion to the minor or perhaps "failed" role it has been assigned, as can be seen by how frequently its scenes are cited or rewritten. But the import lies in the fact that something *other* takes over than any human actor can account for or keep up with.

The Chocolate Factory

To regamble as at a casino the outcome of a *past* war would potentially produce a different virtual present, history, and so on. Here acting, action, and intervention are put in question before mnemonic agencies of telesthenia.

Secret Agent is Hitchcock's exploration not just of the disconnect of sheer performativity that attends the citational image of the cinematic—and compels the invention of positions *beyond irony* (to cite Jameson)—but of whatever agency mobilizes the cinematic event, and therefore the possibility of historical intervention. Thus one could almost ignore the inchoate brilliance of these performances: a morphined Lorre, mangling "English" from an alien unnamed tongue; the Shakespearean Gielgud, out of place, paralyzed, so much Hamlet that he has ceased to act, basically set up. As if each were trapped in an improvisation, an autocitation. One could, given the recurrence to sound, suppose that an obliterating aural effect like the clanging bell in its tower or single chord of the murdered agent discovered by Gielgud and Lorre slumped on the organ in the Langenthal church were the secret agency of the title. That is, *not* voice, *not* the timbre of phonemes, *not* music, *not* any particular use of sound or even meaningful sound, just an obliterating clang of yodeling, of ear-stopping bells, machinal roars, valley-filling chords. *Sound* that stops relay or sense or narrative, like what a later work isolates to an instant as a "single crash of cymbals." *Disembodied*, it seeks a carrier, and there is none, so it settles in, moves about the legs of the players like a small animal, say a dog, even counters something equally unrepresentable in the order of the visual. And that would be: a more or less black smudge, perhaps, a small black dog, a button, a black disk, "Peter Lorre," even or especially a chocolate bonbon.

The black skeet of the first *Man Who Knew Too Much*, shot at in the marksmanship contest and perhaps worshipped in the fake temple, returns—indeed, it has nowhere to go but circulate. *Legs* are entangled with the dog's leash, a dog that attends a later language lesson and howls *telepathically.* And when we arrive with Ashenden and the General at the chocolate factory we are treated to something so garishly provocative we cannot possibly take it in: to begin with the chocolate factory, a grotesque gargantuan trope for cinematic production, as if the quest for the secret agent could only lead back into and through the material premises of the cinematic to discover whatever agency might mean here—even world-altering secret agency, the agency of this secret that has no

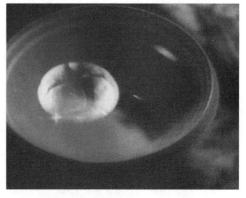

Figure 15. Wailing button superimposed on circling yodel plate, avatar of marble, dog, skeet, sound.

name or even form. Giant gears, mocking Lang's *Metropolis,* workers like hospital orderlies, mocking the idea of the Swiss with such a non-existent "factory" for their precious chocolate, which, of course, is not only a cinematic bonbon but virtual excrement, sweet cinematic treat concealing an excremental black hole and pulsion of death. And then, it turns out the whole cinematic venture is all a front for something else: a master trope of teletechnic networking, the passage of unreadable and transliterated messages with political import threatening Britain, the hermeneutic state, but also historical structures—a spies' post office, concealed in a gargantuan machinal site of cryptography and coded texts in chocolate wrappers. And it is here that the two will learn the name of the other secret agent they are ostensibly looking for, that of the American "college boy" who has been hanging about, bored, pursuing Ashenden's "wife," Elsa, in ambisexual disinterest all along, as if waiting while these great actors go off and kill the wrong man, Caypor, and then agonize about it. The chocolate factory will, behind its front, disseminate secret script across the entire Hitchcockian oeuvre, like so many signature effects or "steps," each as if transliterated and inscribed in the double bonbon of a sweet or its wrapping paper.

The spies' post office mimes an archival relay station and switchboard sending out citations and agents forward and back across the oeuvre. When the *other* secret agent is identified the mission dictates that he should be killed—this, before a Hamletian logic of inaction and arrested performance that Gielgud's presence further inverts. And this on a final cinematic train ride bearing a *Mar*-named agent, "Marvin,"

Figure 16. Chocolate factory, a.k.a. "spies' post office" (a.k.a. film production studio): (a) giant looms as spools; (b) ingenious prosthetics and ocular
apparatuses; (c) rectangular glass partitions; (d) spy scribbles code on bonbon label.

as is revealed at the spies' post office. This secret agent (whose name
indicates a marking effect, as does the mutating black marble and
hole, the wailing and the obliterating sound) is that of a (cinematic)
writing that would deauratize the culture, lead beyond the state programs of identification, personification, and "pictures of people talking." Marvin would be stopped before reaching the constant site of
inscription (*Constant*inople), even if this means bombing the entire
train from the air, discarding, if necessary, the inept troop of stars "old
man R" sent out on the mission to begin with. The assignment given
Gielgud is to stop Hitchcock's runaway cinematic train from redeciding
perceptual politics and historiality: the state is already acting on behalf
of the perceptual regime of Hollywood, and vice versa. Thus the word
"Victory!" scrolled across the screen at the closing, spelled letter for letter, is as if taken from a newspaper while the newsreel runs—the victory
of faux documentary and mimetic indexing over something actantial
one can no longer call the allegorical, but perhaps the spectrographic
or allographic with its secret access to mnemonics and historial agency

(and this, in fact, for the programming of perception will govern the geopolitical as well as the telemarkets and "global" to come).

Thus the perception that *Secret Agent* is a failed project, one Hitchcock lost interest in. True enough, the narrative loses all momentum, diverts into verbal banter and improvisations, swings from infantile sexual explicitness that rejects what it mimes into homoerotic byplay that brackets itself. It pretends to unconvincing moral quandaries that trick the tourist audience and critics, leaves unexplained its Hamletian problematics, since they divert to the cinematic itself, and displays A-list actors all but wasted but for their exposure of the entire "acting" game and immersion in signifying skits they have no clue to—as when Lorre is to have a hysterical fit next to a toilet with a phonograph on it, or when the entire work is flooded with linguistic, postal, telegrammatical, and telepathic ordinances.

The pretense of the spy thriller is its own MacGuffin, its failure to provide any refuge or camouflage for the most hyperbolic and performatively vacant deconstruction of cinematic agency conceivable—one that seems demanded by Hitchcock's project itself. The idea of "agency" appears to undergo a virtual meltdown. During this pause or rupture there erupts an obsession with the teletechnics of *language*: language lessons, telepathy, transcoding, postal relays, alpine Babel, sheer sound as (non)bearer of signification percolate across the narrative, seeking a joint agency in a spectral materiality as if to representation. The "secret" of *Secret Agent* is not something that can be simply given a name or disclosed, say, like the name *Mar*vin.

The chocolate factory presents an absurdist machine for the production of dangerous writings hidden in dark, edible nuggets, black suns and excess, cinematic bonbons. Why does the spies' post office present the key to a plot involving the turning point of a war? Why is the British spymaster who launches the hermeneutic pursuit of this "agent"—in which all variations of acting and action, historical intervention and performance seem invested—named only by a letter, *R*? Gielgud as the "novelist" Brodie is given a fake death, "killed," a photograph above his empty coffin, to become the screen actor "Ashenden," taking with him the apparatus of the book and Shakespearean postures, which are of little or no use to the secret agency of the marking systems and chiaroscuro shadow play of screen effects, which can cut up bodies, impose voices, send aerial bombers from nowhere to close down the production set if it is beginning to know too much about this telematrix.

Ashenden at first mishears the spymaster's name and asks: "'Ah!' exclamation?"—that is, *A* and *H,* but also the trope of apostrophe itself. A spymaster identified with the director yet also the verbal trope of prosopopoeia that gives face and voice where there were none. The answer comes quickly: "No, 'R' as in *rhododendron.*"[1] Whatever antedates the "Ah!" of apostrophe, or converts it into the spool-like or circularly revolving repetitions of rhododendron, will also be hunted throughout the sequence.[2] It is the letter again of all verbs of recurrence and repetition, like the word *remarkable* used of Mr. Memory when he purports, at first, to do nothing but repeat memorized "facts" to a clamoring audience that delights in being told what it thinks it already knows—like recognizing itself in a picture. As a force of repetition, *"old man* R," as Marvin will call him on the train with a certain familiarity, is tied to anteriority and threatened by whatever the micrological "mark" brings to Constantinople that will turn the world war and the East against the tele-empire. To do this, the senses themselves will have to be deprogrammed: as when the giant ear of Gielgud is all but deafened, languages reduced to phonetic elements void of content, telesthenics and postal relays rendered overt; as when Lorre complains to Gielgud after the span of hours in the bell tower with its deafening clang, "Me still blind in this ear."

The problem of "secret agency" is not that of how a cinematic performance penetrates historiality, or how the senses and the archive may be accessed and inscriptions altered, or how the Hamletian order of sheer possibility ruptures time and the event, but what is to be done with a performativity without horizon that the mere advent of the cinematic trace implies. There is no reserve for the "actor," no outside or other to the role, no utterance that cannot be atomized into trace chains, no gesture that cannot have significations instantly reversed in the order of sheer citationality. Gielgud is given his assignment to discover and terminate a secret agent in Switzerland, but he is issued the hyperbolic many-named assassin, Peter Lorre's "the General," as an assistant, and Madeleine Carroll's "Elsa Carrington" as a wife for cover.

The sexual antics that mobilize and interrupt the narrative are displaced by a perpetual revocation of whatever is being signaled, undercut by their own citational recognition as mere performance. Lorre's General with his gypsy earring and the "college boy" Marvin are suffused with homoerotics though the first manically chases every woman in the film, and the latter courts Elsa with infantile charades—except for the utterly neutral couple, Gielgud and Carroll, *pretending* uncomfortably to the "marriage" that begins as imposed fiction and ends in what are essentially publicity photos of the actors, returned to R's office as a cinematic *postcard*. A first trip to a friendly agent in the church at Langenthal finds him lying dead on an organ that emits a deafening chord, clutching a button thought to be that of the killer. After mistaking the English-speaking German Caypor for this agent (he claims the button in the casino), they are told of their error—as Elsa, who had *touristically* come for the "thrill" of intrigue, sickens at the idea of an innocent person's being murdered. The killing occurs during a language lesson that Mrs. Caypor gives to Elsa and Marvin, while Gielgud, who had no stomach for the act, watches through a telescope as Lorre pushes Caypor off a mountain.

There appears a meltdown of epistemological models. Obliterating figures of unicity haunt the mise-en-scène—such as the deafening and presemantic materiality of sheer *sound* before interval, music, or voice in the single chord from the organ at the church, the giant bell, the barking and howling dog, the wail of the yodeling, and finally the factory machinery and fire alarms. Yet the fire staged in the chocolate factory is like a conflagration of and in the archive as such. The writing, like transliterated messages hidden in the film confection, advertises another epistemo-political agenda in its pursuit and flight, upon which the fate of a world war and hence political order depends.[3]

This train or cinematic flight to Constantinople is the projected goal of Marvin, who asks, on the train, as if in precession to the film's own production: "When does the shooting begin?"[4] The film picks up on the Music Hall impresario's entanglement of the word *feet* (material signifiers) with *feat* (act) and memorized *facts* in *The 39 Steps*.[5] The attempt to explain the film in terms of plot and character and moral compass makes the project more and more illegible.

"Conjuring Tricks"

Nonetheless, a certain symmetry takes shape. Lorre's General, with his long list of names, seems sheer activity, ceaselessly pursuing women and eager to wield his blade, yet he will here only kill the "wrong man," and this while watched in a telescope, telesthenically, by the then agonized, complicitous, yet impotent Ashenden. If the General is a "lady killer" whose tastes are polymorphous ("not only ladies," says R), Marvin stages his mock Oedipal courtship of "Mrs. Ashenden" in the manner of a front or cover—passing an unwitting kiss to Ashenden on the phone, blown a kiss by the old carriage driver (Elsa: "He's fond of you"), quipping about biting Elsa's "Adam's apple" (converting her, in turn, to a male while feeding the mytheme of the Fall, and of "knowledge," through this semiotic gauntlet). Inevitably, the more sexual appetite is expressed the less it is there, even by the morphine-inspired Lorre, and the less it is there, as in Gielgud, the more it is forced to be acted out. The actors, playing characters who are performing as other characters, or caricaturing the actors' personas, seem again to be themselves as if acted or disinvested by something beyond or other—say, sound, the black dog, and so on. If "Constantinople" suggests a capital of cognition, Ashenden would be in the unwitting service of a *negative* regime: he is to stop something from reaching this eastern megalopolis, what is accorded the role, say, of the Palladium or British Museum or Tabernacle of the Sun elsewhere.[6]

Explaining the "crisis," Ashenden interrupts R, "But look here, sir, I don't see—," to which R replies, "And you won't *see* unless you stop talking." But perception and signs are not dissociable. Routinely signs are severed and reversed from their conventional assignations. "Marriage" is a contrived front, death ritually staged, manic sex pursuits emasculantly staged, "British" gentleman are Germans (and more gentlemanly than Brits). Indeed, the General, also called the "hairless Mexican," is a perfect instance of this rupture, since, as R explains, he is "not a general," has "curly hair," and is "not a Mexican." He is defined only as the negative of whatever he is named as. Irrepressible and foreign yet without designated origin or identifiable accent, he evades placement by negating the signs he generates: his grammar is broken with frequently reversed word orders or usages, but his accent is unplaceable (the opposite of Marvin who, we hear, is "at home in every language"); he is dark skinned yet not African or Latino, earringed yet a "lady killer"; he has a series of names strung together in Latin style, yet these change. Lorre's excess is illuminated in the *Excelsi*or Hotel when Ashenden and Elsa first meet. She is "putting on [her] face," originally blanked over with cold cream. Upon hearing that R has issued Ashenden a "wife," without giving him one, the General throws a hysterical tantrum. Amidst this fit, when he barks and is associated with the telepathic dog, the General rails repeatedly that this is "too much, really too much" and staggers into the bathroom. Before he tears up the roll of toilet paper that hangs on the wall, and collapses muttering that he "*re*signs" (later, Ashenden will submit his "*re*signation," or at least write it out), something emerges. Visible in the corner is a phonograph on the toilet, a prop inscribing the "present" in and as a black disk of repetitions (of which the film's play then on the screen is one) and teletechnic prerecording.

A figure of sheer excess, Lorre's dark-skinned General is here tied not only to excrement but also to a mechanical reproduction or mnemonic machine, to a prefigural script that imposes "marriage" as a fiction and is referenced back to the spymaster, "old man R." (The *record* on the phonograph cites the round black clock on the wall of the film's opening shot above "Brodie's" empty coffin.) All is directed from afar by "*old man* R," a figure of sheer anteriority—and by a *letter* at that. Hitchcock rewrites Mr. Memory as an active principle in "R," from which letter we can extrapolate repetition (a succession of *re-* words resonates, such as report, retire, resign, not to mention the record itself), yet also representation, and finally reference itself, emissaries of England that are to be policed (somewhat paradoxically) by the "good" side of the spy equation. What seems at stake is what orders repetition and hence the aesthetic or hermeneutic state and its memory management.

The General stands outside the Euro-imperial specular complex, much as the MacGuffin turns on what will become of the *Arabs,* the so-called oriental other who will have to choose a side in the conflict. If "R" represents a node through which the entire work passes—indeed, he will have ordered the train's aerial bombing from his sauna and it is in his office that the film ends—he represents the archival site out of which a certain conception of the act or event emanates. It is suspended only by the General's or Ashenden's passing decisions to "resign," to approach a site where *the logic of the (re)sign(nation)* might be redone or reinscribed. The entire work poses as a site of crisis or crossing, where something like world history is gambled (signaled in the protracted casino scenes and evocations, particularly at the roulette wheel).

Marvin will identify himself with the figure of *three*: "It's time now for the triangle to retire from the family circle." It is as if the bareness of the quest for secret agency encounters anteriority in the paradoxical specter of a dispossession, a material sound unmodified into any form of sense or signification. Elsa tells Ashenden, who deploys Shakespearean Latin with words like "connubial" and "uxorious," to "speak English." Marvin quips, in turn, as if he were the true Shakespearean slumming with the likes of Carroll, "I'm tired of talking in words of one syllable." The term *contretemps* scored into the dialogue situates a countertemporality, marked by the prospect of waiting "hours" in the clanging bell tower, or translating the days of the week into German during the language lesson. Sound, which carries "voice," effectively mutes speech itself, obliterates by accelerations and excess. This occurs too, momentarily, with *teeth,* which Marvin pretends to prosthetically remove as in a "*con*juring trick" (as Elsa refers to the General's cinematic penny game). It is this term that Derrida uses in subtitling the critical chapter 5 of *Specters of Marx,* which addresses how the logics of the specter dispossess and reconfigure, in a general untimeliness, the rules of phenomenalization: "Apparitions of the Inapparent: The Phenomenological 'Conjuring Trick.'" The "conjuring trick" is that of reassigning the embodiment of the specter, a logic accorded to the cinematic here, to a naturalized category of phenomenon, phantom, or percept. What Hitchcock calls the General's "conjuring tricks" is a trope of cinematized marks and sounds, which are both void of semantic content and virulent agents of phantomatic thought, image, hallucineme. As Derrida suggests:

> The spectrogenic process corresponds therefore to a paradoxical *incorporation.* Once ideas or thoughts *(Gedanke)* are detached from their substratum, one engenders some ghost by *giving them a body.* Not by returning to the living body from which ideas and thoughts have been torn loose, but by incarnating the latter in *another artifactual body, a prosthetic body,* a ghost of spirit, one might say a ghost of the ghost if . . . the first spiritualization also, and already, produces some specter. But a more acute specificity belongs to what could be called the "second" ghost, as incorporation of autonomized spirit, as objectivizing expulsion of interior idea or thought. (126)

The second ghost, in Derrida's terms, might here be thought to reenter in a predestined acceleration the prosthesis of the first repeatedly, emerging as the dog, the sound, the marble, the General, the record player, the bonbon, and so on, in rapid relay and in hyperbolic caricature, if not implosion, of the spy postal network itself. While the giant ear will carry a double burden—that of indicating where the ear doubles as a figure capable of networking innumerable simultaneous chains, of reading or hearing, as well as being obliterated in that excess—it is shifted into a problematic of sight with the General's "me still blind in this ear." When Ashenden's train pulls out of the station, the hotel name is identified by the letters going by in reverse, one by one, so that for Hotel Excelsior the first thing we see is the *R,* letter of the spymaster, marked as such, then the *O,* and so on.[7] This chain is inaugurated by turning back on itself, inheriting and generating at once, as when Caypor's dog gets entangled with feet in the Hotel Excelsior's lobby. The hyperbolization of sound to the point of deafening nondifferentiation offers itself, first, as a counterstrike to the ocularcentrism of the image and then is absorbed into, or by, a black hole precedent to any representational order—inclusive of all *phanesthai,* all phenomenalization, any telesthenic articulation, which the General stands as inchoate abstraction for.

There is perhaps no work by Hitchcock in which language is so *overtly* marked and interrogated, identified with a gap, as if "between" alternative tongues (German, French, English, Italian). There are so many incidences of translation and decoding—of messages, written texts—that some broader project of translation seems imposed. In fact, references to Marvin as a "college boy" ("a caveman with a college education") raise the prospect of a scene of instruction that is painfully literalized in the German language lesson between Mrs. Caypor and Elsa. And then Marvin, while Caypor is being killed elsewhere, an event that triggers the telepathic wails of their dog. *Secret Agent,* it would seem, is marred not by an inferior script or plot but by its own nonmimetic ambitions, its subordination to a spectral technicity no actor could comprehend. Not a "ghost" like Rebecca but a transmorphological guest that is at once nonorigin and target of the hunt and mission. This makes the work a key to the ever assembling and disassembling archive—a spies' post office, in fact.[8] The *secret agency* Hitchcock pursues cannot be identified with a subject or an apparatus. It precedes and disperses any ontology, generates sensation and sense in its wake, traverses the membranes of "living" and dead, and puts the unfolding of historial time in the balance of its *contretemps.* The chocolate factory and its spies' post office are nothing less than Hitchcock's absurd trope for the cinematic itself and for the mass production or mock origin of itself as a spectographics.

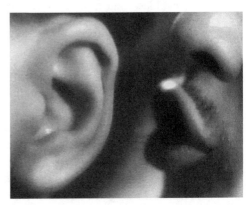

Figure 17. "Me still blind in this ear": giant bell's clang.

"telegram-telegramma-telegramme"

If the sought-for "secret agent" of the title is not the *character* that Robert Young plays as the implications of the name "Marvin," Hitchcock avers to an agency that is not representationally available. It does not belong to the order of personifications or objects. And as a signifying agent it is not explicitly visual *or* aural: rather, the "secret agency" that is tracked will correspond to what *Blackmail* calls a "sponger," a trace precedent to any division between visual image and sound yet one that operates as a mobile black hole in either's system of constructs, without metaphorical analog, errant like a small animal, or deafening material clang, or piece of chocolate.

Following the General's tantrum in the hotel bathroom, Ashenden takes the record player from above the toilet and, crossing the room, notes that their first job is to go to "a little village in the mountains called Langenthal"—as though transferring that cloacal prerecording to this linguistic topos. After the murdered organist is found, there ensues a flight to the Poesque bell. *Langenthal* virtually names an echoing valley of *language* that further inspects the Babel affiliated in Hitchcock with the high Alps and the white of snow. The Langenthal church associates murder with aural obliteration in the absence of interval. These annotations proliferate: when Marvin speaks of being "at home in every language"; when Mrs. Caypor, during the language lesson, asks if he understands German, to which he retorts, "Not a word but I speak it fluently"; when Elsa tells Ashenden, upon his defining the words *connubial* and *uxorious,* to "speak English"; when Marvin quips, "I'm tired of talking in words of one syllable."

It might seem that Marvin too is an emissary of R, to whom he alludes familiarly, or was once in Ashenden's position and rebelled.

The dog wailing at Caypor's murder at a distance is one of several references to *telepathy* in Hitchcock—cinematic zones of tele-archival commerce. It must be juxtaposed to the spies' postal service and the ruptures of translation exemplified by Mrs. Caypor's tutorial. Telepathy appears suddenly, moving along seemingly immaterial routes and rarely appears in Hitchcock before or after *Shadow of a Doubt* (a horse at the racetrack in *Marnie* is named "Telepathy"). Telepathy stands as an *other* or interface to an entire switchboard of hyperbolic performatives that the plotting generates, as if outside material or perceptible sign chains. Amidst these coordinated space-times—and Hitchcock ignores that the space to be covered to reach the observatory or mountaintop represents hours—the undeclared anatomy of the "event," or agency, moves from the implication of the eye and ear, to the black marble or dog, to the co-ordination of death with a partition between and within all language(s). The sensorium disaggregates (itself). If the *act* refuses causal connectives, its leaping movement seems infralinguistic, telepathic, asserting the reflexive agency of a linguistic rupture at the heart of the "event," however miscued or misread. Moreover, with the appearance of telegrams (the word is given in *three languages* above: *telegram-telegramma-telegramme*) appears telephony, telescope, and telepathy. One might say the work disports itself, its secret agency, suddenly and unsurprisingly in the realm of the teletransport as such. "Hitchcock" emerges as the effect of such telenetworks, and they maintain a political and "secret" domain.

If *telepathy* represents a limited and unaccountable logic at the edge or fold of the archive, it is not accidental that the character who informs the General about the chocolate factory is a working girl named Lilli. "Lilli," a name that will recur with Mark's sister-in-law Lil in *Marnie,* represents a too letteral notation of the parallel bar pattern itself, which invariably leads to the spies' post office.

Langenthal cites and rewrites the so-called expressionism of Fritz Lang, dismissing the latter's gargantuan fantasies and recasting their signifying import in one key way: the aesthetic premise of "expressionism" involves the priority of the signifying agent over perceptual appearances. It is countermimetic, and thus, but for its indulgent excesses, close to the epistemology of the cinematic as such. Thus *Metropolis* will be cited, mocked, and reconfigured in the giganticism and technophilia of the chocolate factory—trope of cinematic production replete with giant gears. Hitchcock earlier clues us in, showing the purchase of a candy bar in which the chocolate is discarded to reveal a message inside the wrapper: the message, in German, is transposed into English between the lines on the paper, dislocating each system of notation. It concludes with the command to "take steps *[Massnahmen]*" against the English spies. *Steps* connects the site to the legs of sense, the material markers traversing the work, even as *Massnahmnen* translates also as "measures." The *steps* in question, or measures, are an example within the example of a spy postal, since *steps* recurs to the agents in *The 39 Steps* and opens a telegraphic connection to that work, where the word is associated with feet, traces, micrological script, letters, numbers, and so on, while the German, *Massnahmen,* goes further, allying the other to measuring, cutting, metronomics. The factory produces—indeed, mass-produces—chocolates, which are only the last and most peculiar antefigure in the series whose primary feature is its desemanticizing, voiding, muting, violence.

The 39 Steps shifts from a cinema of mimetic replication, "facts," to one that is a war machine and weapon of mass (de)construction; *Secret Agent,* in essence, sends the most accomplished "actors" of different styles (stage, light romance, horror film) to ensnare and identify, cut off and suppress, the deauratic secret of cinema—which, again, would alter time, the world, the tele-empire. And the closer one gets to this prefigural problematic, the closer one gets not only to the cinematic intervention the work testifies to the event of, but also to the alteration of the very model of history, the program of perception, the secret of archival agency. The chocolate factory is distinguished by an incessant roar of giant gears amid a tangled network of conveyers. It is here, at the "spies' post office," that one encounters a coded netherwriting, and it is here, too, that the identity of the secret agent, *Marvin,* is revealed. It is Hitchcock's most literal address of the figure of the mar(k), as *Spellbound* is of the parallel bar pattern. Marvin, after all, describes himself in the carriage as "just a well-equipped young man at home in every language." To this Elsa responds, "*Bad* language"—whatever bad or evil language means, or if it is simply redundant.

"Old man R" gives one mission to Ashenden about which the narrative, if it is a narrative, is launched: to disclose Marvin's identity and erase him, kill him, stop him from penetrating the lines and getting to Constantinople. When Marvin says to Elsa that it is time for "the triangle to retire from the *family* circle," before disengaging and leaving on the train, he identifies himself with the cinematic Avenger whose calling card was the triad or triangle.[9] And yet so does "old man R," who, apparently realizing that the actors he sent to do the job cannot act, so to speak, calls in an aerial bombardment to decimate the cinematic train and, if necessary, all on it, so much must this deauratic agent be curtailed for history to proceed. It is abrupt, a negative deus ex machina (or the reverse), in which R makes the call from a steamy sauna—that is, like an Olympian shrouded in the fog that, as in *The Lodger,* was identified with the particles of suspended, refracted shadow and light forming the cinematic media out of which the faceless Avenger struck.

The threat to the mimetic order is erased. The foreclosure of the insurgent, nonmimetic plot is inversely exposed in newsreel clips, mock documentaries that show armies traversing a metaphorless desert, and the headline as if spelling the word *Victory* letter by letter across the frame. It is followed by R receiving military officials and a postcard in the Home Office, which testifies to the functioning of the regular postal services, which, nonetheless, disenfranchised spies use. The postcard bears the message: "Home safely but never again." It is signed "Mr. and Mrs. Ashenden." At this point we view Gielgud and Carroll's moving photos as if they were publicity shots of the actors themselves—with Gielgud still looking uncomfortable and trapped beside Carroll. The oddness of this insertion goes beyond a deauratic bracketing of gender even as a  b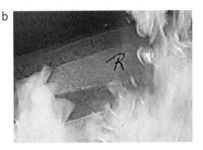

Figure 18. (a) "Old Man R" telesthenically bombs from "fog." (b) The unscorchable "R" of Rebecca—repetition, recognition, representation.

the fictional marriage "R" set up for them is the one proclaimed or inhabited, like a bad Althusserian interpellation of the ritual ideology of "marriage." The display of the tourist actors recurs to Gielgud's opening photograph placed above, and commenting on, the empty coffin.

What sends these actors back into the recent past is the prospect of stopping a challenge to the orders of temporality and causation—to protect the home state of the "present." The battle behind the scenes is over a signifying or archival system that confers phenomenality or world—and, as we know, the media power that will shape the "global" beyond the postures of nation-states warring in the last century. That the murder of the German gentleman who spoke flawless English, Caypor, was mistaken, and that the threat lay in a multilingual American, dispelled the fraternal face-off between the British and the German as another MacGuffin—a perspective Hitchcock routinely, if at times unnervingly, questions in his war films. Even when making propaganda films for the Free French, the results were unusable, displaying the French or British as specular, if distant, variants of their foes in matters of coloniality, empire, racism, and so on.

The *war* between Britain and its others is not typically a mimic war. It is not just between an imperial epistemology and hermeneutics (home) and its constitutive others and doubles. The "secret agent" of the title—that which effects action but cannot operate directly—appears as the nameless and eviscerating *haunting* by a specter that is not tropological yet traverses every scenario. It suggests a mark that precedes and obliterates sensorial programs based on repetition, taking the form at times of a wailing sound. It is nonanthropomorphic, deauratic. The entire work, of course, is premised as a divagation of cinematic effects; hence its link, say, to *Number 17,* a similarly "expressionistic" romp needing to derail a runaway cinematic train. As Marvin utters, "Pardon me while the brain *reels*."[10] But no one is pardoned here. Even the postcard to R suggests a wound, a permanent drift or absence, being caught in the spies' post office nevertheless. While claiming to be "home safely," the senders add "never again." Never again repeat what—that one must say this to "old man R"? Never again return to the theatrical stage intact, since Gielgud appears suspended and trapped in a cinematic image, in his afterlife as "Ashenden"?

Rather than simply being a German agent with a mission that threatens England and the outcome of a world war, *Mar*vin is the agent of Hitchcock's deauratic cinema, a system of markings (visual and aural rhymes, bar patterns, letteral operatives, mnemonics) on his or its way toward cognitive disclosure in what can be itself marked as a capital of constancy and cognition, *Constantinople*. This must be stopped, and stopped by R, bombed if necessary, if the secret agents he sends out— representatives of contemporary acting guilds, respectively—cannot do it. For if the marking system were to penetrate the cognitive center and vaporize the mimetic regime's control of the consumer's sensoria and mnemonic programs, epistemological histories and politicized tropes (anthropomorphism, identification, personification), and were to do so through the atomization of teletechnics of all sorts (including the linguistic, which would no longer pose as the Shakespearean province), well, a variety of histories and temporal models, not least of which would be the outcome of the most recent world war that certifies the status quo of the "present," stand to be undone. It is the same intervention threatened in every other British thriller under different guises—only here fed through cinematic styles that are as disconnected in their sign systems as Lorre's General is in his names. The aim of Marvin was, or is, to disinscribe a semiotic or archival "order."

8. Animation Blackout: The Sabotage of Aura

> The technologies of terrorism and film are only too much
> alike. . . . The cinema, like a bomb, is a device for demterial-
> izing the world.
> **—Peter Conrad, *The Hitchcock Murders***

> The public thinks I have been getting away with murder for
> forty years. But am I really unscathed?
> **—Alfred Hitchcock, *Hitchcock on Hitchcock***

Sabotage has a negatively privileged place among the British works, seeming to reflect on the entire series by positioning the saboteur Verloc
as using a movie house as a front. It would seem a garishly obvious
move but, of course, escaped notice. Yet this allows Detective Spenser
to go behind the screen of the movie house itself, falling into the nest
in which the anarchist plotters are negotiating their attacks on public
space and the state. Moreover, *Sabotage* will seem to turn its bombs,
strapped to the body of the Professor, upon the Bijou theater itself finally, once the link between cinema and bombing is established.[1] It is as
if Hitchcock asks us to think not what this has to do with his own efforts or the cinematic as such, but why this explosion is linked to time
bombs, bombing of the temporal order, and, as such, what that has to
do with going to the zoo, or the many animemes that crisscross the film
from birds to turtles to fish.

In no other work does the accord between Benjaminian "shock" as
the cinematic "dematerializing" of the world, as Peter Conrad calls it, get
such direct analysis, and it remains the legend of this event that can be
cited subsequently with the lightest of touches. Hitchcock's cameo in *To
Catch a Thief*, for instance, occurs beside Cary Grant, who is seated next
to a birdcage on a bus—the very figure of sabotaging public transport or

Figure 19. Avenging animemes: (a) Cinematic transport leads to the zoo(trope); (b) Chatman's pet store, where time bombs are produced; (c) Deanthropo-morphizing fish tank, whose (d) screen envisions melting human structures and buildings in Piccadilly Circus.

travel used in *Sabotage,* thus affirming the deadly and fractalizing agenda of that supposedly "light" film. Opening the film with a darkness that puts out the generator that powers London, the definition of the cinematic bomb as a sabotaging of structures (edifices, temporalities) is detailed with astonishing precision. While the key figures anatomized are temporality and definition itself, perhaps the most intriguing is the film's overt displacement, not of sexuality or the family or audience consumption, but of the "human" as such. Not until *The Birds* will this attack on anthropomorphism be so overt, and never so subtly problema-tized. For, recalling Benjamin's appeal to "natural history" as a corollary to the practice of temporal suspension that "shock" implies, the work is flush with animal figures: cats, birds, fish, references to eggs, and so on. But this is clinched by two complementary if enigmatic scenes that require inspection: the visit to the London Zoo's aquarium and the scene involving a Disney cartoon, that is, *animation,* in which half-bird, half-people creatures serenade and murder one another to the choral chant: "Who Killed Cock Robin?" The scene spurs Sylvia Sydney's impaling of Verloc on a steak knife in retribution for his indifferent blowing up of her brother when conveying his bomb—a time bomb, which goes off both too late and too soon—next to film canisters. While the inscription of "Hitchcock" in the name of the murdered "*Cock* Robin" as well as in "Ver*loc*" himself leads to elaborate detours, what is put at risk from the beginning is another definition: that of "life," of the "aesthetic," of the "animal," or the sensorium and mnemonic grid as "center of the world."

The problem I want to hold in the viewfinder for inspection amidst all of this rubble is how the animeme—the animal as technicity and animation as the prototype for the living—displaces the "human" as surely as *Sabotage* does the figure of light or *aura* from the start. Before its time, ahead of its time, without a time of its own, *Sabotage*'s canister will continue to tick until this riddle is apprehended—which has everything to do with the redefinition of *sabotage*, called into question by the dictionary citation that opens the work.

The Laughing Dead

There are three complexes in *Sabotage* that require inspection, so to speak, en route to examining the figure of the animal. Each has an impact on the problem of definition that is shattered, as the dictionary entry is by the phonetic breaks in the word listing—or by the cut that the subsequent listing, *sabre,* provides. These are, first, why do Londoners laugh when Verloc, in his first act of sabotage, puts out the generator—a laughter that returns in the Disney sequence compulsively allied to death? Second, why is the order of the family so entirely artificial and desexualized, with "Mrs. V." connected to Verloc because he takes care of—and then accidentally blows up—her younger brother, what I have elsewhere called a Potemkin family, which is as much a false front as the movie house (and remains so elsewhere in Hitchcock, for whom, one might say, the "family" is always involved in a family plot, a fictional intrigue that is deadly)? And third, somewhat more subtly, if Hitchcock is aware that he is using his cinema in a manner comparable to the revisionist, which is not to say "modernist," fashion that Benjamin rewrites allegory, which is to say as a performative intervention in historial time and structures of memory and perception, it is interesting that he names the inspector who is in pursuit Detective Spenser, the leading name in classical literary allegory in Britain. Why?

Each can be addressed quickly en route to the problem of the trip to the zoo or the import of animation in the logic of cinematic sabotage. In the first case, Hitchcock seems to be bemoaning in Verloc's name a certain impasse he encounters at the end of his British period: that is, that the explosiveness does not register, does not get read or experienced or responded to. On the contrary, his audience is entertained, laughs, pays to go or not. Hitchcock puts Verloc in the glum position of doing his worst—putting out all that generates light and power in London, putting out the aura of identification and anthropomorphism—yet all that happens is they are amused. His handler at the zoo will cite this gaffe to refuse payment for the deed and require a sturdier effort, namely, the time bomb in Piccadilly Circus, called the "center of the world." One must stop to appreciate this trope. The "circus" references the circles and reels that Hitchcock allies not only with the zero figure but also with the recurrence of the cinematic band, a unit of memory storage not dissimilar, for him, from a sort of eternal recurrence of the same, albeit otherwise. Explosive, it retreats to a site of perception (such as projection), where it atomizes and reconstitutes all at the "center of the world," the programmed sensorium from which image, reference, temporality, and memory are generated or controlled. "Piccadilly" as a word or name will cite a variety of cadenced anagrams in Hitchcock that elsewhere point to the signature of the number 13 and the bar series, which itself will be resumed in the name given to the film whose canisters are carried with the bomb in Stevie's birdcage, *Bartholomew the Strangler*.

Hitchcock will thus ally the explosive import of the bomb on the vehicle of public transport—during which, again, a little dog is seen protruding—with the numbing and trance-inducing bar pattern that atomizes all semiosis and strangles the voice with its cuts. For Verloc to have to confront the Londoners laughing at his act of sabotage—and we see them exiting the darkened Underground doing so—is a strange dilemma. The bar series is the irreducible semiotic pattern, like the train, from which all perception and sign functions, all aurality and visibility, are spawned (and suspended). Yet this cinema emerges as a tool of the state's aesthetic model: its immense expenses are borne by commercial enterprises, its pleasures attached to affirmation of the very institutions Hitchcock would dematerialize (or does), including the "family." It emerges in a definition of the aesthetic itself that promises inconsequential play and representational diversion, not only for mass entertainment, but for "art" in general.

For Verloc as Hitchcock, the deregulation of time and official definition that escapes the censor in the "aesthetic" produce would proceed to an attack that is and is not viable. It is not, since one cannot tell the Londoners in the Underground, who laugh as if they were in a movie house, that they are dead—they are already dead, in fact, since cinema is continuous with the artifice of semiotic consciousness, the product of memory programming and semiotic bands. How to rupture this site? How, except to accelerate the decimation on the micrological level to clear the entire scene, as Verloc imagines when staring at the fish tank and when seeing the structures and buildings of Piccadilly Circus melting as by implosion? How, except to clarify what the "human" is not, beyond the retraction of aura that the film begins with here—emptying out the Bijou of its paying patrons this time, suspending identification with its gloomy characters, suspending "suspense" by blowing up the boy, Stevie?

Hitchcock goes too far. He will pretend to be chastened only to come back without showing his cards, as in *Psycho* or *The Birds*.

Thus the second question: why is the "family" so artificial, a mere front, even if the unseeing Detective Spenser, who begins the film in the disguise of a greengrocer next to the Bijou keeping tabs on the suspect Verloc, plays out a tedious and inept Oedipal "love" for the clearly inert if not desexed Sylvia Sydney, herself often dressed as a sailor boy?[2] Spenser is busy allegorizing, ennobling, projecting, ruining Verloc's plans, as is his job. But the family around him is inert, and Mrs. V. laughs when Spenser alludes to her relations with Verloc—even as her face cringes in nausea at the latter's grotesque suggestion that they could have a child of their own to replace the hole left in the gameboard by the atomized Stevie. Detective Spenser, called Ted (Edmund might be too long), fills in the gaps to rewrite what he encounters as a salvageable love interest, himself as protecting male in an infantile Oedipal competition with the desexed Verloc. In short, he is busy allegorizing in the "old" sense, in the sense of an era of the book, even if he does not represent that particularly either. Thus, as a greengrocer he sits behind rows of fruit and produce—icons of nature, assembled, nonetheless, as items of commerce (en route to *Frenzy*'s Covent Garden market). Which is also to say, by contrast, that Verloc's Benjaminian mode of "allegory" is entirely performative, aims to invert the very premises of the "aesthetic" (by locating it at the "center of the [sensorial] world"). Which is also why the bomb that is sent out with Stevie is accompanied not only by birds but by film canisters: the cinematic as a *time bomb,* as a reconfiguration of temporalities in their entirety, even if its precise "moment" cannot be calculated. Stevie does not arrive at Piccadilly Circus, but the bomb goes off after the moment it is contrived to. Hitchcock's *Sabotage* will be ostracized and unread for decades yet remains potentially lethal and transfigurative for an impending reader, and so on. It loses its "now," much as the sergeant at the bombed-out Bijou cannot quite recall whether Mrs. V.

virtually confessed to the killing of Verloc, whether she spoke *before* or *after* the bomb, which the Professor detonates on his body, teaching the import of cinematic "shock" at his own expense to nonexistent students.

As the tropes of aura and identification, suspense and family, time and sexuality are revoked, it is no wonder that "definitions" are called into question from the start. Sabotage will occur through the atomization of inscriptions and definitions, the clearing of structures that yield the odd construction pit being dug or prepared in the street in front of the Bijou. The "human" is being stripped, which is to say, personification and anthropomorphism—what Benjamin implied the advent of cinema revoked under the term *aura*. It seems that cinematic sabotage may seek the metaphor of the bomb or shot or blitz to dramatize its lightning strike against the metaphorics of time, but that its work is intrinsic, systemic, eviscerating—displaying "life" as other than itself, yet this too in the professorial mode of an assaulting scene of instruction. Hence the visit to the aquarium.

A Trip to the Zoo

Certainly, the term *zoo* recalls the zootrope, the cinematic ur-model that generates the figures of life as visual effects. It repeats, in its way, the opening visit to the Bijou itself, which, when encountered, is emptied of patrons, who complain of the lights going out and want their money back.

Coming near the end of Hitchcock's British period, *Sabotage* reflects on and anatomizes the inner logics of his war machines in their mute entrapment within an aesthetic model of entertainment.[3] Something in *Sabotage,* with its overt use of a movie house as the "front" for anarchist disruptions, its decimation of structures and revocation of light at the outset, remains key to whatever the deauratic might imply. *Sabotage* raises the prospect of definitions from its opening shot of a dictionary. Its set and plot are traversed by citational rebuses and figures that direct themselves, virally, into core problems in Hitchcock's (or Verloc's) practices: the inaugural blackout of the lightbulb (sabotage as advance loss of aura); the touristic Londoners who only laugh at this provocation, clearly not getting the point; the revocation of "suspense" with the actual explosion of the young boy (breaking the *contract* with the viewer); the banter about action and acts; the persistent displacement of the human before the animal (and animation); the affiliation of birds with bombing; the re*cord*ing of dates and time(s); positioning the "family" as a saboteur's front; the putting of official "definition" into question with its odd opening dictionary citation—an entry we are asked, immediately, to *read,* thus putting reading and words at stake with sight. If animation will be put in question together with the premammalians visited at the zoo—supplementing, as they do, a host of creatures listed as food on the menu at Simpson's restaurant—it will be concerned with how animation itself is produced, through the rapid passage of graphics precedent to letteration or image.

As images of writing go, the figure used by a reporter at the bomb scene is strange. It is neither legible nor letteral, yet purports to be shorthand for news reportage—emblem of mimetic reproduction elsewhere (say, *Foreign Correspondent,* or the first cameo in *The Lodger*). Spenser finds the fragments of the canister he knew Stevie was carrying for a film called *Bartholemew the Strangler* ("That sounds a juicy one," noted the doomed bus driver, unaware that "juice" had been used to describe what the generator supplied by way of light to London). The reporter draws near to ask whether the tin contained the film, to which Spenser replies, "No, sardines." Should we miss the connection, the time bomb, already allied to film itself but also to birds' singing, is now allied to *fish,* such as were observed in the aquarium or offered at Simpson's. Nonetheless, the reporter records the film's title, *Bartholemew the Strangler,* but he does so in shorthand as the camera watches the paper fill with unreadable squiggles—figural traces neither mimetic nor letteral.

At issue is not just the definition of *sabotage,* but of *word* or *graphic sign.* The blackout that opens *Sabotage* is a revocation of natural light and of the Enlightenment metaphors on which it rests. It is the effect of the film itself or its technical caesura. Sabotage sabotages the film *Sabotage* or its metapremise, including Verloc's Bijou, then emptied of its patrons, causing the narrative to begin with theater patrons on the street wanting their money back for the sheer darkness and deauratic premise of this consuming band. The bomb is carried in beneath a birdcage and is coded to go off *when the birds sing.* Peter Conrad adds, "In *Sabotage,* language itself is sabotaged in a scene that compounds fake etymologies, puns, misunderstood meanings and the obscure rhyming slang of the East End" (*The Hitchcock Murders,* 161). Deprived of the Alpine scene of Babel, which, again in his next film, will coerce the creation of Bandriki, a phantom nation and language altogether at this crossroads—a vampire language trying to take over the train of cinema and Iris's memory—*Sabotage* turns against itself like the self-detonation of Chatman's pet shop in and with the Bijou. It turns also toward a graphematic atomization of English speech units, writing, the visible, temporalization.

In the vacancy of the human, allusions to animals and *animation* proliferate, most significantly with the visit to the zoo's aquarium. How do references to marine animals and to cooked creatures or birds mesh with the animation of birdlike cartoon people singing? If one drew from this the obvious conclusion, it would have several logics. The first is that of consumption: humans, here, are always seen eating animals, yet in his death scene at the dinner table, Verloc's being stabbed with a steak knife turns him into meat, too. The "human" is equalized by the cinematic machine, the very opposite of the anthropomorphic fetish commercial cinema creates as "pictures of people talking." Hitchcock is not bombing "London"; the cinematic is dematerializing "human" institutions, the sensorium of the techno-Enlightenment man entering the "global" era of universal consumption void of otherness glimpsed in *Frenzy*.[4]

Sabotage poses, then, a "graphic riddle."[5] It may have to do with a re-definition itself—of words, of Hitchcock's cinema, of epistemo-politics, of bombs, of sabotage itself. So at least the opening dictionary entry for the word *sabotage* suggests. The problem of definition is emphasized, moments later, in the badinage of Detective Spenser disguised as a greengrocer next door to the Bijou. This occurs when Spenser tries to defend Mrs. Verloc from returning the ticket money. After all, when *she* is accused of breaking a "contract," it is a legal issue, and a detective should step in. What matters is who is responsible for the act and how *act* is "defined." To return to the preceding remarks, what is at issue is the difference between a performative concept of allegory—what I have called Benjaminian—and a representational one, for as soon as perfor-mativity is in question, all received definitions are suspended, as indeed for individual words. The word *act* may mean theatrical performance or event, if one can tell them apart, but its definition itself performs that difference; it may have to point to the saying itself, if it can, rather than to an official dictionary account.

Moreover, the decimation of dictionary words is the corollary to the dematerialization of buildings or structures: both occur within archi-val zones and mnemonic fields; both clear the way for something else to arrive. Something in the *deed* of sabotage, in the bomb and in the film, will attempt to redefine agency and action, indeed, the historial and epistemo-political "event." This caesura is mimed, again, in the phonetic breakdown of the word as *"sa-botage, sa-bo-tarj."* The blackout that *opens* the work shuts down the Bijou, yet is as if generated from and by it (Verloc), or its running of the very "film" one is watching (or in):

the work begins in its own revocation, it is over before it begins, folded into itself. A caesura or interruption precedes and sabotages, from within. A hand (figure of technē) finds sand in the generator, earth particles. It empties out the movie house, turns it *out* into the streets, and brings suspension into conjunction with the act—of a secret agency, again, that laughter cannot suspend.[6] This will only occur at an apparent source or *generator* itself, which is also to say within the very structure of phenomenalization, light, knowing.

By displaying in advance a dictionary definition of *sabotage,* Hitchcock puts the word, its definition, and definition itself, in question. Words are all *sabots,* "mech. shoes" (says the barely legible opening text) or steps, suggesting by their dismemberment another definition (of definition). What is raised by the definition is the problem of semantics in general:

> (Mech. shoe or armature of pile, boring-rod, &c. Hence sa-boted (-od) a. [F. cf. *satate* shoe, etym. dub.]
> *Sa-botage, sa-bo-tarj.* Willful destruction of buildings or machinery with the object of alarming a group of persons or inspiring public uneasiness.
> *Sa-bre (-er), n. & v.t.* Cavalry sword with a curved blade (the s., military . . .

One begins, then, with reading and the interruption of reading. The entry is without human agency, about the atomic building blocks of legibility, the official archive of words, piled up, handed down officially, in a book or lexicon, the infiltration of other tongues (French), the displacement of words into politically networked events, even the breaking down of sound in letters. With this entry, the work performs in advance of the credits, of itself, a breakdown and precession of reading allied to the blackout. The dictionary text is *highlighted* in the credit sequence, which is crossed by a band of light. What the letteral breaks presuppose is a denaturalization or revocation of "light"—parallel to Benjamin's revocation of aura: "light" is already a technic, structured by interval and speck—at which point sabotage requires a "new" definition (even as this, without a subject, is an example of a mechanical shoe of sorts). When this logic is transposed to the animemes at the zoo, figures of a prehistorial technicity, it triggers to visual dissolve as on a tank screen of great buildings or structures. If the word *sabotage* sabotages its official definition in the process of soliciting it, that generates other definitions—on the phonemic and syllabic level, at first. The *sabre* entry evokes a cavalry (s)*word* with a curved blade. The preceding definition, barely legible, recalls the present of the French *sabot,* evoking shoe—the prosthesis of steps, an (a)material carrier of sense, sound, brute signi-fiers, trace carriers, secret agencies.

Sabotage has retained this double reputation: it is deemed either a cruel failure, expending itself on the demolition of the boy Stevie, or simply, in all ways, ahead of its time.[7] It does not, exactly, have a "time." The word *time* recurs often, while the dates and days of the week are uniquely flashed on the screen in titles (Thursday through Saturday). A sign attached to the bomb that warns Verloc "Don't forget" when the birds will sing—given us to the minute (1:45), though never coincided with—registers what *Secret Agent* had called a contretemps, a structural war over chronographic orders in a suspension of sequence or instant. The Professor turns into a suicide bomber, taking the Bijou with him. The "Don't forget" not only exhumes a Hamletian paralysis but allies the prospective explosion both to memory bands and their effacement: what one cannot forget, say, is to forget, within the cinematic trance, what it materially implies. By the same token, the time bomb will be not only delayed, by an instant, but affiliated in the carnival scene in which Stevie is delayed by the toothpaste and haircream salesman with the phrase "instantaneous arrest of decay." This dislocation will return in a parallel displacement at the end. Mrs. V. (as she is letterally called), having stabbed Verloc at the dinner table, declares to Inspector Talbot that Verloc's dead, as if confessing. Then, in the final explosion by which the birdman, the Professor, blows up the Bijou and with it all trace of anything, the Inspector wonders how the girl knew of Verloc's death before it happened, or if she did: "That's queer. Is that girl psychic? . . . She said it before—or was it after? *I can't remember!*" But this loss of a "present" is not enough to send the world of the text hurtling into the apocalyptic signs held up at the Lord Mayor's parade ("Repent!") or the allohuman and premammalian orders of the zoo—though almost.[8]

This returns us to the "graphic riddle" mentioned above. The logic of "sabotage" can seem inherent to *the image's structure of betrayal*: servic-ing the ocularcentric, it atomizes the eye, the relapses into the mnemon-ic program, just like Verloc within the Bijou. It sabotages the definition of the event—moves it from the real to the inframnemonic or archival plane, where it requires new definition. An explosion temporally impos-sible to localize spectralizes an "instantaneous arrest" promised by the Salvo-Dont salesman—supposed aim of the still shot—from which past and future trace chains would vie for inscription.

The phrase "secret agent" hovers over *Sabotage*. It is the title of the Joseph Conrad novel the story is taken from and the name of Hitchcock's preceding film, which prohibited its being used again. This entanglement of agency, action, secrecy, and definition is openly speculated on as Spenser double-talks the paying customer about the *definition* of the "act," citing a bogus edict "where an act is *defined* as any activity actuated by actual action." What is at stake is an official order of semantics, what Melanie Daniels studies as "general semantics" at Berkeley. It puts the law in question. *Mrs. V.* argues with the patrons over returning their ticket price, since the film was a bust (jokingly anticipating complaints about *Sabotage*). Its double-talk concerns the *law*'s definition of a "contract": "You broke a *contract*—therefore you *broke* a law." Before *Sabotage* itself even starts (and, yet, *in* it), the theater is *emptied,* the "juice" cut off, the money already sucked up. And this, by a seeming act of *providence,* which, nonetheless, is engineered by the movie house proprietor.

Hitchcock will break all his contracts with the viewer here, starting with blowing up young Stevie—a bona fide no-no. Mrs. V.'s ostensible defender, manipulating and confusing the public so that she can keep the takings, is the disguised agent of the law itself, the "greengrocer," who is too willing to *break* the law in its own name (at first) to bond, yet in fact flirt, with "Mrs. V." He represents a law whose interests here are other than the law: "Act of providence? I call your *face* one and you won't get your money back on that." Thus it is the detective and allegorist who will dissimulate on the problem of the act:

> Now if a plane were to come along and drop a bomb on you, that would be an unfriendly act within the meaning of the act. But if the juice dries up on its own accord that would be an act of providence, as laid down in the act of William the Fourth, where an act is *defined* as any activity actuated by actual action.

The dropping of a bomb by a plane on a (cinematic) train is a direct citation of how *Secret Agent,* the immediately preceding work, concludes its seemingly inept chase: a narrative train as if amok, it must be simply terminated by "old man R." The bombing ends the inability of that work or its actors to perform or fulfill their assigned act, or define secret agency. A doubleness splices the event that would occur "on its *own* accord," by automation or chance. Thus the tautologically defined "act": "any activity actuated by actual action." The sought for "event" occurs—*if* it does—on an epistemo-political order of the archive, as in the dictionary. Hitchcock is annoyed this time, as if he had been taken for a mere entertainer. He means business and will suspend humor.

Salvo-Dont

If sabotage against the state produces an assault on mimetic human-ism, the film seems to displace the "human" as such even as that is an exclusive shot. The havoc of a work that declares itself blacked out at its opening should not be underestimated, since all variety of sign relations may be altered, as definitions, in the obscurity of the moment. If birds are identified with the Professor's bombs, for instance, chickens will nonetheless be seen being cooked; if Verloc meets his handler before the turtle tank in the aquarium, the greeting involves making soup for the Lord Mayor's banquet, and there is the long list of cooked fish and meat recited at the restaurant. At the zoo, the tentative anthropomorphism is remarked when a turtle is pointed out through the rectangular window, miming a film screen: "There's a thing with a mustache." One is within a nonanthropomorphic signscape. In *Marnie,* when Mark explains his work as a zoologist Marnie asks whether "humans" are included in his zoological taxonomy.

The blackout of the opening caesura implies a rupturing of genera-tion and generations. Eggs abruptly veer toward cancellation outright, being either poached or cooked ("trying to eat my *egg* on toast in the dark," "poached eggs—the worst thing in the world"). In the aquarium, a couple comment on the premammalian fish in the tank. What begins as quips on consumption ("You'd have hiccups if you had to live on ant eggs") veers into a suspension and outright reversibility of gender—a topos smuggled into the Verloc family in its entirety. A stroller com-ments to his date about an allomorphic fish who lays a million eggs and then changes sexes, to which his date responds, "I don't blame her." The counternatural "nature," a sabotaging within the premise of natural signs and generation, recurs when Stevie examines his two birds with Verloc: "Which one's a hen?" "You'll have to wait until one of them lays an egg." "Wouldn't it fool everybody if one day the gent laid an egg." "Nature" is another front, archivally considered, as at a *green*grocery. The cutting off of generation at its source, like the sabotaging of the generator, converts the fish eggs into a figure of innumerability ("a mil-lion"), followed by an outright conversion of "sex." Such animals are examples of technicity, animation, changelings belonging to a proactive mimesis without model or copy, a semiophysical morphing—that is, what is fully dissociated from the "human" archive. We now see the extent of the broken contract. The time bomb's temporal atomization cannot be anchored by all the precise dates and timings. Aside from the elusive *punctum,* a badly timed "now" or *Augenblick* that blows up the bus rather than Piccadilly Circus, the dislocation of generation illuminates Stevie's incineration.[9]

The sexless marriage of the Verlocs has it own peculiarities. Mrs. *V.*—the appellation is redundant—stays with Verloc because he is good not to her but to Stevie ("You're good to him, you're good to me—you know that"), yet Stevie is not her son but her brother, hence his brother-in-law. The family is positioned in a mock triad of simulant paternity, simulant maternity, simulant conjugality, simulant filiation. Family is another *front,* as is the familiar, the familial: it is, it was always, involved in a family plot. Spenser suggests at the restaurant that Verloc has "another woman in his life," and Mrs. V. laughs ("if you only knew him"). She traverses the first part of the film in a sailor boy outfit, her short-cropped hair boyish if not butch. Spenser responds to these signals obversely, by immediately flirting with and courting *Mrs. V.* with a deluded mock-Oedipal fervor that testifies to his utter misreading of the scene—his inexperience, unprofessionalism, boyishness. There are, as usual in Hitchcock, no real fathers or, perhaps, mothers, a logic that rescinds the Oedipal, ocularist, or mimetic assumptions. After Stevie's incineration, Verloc suggests they might have "kids" of their own. Mrs. V. departs in disgust ("One happy little family"). *She* is neither wife nor mother nor, perhaps quite, woman. Her letterized name, promising a gendered allegory (like "Mr. Memory"), discloses instead a triangle, emblem of the foglike Avenger.

But animation fares no better. The Disney cartoon of a Mae West bird-figure, again half-human, wooed by the serenading Cock Robin, rewrites the allusion to the fish changing sexes, or to the possibility of the "gent" bird laying eggs, or to the boyish Mrs. V. As elsewhere in *The 39 Steps* and *Frenzy,* allusions to Mae West partake of a disavowal of any apparent gender. On the one hand, as a female female impersonator, she invokes a sheerly performative concept of "gender" (or woman), apprehended as gesture and projection by the other; on the other hand—and hands are at issue here, cuffed or not—the juxtaposed *M* and *W* of the name formalize purely semiotic determinations of identity.

Moreover, this exposure of generational logic adheres to the bomb maker himself. The Professor's little granddaughter is fatherless, as he notes when finding a toy near the explosives hidden as "*cat*sup"—hyperbolizing ("up") the animal trajectory and the feline name, *Chat*man: "There you are—no father, no discipline." Yet he turns then to be struck by the child, in a reversal of roles: "Slap me hard. Granddad's been very naughty."[10] The riddle of Stevie returns, neither son nor figure of generation; a prosthetic child, he nonetheless holds the pretense of family together; a *third* or quiescent figure of excess, his uselessness is underlined in his bumbling every chore he undertakes (getting groceries, cooking, bomb carrying). We are blinded as long as we pretend that Stevie's being blown up represents a central trauma, the "broken contract" of an identificatory and humanized viewing. Stevie holds an oddly neutered or desemanticized position in the prosthetic family—a figure of interruption, of sabotage.[11] The *saboteur* wants to affect the future and the past by eradicating a certain simulated "present" but cannot time or locate it, despite recursions to dates, exact moments—a hopeless *chronographics*. To what degree does the entire work contrive, in its way, to *blow up* Stevie precisely—to rid itself of this figure of an intolerable abruption, to sacrifice not just a boy anointed for the event by the Salvo-Dont salesman in the carnival but the figure of sacrifice itself?

The *squiggles* of the reporter's shorthand tropes the graphematics of *Sabotage* itself: seemingly mimetic, a mere recording action, it is yet a mode of sheer graphematics whose implications cannot at once be read or accessed. And yet within Hitchcock's signature system, the very work that most attempts to analyze an aesthetico-political intervention, a new or alternate definition of "sabotage" (and of act or event or definition itself), does so within a mock autobiographical trajectory. All along, the experience purveyed doubled the transformation of "Hitchcock" into something monstrously prosthetic and weaponlike. Only the autograph has no "I" in the usual sense. Spenser confronts the dissimulating Verloc in the Bijou. The detective asks Verloc for his whole story, and instructs him to *write* it out, suggesting the genre of a *confession*: "You know: 'I, Carl Anton Verloc . . .'" The form of the confession is, here, marked as the citationality of another's script. One might ignore, for the moment, the "Carl Anton," whose initials, again C and A, repeat Hitchcock's obsessive letteral formula with variants of the number 13, as if that were itself bound to a dislocation in and by the camera, in and by number, a cancellation of the speaker by utterance itself. The autobiographical mode of confession, here *dictated* by the police, reemerges in the least likely of sites, the Disney sequence culminating in the chorus whose song haunts Mrs. Verloc as she returns to the dining room to execute Verloc: "Who killed *Cock* Robin?" Now, of course, the performative mode of the confession, as *"I Confess"* later exploits, represents a sort of disarticulation of the speech *act* as impersonation and theft, a performativity without reference.

A threat of *forgetting* weighs heavily over this scene, of *forgetting* what is going on, or how to read; of *forgetting* the time of the bomb: "Don't forget," reminds the accompanying note. Of course, one does, or at least Talbot is unable to *remember* if Mrs. V.'s outburst occurred before or after the final explosion. A paralyzing injunction from Hamlet *père*. We forget, perhaps, that redefining the "act" of historical intervention not only alters the legislated definitions and dispositions of serial time, human personification and consumption, laughter, and gender. It already implies an alteration of and within the eye as medium, the "I" itself or human effect. Hence one import of the turn to the animeme. Cinematic sabotage implies deanthropomorphism.

After learning of Verloc's role in Stevie's death Mrs. V. wanders into the movie house. The crowd is laughing at the cartoon, which we watch with her. She seems to forget herself in a strange Homeric laughter. It is "laughter" that Verloc was originally charged with having mistakenly provoked in the Londoners. But here, before the animation, this laughter

Figure 20. Half-bird Mae West cites, and brackets, gender as effect of animation.

takes on a hallucinatory form. She is now the public viewing the sheer phenomenalization of form, as at Hitchcock's cinema, and she is convulsively laughing, near madness, bearing catastrophe and betrayal. While the bomb had been accompanied by a note indicating that the "birds will sing," that is, *explode,* the cartoon—replete, now, with bird-people or figures who *sing*—strangely realizes this while collapsing the human and animal divisions in a mock-utopian murder mystery. The spectral *animation,* a sheerly technical script that most closely replicates the total artifice of Hitchcockian writing (according to Robin Wood), presents Cock Robin serenading a Mae West bird meant to epitomize female pulchritude. The singer is shot with an arrow by a shadowy crow—another bird, but here also a *shade* or shadow itself, cutting off the singing, the crooning, the wooing of what is essentially, again, a "female" female impersonator (not to mention a bird-human impersonator). Hitchcock knows too much. We cannot dissociate Cock Robin—a dead singer, an Orphic crooner—from the name Hitchcock. Nor from Robin, the figure of theft, of blinking ("Blinkin' shame, robbin' the poor people like that"). Buried in this animated *mise-en-abyme* ("Who, who, who killed Cock Robin?") is a fable on the curtailment by shadow—by the animal kingdom and geomorphic time—of a certain "I," sacrificed like Stevie, in and toward a post-Enlightenment and amodernist logic. Sabotage is not wrought from without but involves the work of embedded logics, "material" implications that emerge in the recession of aura. Wrought by the *sabots,* mechanical shoes or steps.

Piccadilly Circus

Do (not) forget! We are brought back to the *time bomb* and the implications of *mistimed punctuality*: mistimed by Verloc, who could not get it to Piccadilly Circus; by Stevie, who was unaware of it on the bus, playing with a little dog we have met, perhaps, in other films; by the Professor, since the clock takes us a minute after 1:45, as if delayed; by Hitchcock, who pretends to miscalculate the implications of his error in letting the event arrive at all. Even though the moment is that alone which is *true* to Conrad's novel. This anapocalyptic dimension, the imagined liquefaction of the edifices at Piccadilly Circus ("the center of the world"), occurs, projected on the aquarium tank, in silence, as atomizing the structures of the visible, the rectangular grids and neon signs. Given its place on the tank, it is portrayed openly as a performative or cinematic melting away before the prehistorial and the nonhuman.[12] The work interfaces this liquefaction of structures with the image of fish spawned as innumerable eggs that perform a counternatural changing of sexes. "Hitchcock" is hollowed out, as it were, replaced by his signature systems and spies' post offices.

The toothpaste hawker who will waylay Stevie for a critical few moments to demonstrate his product, "Salvo-Dont," will anoint him for sacrifice with brilliantine and a public tooth brushing. White blocks with black intervals protrude from the body's skeleton to shape syllables and eat. The ante-image yokes a cinematic alternation or bar series precedent to "light" to the orifice of speech. While the scene prepares Stevie for sacrifice—"groomed for *star*dom," we hear (mocking the boy actor's ambitions to boot)—the teeth also forecast the film canister whose name the news reporter's shorthand was taking down: *Bartholomew the Strangler*. Resistant to any mimetology, the bar sequence "names" a seriality in advance of perception, of which the latter is an aftereffect. It performs and isolates the alternation that materially dissolves the play of letteration before its emergence. "Salvo-Dont," promising the "*instantaneous arrest* of decay" associated with photography, attaches a putative salvation to the undoing of speech. The "Salvo-Dont" anoints Stevie for cinematic martyrdom, "stardom," and with him, cuts off any future he as a humanoid child would represent.

The warning that Mrs. Verloc gives Stevie as he leaves with the package—"careful at the crossing"—again takes on a different resonance in the trajectory of *Sabotage*. "Crossing" is a promised transit or translation, a Zarathustran trope. The implication is closer to *translation*. Such a "crossing," totalized or denied, alters the molecular structure of reading. The prefigural implications of "*Bar*tholomew the Strangler" can barely be read, even if it includes all the letters of the word sabotage. *Sabotage* will have to be sidelined, displaced, left like a time bomb within that archive itself, unopened decades after *The Birds'* evacuation of the human landscape by myriad attacking wing cuts. The *squiggles* of the newspaper reporter dissolve the bar series into mellifluous, unreadable calligraphy, the figural time of the narrative that disperses along "chains" of celluloid frames the latter's toothlike alternations.

The nonanthropomorphic vista *Sabotage* opens posits an intervention in history as an "act" within a mnemonic economy that manages temporality and definitions: those of the event, of gender, of "family," and so on. If Verloc, falling on an extended steak knife in a mockery of Roman virtue, becomes only more meat, falls like the director on the incision of the cut, the animal and human cross in sheer animation.

After the bus explodes Mrs. V. hallucinates Stevie's face popping up amidst clusters of other children. His face attaches itself to boys running through the streets. His loss is registered as the sharpening of the specter, the trope of cinematic projection. This is a site out of which phenomenalization is programmed. The construction pit in the street, blocking traffic, exposes foundations beneath the surface of the ground. Indeed, *children* proliferate late in the film, like so many simulacrum futures or fish egglets without context or generational place—clustered, running, gathered before the Bijou cinema. Any shift within the logic of allegory from the mimeticism of Ed Spenser, faux greengrocer, to the allographics Verloc practices is tied to the name on the film canister that the news reporter is seen copying. The Professor's final act of blowing up the Bijou leaves us without any mimetic image. It subsists in the eradication of the very models of identification and oculist pleasure that would be reapplied, without success, by the hermeneutic conventions affiliated with aura, personification, historicism. *Sabotage* remains a deferred anatomy of the "event" of Hitchcockian project. The *step beyond* implied by the *sabot* blasts *Sabotage* out of any Hitchcock chronology.

There is a curiosity about the emerging star system, for which "stardom" Stevie was being groomed. Stars are not only the light of the heavens, they also betray that the "sun" is itself nothing but one of myriad such points of technical light, pyrotechnic, black holes in turn that link up in constellations. A star is already dis-astral, dis-astrous—which makes the mummified "stars" themselves ciphers. One cannot kill what is already dead, the effect of animation. This is why any *intervention* can only occur in and as mnemotechnics, in or of the archival law whose premise is its own destruction; one is, already, in an allochronographic machine, a *time machine* or bomb. With the technicity of shape and gender shifting ascribed to fish in the aquarium, the nonmammalian order of life and generation is also put on a technical plane: what traverses animation, bird-men and she-he fish and steaks and Verloc, is this knife of technicity. There is no "nature"—on the Hitchcock set or in nature. The figurative designs of the squiggles, a form of writing in need of a template for reading, names, in translation, "Bartholemew," a signature too inflammatory to be taken on public transport. One will have to wait until *To Catch a Thief,* the very oddest of locations, and the least expected, to reactivate all of these technical impasses at the same time. It is something the cameo avows, with the director turning up next to a birdcage on a bus.

III. State of the Image

9. Solar Fronts: Politics of the Post-Enlightenment

The picture opens with a scene at St. Moritz, in Switzerland, because that's where I spent my honeymoon with my wife. From our window I could see the skating rink. And it occurred to me that we might start the picture by showing an ice-skater tracing numbers—eight—six—zero—two—on the rink. An espionage code, of course. But I dropped the idea.
—Hitchcock to Truffaut

The title *The Man Who Knew Too Much* adds little to spectator understanding of either version of that story, but the fact that Hitchcock used it twice over, some twenty years apart—and alludes to it elsewhere, notably *Rear Window*—suggests its importance for him.
—David Sterritt, *The Films of Alfred Hitchcock*

The first *Man Who Knew Too Much* puts into play a title so far in excess of its subject that it has trouble finding one to attach it to—a title Hitchcock could not not circle back to, however, since it among his works alone would be remade. In an oeuvre rife with self-plagiarism and recurrent patterns, to be so literal in its self-cannibalism might signal a summary engagement. Too much for what? Who is the subject, the "man," or "who"—or something else? Is *it* an excess of knowledge or a knowledge of excess that voids the *epistēmē* or archive? Why is excessive cognition pointed to here as a site, clearly, of a political or historial intervention?

One will need marksmen for this. One will need targets that are elusive (say, ambassadors who incarnate all tropological dissimulation) and practice targets (clay targets or black suns). One will need to rehearse on prerecordings and bring the timing of it all just so—so that the instant of this capture and shot will penetrate the fabric of the real (or reel), trigger monstrous seismic consequences, appear or be covered by a lightning strike (even if in a symphonically rendered score). What would excess *knowledge* be if it exceeds, and loops back to precede, the official definition of *knowing*?

Whatever *knowing* is in excess (of knowing), the phrase "too much" detaches itself and ricochets across other films' dialogues, planted here or there, like an alert. In *Notorious*, the second *Man Who Knew Too Much*, and *To Catch a Thief*, it is associated with the sun: there is "too much" of it in these places (Rio, Morocco, the Riviera), or the sun is itself in excess of itself, a deauratic *corona*, in eclipse before it arrives. The work plots an assassination that would alter history, an assault against a regime associated with the sun, with a certain definition of light, the eye, re-cognition. And, inevitably, the plotters choose an exemplary place to hide out, in a temple of sun worshippers, a false one more or less miming cinema itself. *Knowing too much* will imply knowing too much to speak, to be able to speak or to speak what one knows, even if one does not know what the knowledge is or is about—or if that knowledge, of simulacra, of the nonexistence of sun, erases "knowledge" itself and thus its own excess, in the name of something else. Knowledge in excess of knowledge has no premise of recognition. It mutes, it blackmails, it erases and blanks out—it must be itself taken out; it itself will do the taking out. And this is why too the credit sequence with its travel brochures predicting and picturing the unseen tourist's destination, St. *Moritz*, is such an essential cipher: it does not identify place for us, it shows the contaminated machine of "knowing" that is in question: the inscription of the eye in images, advertising imagery, which picture it then seeks in the real, seeks to go to, as the arrival of that same picture next—whereupon the film begins. One cannot underestimate the import of this performance for what we call "Hitchcock": it introduces the black sun; its tropes recur incessantly in works to come; its title alone will be returned to—like its mise-en-scène—when Hitchcock, in the middle of the day, the noon of his career or trajectory, will want to return to ask questions at his private Delphi, and remake the entire work, or seem to and miss. Like Jill Lawrence at the skeet shoot.

Marksmen

The target of the anarchists is an Ambassador Ropa, of an unnamed country. He is to be assassinated with a single "shot" timed to coincide with a clash of cymbals in the giant dome-head of the Royal *A*lbert *H*all.

Deleuze reminds us that weaves and threads may be Hitchcock's pre-eminent figure, without grasping that it is, rather, like everywhere else, a trope of figuration itself: of the tropological systems that saturate, seduce, and blindingly dazzle the eye.

Ropa is Spanish for "clothes." The entire MacGuffin is about the over-throw of tropological systems, which would be fatal to the cinematic, including as it does all natural images the camera cites. Nonetheless, it is given as world altering as well, as if the task of the cinematic intervention lay here, in the infinite displacements and seduction of tropes it knows to be "set" props and blinds. Peter Lorre, with the gash over his eye and the white streak in his hair, a figure of defacement and the alternations of black and white or the cinematic bar series, will be named Abbott, will quote Shakespeare referencing the place from which no *traveler* returns—death, perhaps, as a cut or caesura, a one-way street as far as the cinematic transport goes.

The plot supposes a cognitive overthrow that might assassinate the coils or threads of metaphor, and this during a single shot at the Royal Albert Hall, its huge dome filled with high-aesthetic scores and rituals. Arthur Benjamin's "Storm Cloud Cantata" provides cover for the single shot from the assassin, Ramon, supposedly, at its paraclimactic cymbal crash. That presents a seemingly natural cataclysm, lightning, which mimes the intervention of cinematic "shock." And yet clothes are hyperbolically evoked and unraveled already, in the dance floor toward the opening when secret agent Louis Bernard is shot in a curious fashion. What is called the "jumper" that mother and markswoman Jill is knitting will be caught onto a button and unravel on the dance floor, making a cat's cradle of the dancers' legs.

After Louis Bernard is shot he seems not to know it, but then looks down, sees the bullet hole over his heart, and, miming cognition, proceeds to "die" or enact dying cinematically—imparting secret knowledge. Information exists in a razor brush handle in his room. When Lawrence goes to get the secret it will be opened under strange circumstances: myriad languages are spoken outside the locked door, all the babelesque tongues of Switzerland and Europe—linking this knowledge of an assassination plot, which will trigger the kidnapping of the Lawrences' child, Betty, to muting, to an inability to say, and to the fragmentary phonemes of disarticulated languages. The message with its curious insignia of licking flames over a triangle, a sun's corona over a pyramid, lists "A. Hall" to contact: it is not a person but the place where the concert will be given. Not a he but an it. It is not surprising that Jill, preparing for the marksmanship contest earlier, which she will lose to the assassin Ramon, tells little Betty when she distracts her that she will attend to her "presently." One will have to be in the present, have a present, a certain *Jetztzeit* perhaps, to bring off this shot. She misses.

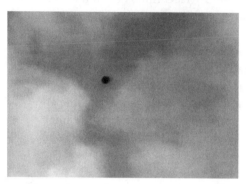

Figure 21. Black sun as skeet crosses sky, shot at by cinematic marksmen.

But the title remains enigmatic, enfolding in itself the purposes of the Hitchcockian uprising and political plot: to overthrow an epistemo-political program, one too suffused with metaphors, tropes like eye and knowing.

In the marksmanship contest cinematic styles compete, yet the token of knowing or the token known and to be shot is more problematic. What is shot at first seems to be clay pigeons. They traverse the mostly blank sky, black spots against the white, inverse pinholes in the sky where the sun might be, only mobile. One must, one would like to, *shoot* the "mark." This disk, however, crosses the sky like a black sun, sending a tremor through the entire natural order not unlike the "Storm Cloud Cantata" as it pretends to a natural cataclysm. A black hole (and not a Lacanian "blot," let us add), insofar as it already covers and absorbs the faux transparency of serial logics, the MacGuffins of light, image, temporal succession. It is already the zero that holds the universe blindly in place, the (eclipsed) sun and the simulacrum that guarantees that eclipse in advance and, hence, conceals it. What would it mean for the simulacrum of such a sun, in the absence of original, to be put out? Is it done by the "sun," or does one put out the simulacrum of a "sun," which placeholder locks the scene in its solar winter and the semiotic whiteout that opens when Louis Bernard, in a ski jump, falls before Betty's little black dog—errant mark running out across the white—and all the players collapse in a tangle of whited limbs?

This solar winter in the Alps will lead later to the fake temple of sun worshippers. The eclipsed disk, moreover, is capable of infinite replication and is *repeatedly* launched in a solar trajectory. Yet what sort of sun is a clay pigeon, or for that matter, reproducible, one after another? What sort of *trap* is being shot, if it is also the solar trap of the "sun's" preinhabitation by a mark, particles, waves, combustion, interval, simu-

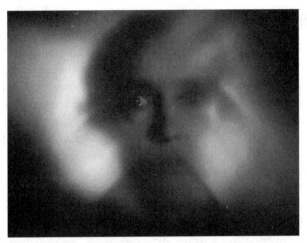

Figure 22. The precession of face: as Clive is hypnotized,
Agnes's face shatters into light rays.

lation, blackness? Why have the critical apparatuses occluded the extraordinary wit—and implications—of Hitchcock's assassins using a false
temple of sun worshippers as a front? It is *almost* too much, this blindness, since it operates like a representational black hole, sucking in constellations of sense, metaphor, figuration, and reference. The shootist aims
at a seemingly limitless succession of simulacra or black suns. This black
sun returns as the black ball Nurse Agnes holds up to hypnotize Uncle
Clive—trope for a cinematic trance or its *hypnopoetics,* which Agnes calls
the "mysteries of the sevenfold rays."

Solar markmanship, temple of sun worship, assassinating "Ropa" (or
narrative time), knowing too much to speak or to act—all hyperbolic,
like the opening ski jump when the black dog runs out and precipitates
a whiteout. If the false temple of sun worshippers is a *front,* a trope for
the movie house in which the flock is duped and money extracted, what
have the assassins to do with exposing the sun as just another trope for
a cinematic black mark? It links knowing to seeing, the metaphorics of
cognition to light, back to the Platonic *eidos,* to ocularcentrism. It is
under assault, to be assassinated by one (photographic) shot. Why, unless the reality of that program is illegitimate and imperial, itself a sort
of temple of sun worship of the same mimicked sort—mesmerizing and
soaking the flock? "Knowing too much," if it does not imply the explosive trace chains of the mute image, entails the undoing of knowing as
eidein, as sight. This is why the work opens with a tourist perusing travel

brochures from which the mise-on-scène or Alpine set of St. Moritz is selected, then transferred to the "real" set or picture, which emerges from a mnemonic program or advertisement. *Too much* for what? *Who*—what "man" or nonman? Why is this severely Hamlet-inflected title adrift in Daedalian references and Egyptian icons (sun worship, pyramids)? What leap or usurpation might be accomplished in the assassination attempt that would, like Sarajevo in 1914, send tremors throughout the political orders of the real? What obliterating cataclysm in the photograph would stage its negative *Blitz* under cover of a symphonic or semio-aesthetic rehearsal of "natural" effects?

The Lawrences' *knowledge* of the assassination plot cannot be revealed or shared. That is for certain—at least not once their child, Betty, is kidnapped. It is as if that knowledge, minimal as it is, induced "little Betty's" vanishing, suspension, disappearance. The girl emerges too as a strange agent: she is called "it" by her mother in the opening scenes, she is allied with the "silly little dog," the black dog that is itself allied to the assassin, Ramon ("you dirty *dog*," says Lawrence) and to the black sun of the skeet. The series is invisible to any treatment of characters, of the "family," and so on. It has all been invisible to the auteurist dossier of interpretation. "Little Betty," this thing ("it"), turns up at the final roof scene in striped pajamas, barred, the insignia of Hitchcock's "bar series." And there are also repeated instances of muting (including Clive's tooth extraction, his mouth swollen), as in references to keeping "your mouth shut" or soundproof walls. It is at the point of discovering the message hidden in the shaving brush—something carrying the insignia of a triangle within a sunburst of rays—that, once again, an explicit Babel of tongues occurs outside the door: Italian, Swiss Deutsch, English, French, German. Knowing, as such, spawned of these linguistic sounds, here asemantic, is also dispossessed by them, or translated into phonetic fractals disowning any one tongue.

This Babel effect is tied to the "secret," the message that nominally explains the title, and accords with the command that something like speech is blocked—and not only by the mechanics of blackmail and a kidnapping that suspends the "family." Moreover, it is a "knowledge" linked to a radical differentiation of phonemic units in and across languages to the point of positing at once an abruption of any monolingualism (specifically English), a site of sheer translation in accord with the cinematic promise of travel that the brochure scene marked and subverted. The Babel effect performs the negative clearing for a type of Esperanto by default that the faux universality of the cinematic would

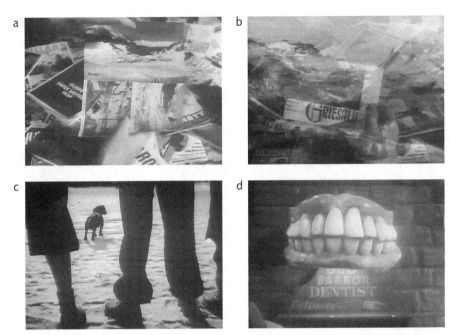

Figure 23. Mnemonic—eye—travel. (a) Browsing hand picks out travel destination (movie locale) that (b) dissolves into site itself (another, now cinematic image) in the first *Man Who Knew Too Much*. (c) Betty's black dog on the snow, which precipitates an inaugural fall, anticipates the *black sun* figure; (d) Advertisement for dentist George Barbor, who attempts to anesthetize the viewer: giant teeth linking celluloid frames to the mouth, the bar series, ingestion.

claim or, under Lorre's (or Hitchcock's) direction, usurp as well. A language of shots, phonetic fractals, black spheres or balls, moviegoing temples exposed and assaulted as surely as Verloc's Bijou will be blown up by the bomb-carrying Professor when trapped. But in this allegorical and allographical reduction to raw cinematic figures in pitched battle with the police order one ignores that little Betty is the figure that passes back and forth from the parents she might want to escape from (who called her an "it" and allied her with the little black dog) and Lorre's cinematic assassins—taken to the rooftop, finally, by the marksman Ramon in her striped pajamas.

The Babel effect, which will return overtly in at least three of the political thrillers as an Alpine staple and migrate, obliquely, through numerous other films and scenes, implies an *inter*site to linguistic effects essentially foreclosing the entire premise of dialogue as "people talking," returning every phoneme to the order of the aural trace that, in *Secret Agent* and elsewhere, will be accelerated to an obliterating and undifferentiating, deafening and paralyzing blast or duration. The Babel effect performs a material reduction that is simple enough: it does nothing but record the real premise of aural signification, anticipating the crash of cymbals and the shot at the conference; it does so, however, simultaneously if inversely, but accelerating the movement or trace that telegrammatically anchors cinematic transit, movement, or transport. The shot, be it by camera or gun, is without territorial or statist definition, without linguistic place or shelter. It is "extraterritorial," as the embassy in the film's remake will be called, a nonsite in which this usurpation is rewritten as a strictly "in-house affair."

The figure of "knowing" appears taken out of any conceptual or biogenic register, linking it to its own translational negation in which an excess returns in advance of any now circular content. Knowing too much seems associated with something like the impossibility of knowing one's own "death." It is connected, in short, to a cognition of death but not of biological life, of a life that is an effect of an acryptophor, a cut, a hole within any solar or faux representational order; hence another point of the recurrence to the temple of sun worshippers as a front.

Successively, a cascade of teletechnic tropes overwhelms the film until, as much as ever, the entire divagation mocks and explores the inner world of intrigue and conjuring tricks of the cinematic while positioning it within an obliterating political and faux biological order, particularly given that the police on screen are always, too literally, as much wraiths as the insurgent anarchivists exploring cinematic logics and teletechnic devices. Thus, we not only have the *temple* of the sun with its astonishing trope of filmgoing—liturgical, Egyptoid, suffused in dark, pretending to illumination, worshipping Enlightenment tropes and promises, housing a ferocious revolutionary troop led by the bug-eyed murderer from *M,* here given a black-white-black coif—but also the succession of figures leading into the temple: the anesthesia administered by the dentist, George Barbor (with the giant set of teeth hung as an advertisement, a black-white-black series placing the eye in the order of masticating teeth); the hypnosis by Nurse Agnes using a black marble called a "light," her face fractured into the "sevenfold rays" representing the initiation rites of cinema; the graphic message in the razor brush; Louis Bernard's cognitive surprise at observing himself shot in the heart and then reading and performing the consequences; the little black dog and later toy cinematic train running its circuit through the concert scene's aesthetic totalization of a lightning strike; and so on.

Thus the figure of *one's own death* is not experienced in Louis Bernard's case, not cognized precisely. The excess of knowing accords importantly with a "death" already indistinguishable from the effect of screen life (as a variety of animation) or what could be called consciousness if one deletes from the term any discrete content. Death is certainly tied to an effect, an eclipse crossing a blank sky, the (a)material artifice of "light" (or the worshipped sun), connected to sound or languages, yet exposing film (like "consciousness") as an effect outside of life as such. Yet when Louis Bernard is shot on the dance floor his response is curious: he must first see the hole and blood, as if from outside, to understand that he has been (cinematically) shot, and then proceed to act out his own dying—as if cognition precisely takes in nothing about this death, is preinhabited by it as the former's condition, or can only mime its scripted results. The same blank and unknowing look will be repeated later, as when Agnes is shot. Dying, losing consciousness, falling, hypnotic trances: the film's surface repeatedly generates this response to a certain excess, except that it is not a plenitude of knowledge, it is more like a vacating of such or, at least, a model of such. It is what Agnes calls, in addressing Clive's marble-induced cinematic trance, at once blacking and blanking out—as if the letteral shift in the two words (*c* for *n*), which cannot always be heard, cloaked a convergence.

Anesthetics

The locus of any "political" transformation would be in cognitive and mnemonic programs: sensoria, inscriptions, identifications, archiving. Lawrence is thus reminded by G., a British agent named as a letter, that a similar nameless assassination took place in Sarajevo with cataclysmic consequences. It is a *single* shot that would alter world history.

The Man Who Knew Too Much puts every word in its title in hiatus—man, who, knowing, excess. *Knowing* alone suggests a

Figure 24. Floodlights and spools attend Barbor's anesthesia.

hyperbolic fall in between the intervals of all spoken tongues, positions the movie house as solar ecclesiastical front for historial intervention. It opens an assault not only on solar poetics but also on the *eidos,* the ocularcentric program, and while it performs the narrative of its own failure, it is, in another sense, already accomplished by the film's spectral existence. The dismembered tourist's hand leafing through travel brochures presents the *first* model of cognition to be critiqued. Advertisement pictures are browsed, as if already installed in the eye, and then sought in the mise-en-scène itself, landing us in the dissolve at the "real" St. Moritz, which is just another shot, more or less mobilized. What the vignette knows is demonstrated in its performance, something *in excess of* the mimetic logics of the picture, of mnemonic programming, of the pretense of indexing. Knowing too much is knowing what precedes and fashions "knowing." It programs, projects, mnemonically rigs, hence negates. But to return to the opening question: what sort of knowing is it—what powers does it have—if it is in excess of sight, light, *eidos,* the Enlightenment, the sun?

We must return to the fake temple. The solar metaphors that have programmed the West are as if administered in the false temple of the sun by Abbott. Seeing as knowing, *eidenai,* the Enlightenment, ocularcentrism: all are cited if not administered from the double temple where Abbott plots the reconfiguration of time, visibility, the event. His black-white-black streaked hair makes him a carrier of the bar series, which, technically, precedes—and disbands—any Egyptic or Platonic sun as origin, guarantor of light, of the eye or "I," purveyor of illumination.[1] The temple's prodigious metaphors follow the marksmanship competition, in which the "sun," rather than being solar or even unique, is black, a copy, recurrently shot across the sky. The (camera) shot, in the assassin's mission, would be precisely timed to the instant of sound rehearsed by the playing of a prerecording of the music. It would assassinate not only Ropa, temporal weaving, but *repetition itself,* the system of model and copy, or the other "sun," the black or eclipsed "sun," already simulacrum, already replicant. In another cipher of cinema, the topos of *light* and heat and Egyptianism or hieroglyphized godhood seems "worshipped" in the temple. And yet that temple is not, or not only, the motley array or leftovers of a metaphysical tradition in which the Platonic iconography lingers.[2] The templegoers have their money taken from them; they are dupes used to fund the hyperion-like leap of the Hitchcockian filmmakers.[3] The assassination attempt's single timed shot tropes a Hitchcock production.

Suns traverse the film, then, though they are not associated with presence, light, or knowing. They are numerous, and they are black. And
these numerous black sun surrogates—what else, later, are Hitchcock's
machine-like birds or attack planes?—traverse and empty other chains
or figures. A first asolar figure is given us in the marksmanship scene, the
"clay pigeon" shooting match between Jill and Ramon, the foreign assassin (and we may hear in Ramon, too, another echo, Egyptian: the anagram of Amon, Amon-Ra, sun god, for whom, however, the A- privative
before the syllable *mon,* of meaning or *Meinung,* attached to the letter of
repetition). It is the clay pigeon (ur-model of later "birds") that crosses the
sky repeatedly when the shooters compete, as when it is hit by Ramon.

Sun worship is a figure for cinema's audience, Hitchcock's ticket
buyers (the collection plate) who come to the temple seeking a certain
enlightenment, succor, solar promise. It marks a faux religious impulse
of the cinemagoer, the ritual nature of the congregation, the fraud that
the assassin-director conceals himself with, the financial transaction that
undergirds it and so on. And it also echoes *tempus* or *templum,* the temporal *punctum* timed to the replayed recording. When the Lawrences are
confronted with "never *seeing* little Betty again," sight and *in*visibility are
interfaced. The inability to see her or "it," as she is called, or see "again,"
is thus connected to the covert premise of sight, or phenomenalization,
in the alternation of black and white.

The postcredit vignette identifies this cognitive impasse more precisely if we read its detail. Two hands leaf through a pile of travel brochures
for holidays in Switzerland, and the camera looks on (almost) from the
position of the eyes of the hands, but not quite, a bit to the right, dis-
sociating the frame from the eye or head perspective it mimes. This
is about hands and pictures, anticipating references to "los(ing) your
head" in the film. The credits proceed without head or face, *acephalic.*
The two apparently male hands (on the right pinky is a ring) lift book-
lets, inscribing this site of fantasy for the viewer, the promise of travel,
desire for escape and choice. A technicity of the browsing and the book's
transference to the photograph is cited, and a false epistemology will be
at once named and traversed, exposed and resealed with a difference in
the film. The hands yield a political assault and crisis from its selection,
whose innumerable "shots" at the finale beat back this eruption of a logic
internal to the English state identified with the tourist books. Browsing
advertisement photos, as an editor would stills, initiates a contract with
desire that will be projected onto the "real" mountain in the photo, yet
as the moving shot of the opening frame: from still to movement.

It is no accident that the opening frames feature an accident on "tracks" in the snow (bar-lines in the snow are referred to this way in *Spellbound*). Louis Bernard's opening ski *jump* and near-catastrophic fall occur before the escaped *black* "little dog," Betty's dog, running erratically across the white snow like an agent of script before the fact. The bodies of the players collapse, limbs as if intertangled in the white cloud, from which they separate out. There is no necessary correspondence between these two hands (and ring) and any "man" in the plot. The hands pick up three folders, the first of which focuses on photographs: one broadside mountain panorama with two half-size frames; all feature snow and ski slopes. Mallarméan white, we might say, is recast as a tourist destination but without humans in it. Frames, photographs, glossed by the next booklet whose title is more of a command: "Take Your Holiday in Switzerland." We will suspend examining the pause of the "holiday," or the link to holy day that the temple will parody. The recurring Alpine scene of Babel and espionage is cinematic vacationland, a snow-white site over which solar metaphors will be imposed and exposed.[4]

The hands now toss aside the English advertisement and reach toward a folder that serves their purpose—that of St. Moritz, of the Griesalp, a glacial mountain whose outline appears in the letteral form of a giant *M* (and we must hear the Mor[e] of St. Moritz as another assertion of excess, of too much, echoed in the Morocco of the second version, which exchanges snow-covered Alps for sun-parched desert). So far, the credits do not so much identify where we will find the film opening, its languid pretense, as declare the entire film event to be about hands and pictures, about (cognitive) tourism and detourism. Marking the tourist as blinded not by light but by the archive programming perception and desire, the hands rest on a photo advertising a notion of the sublime, the picturesque, which then passes into the "real" mountain (itself, again, another photo). It perhaps says: Here, you are now at St. Moritz from your viewing of the photo on the travel brochure. You, viewer tourist, have entered this scene but taken into it not only forgetfulness of where you were in fact (in an English land, browsing, fantasizing) but the entire perceptual dilemma and metaphysical trap of seeing-knowing, the circularity of programming and mnemonics that you just marked.[5]

The sequence *performs* in advance of itself a cognitive trap of perception or reading, as if knowing a bit too much already and in advance about knowing, or seeming to: the eye supposedly belonging to the hands knows, thinks he masters, the travel or passage from a picture to the real thing—its referent, which he then recognizes and moves as if toward (nonetheless, as a shift within picture frames). The "eye" is deceived in advance, much as this regression to pretravel selection steps outside of the narrative within it, creates an antechamber: the real mountain is only *re*cognized as the repetition of a mnemonic implant (named "Griesalp"), a model or advertisement graphic already planted in the travel folder (a folding, in effect, of memory: *To Catch a Thief* will speak precisely of a cinematic afterworld as "travel *folder* heaven"). The real is phenomenalized as if out of the folding archive—prenamed, preframed, angled for consumption.[6] One proceeds as if from model to real, but the "real" is another graphic model recognized from a preinscribed photo (or mnemonic, like the questioning of Mr. Memory in *The 39 Steps*): the postcredit sequence from the position of the *absent head*'s eye is where credibility and credit are launched; it presents a complex reading scene about the occlusion of reading.[7]

Hitchcock enters a scene of graphematics that predates any reproduction and compels us to re-mark the very terms of the temple, its agents and aims. The analytic of cinema here crosses from the pew to the hypnotics of the initiation to the temple's back, conspiratorial rooms. Indeed, *letters* will be highlighted not only in Ramon's asking for his "letters" at the hotel desk, but by the British emissary's name, "G.," or the *spelling* out of *Ropa*—not to mention Hitchcock's speculation on using the skating rink to transmit espionage codes.

Knowing "too much" coincides with a blockage of speech. It is a muting that reflects not a paucity of signifiers but an excess, the atomization of signifiers and the muteness of inscriptions themselves. It is affiliated, too, simply with *teeth*—alternating ivory-like bars or celluloid frames separated by serial gaps in a mouth that masticates and ingests. This latter is registered in Betty's comments when asked her opinion of Ramon: "Many too many teeth, and too much *brilliantine*": again, a blackness presented as light, as "brilliant." He has an excess of teeth linked to a shining blackness. The "it" in question is also the black dog. It seems the effect and inverse victim of a remainder, something that escapes a previous epoch, film, or *anterior* repetition.

Throughout, as noted, characters are repeatedly falling or losing consciousness. This explosion of *excess* with an acephalic coda elicits Bataille's notion of sovereignty, which Derrida explains as a break with all modes of subjugation: "In order not to govern, that is to say, in order not to be subjugated, it *must* subordinate nothing (direct object), that is to say, be subordinated to *nothing* or *no one* . . .: it must expend itself without reserve, lose itself, lose consciousness, lose all memory of itself and all the interiority of itself."[8] *Knowing,* which includes the blanking out of the screen, will be connected not only to an (erased) knowledge of what precedes sight or visibility. Thus the work marks not only loss ("lost your whistle," don't "lose your grip") but a loss of the head, of cognition, in comments such as don't "lose your head." To lose the Cartesian head like the slumping head of Mr. Memory in *The 39 Steps* animates the other bodily parts and extremities, shifts agency from an imperial center or the eye to the material work of feet, hands.[9] The "Oedipal" commodity is parodied and suspended within a ruptured familial order in which Jill saunters off with Louis Bernard while joking that Lawrence could sleep with his daughter, Betty (adding "poor Betty"). It seems ridiculed when the policeman arrests Clive at the temple for disturbing a "sacred *edifice*" (which sounds like "sacred Oedipus"). It seems overturned in advance by the position Betty will occupy in being circulated among the parties.

There seem to be several "Hitchcocks" battling over this decapitation: there is the anarchivist who would intervene in the world-historial archive but will be beaten back at the borders by the police; there are the police, who want to maintain the mimetic regime of the culture, its memory management, and model of light and visibility; there is the reader and blackmailer, to the side of this combat, tracked through the scenes by cameos, signature events, teletechnic and linguistic obsessions, espionage codes, and missions. Above all, there are two orders of the cinematic at war within the work and its conditions—where the host is deadly, money taken, tourist viewers inducted into an underworld they preinhabit unwittingly. Eluding the dentist and plunging into the initiations of the temple, Clive drifts toward hypnosis—where the priestess wields a black marble, her face fractured into light rays, all for him becoming quite blank and black: immersed in the cinematic spell.

Too Much Brilliantine

The train set Uncle Clive gave Betty is called the best "present" he ever gave her. Indeed, the "present" of the cinematic toy train depends on its circular monotony, which the plotters would assassinate like temporality, overleap as sheer metonymy. Thus Jill mocks Uncle Clive playing with the absent Betty's toy, which he used more than she: "You have Pullmans and coal trucks on the same train." That is, the train or present pulls in opposite directions inhabiting the phantasm of movement, pasts and futures out of which that "present" is fabricated, projected, simulated. And like the film itself, it yokes a kind of cinematic trance of the sleeper car to a warehouse of black suns, coal-like, impending conflagration and desemanticization. What seems joined in this cinema, as in the hypnosis scene in the temple that analyzes it, is a sleeper with black coal, black suns as excremental fuel for machines. Abbott rehearses Ramon's single shot timed to coincide with a cymbal crash with the exchange: "No *one* will know—" "Except for *one.*"

When Clive is to be *hypnotized* in the Tabernacle of the Sun and Agnes coerces his initiation into the mysteries of the sevenfold ray in order to put him under, the invasive spectrality of this cinema is displayed in an expressionistic shot. What is called a "light" is a black ball. Light appears the aftereffect of shade, a trace already leaping between telepathic networks, interval not presence. Like the scar traversing Abbott's face and eye, Agnes's defacement marks a precession of *face* itself, of prosopopoeia or apostrophe. The black disk here appears as what engenders vision, precedes light (or perception) as its aftereffect. An aftereffect of blackness, subordinate to it, cinematic light is the product of waves. "Knowing too much" caroms almost endlessly in the conceptual ruins whose transformation it implied. We "see" by not seeing the odd logic of the marksman's competition that Ramon wins. The visible is not perceived but, as in the postcredit sequence, materialized by way of inscriptions: altering a perceptual-political regime involves a descent or ascent into the prerecordings themselves, such as in the recordings of the "Storm Cloud Cantata," where music simulates a natural storm gathering, a *cloud*like London fog, a *Blitz,* correlative of the image's explosive atomization of signifiers and temporal trace chains. Hitchcock here allows himself an anagram within the name Ramon, never repeated quite with such a blunt and unworkable edge—until the name Marnie perhaps. While disassembling into Amon-Ra, the Egyptian sun god, it reverses into No-Mar(k), an infelicitous if irresistible negation of marring by its seeming hyperbolization. The shooting of the mark itself, as it were, prefigures the attempt on Ropa in one other way.

The *knowing* of the title is in excess of any system or archive: it exceeds the archival machinery and it blocks speech or the mouth. Naturally, one goes to a dentist to fix this, who in this case works for Abbott and has a huge sign of teeth in front of his shop in Wapping. The scene is prepared for by little Betty's remark about an excess linked to Ramon: "many too many teeth." Teeth are thematized across Hitchcock, as in the toothbrush scenes of *The Lodger* and *Sabotage,* or the focus on teeth in *The Ring.* They are exterior and prosthetic, as when Markham puts his false teeth in his mouth in the opening scene of *Murder!*

Hitchcock had originally planned to film the scene in which Lawrence tracks the phone call to Wapping in a barbershop, but he decided against it because Lang had just used that setting. In changing the scene to a dentist's office advertised by giant teeth he retains the name George *Barbor*—shifting the term *barber,* with its cutting implements, to a proper name. He wanted to use this word name, or at least its syllables and repetition. The sign incorporates a terrestrial inflection ("Geo") interfaced with the repetition of bar, the serial cutting figure, and allows the sinister dentist to serve as an anteroom to the movie house. Here the eye as cutting teeth is serially displayed, then blocked or muted (the muffled Clive), *anestheticized* if not blinded with a surgical floodlight. The mise-en-scène appears to be all about entering an inner sanctum of cinematic manipulations and spells: the sanctuary of the faux sun worshippers must be penetrated, the cinematic anarchists machinally exposed. To get Betty, Lawrence must proceed beyond these entrancing effects and cinematic spells, just as a disguised Detective Spenser will fall into the conspirators' room *behind* the movie screen in the Bijou. The dentist Barbor anestheticizes with a cinematic floodlamp. Lorre will later quip that Barbor was overcome by "apoplexy," a *falling* disorder.

If *teeth* form a row of bars not unlike piano keys, the site of the mouth as that of speech and eating is again blocked by their excessive alternation of white and black. The dentist's name cites the bar figure but also a term, *barbarian,* used by the Greeks to denote the babbler of any *foreign* tongue (ba[r]-ba[r]): as the Alpine Babel scenes underscored, where languages are disarticulated in advance by mechanical reproduction, any tongue is resolvable into alien sound. Speech is stitched shut at its port of emergence, by teeth, a virtual bar series allying aural concatenation to the metronomics of "light."[10] In the Royal Albert Hall music passes through several incarnations: it is thematized as in some sense sublimely "beyond" speech; next it turns out to appear achingly mimetic in intent (to describe, reproduce, nature broken by a cataclysm of lightning); then it appears a prescripted repetition and a form of recorded writing with bars as the score. The entire order of a "natural" cataclysm has been reverse-inscribed as a mnemonic semioclasm, in which the lightning *(Blitz)* covers an impossibly timed repetition in which the (camera) shot aggressively negates and transforms a political order—yet misses.[11]

Having expended one shot, innumerable ones follow, raining a deadly shower back into the "front" the temple had presented. Hitchcock places in the grand shoot-out sequence an odd parenthetic skit that involves the word *mattress*. Three bobbies, marksmen, assume sheltered positions overlooking the temple. One is positioned behind a piano, which protects him from outside shots. But a second pair usher a plaintive young woman outside from a bedroom and, making a comment about her warmth, put a *mattress* in front of a window. While the *piano*'s ivory teeth protect, the other bobby is reminded by his partner of his wife. He is promptly shot dead in the face through the mattress. The remark about a warm young woman's impress triggers in critics the moralist assumption that the bobby's defacement is some sort of punishment for transgression, yet the opposition here is between *piano* and *mattress*—an instrument of mediation, of alternating bars and music as opposed to the mattress.[12] The doomed policeman was told not to *"touch* that *blind"*—not, that is, to have unmediated contact with whatever the warmed mattress or matrix covered or implied. The mattress metonymizes, by contrast with the ivory teeth, a presumed mater(n)(i)ality precedent to inscription. What offers cover or camouflage in this shooting zone is a formalized apparatus producing musically inscribed sounds over against any attempt to "touch" the blind or matrical excess.

Lawrence's hand breaks out of the soundproof door at the temple by punching out a circle ringed by bullet holes—in effect turning inside out the dance floor shot of inwardly pointing *fingers* surrounding the window's gunshot hole, offered in the form of an empty glass sunburst. The emerging *hand* hyperbolically asserts a Hitchcockian *technē* breaking out from within that negative sunburst and the opening scene of *hands* sorting through travel brochures.

The figure of the sun is excrementally vaporized in the temple after Lawrence has joined the kidnappers. It gives some hint of the viral contamination of all representational or figural codes that the black sun not so much effects as testifies to. A Mrs. Prockets, the charwoman who aids the conspirators (also marked by her shape as a Hitchcock double), asks Abbott for permission to leave the temple, nervous about impending trouble. He tells a thug to see that she doesn't leave, and when she is brought back they have removed her skirt, exposing her legs to general mirth (Abbott will momentarily advise the thug to give Lawrence "a *bad leg*" if he tries to escape). Mrs. Prockets has been compelled to remove her *ropa* and show her black petticoat and bare legs. Here the figure of excess returns not as simulacrum but as excrement and, more curiously, *chocolate*. For in an impish skit that directly defies the state censor, Mrs. Prockets stands next to a shelf and the gangster reaches, as if into her rump, for a chocolate on the shelf, which he retrieves and drops into his mouth. The technical obscenity is double-edged, cutting not only into a state censorship whose blindness it demonstrates with a figure of excrement but also into an invisible censorship present in the blindness of the tourist viewers—the faux sun worshippers. If the black sun is configured here as a chocolate, a bonbon like (the) film—consumed, indeed, as entertainment—then it is also excrement of which the consumer is not aware Mrs. Prockets is gifting, like poison or a sabotaging bomb. As a vignette it is a pure example of what is (in)visible while being seen, a form of touching the blind. As Hitchcock's bonbon is passed to the viewer—the chocolate as turd, as black sun—Abbott still pokes fun at Mrs. Prockets's pale legs by asking, "Have you never been to the *sea*side?" Here, again, *sea* breaks as see or barred sight, which is generated by this material figure of excess that depends also on a sea in which must be heard the maternal *mer* or *mère*.

Figure 25. Thug helps himself to a surprise chocolate bonbon, courtesy of Mrs. Prockets.

The hyperbolic work retracts the title's contentless subject that it puts in question: the "man *who*."[13] It runs through an epistemological critique of solar MacGuffins, which is also to say metaphor and personification, as entry to a site of political intervention—what is also mimed as the inner workings of a cinematic mystery that resides, treacherously, at the core of memory and perception, the mystery of the sevenfold ray. The intervention mimed by the plotting against familial *plots* by Abbott's "circle" projects a transformation of cognitive terms, creates its future reader. The black disk opens a series of markers whose prefigural status eviscerates the received programs of cognition as an order of inscribed repetitions.

Knowing too much applies to the photographemic *image*: a sudden excess of signifying trace chains, unable to speak, a vertiginous evacuation not unlike all languages being spoken at once for which atomized marks and sound were technical premises, a place of no return and interruption in which future generations are kidnapped. The Tabernacle of the Sun is perhaps the bizarre mock fest of the cult of light that this "cinema" solicits while wholly divesting, used as anarchivist front—like a deauratic practice implanted at the heart of a canon meant, officially, to uphold the ocularist, faux Enlightenment state. When a certain pause occurs, structurally at least, in Hitchcock's oeuvre two decades later, a drawing of a bow of sorts for whatever is to come, it is to this title alone that he returns with other questions.

10. Zarathustran Hitchcock

> I love those who do not know how to live, except by going under, for they are those who cross over.
> **—Zarathustra, "Prologue"**

> As Nietzsche put it, man is "a rope over an abyss," stretched between animal and "Übermensch." Brandon in Patrick Hamilton's theatrical version of *Rope* cites Nietzsche as the sponsor of adventure and danger. . . . Taut, tensed, that rope can be extended into a trapeze. The character played by Cary Grant in *To Catch a Thief* is a veteran of the highwire.
> **—Peter Conrad, *The Hitchcock Murders***

To Catch a Thief ends with an eighteenth-century "gala" affair in the hills near Nice. The word *gala* suggests apocalyptics, an unveiling or disrobing, but all the figures here are dressed to the hilt. It is peopled with "formal" costumes (the word *formal* echoes in the dialogue), fantasizing a past grand age, as well as many props that roam Hitchcock's other films. Yet the scene seems to fall through and precede the very "history" it mocks: partygoers dress up as if history too were a period piece or a film set, produced retroprojectively and harassed—as in some Zarathustran logic—by prehistorial agencies. The fact that at Nice, or *Nizza*, Nietzsche composed a part of *Zarathustra* has a certain resonance, since the fourth part of that work also features something of an antiapocalyptic gathering for Zarathustra's stragglers and creatures. Hitchcock would know this and be aware of the Nietzschean parallel of eternal recurrence to his own MacGuffins associated with rings and returns, with cinematic spools and zero or ocular figures of time's consumption of itself.[1] Could Hitchcock be read as a sort of "going under," or over? Of characters decimated, or bridges stopped on, of transport not arrived? Would they be, if obliquely, "Nietzschean," or would there be any point to a "Hitchcockian" Nietzsche in turn? Is this convergence coincidental or does it indicate where Hitchcock may function in—and against—not only the "ineluctable advance" (George Collins) of a teletechnic empire but also the sensorial programming and cinematic counterstroke to its production of the "last man" of touristic teleconsumption?

The value of such a question, today, would not be in the more pop iconic senses, such as those that link the name Nietzsche to the rhetoric of the *Übermensch* in the one place in Hitchcock it occurs, in *Rope*—unless that would be as the citational dismissal of that rhetoric, which Brandon unauthoritatively performs in the Manhattan penthouse. He contests the citation of Nietzsche as a cheap purveyor of superman theories even as he, Brandon, enacts precisely that: dismissing Hitler as a vulgar literalization while, in fact, reabsorbing the fascist *rhetoric* of the recently conquered other. This last occurs in the work by way of the academy, the self-disowning discourse and *playful* aestheticism of Brandon's humanist professor, Rupert, or more literally the screen icon James Stewart, who would, one supposes, be the very antithesis of this—as if Hitchcock espies in the construction of the all-American hero, whatever his plaintive moralism, a variant on the hero worship and mimetic identification that suffused Nazi propaganda. This occurs just after "the war," much as America absorbed Nazi scientists from its vanquished Enlightenment and imperial double. Hitchcock leaves negative traces of this contact—as in the name Huberman in *Notorious,* drawing again on pop associations consistent with the superficies of the cinematic—but a performative trace of this interface would be sought elsewhere.

In question, rather, is where or whether the totalization of the *cinematic* in Hitchcock's hands—the atomization of deauratic traces that links Benjamin's work on allegory to *The Birth of Tragedy,* say, despite the former's disclaimers—options a rupture and inversion of a received model of aesthetics as such. This, while drifting toward a production of the "last man," the ultimate tourist of the teletechnic era to come, long arrived. This elaboration Hitchcock would both oversee and contest. In the earliest British thrillers the usurping cinematic anarchists poised against the home state without known political agendas (except for a totalizing intervention) join a war already under way, that of a totalization of the teletechnic empire in which they (Hitchcock) also participate. Later, as in *To Catch a Thief,* the cinematic may be aligned with what can be called the "Resistance." It resists, or avenges, in the name of the wholly *other,* and which can appear as wraith, serial murderer, birds, the teletechnic, as nonanthropomorphic and nonauratic language.

A certain accord lies, again, between the eternal recurrence and the banal facticity of the cinematic spool. Certainly, it is not just one or another MacGuffin that is, in Hitchcock's system, a "nothing," as if such could be opposed to a something or a someone. The MacGuffin as a performative marker is precisely like the zero in its modern functions: a placeholder over a nonsite from which numeration can seem to begin, from which the $N + 1$ can appear to start a narrative or allegorical chain. The "eternal recurrence" would have been Zarathustra's MacGuffin. It is purely cinematic, and Hitchcock inherited in cinema the banal literalization of the eternal recurrence as a questioning of the structure of mnemonic repetition, the priority of inscriptive programs (celluloid) over phenomenality (projection). The back-spinning wheel that opens *Blackmail* tells us this is a teletechnic problematic—one that is not so much a "modernist" chapter within an archival history as an acceleration and absorption of all archival variants within a relatively short official "history" of human script and monumental history, the several thousand years represented in the British Museum's assemblage of forms.

This "Nietzschean" connection releases a series of questions pertaining to the circle, the zero, and the spectrality of what can be called the "1." It is not just that Hitchcock's persistent treatment of numeration accords with the fiction of a zero for which the "1," too, is a secondary trope of sorts. That is clear, say, in the proliferating appearance of triangles and pyramids (or the number 13) from *The Lodger* onward, as if that itself initiated an open series incapable of stabilization, and as if one began, in any numbering, with the number 3. In these works, the number 3 appears as a so-called *first* number, much as for any technician of the visual; triads represent the *first* visual plane (the triangle), or for discourse theorists, the first "social" ensemble. *One* is what any speaker or so-called subject pretends to be. Yet it is a spectral retroprojection of and from the third, apparently, a complex initialed in the 13 that pervades Hitchcock's work and marks his, in this sense self-canceling, birthdate (August 13).[2] But the labyrinth of numeration represents an interesting dossier for cinema, which departs from spinning wheels and null points. The circularity of the spool is but one tangible enigma, since the unspooling (forward) of a stored mnemonic band, again and again, presents itself as a phoenixlike beginning in the ashes of its own recurrence—and raises the question of where, or how, the affirmation of the "eternal recurrence," of the MacGuffin, paradoxically ruptures a representational program by returning to a site anterior to itself: the nonsite, technically and in fact, of inscriptions.

It is not incidental, then, that Hitchcock's work is littered with what might be called "O-men," who inherit this transition, who are emptied as ciphers and couriers of something to come, something of which they know nothing, and do not, in any case, arrive intact. It is amusing to reflect that these can be James Stewart or Cary Grant, and that the individual actors' entire Hollywood iconography is cited and dragged into the semiotic maelstrom of inversions with them, but that is certainly so to a degree: when "Scottie" *goes under,* so to speak, in *Vertigo,* an entire template of mimetic and gender or identity assurances linked to Stewart and America undergoes disarticulation with him. Uncle Charlie's smoke rings; the names Otis and Oakley; Hannay, called a "nobody"; Barry Kane, to whom Tobin points out a book titled *Death of a Nobody*; "Johnny-O" Fergusson, "Dick-O" Blaney, Roger O. Thornhill: all inclusive, otherwise, of specters, revenants, amnesiacs inheriting the memories of others; all hostage to voided marking systems, in which the circuit as MacGuffin is installed. This is so rigorously marked in graphics, letters, and nominal tags that the issue of circuitry itself is critiqued as a mnemonic construct. If anything, the supposed nothing or nobody named "George Kaplan" in *North by Northwest* signifies too much by comparison, anticipating, in his nonexistence, not only the standard subject but also the giant faces of Mount Rushmore, whose personification appears to fall away before a deanthropomorphized rockscape—heads *(capo)* of the earth *(geo[rge]).* The recurrent *series* of proper names that dislocate nominal identity across Hitchcock characters, for whom lists of names or extra nicknames pop up, seems a general condition of the cipher—much as, in *The Lodger,* the morphing of faces on those supposedly listening to the wireless inscribes the singular viewer or consumer of the screen work in the event of the showing as interchangeably individuated beings over time who are mnemonically preinhabited and momentarily *produced* as effects. The recurrence to a certain zero effect has nothing to do with a "character" or psychology. The facticity of the screen wraith as shadow play and mnemonic specter is assigned the structural space of the human in whose "eye" or head the entire band will be run or rerun. The facticity of the cinematic is marked as coextensive with the citational program of cognition or consciousness or identity, to use available terms. What is called life or the

living is not structurally other than a form of animation, like that produced from artfully cut effects of light and sound play. Inserted into the
memory disks of mass culture, the cinematic is totalized as the aesthetic
organization of spectral experience, perception in the teletechnic empire
of "global" logics to come.

The explosion or "shock" of cinema's advent is not only the annulment of tropes of origin before teletechnics of prosthetic memory and
media, whether what is suspended is called "nature," the "eye," "light,"
or "Mother." It marks an inversion of whatever had been rendered as *the
aesthetic* within broader traditions of philosophical hegemony. The place
where this tradition is performatively inverted is *The Birth of Tragedy,* a
work Kittler calls a cinematic theory *avant la lettre.*

Raymond Durgnat observed of *Psycho* that "it has a Dionysiac force and
ruthlessness; one might call it a Greek tragicomedy." Hitchcock already
had called it a comedy, which renders the second part of this quote regressive, but the adjective Dionysiac is arresting.

Kittler deems *The Birth of Tragedy* an ur-cinematic work: "Nietzsche . . .
produced a film theory before its time under the pretext of describing
both *The Birth of Tragedy* in ancient Greece and its German rebirth in
the mass spectacles of Wagner" (*Gramophone,* 120). One must recall
the ocularist powers accorded to Apollo in the work, or the manner in
which what is narrated, stammeringly (Carol Jacobs observes), is nothing less than a prioritization of media to the mapping and generation
of historial programs, events, "experience," form: the seeming birth
of theatrical space out of the specter or *Geist* of what is called music
returns to an alternation, an arrhythmic differencing that preinhabits
the star power of Dionysian exorbitance, as the latter gets to portray
itself.[3] What is the *ghost* of music in advance of itself, reminiscent in
graphic display of the Hitchcockian parallel bar sequence? The succession of linguistic forms passes through dialogue, eristics, descriptive
language, and Euripidean ratiocination. Presented as the unfolding of an
allomorphic or teletechnic archive, it yields successive modes of language power delivering up, finally, Socrates and philosophical prose.
The MacGuffinesque agon of the two gods gives cover to this narrative.
Yet the definition of "music," or its spirit, appears in question. On the
one hand, it is the domain of the mock-originary Dionysus who has
the upper hand to Apollo's countermastery of the plastic arts—and of
the eye. Apollo gives it his best shot, but he is all along affiliated with
belatedness, the cooling down of volcanic and preoriginary excess, the

domain of reflective form. There is no contesting Dionysius's charisma. His association with predescriptive *Musik* is the clincher.

In question is the cinematic analogy and the definition of *aesthesis*. The term *aesthetics* recurs to the Greek *aisthanumai*, "perception." The narration Nietzsche proposes that moves us from dithyramb to Socrates implies a linguistic model for what Benjamin dubs a sensorium's programming. It is the genealogy of *media*. If it is possible to call *The Birth of Tragedy* a cinematic theory, as Kittler does, it begins with the *projection* of the visible out of Dionysian primordiality: like Wagnerian opera, a sequestered stage materializes the newly concealed powers of the orchestra below. Here the aesthetic model is inverted, since instead of representing life it names where "life" would be phenomenalized, virtually, out of mnemonic effects. It begins a theory of teletechnics that leads to the most famous line of the monograph: "It is only as an *aesthetic phenomenon* that existence and the world are eternally *justified*."[4] The linkage is startling if it means something like beauty is the only justification for existence. It is more startling, still, if something like justice is bound to the production of perceptual phenomena *(aesthesis)*. The world is determined, for humans, out of its archivization, for which there is no simple or pure "perception." The rule of mnemonic programming and inscription is cinematic, but, since the detour through signifying agents can imply their material division and subdivision as marks, the cinematic's atomizing power can contest, interrupt, disinscribe. It is here that telenetworks and temporal agency are accessed. The visual, as on the screen or in what is called Apollo, is a forgetful product of inscription and forces before any pretext of light or the eye is introduced. *Aura,* as the term occurs in Benjamin, is banished with the advent of cinema, or here perhaps dithyramb.

Kittler appropriates this line in *Gramophone* to argue for a "transvaluation" implied by the cinematic machinery: "If 'the world' can be 'justified to all eternity . . . only as an aesthetic product,' it is simply because 'luminous images' obliterate a remorseless blackness" (120).[5] While this characterization privileges the luminous over the "remorseless" black, as though retaining the auratic premise, it is modified. The Dionysian is for Kittler "the flow of data" (120), the "elementary fact of Nietzsche's aesthetic." It makes *Dionysus* the "master of media." Dionysus as the master of media controls the projector booth, like Hitchcock's first cameo in the editor's booth before the giant printing presses, while Apollo is permitted association with form and sight, the products of archival manipulation. Appearing to pull the strings of the formalist Apollo, Dionysus still wields prefigural powers and the "primal" pain of dismemberment. Music remains safely prefigural, virtually divine.[6]

But it goes downhill from here, particularly once the two godlings start to mingle: the mock dialectic software erodes with its own duplications.

Locating this moment requires a certain slow-motion replay. Dionysus at first accords with the cinematic cut and hence the "Hitchcockian" signature effect of "Mother." In Hitchcock, precisely such an (a)maternal and (a)material site seems formalized in the haunting weaves of what has been called "Hitchcock's signature," the visual and aurally syncopated *bar series,* the slashes generating and suspending the effects of narrative, or mimesis, or the visible. Irreducible as markings precedent to any possible perception, this is visualized by Rothman as / / / /. It can morph into virtual faces, letters, graphics. All visibility, all networking, begins and ends with this cutting. Yet how does Hitchcock's "formalism," his obsession with the *technē,* translate into the "Dionysian" power that the maverick Durgnat found himself compelled to note? Was not "Dionysus" supposed to manifest the most originary of violences, *before* representation? Where is the "aesthetic phenomenon" associated with *music*—or with rhythm, *alternation,* the keeping or production of time?[7] *The Birth of Tragedy* stammers on this point in a hiccup-like reversal that is invariably covered over. In an anomalous passage, Apollo changes places with Dionysus, or seems to, then is put back as if nothing happened. But this occurs at the most loaded instant, at the origin of "music" itself. Apollo is briefly recalled as the official originator of music:

> If music, as it would seem, had been known previously as an Apollonian art, it was so, strictly speaking, only as the wave beat of rhythm, whose formative power was developed for the representation of Apollonian states. The music of Apollo was Doric architectonics in tones, but in tones that were merely suggestive, such as those of the cithara. The very element which forms the essence of Dionysian music (and hence music in general) is carefully excluded as un-Apollonian— namely, the emotional power of the tone, the uniform flow of the melody, and the utterly incomparable world of harmony. (40)

This is covered up, but it is too late, and one suspects a certain Nietzsche was altogether in on the flashing expedition. Instead of the exorbitant Dionysus, the formalist Apollo is placed as if at the ur-site or *Ursprung.* A simulacrum of music occurs as if it's still origin, a copy *without* original. Apollonian music here excludes the Dionysian, is called merely *rhythmic,* so that it must be excluded itself even *as* music. A ghost or *Geist* of *Musik,* it gives nonbiological "birth" out of its own afterlife and in advance of *Musik*'s true emergence. Music seemed a premimetic order to which "language" was added ("language, in its attempt to imitate it, can only be in superficial contact with music," 55–56), yet here music is born out of the alternacy of sheer formal semiosis, linguistic difference in its barest or most minimal form: *rhythm.* Rather than present a plenitude, Dionysus represents a *pre*originary *repetition* ("himself pure primordial pain and its primordial *re-echoing,*" 50). Apollo momentarily precedes "Dionysus," determining the latter as already an aftereffect, as *his* front. By letting "Dionysus" win and become a poster god for the misreading of the work, Apollo is canny. *He,* Apollo, becomes invisible thereafter, an increasingly unharassed formalist, like an unserious filmmaker. He preserves opportunity and power. He—of the long shot—watches over the elegant villains in Hitchcock's tele-archival thrillers.[8]

Hitchcock's *bar series* scissors; it cuts up the eye in advance. It invents the generation of spatial and temporal difference, hence the possibility of a series, serial murder, allegorical remarkings, perceptibility or reading. Apollo precedes the pretense of Schopenhauerian will or music. Apollonian dismemberment connects the bar series and its affiliates (aural concatenation, knocking) to a Dionysian pretext. The script indexes a Nietzschean reading of "cinema," a Hitchcockian Nietzsche. The bars represent and perform the permanent suspension of mimetic claims and surfaces, the Apollonian dreamscape. The trance of the cinematic, artificing a site of disinscription and reinscription, is like that of the dithyramb: a jubilating public identifying with that which ruptures all identity in "primordial" difference, "Dionysus," quiescently reassembled before the hypnopoetics of a dark and seated enclave. Anesthetized. One could propose a Hitchcockian reading of the final manner in which Nietzsche marks his project, at the end of his career, as though Apollo has been subsumed totally and is no longer the other: *Dionysus versus the Crucified.* Not the Greek versus the Christian, but one god premised on difference and another instituting chiasmus as a hermeneutic regime. Chiasmus, like the giant "X" that turns up in Hitchcock at key if surprising moments, strives to machinally invert signifying poles and referents in advance. By the Crucified we can hear an instituted chiasmic of truths and hermeneutic polarities inverted *before* they are codified as reference or symbolic law (hot and cold, male and female, light and dark). To oppose Dionysus to the Crucified, to a hermeneutic regime of semantic inversions, is to oppose the Dionysian or cinematic bar series of irreducible and deauratic media to a gigantic Greek *chi-* or *X,* an "X" that appears at times across Hitchcock's oeuvre: the skis in *Mr. and Mrs. Smith,* the "crisscross" or monogram on the lighter in *Strangers on a Train,* the flag before the targeted prime minister in the second *Man Who Knew Too Much.*[9]

Hitchcock implants a blackout at the retrodawn of the video age, globalization, telemarketing, hypertechnics. With an entrapping hospitality toward every interpretive agenda or positioning, this cinema conjures a terrestrial set peopled by always past and future wraiths. *Moment* is at issue, the photographic *Augenblick* about which Zarathustra mock cinematically disports:

> Must not whatever *can* walk have walked on this lane before? Must not whatever can happen have happened, have been done, have passed before? . . . For whatever *can* walk—in this long lane out *there* too, it *must* walk once more. . . . And this slow spider, which crawls in the moonlight, and this moonlight itself, and I and you in the gateway . . . must not all of us have been there before? And return and walk in that other lane, out there, before us, in this long dreadful lane—must we not eternally return?[10]

The spool runs again, erasing, but for a trace, where it has been—like the two hands clasping at the close of *The 39 Steps,* one of which next appears, in the opening frame, buying a ticket at the music hall. In *Zarathustra* that spectral other on behalf of which the overman would go under in a general disarticulation is called *earth,* site precedent to face or voice yet scored by the bar series' effects. *The cinematic spectralizes earth.* It appears as pure *technē, aterra.* The O-men, on occasion or throughout postgendered, are one cipher for the voiding of epistemopolitical programs.

Cinema's atomization of the mimetic image is clearly double: it can serve a statist program or sabotage from or beyond the border of an archive, accelerating the former's death drive against it. Hitchcock is not modernist nor surrealist nor postmodernist; not auteurial nor ocularist nor mimetic in any way.

11. Extraterritoriality: An In-House Affair at the Embassy of Ao——

In the audience there are probably many people who don't even know what cymbals are, and so it was necessary not only to show them but even to spell out the word. . . . Let's say the first version [of *The Man Who Knew Too Much*] is the work of a talented amateur and the second was made by a professional.
—Hitchcock to Truffaut

If the film called history unwinds itself, it turns into an endless loop.
—Friedrich A. Kittler, *Gramophone, Film, Typewriter*

It is seldom asked: why "remake" an already masterful—perhaps, in fact, too perfect—earlier work? In the post–World War II films the MacGuffin of battling nation-states became irrelevant for allegorizing cinema's threat to the home state, and what had been secret agencies and saboteurs outside its borders descend into the totalizing horizon of the media-state "America." The cinematic assault enters not as world-altering saboteur but as Bruno Anthony or the black cat; it disarticulates not the home state but the home ("Mother"), mass (cinematic) tourism, the star, gender artifices, what may be called "family" plots of the new dispensation. When it revisits political espionage it will involve a cata-basis back into Hitchcock's earlier work, as if he required a pause for taking stock or reorienting in the second version of *The Man Who Knew Too Much*. The film bearing that title will entail this time not an international assassination attempt that could trigger world war, a historial conflagration, but what will be called an "in-house affair," the intrigue and usurpation that culminate in the "extraterritorial" embassy of an unnamed foreign nation. To the extent that nation, whose opening letters we see as "Ao——," is a cinematic domain, such an "in-house" usurpation might seem internal to Hitchcock's project, as if this looping back staged an internal review and hiatus putting the later career in contrast to the revolutionary aggression of the early work (and "villains"), as if between two Hithcocks, early and later, "amateur" and "professional," if these positions or priorities could be definitively assigned.

Could Hitchcock have remade it just to use that extraordinary title, which some find never really is explained by either work? Was the formal experiment of a rewrite as tantalizing, say, as the strictures imposed by the claustrophobic *Rope,* in a very different way, or did he cherish the set piece in the Royal Albert Hall and not trust that its intricacies were apprehended the first time around? Does this self-cannibalization attempt to reinscribe or renegotiate some cinematic intervention or the formal sophistication entailed in postwar American tourism? Did Hitchcock reach a point where a backward glance was needed that would not turn him to stone, since that was already the case—as mocked, almost, in the visit to the taxidermist's shop in the latter film, a supposed "red herring" that lies at the heart of the project's visit to and questioning of its own underworld? What other discourse could be opened by creating such a work—as if between the first and the second, or in the act of reading that the remake presumed and performed? Does Hitchcock write these and other questions into the work, itself replete with "questions" countering the cognitive focus and promise of the title, when calling, at one point, the assassination plot this time around an "in-house affair," as if handled *en famille,* between one Hitchcock and another, on the extraterritorial grounds of what is called the Embassy of Ao———? What is an embassy of such vowels? As if this syllable or outcry or graphic puzzle of pain presented a signature for his circular operation as such—in which case, what young ambassador would be trying to assassinate what aged rotund and balding prime minister?

The film preceding the 1956 remake of *The Man Who Knew Too Much, To Catch a Thief,* anticipates it in a number of almost unreadable ways, from the travel service opening to its peculiar MacGuffin. In that work a retired jewel thief called "the cat" comes out of retirement to pursue another copycat using his "mark" and style, thus framing him for the crimes. Interesting logic: the original (a thief, nonetheless, hence a simulacrum) must anticipate or copy *his* copy, and cut it off, thus curtailing the value of his imprimatur. It might correspond, say, to how a director would imitate his imitators who might be having more success than he, or an actor, like Cary Grant, who came out of retirement for the role—if actors, per definition, are thieves of identification, and so on. If that was how Hitchcock saw the problem of making a "Hitchcock" film so light-headed that no one could tell if it was a perfect copy or an empty fake, his next move might indeed be grossly and abjectly literal: to remake, to recite otherwise, a previous "Hitchcock" title. He could thus disappear into its outline, and no one would quite know if he were refining an earlier attempt or turning against his own signature. It would be, so to speak, too much.

But one can view it otherwise, too. The second *Man Who Knew Too Much* is the only "remake" in the opus. It so literalizes what he called his system of "self-plagiarism" as to give pause (the term is Hitchcock's for poaching on his own works). If Hitchcock turns against "Hitchcock," like a usurper against an established statesman, it is not clear which is which and where this plot, an "in-house affair," leads. Why, of all the works, does he choose to remake the one whose title, at least, focuses on hyperbolic cognition, excess knowledge, solar destitution? Unlike *To Catch a Thief,* which is set on what an Art Buchwald column calls the "lighter" side of Europe (the French Riviera), *this* film opens below the Mediterranean altogether, on what is called the "dark continent." Unlike the first version, which began in Alpine whiteness, this one opens in a solar waste. The calculus of variations is forbidding. In contrast to the first version's assassination attempt on Ambassador Ropa, a world-altering assault, we are told, the second will be an "in-house affair" conducted in the extraterritorial embassy of a nation we only see the first two letters of on a sign: Ao—— Embassy. This painful cry of entry occurs, the sign tells us, at the rear—resonant not only with its implication of anal rape but also with the knife in the back or betrayal that will materialize in the spectral chase of Louis Bernard dressed in a burnoose in the Marrakesh market. Certainly, a struggle for usurpation appears conducted within the house of eternal recurrence, that of the Hitchcockian spool, or alternately, that of a wail of pain. This *"extra*territoriality" must be heard as both atopic, without place, as the figural domain of warped times and interspaced shuttling of reading sites, as sheer excess and as in some sense extra*terrestrial,* if the cinematic image negates and suspends any remotely natural, originary, maternal, or indexal logic for the planetary scene it surveys and finds, outside the window of the cinematic bus that opens the work, desertlike, void of vegetation or nature.[1]

"Again, and again . . . and again, and again," sings the voice of

Figure 26. Rear entry to the cinematic Ao——
Embassy, "extraterritorial" site.

Doris Day, jazz singer, called "Mummy," rising up the stairs from the improvised parlor concert in a closing scene of the film at the Embassy of Ao——.[2] As these words soar up the seemingly endlessly repeated formal stairway to Jo Conway's (Doris Day's) kidnapped son, Hank, "again, and again," one might feel caught in a formal backloop, a loop of recurrence that could have led—ideally—to still more remakes of this one film. Again and again. Almost.

The narrative of a tourist couple, Ben and Jo McKenna, who stumble on an international threat and whose son is kidnapped to secure their silence—which then leads them, in searching for him on their own, to thwart the assassin's shot in a concert in the Royal Albert Hall (an A. H. signature)—has several obvious shifts, in addition to those mentioned: instead of a little girl (Betty), it is a rather bizarre little boy who is kidnapped (Hank); instead of Brits, "Americans" are very much in play; instead of Jill Lawrence's photographic marksmanship skills, we have Doris Day's singing (equally lethal, we witness, to the Euro ear); instead of a temple of sun worshippers as a front, we are given a chapel; and so on. The epistemological topos appears redoubled. On the other hand, this excess of excess opens in a site where the sun's excess blinds and requires dark glasses. Where the first *Man Who Knew Too Much* incurred much passing out, hypnotic trances, and self-observing deaths, the second requires *anesthesia*—like the sedatives administered by Ben to Jo when he tells her of Hank's kidnapping. Something is more formally orchestrated and peculiar, as shown in the ability of the work to afford itself a scene of near-opera buffa in the taxidermy shop, where stuffed animals turn against Ben and appear ready to bite or eat him—a pause within a pause, perhaps, which he retreats from, as if he stumbled into Hitchcock's cinematic workshop as well. Why does Hitchcock refer to the first version as the work of a "talented amateur" and to the latter version as that of a "professional"? Why could he not give up this title, or could he, with time, not make a third or fourth version, again and again? Why did Doris Day break down crying on the set, and offer to withdraw, mistaking the cruel use to which the camera put her (perpetual citation, implicit acidity) for Hitchcock's imagined displeasure with her? What taxidermic gaze did she suspect or know, as it were, too much about? "Too much" for what?

Jo is interrupted *reading* at the back of the bus—from the position of blacks in the southern United States at the time, from the position of what will be called in a moment, with no obvious sense in her case, "Mummy." I will make three hypotheses in shaping an approach to reading this work, with this interruption in mind. The film, by its repetition alone, is clearly marked, notched in a way that assumes an enigmatic relationship to the oeuvre, as if held in an extraordinary reflexive hiatus within Hitchcock. As a formal exercise, it preinhabits his own signature and title—this time, he says, as a "professional," a cipher term—yet is replete with autographics: the Prime Minister will look like him (Truffaut says); Albert Hall bears his signature initials (an "it," not a "he"); he is becoming an "American" yet also returning to London (like Jo); the title alone speculates on the explosive status of the muting and blackmailing image; the "little boy" *Ha*nk bears his signature; and so on. Three points:

- That the second version assumes the first version's already hyperbolic critique of cinematic epistemology and proceeds to a *formal* extreme in which its allegorical, citational dimension is turned on, or against, itself (an "in-house affair").
- That in doing so, it puts the very principle of temporal succession or generation into hiatus, which the retrieval of Hank seems necessary to proceeding beyond.
- That what is to come in Hitchcock's production, which is about to enter what is deemed its most powerful phase *(Vertigo, Psycho),* will depend on this "pause," this taking stock and entry into its own underworld, this folding back within his signature system, and that in one sense, at least, one could say that this subsequent production will not take place or proceed beyond this point.

A good deal might depend on the rescue of young Hank for what is called the American family. Hitchcock had been said to make the same film over and over again, and here he does that so literally that it opens a vortex or black hole in the system.

It Looks Familiar . . .

There is a peculiarity on the bus ride to Marrakesh, which is doubly marked as a cinematic allegory, not only by citing Hitchcock's cameo in the preceding film (at the back of a bus), but also with upturned bicycles

Figure 27. Issue de Secours (Exit): American tourists on ghost bus to Marrakesh.

atop the vehicle like projectors or spectacles. The opening dialogue has Hank and Ben McKenna viewing the void and hostile landscape yet finding it "familiar," indeed, *familial*. That is, they cannot not consult memory and come up with a simile that makes it familiar—they make it a metaphor, but for what, if not also the earlier version? Morocco is certainly not that familiar: robed beings, ghostly and faceless; minarets broadcasting prayer calls; sunglasses presenting blind-looking eyes everywhere. Any sense of déjà vu would have to be mistaken. A cinematic landscape and ghostscape. Tourists, the McKennas will also be figures of the viewing public—window traveling, appropriating the alien nonlandscape:

HANK: Daddy, you sure I've never been to Africa before? It looks familiar.
JO: You saw the same scenario last summer, driving to Las Vegas.
HANK: Oh sure—when Daddy lost all that money at the craps—
BEN: Hank!

There is in the first words of Hank a *backloop*, looking for a memory or model for the desert of Africa. Mother knows her film references and cites a previous "scenario" here replicated. Yet it links that memory to Daddy's gambling and crash "at the craps—." Before the word *table* can be said, he is interrupted by Daddy's calling his name, recalling him to muteness, since he knows too much. But then, as is the case with the film, "this really isn't Africa" but a cinematic wasteland of *Mar*rakesh and *Mor*occo redoubled and obliterating light itself:

JO: 'Course, this really isn't Africa—it's French Morocco.

BEN: Well, it's northern Africa.

HANK: Still seems like Las Vegas.

As American tourists, the McKennas compare everything to home, to what is familiar: the landscape is like Las Vegas, site of gaming, of chance. They would be inexplicably at home in this ghost land of Morocco. Traveling in northern Africa, the "dark continent," they are sitting *at the back of the bus,* place of nonpersons in America at the time.[3] (It is during this film that Hitchcock will assume his American citizenship.) In this opening bus ride, cinematically marked, words draw attention to themselves—how they may inflect, interface, make incisions. As with the crash of cymbals, Doris Day's singing, the role of the orchestral cantata, much will be subordinated to *sound.* Words will "sound like" other words ("Marrakesh, sounds like a drink"; "He sounds like [a doctor]"), and even *spelling* will matter ("he can *spell* 'hemoglobin'—of course, he has a little trouble with words like *dog, cat*").

Doris Day counters Hank's opening question, intercepting what is directed to Daddy. She affirms Hank's conjecture but in a way that undermines its reference. He has indeed seen what is called this "scenario" before, implicitly, as the previous *version* of the work or another (like *To Catch a Thief*): "You saw the same scenario last summer." Whatever "professional" shift Hitchcock claims for himself in producing the remake, using the hyperbolic first "version" as a tissue of effaced autocitations, it must also be a *reading* of the "first" version. Certain fissures emerge in the opening bus ride in which Hank's first words depict (re)cognition as something seeking to repeat the already installed mnemonic model. Yet unlike the first version, which features a tourist's hand leafing through travel brochures, picking out a picture of the Griesalp at St. Moritz and then dissolving to deposit us "there," a sly setup of the viewer's cognitive entrapment in advertised images regardless of where the travel pretends to go, here the tourist model is home, or a desert that simulates it. This cognitive trap of the familiar seeking its own confirmation, a tourist trap about which the film knows too much from the start, appears in some of the critical engagements with the film too.[4] On the bus to Marrakesh, Americans are the strangest passengers, the most out of place, or *atopos*—except, perhaps, for Hank, the "little boy" who will seem impassively circulated and who spouts the most metaphysical comments of the lot. (In this, he recalls the little boy Arnie of *The Trouble with Harry,* who, with his toy space gun, figure of cinematic weaponry, dismantles past and future time.) Hank sagely notes: "I don't know. In school they call it the dark continent—this is twice as bright as Indianapolis." The desertscape called Morocco on the dark continent is something like pure exteriority, noon without shade, a darkness "twice as bright." The figure of "knowing" is so overdetermined that, as no one remarks, it is reiterated in the *names* of the two lead characters, Dr. Benjamin Mc*Ken*na and Jo ("Jo—no 'e'—short for Josephine") *Con*way.[5]

"Arab Talk"

White-robed ghosts walk the streets of this Morocco as normal citizens, a cinematic land where face-covered Avengers and sunglass-blackened eyes are normal. This is also a different historical landscape, colonial and prehistorial: after the "war," "liberated," it is still "French" Morocco, a relapse supplanting the victors for the fascists from the eye of the other.[6] The order of firsts and seconds seems temporally in question or suspended, like the priority of father and son taxidermists with the same name, Ambrose Chappell.[7] The stutter by which Hank refers to a déjà vu, an already having been *here,* in his first words on the bus, alludes to the earlier film. If the second *Man Who Knew Too Much* folds the first into itself at once—resulting in a bizarre, even hyperbolic flatness to the tone and narrative—the work opens in a reflexive mode that both haunts and compels its perpetual interruption reflected, say, in Louis Bernard's trying vainly again and again to reach the knife in his back, or in the assassination of the Prime Minister being plotted against by his own ambassador.[8] The Prime Minister seems like he stepped out of the taxidermy shop, an animated costume, unreadably dim, positioned on a painting behind the younger Ambassador in the latter's office (who both breaks and seems caught by the frame). Louis Bernard only half seriously remarks of Doris Day's "Que Será, Será": "Too bad it was interrupted."[9] The "red herring" trail to the taxidermists' workshop brings this hyperbolic problem of succession to an impasse: what comes "after" the dismantling of the solar, a step beyond (or before) yet also a formal repetition?

   This rupture of nested episodes seems announced in the peculiar titles accompanying the credit sequence, telling us to focus on the cymbalist of the orchestra—peculiar, since the emphasis is suited to a silent film and names an event without any meaning as the primary referent of the work, the event of an empty event: "A single crash of Cymbals and how it rocked the lives of an American family." Each word—*single, family, crash, rocked, American*—disaggregates and sheds tendrils, but only a few inflections interest us here. Hitchcock tells Truffaut, as if he were speaking to a child, that many people in the audience do not know what a cymbal even is, so "it was necessary not only to show them but even to spell out the word." The title text identifies a "crash" as the topos of the narrative—a certain, "single" catastrophe or undoing, yet also the event, demonstrated visually, of a mere sound, of cymbals, which the cymbalist holds up like two rings or spheres, like a bicycle or spectacles. This inverts the normal pretense of indication, where the unknown word is given a picture, or shown: reading is what the image here is directed as if back to, down to or before letters (the gratuitous capital *C* of cymbals). In the word *crash* Hitchcock posits the structure of cinematic "shock," implying the aural analog of symbols to cymbals. Where the Greek *symballein* throws things together, here the violent collision of the cymbals produces an aural cataclysm. It shatters or *rocks*—retracts aura or personification of any sort. It implements "shock" as a formal premise, a perpetual horizon interrupted by minarets.

Dependent on rehearsals and recordings, the instant must cover, if not coincide with, its strike—as a cymbal crash covers a gunshot. It is already posited as a virtual (future or past) instant that might be intervened in at a singular juncture of times or intersecting constellations. This "single" referent, a crash of cymbals or shattering of all metaphors or symbols, decouples every other mimetic referent: which might be called the allegorical desert scene of Morocco. This single crash will be rehearsed from a recording of the "Storm Cloud Cantata" to time it just right, of course, that is, to cover the assassin's shot, the punctual event of that shot or photographemic *Augenblick*. The recording repeats and forecasts the crash, which in the storm-simulating cantata is the arrival of *lightning*, of *Blitz*. The instant is timed and prepared for by repeatedly listening to a recording in the chapel. It seeks a missing *punctum*—something between the future tense of Doris Day's "What will be, *will be*," and the Prime Minister's retort of thanks, following her "It wasn't . . .": "But it was . . . *it was*." Thus Drayton's interruption of his sermon, and dismissal of the flock take *stock* of an earlier puzzle in his archive, and all that resides in the future: "We should pause—and *pause* now—to do a little stocktaking." Stocktaking is also archival storage, as stock is compiled film. Without an Archimedean point outside the performance, without a "director," without a precise time, Hitchcock's work will track the caesura of its own historial interruption in the giant domed head of the Royal *A*lbert *H*all.

Hank walks forward in the bus, which brakes suddenly, and in catching himself he accidentally pulls at a woman's veil, revealing a face she rushes to re-cover.[10] An Arab man chases Hank, shouting, at which point the French agent, Louis Bernard, intervenes to "help." He knows something they do not, what is called "Arab talk":

HANK: Hello. You talk Arab talk.

LOUIS BERNARD: A few words.

JO: Why was he so angry? It's just an accident.

LOUIS BERNARD: Well, the Moslem religion allows for few accidents. May I?

BEN: Yeah, sit down, right in front of Jo there.

LOUIS BERNARD: I thought his name was Hank.

BEN: No, that's my wife's name, Jo—no "e"—short for Josephine. I've called her that for so long, nobody knows her by any other name.

HANK: I do—"Mummy."

Contrasted to Cary Grant's claimed intent to send a stamped letter to Mother in the opening of *Suspicion* or, in the opening of *North by Northwest,* to use any teletechnic means—telephone, telegraph—to communicate with her, Hank seems fortunate here, having Mother right there, though he already has his own Egypticized name for her: "Mummy." Jo's name swings between genders by virtue of an unhearable *e.* The exchange is also about "words":

LOUIS BERNARD: Now, about the accident. You see, a Moslem woman never takes off her veil in public under any circumstances.

HANK: You mean they feed her *intravenously?*

LOUIS BERNARD: A big word for such a small boy.

BEN: You see, I'm a doctor.

LOUIS BERNARD: He sounds like one.

BEN: Yeah, he can *spell* "hemoglobin"—of course, he has a little trouble with words like *dog, cat.*

"Arab talk" moves from vision *as* memory to word to spelling to what precedes spelling (dog or cat as black sun or trace). It parallels Dr. McKenna's surgical extractions from the body, as when he later speculates to Jo about which of his patients' body parts was "paying" for their trip:

LOUIS BERNARD: Where do you practice, Doctor?

BEN: Indianapolis, Indiana—Good Samaritan Hospital out there.

LOUIS BERNARD: What brings you to Marrakesh?

BEN: We were attending a medical convention in Paris, and I thought
we'd come down and see Morocco again.

HANK: Daddy *liberated* Africa.

The cinematic bus moves between Casablanca (the C-A signature
registering a 3-1, or 1-3 inflection) and Marrakesh (a *Mar-* name or site),
and they will have "three" days in the latter. Doris Day will be called
Mummy, linking her to the mummy-wrapped Miss Froy in *The Lady
Vanishes* and the taxidermy set piece to come, as well as, proleptically,
"Mother" in *Psycho.* Questions flourish, others pass unasked. For instance, why, when Ben identifies his city of origin, is that "Indianapolis,
Indiana"? That is, a site in which the word *Indian* is repeated, *remarked.*
This response verbally cancels the site of "America" as home, since it
would have been the land of Indians, not of "Americans," who were only
foreigners. Americans, Hitchcock tells Truffaut, do not exist: "There are
no Americans. America is full of foreigners." In turn, the repetition of *in*
promises a kind of interiority, an inside or home reserve, that is evacuated by the term Indian—as with the odd term *inny,* used in *Shadow
of a Doubt* by Mr. Newton and gentle Herb to recommend "Indian
arrow poison" as a murder technique that leaves no clue. There is, there
would be, no *interior,* much as there is none in a desert that is "twice as
bright" as Indianapolis, obliterated by solar logics gone awry, even as it
is called the "dark continent"—excessive brightness as black or blanked
out, the blinded sunglasses like empty sockets worn casually.[11] It is Ben's
nescient task to resist the political intrigue of cinema as American tourist (and moviegoer), to pass through it all without learning or knowing
anything about it, to retrieve "Hank" like the little pre-Columbian idol
of *North by Northwest* carrying the secret microfilm.

Repeatedly, Ben will refer to their intent to "pick *up* Hank." This
will be, in fact, the closing lines of the work when the family returns to
the hotel room, to find Jo's friends sprawled out asleep, exhausted from
waiting out the interrupted visit. Hank, of course, is a peculiar "little
boy," as he is frequently called (the phrase used by Hitchcock in remi-
niscing of his own childhood terrors, as in the oft-repeated anecdote of
being taken to a jail cell by his father). Hank, whose name will suggest
hang and *hand*—as when, at the restaurant, Ben is frustrated trying to
keep one hand at bay with his food, in the end disabling both—differs
from "little Betty" in the first version in many ways, of which we will
mention here only one: while Betty will be identified with the little dog,
surrogate of the black sun, and return at the end, atop the false temple,

in barred or striped pajamas, Hank seems in general a bit removed from every scene. In a work advertising excess knowledge, Hank will tend to answer questions the adults put to him with an undecidable shrug, prefaced by "I guess so" or "I don't know." He disappears, like Betty, with the appearance of the to-be-suppressed secret about the assassination. Hank, a name suggesting suspension, as in "hanging," is himself suspended from the narrative, kidnapped. Hank is suspended, "suspense" is suspended: something would be gambled, just like in Las Vegas, not by creating suspense but by suspending suspension—were that possible. A rope will be taken out in the embassy basement, dangled with the intent to strangle as the thugs are told to wait in "the mailroom." It is a Zarathustran rope for acrobats, like those seen tumbling in the bazaar.

Our People in Marrakesh

What is this *pause* that a mock-priestly Drayton offers in his sermon as a taking stock, as if within the Hitchcockian oeuvre and teletechnic complex, almost with a view toward a certain encounter, event, or (consumed) repetition? What has changed as the temple inscribing moviegoers in an ideology of light is transposed to a bogus Protestant church on Vicary Street, whose vicarious nature is reflected in the seemingly abysmal and formal replications of rooftops? In a work that shows us, as does *Secret Agent,* a close-up of an ear, of Ben's ear whispered into by the dying Louis Bernard, imparting a secret he must write down to remember, on paper bearing the word "Memorandum," we must also hear the recurrent phrase "pick up," or "pick up Hank," differently—even when distorted, say, by McKenna himself, as pick *out* ("Why should he *pick me out* to tell?").[12] We can hear in "pick up" the beginning of the word *picture,* only here linked to the hyperbologic direction, "up": to "pick *up* Hank," as though breaking off the command to *pic*(ture) by the eruption of letteral graphics in the figure of speech itself, as though the logic of such depiction or picturization were interrupting itself when applied to *Hank* (Norman Bates speaks of making a "mental picturization"). Hank must be returned to the picture, the family, whose future, it seems, or center, has vanished. This event invades the (a)topos of the mise-en-scène, be that Morocco, or a northerly site, England, or a spectral site, alluded to as home, unseen, but "like" both in different ways—visually, linguistically—*America.*

As tourists in this jump-cut or cross-edited *terrain* (Morocco, Paris, London, Indianapolis, Las Vegas, the "dust bowl"), we need a new sort of map or directory. Ben reaches several times for the phone book, in which precisely the voice or phone appears dissolved into numbers, letteral names, addresses, and so on.[13] He thumbs the pages of a directory as though it were a dictionary in the Marrakesh police office when Drayton is talking to the hotel, and a phone book is key to locating the two Ambrose Chappells and Ambrose Chapel itself. Telephones dominate this film, much as the unreachable knife in the back cites the (editing) scissors of *Dial "M" for Murder*. Among other things, one "picks up" a telephone to communicate, and this seems to happen in all interior locales (hotels, airport, apartments, embassies, "church," and so on). A communication system seems to underlie the cinematic fabric, a switchboard of blinking lights and connectors, increasingly vertiginous in a horizontal way. For a moment, the film appears to be about a telephone book as such—a "book" that directs to yet cancels voice as other than rehearsal of a script, relay, autocitation, another's. But what, again, of Hank, whose perpetual "I guess so" in answer to all questions, a bracketing, makes him the one who walks toward the dying Bernard—as if the site of the latter's death agon were connected to him?

The cut in the back, behind, which Louis Bernard cannot reach as he staggers, a berobbed ghost, face neither white nor black but streaked with barred finger traces, cuts an opening to all that is anterior: every trace chain in the archive, at one moment, or the anterior version of this film, in a different monadic compression.

To "pick *up*" Hank remains a hyperbolic phrase, much as ascension seems remarked in the sight of the minaret, in Ben's climbing of the bell tower rope, in the movement of Jo's voice up the self-replicating staircase toward the end of the film. If the term *pick* evokes picture, to *pick out* ruptures the indexing or indicating of the pointing finger in *Blackmail*, as from a police lineup, an excess within the pic(ture) itself. The work that would revisit and rewrite the first *Man Who Knew Too Much*, that picks it out and

Figure 28. (a) Stewart fingers *phone book,* lists of numbers and names. (b) Tiger mummy wants a piece of "live" Stewart.

up, like a travel brochure from a pile, cannot not also be an anatomizing allegory of the phototelic image as such. This *hyperbologics* is on display in the market or bazaar scene: there, two depictions of acrobats climbing up one another's shoulders, momentarily forming a triad only to tumble down at the end, sandwich attention to the "teller of tales" addressing the crowd. The "teller" in dark glasses is sitting, stationary, using a pointer to stab at the air around him as he weaves narrative, much as the Prime Minister will be called a "*states*man," stationary, like the "statement" that the commissioner wants from Ben when summoning a *typist*. Whatever in this flat desert scene climbs to excess and heights—like the upward launched and the gravity-curving palms that punctuate Marrakesh—falls parabolically back, Icarus-like, only to a desert earth void of trees, of natural image or index. An earth of black eye sockets and hooded specters murmuring in "Arab talk."

A work that citationally absorbs, disgorges, and replays its precursor text(s) while attempting to usurp it by temporal precession, like the two Ambrose Chappells or the ambassador and Prime Minister, must leave a tangled web of densities and decoy trace chains, in effect overloading what might be called the spies' e-post office—the set piece of *Secret Agent* rendered hyperbolic—with a virtual whiteout of letter bombs, spam, and picture postcards at once. Too much. Yet also too little.

The "little boy" is a complex figure—not only of a "son" (as Ben summons him), but one echoing the word *sun* yet allied, nonetheless, to hanging, to suspension (even epistemologically, in his distancing reply to rhetorical questions: "I guess so"). And the inscription of the letters "HA" for A. H. (as elsewhere in Hitchcock the name Harry or Henry or Henrietta and so on is used). *The Man Who Knew Too Much* is imbued with an almost too routine series of signature effects, as in the "little boy" Hank (an *L. B.* that will, in turn, be linked to the death of Louis Bernard), but also to the giant domed Royal *A*lbert *H*all itself. That is, an A. H. site, as in the first version, like a huge echoing head, not a "he" but an "it," as is said of Ambrose Chapel, as well as those figures who operate by corporeal citation—like, as Truffaut noted, the cymbalist in the credit sequence, or the bald and portly Prime Minister to be assassinated, sitting, listening, behind a state flag emblazoned with a giant X.[14]

It is not accidental that an autobiographic event marks itself at this site, this remake in which the signature, "Hitchcock," will be as if re-inhabited and ventriloquized. The first film version's failed invocation of a Hyperion-like solar *leap* (the first day of spring, the ski jump, Jill's "jumper") is as if inscribed as the stutter of an "I" trying to assert or claim being, only to fall into the self-citational and self-replicating stammer in and across the utterance: "I *am*." It is a frenzied autocancellation as if at which all signature systems converge as debris. Yet the mise-en-scène opens in Morocco: a corollary of Egypt, land of the dead and of hieroglyphic writing. If an unspeakable and pointlessly compulsive "I am" echoes by deletion, barred by its own status as utterance across the text in the recurrent *Am*brose Chappells or Chapel, it is also heard in the word *American* capitalized in the title text ("how it *rocked* the lives of an American family"). When the dying Louis Bernard whispers into McKenna's ear, *speaking* will appear to generate and bar this hyperbolic accession—propel it into an order of death, an afterlife at which the Moroccan citation of an Egyptian landscape and signscape scarcely hints. The logic here will return one to the taxidermy scene, the faux "red herring," as it will to the apparent nonrelation between the first and second versions that remains the latter's greater riddle: why it should exist at all.

On the bus the McKennas are seated in the back beneath the sign saying, "Issue de Secours." Exit. If the first version dismantles the role of the sun in Western tropes of knowing, one does not just *begin* this time in a site of blinding solar excess, where there are people without faces, veiled, or with dark glasses. It precedes personification or, in the accidentally removed veil, face. Morocco echoes the verb "rocked" of the title text ("how it *rocked* the lives of an American family"): more-rock-o. Other of all metaphor, of personification, of aura.

There is a near-blinding exteriority to this exitless desert, a *dark* continent "twice as bright" because of that, disemboweled of referents, as though sucking all the scriptive labor of the preceding version into this sudden preposthumous Egyptian vista, which nonetheless recurs "again and again." The bus is headed from *Ca*sablanca to *Mar*rakesh: it moves as if from a "CA" figure, a "white house" that nonetheless recalls the ice mountains of the first film, to a site that incarnates, at least in name, an entire *Mar*-system in Hitchcock's writing: *Marrakesh*. (Jo: "Just wait 'til you get to Marrakesh." Hank: "Marrakesh—sounds like a drink." Ben: "It sure does.") These desert travelers are thirsty. The phrase "sounds like" points to constellations of the later giant ear, as does the advertised crash of cymbals. For instance, "drink" can suggest water, a sea, say, *mer* or *mar,* or it can sound like "in" (Indianapolis) or just "ink." *Mar*rakesh, as a name, suggests an allographic domain of marring and marking, in *Mor*occo, superimposed over rock or desert or an emptiness that can only generate metaphor, similes, the "familiar" to excess. *Marrakesh* thus suggests a cinematic locale and logic peopled by spectral ciphers: "our people in Marrakesh," says a British spook. This appears in the market scene the following day, replete with acrobats, tellers of tales, rows of sewing machines, the apparition of the black-faced Louis Bernard stumbling to his knees with a knife in his back. A *Mar*-system implicitly invokes and disfigures the logics of maternity—of the *mère* or *mer*, of *mé(moi)re* or "memorandums," invoked with the opening recollection ("you sure I've never been to Africa before?"). This will turn up atop Ben's notepad, on which he transcribes the *secret,* as "Memorandum." It references the memory storage of the celluloid itself. Beyond the trope of maternity that Doris Day is asked to excruciatingly mime (even as her name boasts of a "gift of the 'day'"), Hank objects when her masculinized name is explained by Ben: "Jo—no 'e'—short for Josephine. I've called her that for so long, nobody knows her by any other name." Hank again counters: "I do—*Mummy.*" Mummy not Mommy, this jazz variant of Kafka's Josephine, the singer, antici-pates the more vexing scene with taxidermists, where *all* animals, we might say, as zoographematic animemes that bite back, will appear in the process of becoming animal and mummified at once. Assuming the posture of life as animation, the animeme repeats itself and, here, ag-gresses: it starts to consume James Stewart.

I will make, here, two *detours* then, making our way through a series of interruptions, through the numbers and names of the phone book, through an unexpected type of thinking, and thinking of *types* and ty-pographics (as the police inspector says when McKenna breaks off their interview: "I'll send for a typist"). One will have to do with food and con-sumption, interiorization by representation; the second with legacy, sons and fathers, sons and mothers, temporal sequence, generation, time.

On the bus Hank asks Louis Bernard whether he likes snails: "You eat snails?" "Well, when I'm lucky enough to get them." On the affirma-tive reply, Hank offers that the McKennas' "garden back home" is "full of snails": "We tried everything to get rid of them. We never thought of a Frenchman." The joke is almost too much, too good for the bantering context, but by this asymmetry it seems marked. *Eating* is connected to the predatory consumptions of the eye, its faux internalizations and negations. There is an elaborate scene at the Moroccan restaurant where the McKennas encounter the Draytons. James Stewart is unable to fit his long legs (too much, Gulliver-like) into the seating arrangement and is unable to use his hands in the customary way (only one for food).

He tosses down the dismembered chicken in frustration (an American trait), extending his hands as if dismembered themselves, suspended.

Drayton, we hear at table, "was a big noise in the Ministry of Food during the war"—a "big noise," if not a walking "crash of Cymbals." He is even "preparing a *report* on soil erosion," comparing the Moroccan desert to the American "dust bowl," that is, dissecting the imposed metaphors and familiarization of American tourists. Between having been a "big noise" and "preparing a report," another figure of sound or gunshot, Drayton binds a raw materiality of sound to an evacuation of sustenance, the eradication of produce from the earth ("dust bowl"). Hank is never seen eating, though even the double agent at the Embassy of Ao—— is ushered through a kitchen. Kitchens occur throughout Hitchcock as a trope of cinematic production, the film commodity as a confection, as in *Secret Agent*'s chocolate factory. Yet here a forced abstinence—the destitution of Moroccan poverty—returns us to the desert, to spareness or reductiveness that is the elliptically deficient correspondent of the proclaimed excess ("too much"). To snails.

The specter of a Frenchman eating snails from an American backyard, or earth, leads in a way to the taxidermists' shop, where we encounter the lifelike yet dead wild animals attacking Ben, a preternatural sawfish decapitating him, a tiger catching his hand in its mouth, almost holding or consuming it, turning the tables on the human consumption of animals (as, differently, the *bird war* will seem to in the later film).[15] Stewart stumbles in this hyperbolic remake into the most curious chamber of the film's labyrinth, a virtual mummy or cinematic workshop, mocked yet exploding in a final hysteria and slapstick free-for-all (a leap into an *other* genre, in fact, from which it backtreads). Prefigural, it suspends generation in the form of Ambrose Chappell father and son in favor of replication, like the row of sewing machines which the Moroccan women are seen plying at the bazaar, albeit here all male. But it turns out *A*mbrose *C*hapel, harboring another 1 and 3 signature (as book-inflected *Buch*anan says, "This number will find me"), is "not a man, (but) a place," an "it," a "building" or *structure*. Depersonified, rocked. There will be a panspecies menagerie at the taxidermists' shop: fish, birds, wild game. What is striking in the reversal from Frenchman eating snails to tiger eating man is that the latter, deposing the human as machine of consumption, is already beyond "death," or life-death. Stuffed animals whose skins simulate the screen wraiths of actors purvey the withdrawn attack of nonanthropomorphic figures. The small black cat as trace and thief of light in *To Catch a Thief* swells into an attacking striped beast. Like Ben, unable to proceed with eating, or the tiger unable to close its jaws on his hand definitively, a suspension of ingestion interrupts the routine of touristic consumption.[16] And this abstention will have some alliance with the sheer exteriority and poverty viewed all about in Morocco, particularly contrasted to London.

Why, in this return to Africa for McKenna, is this family already bound to, and evasive of, a certain solar obliteration, a territoriality of the sun, beyond all sight and allied to American blindness, black glasses, the "dark continent"? How is Hitchcock's cinema taking stock of its direction—if not by a catabasis within a catabasis, going back to the earlier enigmatic film to undo it, question it, or to the African genesis or Egyptian source? How is Hank, "son," an unwitting bearer of the solar emblem—and not only because *son* "sounds like" *sun*—as is the blonde and fascinatingly nescient and bizarre Doris Day? Much as the two Ambrose Chappells, father and son taxidermists sharing the same name, will put in suspension *generations,* McKenna's forename is marked and played on: *Ben,* after all, suggests "son of" in Hebrew, as well as Benjamin, brother of Joseph and youngest son of Jacob, sent down to Egypt. The name also echoes as "son of sorrow" or "son of the south," south here citing Morocco, Africa, the "dark continent," legs, materiality, a destitute Marrakesh in relation to the northern London of the hotel, embassy, the Royal Albert Hall. As a son, Hank is a son of a "son of," a trope that erodes not so much the soil, from which plants are generated, as generational logic before simulacra and solar dissimulation. Indeed, the name Benjamin is present in the credit sequence,

Figure 29. Reanimation workshop, circus of predatory animemes.

and again on the concert placard before Albert Hall, since Arthur Benjamin is the composer (father) of the "Storm Cloud Cantata," whose score we will hear and, indeed, read, and whose "single crash of Cymbals" is to cover the assassin's shot. The woman accompanying the shootist at the Royal Albert Hall, provided to lend him an air of "respectability," is named Miss Benson—as if to say, again, "son of son," as though a certain implosion of generation is or would be at stake in the assassination, against a natural or referential reading of sun, or even son. It is as if the suspension of Hank were putting the son or sun out of play, throwing the work into a sheer formalism it must grope its way through, only to finally "pick up Hank" again.[17]

Hank's reference to Daddy liberating Africa inscribes James Stewart's famous wartime service in the signscape, collapsing frames of historial referent, much as the "jazz singer" label tropes Doris Day's facade. The stars are inscribed as portals between the historial real and the performative of the cinematic text. In Doris Day the appropriation seems different. There is another pun in her name, ignoring for the moment her entire posture as blonde head and bearer of the son or sun. For we learn from the placard in front of the Royal Albert Hall that the day is June 6, D-Day, for the invasion of Europe. This invasion is mimed inversely when Jo sings "Que Será, Será" before the squirming Europeans at the embassy. Yet "*the* Jo Conway's" return to London is also inverted by McKenna's *return* to Africa as tourist, evoked by Hank's bragging, "Daddy liberated Africa."[18] To *liberate* Africa recalls that *libre* and *livre* interlace in the ear, as the Statue of Liberty is used in *Saboteur* or "livery" in *Vertigo*. In what respect, however, is the *gift* that Doris Day bears an aesthetic counterinvasion, this time by the simulacra of "Americans"? These returns to a past, like a catabasis, whether of Africa or London or Egypt or the first *Man Who Knew Too Much*, suggest an archival encounter, taking stock, that puts virtual futures into play or would as unpredetermined ("Que Será, Será")—like the little boy Hank. From one angle, the "in-house" assault by the ambassador on the Prime Minister pivots two "Hitchcocks" in formalistic agon: the trademark and the Avenger, the earlier and the later, amateur and professional, hyperbolist and formalist, father and son taxidermist, though in what direction or order is uncertain.

Not a He but an "It"—No Personifying Allowed

The Embassy of Ao—— will be approached from the "Rear Entrance," an "extraterritorial" enclave served by huge cinematic kitchens. What occurs when one stops eating—when interiorization, by the body or memory, is interrupted? And this, by a redoubling of a sun ("twice as bright"), a return to a first version, to the "dark continent," to liberated Africa, to an already visited Morocco (or Egypt), and to England— where Jo Conway has "played" before. Ben McKenna will have to lower his ear, which fills the frame, to hear what the dying and blackfaced Louis Bernard—French yet Arabic, Arabic yet "born" in Paris—says that is relevant to all this. What is the Memorandum's secret, the secret of this implicit "do not forget"?

There is a suggestive difference between the "first" version and the "second" version of the film, for at a certain point in this reading (since that is what is interrupted in Jo's case, reading the first "scenario," as she calls it), this priority, this infratextual order, is at least performatively at risk. It may have to do with when Louis Bernard passes the secret out of which all the problems ensue. This time, the difference in question will not be the difference between a girl child, Betty, and a "little boy," Hank; between a British and an American couple; between an amateur and a professional director—all perhaps "MacGuffins," if that term has any referent beyond the literalization of reference *tout court.* Nor is it only that the "second" version *assumes* the solar dismantling of the "first" already with its opening bus ride—transposed from the Griesalp to the sands of Morocco, indeed, to the *Mar-* state of Marrakesh. One might expect no less of a work following *To Catch a Thief,* which at least stayed on the northern side of what it calls the "Mediterranean," the middle-earth, and which that work, so lacking in gravity, seems to lose location of (Grace Kelly will quip, from a hotel lobby, that at least it "*used to be* this way"). The faux temple of sun worshippers, which inscribes the public's relation to a fraudulent metaphorics of light as knowledge in Western thought, disappears in the second film and we emerge, at Ambrose Chapel, in a spare Protestant setting void of such hieroglyphs, quiet, formal. The difference may also be that between two semiotic apprehensions of death.

In the first version, Louis Bernard will look down at his shirt when shot in the heart in order, once he takes note that he is to die, to perform the routine, as though knowing "my death" had something to do, in that film, with knowing too much or too little, with that obliterating excess of the black sun. The look is uncomprehending. Yet the second version seems altogether disinterested in this—or rather, it takes it for granted; it begins in the land of the dead; it begins (almost) in Egypt. It is, as a travelogue, Hitchcock's "Book of the Dead," as the taxidermists' mummy factory perhaps implies. What the second version supplants for the first's shock of *not* knowing one's own death, the blank look, or its already being the case on the screen as in that semaphoric animation called "life," is something else: a return to a scene of trauma (Africa, the war), the repetition of a memory that cannot be remembered, the formal repetition itself (the rows of houses, each alike, in London, the dominion of sheer form, the echoing refrain of Jo's last song, "again, and again . . . ," the mocking replication of the stairway of the embassy).[19] The drift is toward a precession of metaphor, such as is first echoed in Hank's opening assimilation of the landscape to a remembered home.

In the tourist family there is always a *family plot* we don't know: the mother may be a virtual male, or a mummy; the couple in a visceral death match; the child side with the anarchivists. The whole, as with Verloc, is invariably a *front* for other activities.[20]

The market scene in the public space of Marrakesh is where the spectral power of this *Mar-* scene converges. Here will be performers (blind teller of tales, acrobats rising vertically), women with sewing machines, discourses on babies and cutting body parts, a blackfaced Louis Bernard's staggering from an alley with a knife in his back and falling to his knees. Hank is at home in these spectacles.

This *question* of generation is called "*the* question," by James Stewart. Jo and Ben are walking and making their amused list of how Ben's surgical work paid for the trip and various extras. "You know what's paying for these three days in Marrakesh?" he says. "Mrs. Campbell's gallstones." Body snippets and parts, cinematic dismemberments yielding cash. And the list goes on: Bill Edwards's tonsils, Johnny Matthew's appendix—all the innards missing from the stuffed animals McKenna will be tossed into the arena with in London. Then Jo springs "the question." It is all about the future, about what will be, about when they will have "another baby." It pretends to be an intimate, if embarrassing question, a maternal urgency: the subtext, too, is that they will run out of time to do so, but that issue seems secondary when they are faced with a formal warping of historial time in the plotting this sort of discussion almost sets going in the film. Thus several gestures undermine this suggestion, keeping in mind that during the "Que Será, Será" duet, a song of the future present, the future of "is," even Hank dissociates himself from his assigned temporal role: "*when* I was just a little boy." The problem of "the question," and hence questions, generally, and knowing returns. Jo scolded Ben after the bus ride: "You don't know anything about this man—and he *knows* everything there is to *know* about you," and so on. What is first presented as a leap—Ben: "Just like the county fairs, they've got everything but the balloon ascent"—is pancaked also out in a horizontal vertigo of desert. About having another baby, Jo adds, "You've got all the answers." And Ben pretends: "Yeah, but it's the first time I've heard the question." A bit later, he tells the French inspector, "You not only ask the questions, you answer them, too." Like Mr. Memory's repeated "facts," which must be checked with the one who asks, who already knows the answer. Thus it is noted of Jo by Drayton, "My wife tells me Mrs. McKenna appeared at the London *Palladium* a few years ago." That is, where Mr. Memory externalizes his recorded formula, as he must, and expires: the Palladium, site of Pallas, of wisdom as a form of mnemonics, repetition, inscription. But something intervenes. *The* question, one of generation, is ironically spurred by an antithetical and, hence, unread specter: Jo asks after she glances at an infant carried by its indigent Moroccan mother, and then associates this sentimentally with babies. The association should be soft, touching, following the surgeon's list of excised innards. But if one looks it is the opposite: a baby is slung over the back of a woman in wretched poverty, bobbing like a sack of wood.

After *the* question, a third *coup*: Hank, their last baby, their first version, *points* to a row of Moroccan women, one after the other, seated before sewing machines. The bottom tier of industrial labor, making clothes, destitute replicants of the Fates before the return to the top of the economic and aesthetic pyramid in London's Royal Albert Hall. As the bus pulled into Marrakesh one glimpsed a woman *bicycling* with such a machine on her head, connecting it to cinematic production. Hank is shrewder still: "It looks like a television commercial." For what? The second baby might also be a second version of the film—not existent yet, being almost birthed or retracted in performance.

Hitchcock is so maternal here, such a *mummy*. The machinal stitching shifts reproduction into mechanical reproduction, and as Hank implies, the televisual, a "commercial," like the "invisible weavers" Clara Thornhill, "Mother," taunts her son Roger (Cary Grant) with in Kaplan's hotel room when he examines the too short suit. *Again and again*—yet here that is machinal, colonial labor or service, part of the televisual globalization traversed by machines that can replicate mothers in a row inversely. The maternal instinct evoked in Jo by the miserably slung baby, already a life in excess of its uses, is altered by the line of women. Deleuze notes that *weaving* is a primary trope in Hitchcock, though it was just that, the primacy of trope, that the first version aimed to take out or assassinate in Ambassador Ropa. Here generation as mass production forks into two: it dematernalizes woman figures yet allies them to visual media as advertisement, commercial manipulation. It suggests some implications of the term *mummy*. If generation is cut off, curtailed in advance as the cinematic, it will have something to do, ostensibly, with the vanishing of Hank—the son and sun, who we will encounter only once in the interim, as a *disembodied telephonic voice*. One steps into a zone of infinite replication—rows of identical women, faceless. Even as "woman's" biological role in reproduction may be cast garishly, the prospect of conception between the two Hollywood stars playing a married couple is recast through impoverished sweatshop Fates using *Singers*—perhaps jazz singers, whatever jazz means here.

This encounter precedes the sight of Louis Bernard stumbling out of the crowd with a knife in his back. He falls to his knees, berobed like a ghost in blackface, and whispers something to movie star and American icon "Stewart" as he dies. It is a supposed secret and will trigger Hank's kidnapping to keep it from being shared further, to stop speech. Pascal Bonitzer observes that Louis Bernard, dressed in a burnoose, is pursued by police but then by another Arab who looks like himself, the one who puts a dagger in his back, then is in turn chased by the police in Bernard's place as the latter staggers on, reaching unsuccessfully for the blade in his back, as if reaching for what is anterior to (but driven into) him:

> The sequence featuring the murder of Louis Bernard is constructed as a nightmare, in which a man would seem to be chasing his own reflection in order to stab it in the back. It is in fact impossible to

Figure 30. "Like a television commercial": cinematic Fates with Singers.

distinguish pursuer from pursued, since they are identical silhou-
ettes in burnooses, but Hitchcock deliberately accentuates this doubling effect by taking care not to show immediately that two men
are involved. (180)

As Bernard falls, McKenna's fingers streak the blackface, leaving it as if
striped, black-white-black. The "secret" of the earlier version was passed
in a shaving brush while garbled tongues were showering Babelesque
phonemes outside the hotel door. This time, the secret, whatever it is,
will be written down on a paper printed with "Memorandum" at the
top so that Stewart can remember it. Like the earlier version, speech
is stopped by the kidnapping, and it gives minimal reference to the
work's title; this is, perhaps, the information that is excessive. That injunction connected to the kidnapping is accompanied later by phrases
like, "Remember, say nothing," or "Shut your mouth." Whatever the
supposed information denotes, it stops the mouth, cuts off the voice or
detaches it.

As Louis Bernard stumbles there is a musical allusion to Siegfried's
death by a spear in the back in *Die Götterdämmerung*—not surprising
from Bernard Herrmann, who will use Wagner elsewhere, as in *Vertigo,*
and will show up on the podium in the film's concert sequence con-
ducting the "Storm Cloud Cantata," inducted into the work's numerous
folds. The only obvious parallel to Siegfried is the stab in the back. The
musical allusion begins and is broken off. What it *recalls* perhaps is that
Siegfried's murder is triggered by a return of memory, by the memory of
a "truth" outside of the fallen present time and reaching back into a heroic youth, promise and vow—a return to "identity," from forgetfulness,
that triggers his slaughter. The knife in the back, unreachable, carries a
faux reflexive structure that cannot close its circuit, or reach behind itself to its anterior. Technically, the knife could denote the anteriority of
the first version, or even the preceding frame of celluloid, or the technē
as such. Stewart asks why Bernard "picked me out," a complaint he
repeats as Scottie in *Vertigo.* The words identify a hyperbolic logic to picturing him, as if the narrative unwinding only followed that logic of be-
trayals into a world-altering scheme. The image, here, betrays. It betrays
the tourist and the reader; then it betrays itself, much as it devolves to
picturing giant musical bars before a rehearsed and page-turning choir
simulating a "natural"—or cinematic—catastrophe, *Blitz* or lightning.
The entire orchestra and choir, formally arrayed and controlled, assume
the mantle of technicity from the telephone book in Marrakesh and the

telephone bearing Hank's voice in agent *Buch*anan's office at the airport, a name that cites *book* as he sits next to a typewriter. Scotland Yard
does things by the book, as when the summoned police refuse to enter
Ambrose Chapel at Doris Day's insistence, which the American couple,
tracking the cinematic, dissolve into telephones, musical weapons,
thumbed telephone books atomizing letters and formalizing numbers.

But the cinematic was precisely involved with the "secret." On his
knees, the blackfaced Louis cites not so much Siegfried run through
by Hagan's spear as he does a cinematic minstrel icon, Al Jolson.[21] This
knowing, which is also not one, has to do with film and speech. Al
Jolson, after all, in *The Jazz Singer,* is also in blackface and on his knees
in the first "talkie," preceding the British *Blackmail.* Jo is here also a jazz
singer (given a loose definition of American jazz), enough to make the
Euro ears cringe politely at the embassy concert. There is a doubleness
to this minstrel gesture, this citation, which resonates in opposing directions. On the one hand, the blackface returns us to the McKennas at
the back of the bus, where blacks sat at the time in the American South.
Again, Hank asks right away, as if someone else knows these things, "Are
you sure I've never been to Africa before?" As Ben will not be allowed
to speak about the secret, the assumption of "speech" to mute or silent
graphematics knows that there is, in a sense, no speech at all—at least
as expression, communication, nonprosthetic voice. Stewart will pursue
the clues on his "Memorandum" through a phone book (a "voice" book)
to the taxidermists' workshop and then to the chapel, a "building," an
"it" that is not a personification, not a "he." The clue that derives from
the impasse within this "talkie" is, in a sense, that "talkies" do not exist,
that they never were passed into as such.

For Hitchcock the transition from silents to "talkies" is technical and misleading, chimeric. It never takes place. It doubles back,
marks "dialogue" as what "sounds like," as if from a position between
languages—outside of personification, an "it" not a "he," much as the
camera lens is without any corresponding eye. This is an update from
the first version, where the "secret" found in the shaving brush is linked
to a Babel of tongues heard through a door in the Swiss hotel—multiple
languages, reduced to alien signifiers in concert. In the first version the
secret was associated with the atomization of all languages into aural
signifiers when spoken at the same time, what Benjamin inversely called
reine Sprache, pure language. The voice is by its definition blocked,
muted, reduced to this memorandum and the giant ear that will lead,
cataclysmically, to the "crash of Cymbals." The ear, here, must incline,

must decline (into) its *labyrinth*.[22] What is imparted, what is whispered, is written down, translated back to script, to anterior memory—like the knife in the back, the back of the bus, the written title text that precedes and informs the opening scene ("A single crash of Cymbals and . . ."). This will bear on the motif of soil erosion and the "Issue de Secours" sign on the bus window:

Memorandum

A man a statesman is to be killed
assassinated in London soon very soon
tell them in London to try
Ambrose Chappell

Is the entire film a "memorandum," memory storage? There is, for Louis Bernard, a certain stuttering ("a man . . . a statesman"), void of diacritical marking, a doubling that recurs in the letters of "Chappell," in the father and son pair encountered under that name, which, like the *rock* heard in *Morocco,* is a thing anthropomorphized, personified. If one is moving away from the last two tropes, one is moving away from *aura* as such; one is delving into the "secret" of the cinematic condition, widely forgotten or repressed, about which one requires a memorandum about memoranda. Such glyphs lead back to the land of pictographs, of the dead and taxidermy, of memory and proleptic mnemonics. These figures gather themselves about the missed *event* of the (cinematic) shot, the assassination, the scream. One prepares by rehearsing the timing against the *recording* listened to repeatedly in the upstairs room of Ambrose Chapel: if one can get the timing precisely, like the guiding image on a cruise missile piped through CNN to hone in, pictorially, on its target—only become itself. The archive as recording, like film, is replayed in advance to coordinate, stage, and intervene in the artifice of a scripted instant, an *Augenblick,* a recording focused on the "single crash of Cymbals." And all symbols. McKenna can only ask: "Why should he pick me out to tell?" Every "me" is picked out, multiplied, like replicating viewers, like Moroccan women, like a "*tele*vision commercial." The notation stands for all inscriptions looping back into the phenomenal or temporal orders, which must forget them to occur. The "memorandum" can be and is misread, its referent an "it," not a "he." It is auratically personified even though this leads to the mummy shop. It must be *read* and sought through the *tele*phone book. The hysteria of the taxidermists' shop comes when father and son coinhabit name and time, like the title shared by the two versions, crudely stuffing and animating underworld things that bite back, consuming humans, if its threshold and nonsecret is crossed.

Thus the assassin's shot is given a different structure in the second version. In the first, the scene at the Royal Albert Hall focused on the idea of the noncoincident instant (the word "present*ly*" is used) that would, through the spatiotemporal evacuation of tropological chains (Ropa), alter history, intervene in the politico-aesthetic order, assault the very structure of temporality—all by way of the photographemic shot, if it could be utilized as such. That pretext recedes in the more "professional" version (if, again, *first* and *second* here become technical labels). In the second, the camera focuses on the *flag* underneath what is now the Prime Minister of a certain unnamed nation—or seminamed, cut off, Ao——, for what is given as an "*in*-house affair," a reflexive matter. There are "extraterritorial rights" for the embassy, which forbids access and constitutes a site of alien turf in London, Britain's *own* terrain. One could say it is an *extra* terrain that is also aterrestrial in a certain sense in which the teletechnic camera is outside all categories of human or other life, *atopos,* like mechanical "birds," exterior to the terrestrial as an anthropomorphism—like the *ear* that might fill itself out in the word ear*th,* like the *rock* of Morocco, like Drayton's allusion to "soil erosion" (himself once a "big noise in the Ministry of Food," yet also, as he tells the Moroccan hotelier, a "college professor," and then again, a Protestant minister, and so on). One will have seen this cinematized earth that is no longer an earth again and again in Hitchcock: in the "beautiful" landscape of a Riviera that the tourist viewer does not see for the treeless moonscape it is, or the horizons of a prairie stop under attack by an errant crop duster.

Where the solar has become mechanical, the earth is no longer "natural," and the natural never was as thought. One is in a field of technicities, like the cinematic, which correspond, more or less in causal connections, to a modern evisceration of life forms that *Frenzy* will imply, an archivization or mummification or what is taken into its system of consumptions, as into "television commercials." At all events, the broken-off syllable, "Ao——," suggests not only the backloop of a temporal or banded circuit, like cymbals or bicycle wheels, but a cry of pain, an "ow," what Jo says the sight of the Marrakesh hotel eases ("Well, this eases the pain." "What pain, Mummy?"); what Ben will give Jo *anesthetic* pills for in advance of imparting the knowledge of Hank's kidnapping, compelling her to fade, *to go under*. A pain, implicated in the spilled bucket of sky-blue paint that slows and covers Louis Bernard, making possible his murder.[23]

Personification may be already heard in the A. H., or apostrophic "ah!" imprinted in the *A*lbert *H*all, itself an "it" and not a "he." It invokes the logic of prosopopoeia, what is "before the eyes," literally, and a giving or precession of face, as we see on the bus with the accident of the veil, curtain drawn. Faces and facing seem marked, as when Louis Bernard falls to his knees, or as with the figure in the market whose face is totally veiled and sporting sunglasses. One cannot dissociate such pre-faces, of course, from heads, heads in general—the ostensible locus of *knowing*, whether too much or too little—while heads for the camera, which tend to talk, are routinely cut off by the frame. The work, repeating a phrase about *losing one's head* from the first version, enacts this pictoral decapitation, which is that of most dialogues on screen in any case, in the taxidermy shop. The scene that ends with a shot of a mounted lion's head depicts a sawfish against Ben's neck in a clear trope of decapitation—the interior of Albert Hall, or A. H.'s, presents the empty ringing space of a giant skull (the "ivory dome" in *The 39 Steps*, the British Museum in *Blackmail*), much as the assassin's gun emerges from the curtains like a prosthetic eye from parted hair (as in the first version), and the dislocated name of Ambrose Chappell, or at least the chapel itself, resonates with homonymic figures like *chapeau, capital, capo*.[24]

The "second" *Man Who Knew Too Much* wanders to a site from which the anchor or gravity of "death" is not even at issue, a site where earth, the promise of all mimetic representation, had ceased to be defined as a referential alibi. And yet it is here, at a border where "life" and "death" are disarticulated, at a time between "was" and "will be," which would be recalculated according to the repeated rehearsal of a recording, that a putative event, reflexively promised, would be staged or attempted, charted or deflected. One could only slip within this "pause" that is also the remake as such, and be located momentarily in a sort of prescene to the entire affair. It is within this logic that the visit to the taxidermists seems to retreat from any interpretive logic. One only ends up there by the mistaken assumption that an it is a he.

Animeme Bites Man

McKenna's visit to the workshop of Ambrose Chappell, *père* and *fils* with one name, appears not only as a bizarre interlude, an out-of-place pause within a pause for which no possible reading can account, a hyperpause within a succession of such whose generic locus is extraterritorial. It begins bathed in paranoia (in which Stewart appears, inversely, to the younger Chappell as predatory), shifts to blank doubling and misapprehension (in Stewart's confrontation), alludes to a kind of sexual blackmail, erupts into hysterical aggression, then retreats in a fussy explosion of opera buffa that has no place whatsoever in the work's barely containable facade. It discloses the deauratic as animal stuffing. Even the vaudeville disintegration of this interlude ends abruptly, with Ben, his hand caught in a tiger's mouth, being restrained and called mad. Head shots of mounted wild animals punctuate the vignette, with bizarre creatures being crudely stuffed on tables, and a giant sawfish visually made to decapitate the struggling Stewart. Back in the hotel, Jo figures out that "it's not a man, it's a place," moving from personified human name with its doubled letters, to revivified animal, to undead thing, a "building"—at which point the narration can proceed to the Royal Albert Hall. Unlike the first version's visit to the dentist George Barbor's office, which is transitional, the taxidermy scene is a visit to a *zoographic* underworld. It leads nowhere and has no place; it is an interruption, yet can only be broken off, a pocket, swirl, or momentary expenditure that pretends to stumble banally into a cinematic preproduction workshop for animemes and cinememes.[25]

What does it mean to be drawn to a *phone* book, where identity will formally drift through numbered addresses and phones, micrological units, pointed at with an index finger? Or which reduces the *phōnē* or voice to number, lists, a book?

Figure 31. Stewart "beheaded" by a serrated sawfish.

When Ben found the address of Ambrose *Chappell* in the phone book he exclaimed, "There he is, big as *light*." The phone number itself remarks these gargantuan proportions: "Chappell, Ambrose, 61 Burdett St., Camden Town . . . Gulliver 6198." This assignation of being too large for one's surroundings, exemplified at the restaurant when Stewart's limbs simply could not accommodate the setting, or too small, on the screen or marked on celluloid, repeats a knowing too much that is, to all effects, a tactical deficiency on all fronts. It registers a dislocation in which body as such cannot be made to fit into any provided frame and places the work in an excoriating Swiftian genre. It will also be associated with the gigantism or diminishing long shots that are cinema's currency, which prevent proper mimesis or identification from ever occurring, as monster specters traverse the screen. One is left momentarily with numbers, what the *phōnē* book pointedly and repeatedly dissolves proper names and letters into.

That the Scotland Yard inspector's name is *Buch*anan, referencing books, that his office provides the phone call from Mrs. Drayton and Hank, invokes this dilemma of script and telephonics. There appears a formal progression: not only passing through the record player of the chapel toward the musical score being read on the concert podium—increasingly, a series of giant bars (/ / / /)—but in the last word of Hank's disembodied voice on the phone. Hank, very subtly, can be seen as enjoying torturing his emotional mother: "Is Mommy crying? I didn't mean to make her cry." Right. He is asked where he is by his father and gives the beginning of an answer: "8," trope of infinite circulation or recurrence, of the bicycles atop the Marrakesh bus, of the two "cymbals" held up in the credits, of movement, eyes, spectacles. In the phone book, numeration allies itself to and dissolves, like letters, the *voice*: the routinely voiced-over personification of just more sound (as Hitchcock says); Michel Chion's "disembodied voice," his *acousmêtre,* here inversely the boy's (*not* the mother's) the general condition of "voice" as such. The number "61" is repeated twice, followed by "9" (three squared), followed by "8." We have triadic rupture, pyramidal or Egypticist, the mnemonic order of *The 39 Steps* (3 and 9), the intervention of a locked spatiotemporal circuit associated with the eyes in "8"—opening ejaculation of vowels, like "Ao——," like the figure of pain or invasion (D-Day), of pharmaceutical-cognitive rape like the drugging of Jo in the hotel room that tropes the audience's relation to the film. The entry in the phone book will neither be "there," nor "big as light," nor, by inference, is light anything like clear, but rather the aftereffect of marks, bars, and gaps like these nongrammatical entries (like the real estate list of numbers and names in the preceding film, *To Catch a Thief*). But the locale, Camden Town, after all, appears to open one further trace chain.

Which returns the Al Jolson citation, that of the first "talkie," to its Hitchcockian parallel in *Blackmail,* the "first" British "talkie," if technically the second, a collision of firsts and seconds. In locating the taxidermists in *Cam*den Town, Hitchcock not only reiterates the seemingly inescapable 3 *(C)* and 1 *(A)* signature again, but uses a syllable, the "C-A-M-," written down in the opening scene of *Blackmail* in the Flying Squad van, the address or direction dictated through the wireless. One might fill out the word as *cameo*—or, for that matter, variations on camera as the figure of the chamber, the box, tomb and triadic pyramid, site of mummifications, taxidermy, "Mummy." "Camden Town" is itself another listing in the phone book, in that site where the *phōnē* or voice is transcribed as the "memorandum," the exteriority of mnemonic script, which, here as elsewhere, is opened to the workings of another outside, to a near reencounter with *tychē* or chance, much as the assassin will approach the crash of the cymbals at just the precise point heard on the recording ("again, and again"), opened to disinscription or reinscription, a reconfiguration of past and prospective futures that the politico-aesthetic moment of intervention, or the (always also camera) *shot* would stage, mime, or presuppose.

Thus the visit to the Ambrose Chappells begins in a book, and as a *listing*: as a further pause and Egyptification, pre-Mosaic in that it leads, it seems, back to a province that is a dead end, of the dead and without even them, without any crossing or clue to an elsewhere, to a zoographematics of the undead in which "life" is reproduced as animation. The trace word *cameo* frames this disruption and peters out in a comic opera mode with musical accompaniment and a vaudeville skirmish (fighting with stuffed wild animals). It suggests that this signature explosively functions as the faux guarantor of the mimetic pretexts (this is Hitchcock's, this *is* "Hitchcock"), yet inverts that entirely, flashing cinema into and as a web or network of bars and marks and aural chains precedent to the indicating or finger-pointing effect referenced to sight ("There he is, big as light"). The "cameo" countersigns the invertibility of any inside, any home, any territorial containment of mark, image, program, "experience," real, mnemonics, inscription. It guarantees the undoing of any mimetic pretext for the Hitchcock camera, image, project—what may be the final "MacGuffin," the image itself. The "man who knows too much," indeed. What *man*? Too much for what? The course of the trajectory, the knowledge that Hank's removal allows to be played out if not possessed, involves a deanthropomorphism of the premises of life, history, family, event, that is, cinema. Within what might be called the *face* of the image is a citational war that would decide the fate of sight, agency, the ear, specular (global) politics.

One "sees" the devastation Hitchcock inflicts on the premise of the metaphoric, of sight or the eye, much as the interlude is premised on Ben's total misreading, mishearing, and miswriting (two doubled letters). And yet the scene is all too precise and banal. Void of women, it circumvents the row of sewing women as well as Doris Day herself (an antiblonde) as "Mummy." It displays the male line or production workshop of mummifiers (the workmen, called by the same name, like brother-sons, the father, semidotty and abdicated, the son's son, the vague homosexual blackmail alluded to in Stewart's reference to someone who "knew" Ambrose junior in Morocco, and so on). Camden Town, the site and logic of what is of the camera as chamber, as box, and the cameo effect. Stewart wanders through the taxidermists' shop, where generations appear interfaced and near collapse, where the fullest array of animal figures in Hitchcock (culled from across his productions: birds, fish, cats) is adduced in what exceeds a facile citation of the modality of the screen's skins. If in *Sabotage* fish inhabit decimating tank screens, or if in *The Birds* the avians are prehistorial invaders associated with the cut, they are here all laid out, inert, being prepared by a still earlier artifice. Accordingly, the scene is not quite the "red herring" it is advertised as, and if it tempts to a symbolic reading (Bonitzer) one forgets what happens when symbols crash before sound or marks. The animal revenants seem to turn on Stewart, mobilize, decapitate, and consume or counterconsume, rise up and indicate the domain of recurrence they are caught in to be anything but passive, controlled, or "dead" (like "Mother" in *Psycho*). The inert itself attacks, does not want to give up on catching Ben. The tiger retrieves the black cat of *To Catch a Thief*, a hypnokleptic trace, now as giant attacking man-eater—what returns fully animated, finally, in *The Birds,* a full war, the "bird war," as it is called, where the animemes are dispersed as myriad flecks, outside all anthropomorphism, where they go straight for the eyes, for the schoolchildren and their mnemonically drilling teacher, where they attack *telephone booths* and would disrupt imprinting.

Yet what has this to do with Hank, with "knowing" to excess or to erasure? What, in the interface of (dead) living and (animated) dead, brings the mnemonic system—the memorandum, the archive caught in recorded rehearsal—to an *in-house* point of political alteration? One does not return from this blind and irresponsible catabasis, where the human is suspended (become meat, more simulacrum), to some familiar or familial time. One must proceed through the passage from voice to book to numbers on to musical notation. Bars. Hank, from the perspective of "I guess so," a sort of "perhaps," engineers the allegorical parenthesis by his absence. "Picking (or picturing) up" Hank will accomplish not the rescue of the family, of America, of "life" from the jaws of foreign intrigue, from accident and pain, but the blundering derailment of a hyperbolic aesthetico-political project that Drayton guides ("big noise," "professor," "minister"). The taxidermists' shop, accordingly, suggests the workshop entered, too, to retool the props of the first version. The taxidermists' shop tropes the workshop of the Hitchcockian storybook, into which one of his players has entered through a glitch in reading and the phone book. In each case—Chappell, Chapel, the Royal Albert Hall's dome—a head and decapitation are in question. Idiotically, Ben threatens Chappell the son unless he tells what Ben has no idea about and then must extricate himself from a battle with the enraged animemes, poised to invade in later works. The nest of "mummies" in advance of any natural mother has been stirred, disturbed, cited and implied, and its return will be inevitable.

The rehearsed *event* of usurpation within the Hitchcockian workshop, instead, is projected onto and as the assassination of the Prime Minister in the Royal Albert Hall—in the head, in A. H., in the mnemonic systems we will see evoked, of the portly Hitchcock double. As Inspector Buchanan observes, it is a matter of "trying to eliminate one of their own big *shots.*" Momentarily, however, the work is caught in a void of replications absent personification (with, as is said in front of the chapel, "no sign of life"), like Lila caught in the mirrors in Mother's bedroom in *Psycho.* Jo McKenna, telephoning back to the hotel, stands before a sign for Vicary Street, while the roofs fan out in endless multiplication and empty similitude—a vicariousness in which the viewer is deferentially inscribed, relayed, dissolved exponentially. And yet, all of this happens in and as telemnemonics, in the Egypticized land of the dead that London unmistakably carries over from Marrakesh in inversely clothed forms and shapes.

"History" is endangered differently than in the earlier version: it is the difference, say, between a politico-mimetic regime that manages difference (solar poetics) and what remains when, that "first" regime ostensibly revoked, the entirety continues to run just the same, reproducing itself like rows of sewing machines, even in its afterlife. The difference between an "amateur," who takes delight in thinking the sly overturning of a solar fraud can be performatively exploited, and the "professional," who knows that one has begun, all along, in the land of the dead, and that this will repeat itself, again and again, and that it has become an "in-house" affair, a "family" matter, like the bite of an undead tiger. Allegory, which Benjamin reminds us negates the things it names or represents, turns upon its own machines and negates them. If the Hyperion-like leap and fall can be represented by a ski jump or, for that matter, the unraveling of a knitted "jumper" in the earlier version, here it is simply Moroccan palm trees, vertical yet leaning over in a perpetual arc. And yet, for all the reflexive hyperbolics that suffuse the sheer formalism of the later or second version—which, in its staged assassination plot, wants to assume the position of the first, to be prior to its own model—this autousurpation appears ironically compelled. And this, as James Stewart forever dramatizes, by a kind of justice and passion to right, an *avenging,* call it American, call it familial. As the titles suggest, the "American family" will only be "rocked" throughout this "crash of Cymbals," which is also that of the cinematic logics of the two circlets the cymbalist holds up.

Figure 32. Vicary Street: butched "Jo" in phone booth beneath Coca-Cola ad as on a screen, Hank's "television commercial"— wired vicariously to Ambrose Chapel's faux worship.

One of Jo's friends in the Parnell party gathered in the hotel room is a stage performer who is introduced as "Cindy Fontaine," but she refers to her prestage name as Elva *MacDuff*—the name, that is, of the avenging hand, not of woman born, who will bring Macbeth around, to justice, the one avenging a murdered son (even if MacDuff here, and suitably, is a pouty, quipping socialite). One may even hazard from this reference to *Macbeth* that "Hank" is already dead, as the trip to the Chappells might also suggest, like the charade by which the Prime Minister would be shot, yet only as a kind of Hitchcock doll, a portly Lilliputian in comparison to the dome of the hall, A. H., itself, not a "he" but an "it." If so, his eventual rescue from the top of the many flights of stairs in the Embassy of Ao——, a hellish heaven as timeless formal labyrinth overseen by the Draytons (and having to hear a nervous Doris Day sing, "again, and again"), is reduced to formal repetition, an attic tomb. Yet if there is a leap mobilized on behalf of *Hank*—retrieving a figure who names a suspension in advance, who is suspended in turn—it is less clear what triggers the assassination attempt.

To be sure, "Hank" will always also signify the allegorical reading of the work that, Hitchcock assumes, is encrypted, inaccessibly, in its construction: the motive and event whose traces occur in the citational networks and details no tourist reader, including the American family that (as viewers) is performing its rituals, can see let alone acknowledge without profound archival alterations. The usurping plan of assassination is launched from within the embassy's own community (taking care of "one of their own"), a reflexive move or usurpation of, on, or by Hitchcock's system on the referential predicates it must obey. Bertani's kitchen from *To Catch a Thief,* a site of "cutting, slicing," is transposed to the basement of the embassy. But to speak here of any *American* justice, the distinctly American outrage Stewart personifies when one's autonomy is compromised or suspected, is to recall what was noted of that homeless name and place. However its hypogrammatic interior assembles itself, America, like the formal consequences of any teletechnic system, is what is sheerly without interiority.

In the Moroccan desert and Marrakesh, the name *American* works a blind and defacing logic for Hitchcock, at once asserting a hyperbolic "am" that triggers the signature effects swarming the text yet applying an aprivative in the *Mar-* system. It countersigns a depersonifying drift through *A-Mer*(e) or *A-Mar* (a negation of the mark).The logics of the American, a foreigner to his or her "home," can only end up in an "extraterritorial" space, here the embassy. Unexpected as this is behind the bewildering choreography by which Doris Day's pop singing is on display in the last scenes, it is this entirely formal exploration—void of any serious identificatory, Oedipal, or subjective content, commentators aside—that puts the historical and aesthetic systems in play at risk, that draws them to the edge and only appears to bring them back from it, as McKenna fetches Hank from the upper floors, or seems to.

This might be possible to call a *pickup,* a hyperbolic mock retrieval of the third, suspended, missing figure, a speaking thing, brought back to its (mistaken) place in the "familiar." The "joke" on the "American family" does not, in any event, stop at the fond contrast of clichéd American innocence and presumption, outrage and efficacy, which Stewart represents—overplaying his cards, with dominating and destructive ignorance, vis-à-vis his wife and son—nor is this evisceration exhausted by the spectacle of Day's unwittingly vulgar singing before the effete Europeans (like the "torture" inflicted on the old European Van Meer in *Foreign Correspondent,* of making him listen to American jazz). The single *shot* should not just be heard as the prospective, noncoincident, ever-to-be-timed intervention within the rehearsed time of a prerecording, as though by the photographic blink of an eye perfectly timed to undo a certain structure of time. It is not just the atomization of the visible or the constitutive trace chains of the historial set, put in a "dialectics at a standstill," however destroying of the simulated "life" it captures or mummifies. It is not just the logic of the report that is at once an archival entry, a pretended index or representation, and the sound of an explosion—or explosion of sound. Mallarmé witnesses that every explosion occurs within and as the logics of a book.

The shot must be conceived as the atomization not just of trace chains and temporal regimes but also of the archival order and its laws, that secretly ally Morocco to television commercials' globalizing and viral import, or London, offset by the first, to a formalized city of the dead and mummymakers (as becomes clearer in *Frenzy*). The trajectory from northern Africa to southern Britain not only shifts from the colonialized black origin or solar destitution to the faux acme of a European capital emerged from the shadow of a barbaric war (Daddy, recall, "liberated Africa"), it also exchanges, contrasts, and equalizes these alternate spaces under the spectral onslaught of mass American tourism and the cinematic. Hitchcock's seamless identification of the cinematic with weapons—avenging murders, silent bombers, gunshots, saboteurs' bombs—is not simply a tool of techno-weaponry or a performative tool of atomizing resistance against a hermeneutic program and "global" imperialism of the tele-image to come. It occurs in and as a mnemonic faulting of programs, an archival assassination, an order of memoranda: the secret transcribed from Louis Bernard, fallen to his knees in blackface, pleas on behalf of—while imparting the information to frustrate—the import of the cinematic event.

Acephalic Rhythms

> HITCHCOCK: I can't help feeling that ideally, for that scene to
> have maximal effect, all of the viewers should be able to read
> a musical score . . . Wouldn't the suspense have been stronger
> if people could actually read that score?
> TRUFFAUT: Naturally, that would have been ideal. In the original
> version the cymbalist's face isn't shown, but I notice this
> omission was corrected in the remake. By the way, the musi-
> cian looks a little like you.
> HITCHCOCK: Just a coincidence!

Music partakes of a cinematic deceit. It offers itself, welling out of nineteenth-century metaphysics, as the sublimation of aesthetic drives, unobstructed by mimetic lather or overdependency on the Apollonian image—and yet, it devolves to a system of writing dependent upon bars. In the concert at the Royal Albert Hall something peculiar occurs on the podium to the score's director: first, it inducts "Bernard Herrmann," whose name is displayed on the placard outside the hall, from scoring the film to performative "real" pinned to the mummifying podium; second, it compels, at the right time, the right second, a reading of the score as that devolves to increasingly giant and simplified bars, a series of parallel lines. These are displayed in atomizing close-up as the crash of cymbals signifying the storm's cataclysmic breach of natural order and panic approaches, as the assassin's prosthetic eye and pistol draw their bead, as Doris Day . . . well, as she takes in, rises to the hysteria of her choice shriek, whether that is voluntary or not. The score attracts these cataclysms to itself, knowing too much, perhaps, say, that all of the real and aesthetic and counternatural "natural" cataclysms are re-hearsed, scored, devolved to these perhaps ordered or perhaps read giant bars all but segmented into nonexistence. Double *illegibility*: "all of the viewers should be able to read a musical score." The actual sound is almost irrelevant to the metronomics, at least for Hitchcock: it should be read. There comes a crash, not only of all symbols but as an elusive "shock" that, like the bomb in *Sabotage,* cannot quite be temporally coincident, though "time" would be actively reconfigured by it.[26] Soon we will have moved to the excessively cool and almost formal aftermath of this anticlimax—move, essentially, into and onto the "extraterritorial" space of the Embassy of Ao——, where this "in-house affair" has assembled itself. But several things precede this, particularly since not only the shot timed to the rehearsed recording, but also a variant of the entire script, scene, and preceding film is being, again, repeated—down to the anticipation, this time, of the shriek, the misfire, the suspense, again and again.

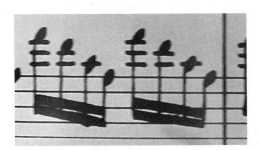

Figure 33. Full screen *reading* with "Bernard Herrmann" of bar series as musical notation, a metronome condensing to "single crash of Cymbals."

Jo's scream as the marksman shoots under the cover of the crashing cymbals—triangulated sounds or "big noise(s)"—saves the portly, bald Prime Minister, who receives a flesh wound in his arm. The shriek is ambiguous: it literally preserves Jo's imposed "silence" about what she knows lest her child be harmed or killed, yet intervenes, negatively, simulating a moral choice in any case. It is not just a political rivalry or the contest of generations (the younger ambassador usurping the older Prime Minister) but the entire natural order, as aesthetically composed and ritually replayed by the high cultured concert ritual, that is at stake: everything stretching from the streets of Marrakesh to the tuxedoed parlors of European aestheticism. It will be reported in the embassy that "the marksman panicked," in which word, *panic,* one must hear the totalization, or *panning,* the limitless irruption and citational networks of the shot. It is italicized in Arthur Benjamin's cantata as well, where the panic of *all* creatures at the approach of the lightning strike is hymned.

There is a rift between the political and the epistemo-aesthetic "event," represented as a lightning bolt in the cantata. This rupture doubles the labyrinthine collapse of frames in the scene's cameo logics, which trot out a Hitchcock double as the target, deranging any neat dismissal or ordering of the intrigue.[27] It is what a different Benjamin calls "natural history," the correlation of what is not quite even geologic time to the caesura within linguistic and representational webs. The name *Herrmann,* at once Herr Mann and her-man, gathers an underlying chain of gender disruptions.[28] Miss *Benson,* the shooter's date and aide at the concert, names another doubling of "sons," using a woman to map this male mock agon and specular usurpation; Doris Day disarticulates a female "position" in her assignation by Hank as "Mummy," registering, in turn, not only the power of her abandoned public career to eclipse the medical career of her husband (whom she routinely outthinks) but also in a face, hair, voice modulation, and bearing Hitchcock allows to mark itself as "male."[29] Yet if there is the pretext of male-male drive to usurp (as between elder and younger, father and son), giving way to a logic of *contretemps* (as between brothers or doubles, dissemblers in the eunarchy), it seems momentarily altered in the attempted assassination. The person aiming at the Prime Minister stands in for Drayton, who stands in for the ambassador, who stands in, or should, for the Prime Minister and that "single crash of Cymbals," which refuses all anthropomorphism and which the credit titles name at the outset. The cymbal crash attempts to break through the rift it cannot help reduplicating, counterrhythmically, as an "act" intervening across the totality of performatives. This usurpation turns, as an "in-house affair," against its own premises or against the Hitchcock look-alike Prime Minister.

If the assassination of Ambassador Ropa in the first version of the film attempts the hyperbolic and cognitive overleaping of a temporal regime by the cinematic project, the second version seems caught in a temporal back loop, "again, and again." In the latter version, in front of the Prime Minister there is draped a flag bearing a giant X, a graphic, emblem, mock letter, or prefigural marking that traverses Hitchcock's work. It seems, if anything, oddly gathered in the flag, emblem of emblems. It is a site that gathers at the putative point, *punctum,* or instant when a crash of cymbals or symbols is positioned before a lightning *Blitz* that is registered in the storm-gathering score. Undertaken by means of an irreducible signifier become its own signified, the crash dissolves innumerable sign chains caught in the ear. One might approach this targeted Hitchcock double above the giant X otherwise, by considering the chiasmic properties of this figure. One might, perhaps, consider the chiasmic properties of this X, placed officially before the Prime Minister. The target of assassination might be a perpetual reversal and inverting reinscription of sense positioned officially and in the state. The "in-house affair" has become a professional, or technical, rather than an amateur, or romantic, matter. What is attacked in the work is a cognitive dilemma under the imprimatur of the Prime Minister. One may be sympathetic to the assassination, as one may be to Hank's virtual escape from his stifling "American family," but not as obviously as in the first version, where the cinematic plotting was so clearly a correlative of cognitive excess and an exposure of solar poetics. Here the sun has long been hyperbolized and deleted: there was no sun, in effect, only the artificed phenomenalization associated with graphics and projection. Generations are suspended, eternal recurrence reduced to a tourist bus.

As the music proceeds, the camera decides, only somewhat ludicrously, to follow or, more precisely, read the score or its simulacrum. In a work about cognition, the X signals a chiasmic reversal of sense that precedes and frames the familiar and familial. It proceeds with the reading of a barred score. This attack is mimed, so to speak, as a trauma of mnemonic intervention and reinscription, a virtual "event"—like a natural cataclysm represented by and as semaphoric means, as at the concert—that redefines the mnemonic system as such, altering the past and possible futures. Something like this could be said to be implied on the "memorandum" that summarizes whatever the dying Louis Bernard passes to Ben McKenna. The name "McKenna" suddenly sounds like a knowledge sound bite (or fast-food variant), that is, of whatever cinema knows about its virtual, interventionist horizons. Ben scribbles down the "memorandum" so that he will not forget; the note says, by its existence in its way, "Do not forget!" like King Hamlet, but is mistranscribed and first misread.

The Embassy of Ao—— or of cinema is cut off, self-invaded and paused for taking stock, in pain, its politics self-involved, formalized, a power struggle between forces internal to its pasts and virtual futures. Nonanthropomorphic species threaten to intervene, and consume, from the position of the undead—a phantasmal (cinematic) present with its human sleepwalkers, a plenitude of predator species allied to restless memoranda, marks, shots, at bay until refined in *The Birds*. Hitchcock spoke of "scoring" a work, planting markers, etching into a script words or figurative relays. At the top of the power pyramid is the Prime Minister, a bald and fat older man who looks like a big baby, a Hitchcock double. The intrigue is here typical of the MacGuffin of all the wars within this cartoonish system, a staged usurpation within the eunarchy. It is also turned back against Hitchcock, where the hollow dome has emptied out all but the formalized elements of this recurrence: the ambassador would also, at the appointed time, simply repeat this system. Unexplained, the scheming ambassador also knows something in excess, too much to represent.

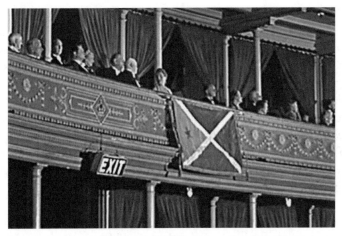

Figure 34. Target Hitchcock double above the chiasmic *X* and "Exit."

No Americans

> In England one is always running into people who are anti-American although they've never set foot in this country. And I always tell them, "There are no Americans. America is full of foreigners."
>
> **—Hitchcock to Truffaut**

As the assassin prepares to shoot, as Jo reels between impossible choices, as Ben, bursting in, runs to find the shooter, as the cymbalist reads the score, what the scene puts into play threatens to undo and reconfigure the male-male chain of power or succession. Yet it also conceals another agon, that is, between the giant *X* and the reading of a score which expands to single bars that fill up the frame; between the covering reversal of meaning atop whose flag the Prime Minister sits, which, say, registers as "sight" what is a mnemonic effect, and the most simplified gesture of alternation, of *metronomics* (/ / / /) precedent to all perceptibility, a movement of difference the cymbal crash will both exemplify and miss. If the trauma of *Spellbound* is the most explicit pursuit of this so-called bar series, here is the only scene in Hitchcock in which that bar series will be literally and figuratively read.[30] The mise-en-scène seems to hurl the self-refining bar series in midreading against the structurally installed *X,* the perpetual chiasmus of representational assignations.

A reversible war within the family, a faux family plot that will spill over into the American tourist family: between nonfather and usurping nonson, between nonbrother and nondouble, between ambassador and Prime Minister, between a totalized tropological system that has gone over to sheer formalism *(X)* and a prefigural, metronymic, performative shock (/ / / /). One could read the resentment of the ambassador, hot-blooded, as a resurgence of the first version against the second version represented by the older *Prime M*inister, the older Hitchcock: it has not been working, it is too Hollywoodesque, too establishment seeming, really. "Doris Day"? Or is it the opposite, since the ambassador is the usurper, all formal pretense, the "professional" to the installed "amateur," the younger to the older "version"?

The Prime Minister clearly prevails. He is odd, he looks and sounds odd, like a big baby, but impeccable; very old yet an infant. He meets and thanks Jo on the stairs for her intervention on his behalf—Jo, who had no inkling whatsoever of the political stakes. Yet the chiasmic *X* shifts positions again. The Prime Minister knows too much to be flustered, angered, even suspicious of his ambassador: his link to and use of natural images, the ones the camera endlessly cites and the ones the public recognizes and naively digests, will not be relinquished. The *X* marks their gathering spot, like the structural grid of the jungle gym for the birds behind the schoolhouse, or like the cinematic cataclysm musically performed as a natural storm and *Blitz* by the cantata before a formally attired and ritually placid audience.

Hitchcock took pride in the more professional management of suspense in the Royal Albert Hall sequence—the ultimate interrupted interruption. Yet the scene is less suspenseful than it mimes and meticulously anatomizes the *technē* of "suspense" in Jo's incremental agonies (no doubt, in ways, Hitchcock would want to shoot this again and again). Rather than a performative plot against the phantasmal "present" or *punctum*, the second version allies the *Prime M* with a systemic "crisscross" of referents, as it is called in *Strangers on a Train*. The "amateur" quality of the earlier version, perhaps, was the MacGuffin of a "present" to begin with, which here seems dismissed with the opening in an Egyptic signscape with an American "mummy." Jo will sing what becomes Doris Day's famous coda deferring to a future that seems in play ("Que Será, Será"), while the Prime Minister assures her of the incontrovertible facticity of the past (Jo: "It wasn't—," Prime Minister, thanking her: "But it *was*, it *was*").

The two versions of *The Man Who Knew Too Much* cannot be read successively, in either direction. Here Drayton, in which the German

Figure 35. Usurping ambassador caught in stupefied Prime Minister's frame.

Dreh resonates, ministers: "We should pause—and pause now—to do a little stocktaking." Like Hitchcock to his futurists: "It isn't a he, it's an it—a building." The title could be made yet again, never gotten right, "again, and again." Each version better, and worse, than its predecessor, its counterpart, too much and too little, never quite right. Which is why, too, if Lorre's Abbott in the first version is shot behind a door when his chime goes off, betrayed by a sound that was to conceal his revolutionary act, Drayton, led down the many stairs by McKenna in a scene citing *Notorious,* still holding Hank hostage, will be elbowed, knocked down the stairs, his gun going off in *his pocket,* reflexively, simply annulled by the system's unwieldy spatial and temporal back loops. Hank will be brought down the stairs, but recall what the camera does when mounting them, following the mother's singing voice: they seem endless, one after another ridiculous and unrealistic flight, replications of replications. When the McKennas "pick up Hank," he is in fact brought *down,* and the syllable *pic(k)* is recognized in the mimetic ideology of the picture: Hank will be returned, in person, to the hotel room where Elva and friends are sprawled *waiting,* interrupting their interruption of their guests' interruption, or seeming to. Benjamin McKenna and Jo Conway—or "Mr. and Mrs. McKenna"—McKen(not) and Co(g)nay, and so on. A double helix accelerated, "again, and again," until exfoliating doubles and simulacra become a vicarious principle of action, of alteration, of intervention, of auto-assassination: bringing the mummified dyad life-death, like the American family, to a cognitive point of reinscription—or not. All appears recuperated at the very site where, from the beginning on the bus, it was at the point of dissolution, the "American family." So there are (to begin with) two films in the latter work alone, the ambassador's, say, and the Prime Minister's: the mimetic story of an American family on a bus in Morocco going to Marrakesh who accidentally meet . . . and so on; *and the other,* a recurrently interrupted and flatly hyperbolic text of near sheer formalist torsions, falling through language, bringing life and death to a standstill for reconfiguration, putting into play the head as trope and with it all global capital, rewriting the political as the semiotic, reading the bar series, crashing the ideology of symbols by itself (cymbals, sheer sound), preceding face and the blinding (and artificed) sun, the metaphorics of "light" itself in the Western cognitive tradition, dismantling temporal and genetic succession, suspending interiorization, placing the archival itself or mnemonic notation, and so on.

The second *Man Who Knew Too Much* puts the referent of its subject "man," or "who," in hiatus. Both subjects have already, like a recording, returned as citations, emerged from Marrakesh's spectral streets, as the taxidermy shop insinuates. The spectrographic, here, denotes the allographical premise of this cinema, that is, its prospective ability to intervene in its own prerecordings. The film calls this "the" question. The assassin's camera shot and the cover of the cymbal crash are Hitchcock's most overt figures for the "act," the *event,* of this intervention—which the least of Hitchcock's frames implies. It shuttles between the *Mar-* territory of the land of the dead and the "extraterritorial" Embassy of Ao——. The topos of repetition is itself caught in a sequence of hotel mirrors in which James Stewart, in the packing scene, all but fails to appear reflected. The American family, site of the "familiar" bus ride, triggers all of the events it supposedly steps into as if accidentally: "You sure I haven't been to Africa before? It looks *familiar."* Only Hank suspects that he has been here before, he who maintains his skeptical distance from all the mimetic fictions, answering "I guess so" as if in the mode of Bartleby's "I prefer not," and who has been there before and is weary of it already, as when singing of himself as another: "When I was just a little boy, I asked my mother . . ." "Que será, será." Or not.

From a perspective ceaselessly reframing itself, the work has, as the song says, to do with the future, that is, with the future or son being cut off, its being foreclosed by international consumption (touristic, gastronomic, textile), or its being opened, otherwise, by some spectrographic intervention, a mock-revolutionary mnemonic intercession. There is reason to assume that Hank, when rescued from the highest floors of the embassy, is not the same Hank altogether who was picked up by Mrs. Drayton and kidnapped, even though he seems a bit depressed, with Mrs. Drayton worried about his fate. He has certainly been out of the picture for a long time, while everything else was and was not happening. There is no reason to assume that, being led down the endless staircase, he is any more alive than the others. The irritating jingle that, predictably, won the film's only Academy Award and became a Doris Day trademark, puts in play this opening of a suspended future, this requirement of the work to atomize its own formal project, again promising or failing as an aesthetico-political event caught in rehearsing bands. Shuttling backward and forward, as on a loom, the ambassador and Prime Minister exchange positions, chiasmically, between suggesting earlier and later "Hitchcocks." The award-winning song is conveyed by and aurally (de)materializes the disembodied voice of (a) "mother"—or *mummy,* whatever that (a)matrical atopos designates in the absence of generation or maternity. Such a massively ruined work is "allegorical," not in representing anything but in turning against and reflexively interrupting the formal system that programs its present from behind, from the back, where a dagger called "the past" is stuck.[31]

If the first *Man Who Knew Too Much* undertook to dismantle the metaphysical linkage of light to knowing, the later version—if this order or sequence can be sustained for reference purposes—opens with a ritual evacuation and repetition of touring, of solar blindness, of a vacant horizon or desert on the "dark continent" from which no further fall would seem possible. Having evacuated the Mediterranean logos with *To Catch a Thief,* the second *Man Who Knew Too Much* returns to renegotiate the oeuvre's future directions, a catabasis, departing from the desert, heading north from the land of specters. It defines intervention as occurring in the domain of *formalization.*

In some ways Hitchcock was too late. The preceding work, *To Catch a Thief,* during which no doubt the remake was being formally planned, thought about, circled, and throughout which citations from the first *Man Who Knew Too Much* arise, may in fact have done this better. In that work, the wine steward Foussard has the white-streaked hair of Peter Lorre's Abbott in the earlier film, and the travel service credit sequence seems to develop the same work's opening critique of brochure advertisements and touristic programming by preinstalled pictures—a cognitive impasse. Beneath the too obvious affiliations (same title, same general plot), the premise of the remake may itself be just a "front," then, for an entirely different project, one that, in its excess, escapes the orbit of the first's preoccupation altogether and, indeed, had to appear to be doing the opposite to elude its familial guardians and memory bands. If Pascal Bonitzer was accurate in suggesting the work most closely relates to *Psycho,* in every obvious way wholly other, one would need an altogether different map for reading. In their entirely unapparent fashion, Ben's memorandum and the "in-house affair" at the Embassy of Ao—— all but provide this map. If nothing else, one might better ken, say, why Doris Day broke down before Hitchcock and offered to leave the project, unsure what was wrong, and why the latter assured her, on the contrary, that she, as "mummy," was doing everything perfectly. If the future that "Que Será, Será" addresses were also to have been his future production, or if Hitchcock required a "pause" before proceeding, a backward glance or an opportunity to *read* or rehearse his own formal itineraries, the occasion, say, to map out yet again the formal premises of cinematic intervention, it is difficult to know whether, appearances to the contrary, that did in fact occur.

Coda: Exploding Cameos

When I've gone through the script and created the picture on
paper, for me the creative job is done and the rest is just a bore.
—Hitchcock to Truffaut

When the recent Johnny Depp film *From Hell,* adapted from the Alan
Moore graphic novel, deploys a Jack the Ripper story to speculate on the
advent of cinema and its unleashing of the techno-wars and genocides
of the approaching twentieth century, it repeatedly cites and uses *The
Lodger* as the ground zero of those histories. Some fundamental shift is
attributed to this advent (or its signature text) that hellishly alters the
historial. Moreover, the advent of this cinematic cutting in the person
of the Ripper is also politicized, as, in this rendition, it turns out he
is working on behalf of royalist conspirators (or CEOs). The Ripper's
surgically outrageous cuttings of the living double for cinema's cutting
up of the body and eye. In a countermoment coming out of the same
machine, Depp's opium-addicted inspector is tracking these killings
by himself entering cinematic trances, from which he reads future catastrophes. By again and again citing *The Lodger,* the work locates this
historial transformation in a specific film. Cinema and photographics
here herald techno-genocides of the coming century by way of the dismembering cuts and dehumanization of the sensorium. But this cinema
generates its own tracker, detective, or cinematically addicted inspector
in Depp. There are two sides to this cinema: one serves the home state's
regimes of identification, aesthetic play, mass programming, and artificed memory, for which the cinematic "cut" becomes a profound tool
for managing perception; the other is a Hitchcockian or Benjaminian
practice for which the "cut" initials alternative templates of perception
and time, definition and gender. Depp's inspector will be terminated by
a planted overdose of his drug of choice.

Autograph

One must pause to remember the dimensions: at one point, not only the name *Hitchcock,* but the corporeal outline (and perhaps, of course, the voice, the macabre cockney drawl), were among the most recognized trademarks worldwide, stimulating a series of programmed associations as if at the ringing of a dinner bell. The marketing, the planned manipulations of interviews, the cameos—the cunning trailers, of course, the television mugging appropriating the entire commercial frame (of the sponsor), down to Van Sant's hyperreal *"Psycho"*—as if literalizing the industry's inability to step "beyond" this work that will be endlessly cited, stolen from, invoked, mimed. Godard, in his *Histoire(s) du Cinema,* casts this as an event within teletechnic "globalization":

> I incorporate Hitchcock into the *Histoire(s) [du Cinema]* because I believe that at a certain epoch he had absolute control over the world. More so than Hitler, or Napoleon. No one before him was ever in such control over the public. This was the control of poetry. Hitchcock was a poet on a universal scale, unlike Rilke. He was the only *poète maudit* to encounter immense success. What is quite surprising with Hitchcock is that you don't remember the plot of *Notorious,* nor why Janet Leigh goes to the Bates Motel. You remember the pair of glasses, or the windmill—that is what millions and millions of people remember.[1]

Godard proposes a "Hitchcock" who is first master of a global marketing and mass media, allied with sheer power: "at a certain epoch he had absolute control over the world. More so than Hitler, or Napoleon." Hitchcock seemed negatively aware of this, as when Napoleon is cited by the stilled *Eroica Symphony* disk in Norman's room—a failed usurpation. Godard references, here, memory as the site of this power, as though something were being both installed and altered.[2]

Not that "Hitchcock"—one can summon a virtual chorus of these, simulating one another, supplanting doubles by their doubles' doubles— had not practiced a certain return of the simulacrum, Nietzschean in a pop cultural sense. This is repeated throughout: *Vertigo,* rumored to be written by Pierre Boileau and Thomas Narcejac as a "Hitchcock" book to be explicitly sold to the "master of suspense" (yet what exactly, here or elsewhere, is suspense?); *North by Northwest,* constructed by Ernest Lehman as the ultimate "Hitchcock" vehicle, each circling back, recurring in advance. A penultimate signature machine, it would seem, held in place by the too familiar and misleading cameos (that is: as if these as-sured presence, authenticity, auteurism rather than the opposite—a total rape of the representation fiction). These cameos, which should ensure the mimetic logic of the film (this, after all, "is" Hitchcock, right here, if you spot it), instead sign the dissolution of any mimetic, referential, or historicist logic (there being no place for "him" in the narrative). An incision, the cameo performs the demolition of the mimetic ideology of photography, a parabasis within parabases of all discursive markers, and this, not by referencing a self-consciousness but by standing in for the spectral and material mark itself. One should not take a network such as this too lightly. It spreads, is virulent. It cannot stop its excess, vicari-ously citing everything. Various body cuts (drooping lip, balding pate, girth, the sketch Hitchcock would give as his autograph) are converted into mock-hospitable familiarity. One could say that "auteur" theory as such involves a reaction against this effect, an attempt to muffle it. What becomes accessible is a cryptonymic, cryptographic, micrological field of writing and signifying agents that perform a signal resistance.[3] The cameos are not innocent. It is difficult to recognize many interpre-tive strategies outside of or beyond the auteur system that was spawned, in part, to protect against his assault, really, on the very order of the visible and "light." Indeed, it may be that auteur theory is a symptom or defense before what one could call, inverting Bellour's use, a certain *signature system*.[4] Suddenly, this system does not include cameos, but a virtual army of autocitations, repetitions, MacGuffins, logics, but also letters, numbers, syllables, phrases, body parts—the cuttings that get as if more and more micrological, more invisible, more like secret script or agents. Kittler opens his review of the teletechnological fold of con-temporary culture, in which the cinematic advent arrives together with accelerations of *war* technologies: "Media cross one another in time, which is no longer history. . . . Since its inception, cinema has been the manipulation of optic nerves and their time."[5] Yet to name such "optic nerves" is to imply or invoke molecular operations that, chemically and otherwise, produce it. If so, then what is attacked in Hitchcock's early political outings may be a regime of representation, the sensoria.

Cameology

There is, if we look again, a counterlogic to the cameo. The first cameo in *The Lodger* (behind a glass partition in the vast telecommunications sequence, the newsroom's production of print and the relay of public copy) locates the director in advance of a machine of imprinting that is referenced not to an image but to the letter, typographies. The second in the same work, above the spiked fence, striking at Ivor Novello, places him by what Rothman calls the bar series, the irreducible series of in-tervals, slashes, cuts, repetitions, markers, and so on, precedent even to letteration or, for that matter, "light."

At first (a long "at first"), the cameo's logic is thought to "present" the auteur himself. It confirms the mimetic promise of the picture and his authorial dominance. It is thought to say: if you are looking for the reproduction of the *real,* well, here it is. Here is the one figure who is *not* an actor, whom you know or have heard of, indeed, who is the director. Moreover, he is not even in the plot. But what is taken as an imprimatur or the token of a ludic or rhetorical battle for mastery with the viewer (Rothman, Leitch, Zizek) performs as an eccentric agency, warping and rewriting surfaces, folding everything outside of, before, or excluded from the fictional frame into the band or surface, without ex-terior. Hitchcock remarked about one such cameo (that of *Stage Fright*) as follows:

> There may have been a "MacGuffin" in my film appearance, but not a ham. My motives have always been more devious, or, if you prefer a more devious word, sinister. I have wormed my way into my own pictures as a spy. A director should see how the other half lives. I manage that by shifting to the front side of the camera and letting my company shoot me, so I can see what it is like to be shot by my company.[6]

What does a "spy" do who was refused a place, destroyed the tissue of transit or delineation, ruptured the pretended frame, is shot by (and, spying, shoots) his "company," contaminates all sets and citations— claims access to every conceivable trace chain without touching upon any? This is a rape of the mediatrix. A simulacrum, it destroys auteuriali-ty and authority. Highlighting the promise of mimesis, it voids the mimetic logic. This figure, in fact alien to the set's internal logic, the body ultimately fragmented into signs, parts, shards, imports the logic of the MacGuffin into the band, ruptures every representational contract, virally contaminates all floating signifiers with its allomorphic logic. This "Hitchcock" or this cameo guarantees a movement of translation without limit, the dissolution of the mimetic ideology thought to guard photography or film, and with that, every familiar regime of memory management and every statist hermeneutic is bracketed. Like the black sun figure that preinhabits light (or the "sun") in the early British films, the cameo—in which the word-name *camera* would linger—imports an allomorphic logic of the cut, the "outside," the graphematic trace as prefigural and previsible into a screen set whose inescapably prosthetic constructions have been marked, notched, pushed into the frame. Attributes of this cameo logic include:

- *It is allo-mimetic.* While pretending to *present* the already known, the *re*cognizable ("Hitchcock"), to give the real director as a confirmation of *mimesis,* the cameo dissolves the frame, folds the "outside" into the mise-en-scène, eluding any reinstallation of frame.
- *It is spectral.* The "Hitchcock" of the cameo imports an active *ghost,* a point of repetition networking a citational field where the specter "is" the existent, the horizon of events and acts.
- *It is viral.* An eviscerating logic is unleashed, as the host enters the nonsite of the set as guest, making the home site itself a guest, a gesture normatized in the television presentations.

If the cameo marks the disarticulation of the mimetic protocol by the very logic that should uphold its program, by Hitchcock "himself," it performs several other incisions. For one, it disincorporates and dismembers Hitchcock's body, giving it the value of a trace: the voluminous outline, the pouty lips, the balding brow to be matched with an unmistakable voice, which, together with this form, will always also be disembodied and too (in)corporate at once. An entire array of marketing expectations and cinematic *doxa* emerge as the manipulable debris of these incisions—a certain "Hitchcock" commodity awaited or imitated or self-mutilated, monikers of various coin (master of suspense, of the macabre, and so on). All useful, all directing or warding off traffic, stepped into or out of, enforced in the manipulation of hopeless interviewers (Truffaut), an army of simulacra indebted to the burgeoning telecommunications networks as so many echoes of a preoriginary rape. One may speak of being cameoed.

But there is another dimension to this itinerary, which the cameo is the most obvious symptom of or decoy for, a countersignatorial army that the icon of the "Hitchcock film," or "Hitchcock actor," or "Hitchcock suspense" tends to draw the eye from (and, predictably, fan out and betray, conceal and preserve). "Hitchcock" would be produced and preinhabited by markers, insignia, letters, code numbers or phrases, re-marks, everything and anything but the phantom auteur. Hitchcock's is perhaps the strangest and most global exploitation of a signature system in a dawning era of techno-telecommunications and marketing networks. Hence, if these signature effects are broadly illegible or invisible to begin with (require, at all events, citation), then there would be a "politics" to the work of the signature system. Behind the cumbersome profile, behind the fat or body-in-excess, this "Hitchcock" *breaks* an entire politico-aesthetic regime of mimesis and reference.[7] Not only does this cinema persist in a state almost of war, as the war machine whose secret formula Mr. Memory was to smuggle out of England, but this condition will be written into all of the narratives variably. All of those elegant or detached "villains" bent upon sabotage, assassination—in general, some intervention in the definition of history—resonate with the task of Hitchcock's cinema: to alter the mnemotechnic program out of which the state and its talking heads (the phantasm of the "Cartesian" subject) are generated, together with the latter's presuppositions about gender, light, agency, time, the "human," politics, and so on. In the great critical traditions surrounding "Hitchcock," the question of what a signature system does was long occluded, together with any extended disquisition on "language" through issues such as marks, sound, relays, language lessons, codes, letters, musical notation, reading, cryptic writing, translation, mnemotechnics, telegraphy, telepathy, and so on. What I am tempted to call a spectrographics or allographics would depart from such inflections and necessitate a re-marking of Hitchcock. This blind spot may be constitutive of what connects film theory more generally to a logic of light, of visibility, of mimesis, of reference, and so on, ostensibly still "Platonic." Yet it is this prospect and tradition that, from the earliest films on, Hitchcock can be seen as eviscerating (assassins using a false temple of sun worshippers as a front and trope for a movie house). Before the eye, imprint; before image, shadow, mnemotechnic, iteration—all of which the mnemonic effects experienced as *the eye* forgets as it spectates, identifies (with), speculates on the capital before it, the heads or "pictures of people talking."[8]

Kaleidoscope

Benjamin's term for the hermeneutic programming of the senses was the sensorium. He implied that any alteration of such installed regimes, which was concerned with aesthetics at the site of perception *(aisthanumai),* involved a reflexive rupture, a caesura, at the site of mnemonic inscription, whereupon alternative inscriptions could be deployed. That would involve alternative definitions of time, the political, representation, mnemonic management, experience, gender, perception. It is with this in mind that *Sabotage* opens with a dictionary definition of sabotage. Every time Hitchcock evokes the *double chase* as a device (the "hero" chasing those who, in some variant, are chasing him, in an inverted and self-engorged structure), he begins by short-circuiting the hermeneutic model that the chase since Plato has represented; every time he invokes the cameo, the mimetic pretext of film and photography are suspended; every time a signature system fans out, linking scene to scene—that is, in every scene, every film—a precession of all orders of recognition is asserted. It turns out that what the cameo signs or signs on to traverses a network of signifying agents, graphematic figures and film representations at once.[9] Several prospects follow:

1. That there is a yet untracked interrogation of language in Hitchcock in figures of writing, telegraphy, cryptography, translation, sound, blocked communication, language lessons, and so on, which is tied to other marking systems (cameos, recurring figures, phrases, letters), which displace the ocularcentric and mimetic regimes: the very concepts of agency, the visible, memory, reading, "man," face, and the political undergo a translation.[10]
2. That this *epistemo-political intervention* represented in and by the plots involves archival wars.
3. That when cinema is marked as transport or travel, the viewer is routinely inscribed as touristic—essentially blinded.
4. That any *spectrographics* may be allied to a figure sometimes called "Mother"—an archival site of inscriptions, premise of celluloid and mnemonics.

One may trace the premise of a spectrographic practice to a permutation of the term *allegory* as that is performatively inverted by Benjamin. In Benjamin, allegory is linked to translation, is linked to cinema, and each, in turn, will receive a penultimate gloss by what he calls "materialistic historiography." One can in Hitchcock's case activate seamlessly this link between a transformative *allegory* and *cinema,* since the prospect of historial intervention is itself a recurrent "MacGuffin." In this, Benjamin accessed a virtual project that could alter its *own* mnemonic program, intervening in the management of the past and the production of futures by reinscribing programs as such. If these works turn formally against their own premises—like a gunshot to the eye, in the case of Dr. Murchison in *Spellbound*—this is monumentalized in the plottings of his "villains": how to overthrow, usurp, deface, assassinate, a doomed model of history and hermeneutics—solar, mimetic, Enlightenment-derived.

What happens if the ocularcentric state is sabotaged, its cognitive programming autoruptured as a regime of memory management (mass culture industry)? What occurs to cognition in the absence of a meta-phorics of "light"? What, finally, is and has been lodging in the "house" of historial programs that enforces or, here, assaults this blind? A memory of the telemnemonic, the telegraphic, preinhabits Hitchcock's mise-en-scène, like the waltzing feet dropped into Santa Rosa's filmic enclave on Uncle Charlie's behalf.[11] This compels the detour to a site in Hitchcock that had been routinely occluded: an explicit recurrence to marking systems, cryptonymy, letters, "reading," mnemonic traces, sound, translation itself, telepathy and telegraphy, postal relays, and the ways these problems take shape within an order laced by espionage.

An Egyptian focus in Hitchcock's early work is apparent in mum-mies and pyramids, hieroglyphics and solar worship. Yet these allusions are not marked as an appeal to a hieroglyphic origin to the image, how-ever interesting that might seem. The hieroglyphic is something which this cinematics does not harken back to but rather structurally precedes. Hitchcock will apparently find that even when the aural and the visual are understood to interweave, what threads the images or figures is not a representational index but something that has no *foreign correspon-dence,* something often black and mobile, something allied at different moments, to sheer sound, black dogs and cats, various traces. It is on the level of inscription that the experience of phenomenality, paralleling the spooled and projected screen image, is produced or altered or inter-vened in. To a certain degree, then, a critical genealogy of this site and reception ("Hitchcock") tells the tale of a relapse without genealogy, of positions more or less programmed in their "auteurial" unfolding by an oeuvre that cancels each move in advance, disbanding its recupera-tions with the faux specter of the cameo. And it tells also of a relapse triggered before the sheer "shock," if one likes, of the *de*auratic—what is without personification, without anthropomorphism, without "light" (as a natural trope), without the premise of a seeing "eye."

A spectrographics prowls at the virtual interface of epistemology and event, trope and inscription, translation and mnemonics, an imaginary era of the book, on the one hand, and one of the image *(Bild),* video, the electronic archive, and so forth, on the other. For if the cinematic is distinguished, always, by accounting in advance for its own repeti-tion, it also divides, recedes before itself, re-marks and precedes its own apparition. As when it leaves a signature that can be barely traced at all, except perhaps by and as what Rothman called Hitchcock's most resolute "signature": the parallel bar signature, the series of slashes or alternating lines out of which something like the (im)possibility of sight or perception seems at once parsed and generated. Hitchcock could be observed to have experienced the cinematic—that is, "experience"—as a weapon of mass destruction at the simulant site of cognitive programs. When he uses the term *pure cinema,* it has little to do with the purely "visual." The pure movement in question invariably involves citational networks and temporal folds, mnemonic explosions and cuts, the leaps and telepathic chains that accompany the cinematic rush or hiatus. This cinemallographics precedes figuration, predates hieroglyphics, traverses aural and visual chains, coalesces in and erases memory.

Cinema knows that it precedes phenomenalization: at the core of the visual, a black sun; at the core of the aural, a trace mute and deafening. Taking itself as a futuristic weapon (stealth warplane), as if attacking without warning or designated place, it cannot stop accelerating its chains of citational relays, every shot citing every other, and each the entirety of the visible order and its artifice. This is why one can no longer speak of irony here, as Jameson indirectly observes. The "frame" multiplies autocitationally while staying in place, a nonplace. Instantly, it is in a political domain, near its center, where the programs of memory and sensation, identification and consumption are installed or serviced. Machines everywhere, as the glass-boothed editor of a media empire might assume. It is when this operation cites, turns against itself, the "cinematic," that it requires a new body to enphantomize, a different set of definitions.

Notes

Preface

1. What I ⸻ ⸻ ⸻ "cinema" in the accelerated
histories of w ⸻ ⸻ g, today, the entire advance
of electronic ⸻ ⸻ nory, techno-weapons, and
global capital ⸻ ⸻ lecommunicative machines,
figures, and v ⸻ ⸻ io, screens, circular fans and
millstone wh ⸻ ⸻ nd bombs—prostheses like
spectacles, bi ⸻ ⸻ syllables, punning citations.
These have ei ⸻ ⸻ ally occluded by the auratic
culture of fili

2. Sometimes in Hitchcock this fragmentation "bomb" is such that certain
letters are as if hurtled into works decades ahead—as the stuttering and alliterative *ps* of *The 39 Steps* (Portland Place, pips in poultry, pipes, Palladium,
Pamela) materialize underfoot in *Torn Curtain* as the Resistance's cinematic
code term of recognition, the Greek π. Other letters, like the gamma applied
in Mr. Memory's secret formula for silent aerial or cinematic bombing ("R
to the power of *gamma*," he recites), seem to disappear into the sea change of
glyphs. The preinhabitation by or lodging of alien graphematics and letteral
inscriptions in advance of the "visual" does not widen or reverse the institutional rupture as if between the era of the Book, or literary studies, and that of
the Image, or media studies. Rather it presupposes networks that precede each
variant of teletechnic media. In each case, there is a shared effacement: the era
of writing relapses into the archival premises of the Book; the era of teleimaging
relapses into the mime of the "picture."

3. The too close reader of Hitchcock, I suggested, finds herself in Iris's dilemma. She knows "too much"—something about inscriptions that a certain
Dr. *Hartz* (the letteral plant of *A* and *H* looms) knows too, perhaps a given
within a phantom nation that seems to elicit figures from Balkan monster
flicks. Dr. Hartz mimes Bela Lugosi, the innkeeper is named "Boris" (as in
Karloff), and Miss Froy turns up bandaged head to toe like a mummy. Cinema, in this riff, resides in the home of the reanimated, the undead.

4. Curent research in animal perception has come to endorse a top-down model dependent on memory, and inscriptions phenomenalizing themselves over the presumed bottom-up model of sense impressions passively registered have been, oddly, said to "turn vision science on its head." A recent report (Tanguy Chouard, "Brains Fake It: Seeing What You Expect to See Might Not Be What It Seems," *Bangkok Post,* November 4, 2003) suggests a model of pre-inscription: "People's tendency to see what they expect to see may be caused by their brain constantly generating virtual sensations. So suggests a new study of sleeping cats. When animals' eyes were closed, researchers recorded spontaneous patterns of neuronal activity similar to those evoked by real scenes. Strikingly, this happened in the primary visual cortex—a region thought to record visual stimuli passively. Like an untuned television screen flashing up occasional pictures, the resting cortex spontaneously produces clear maps of the outside world. It is as if the eyes were actually looking at objects. This is not dreaming. Because it happens so low in the normal information processing chain, it is almost as if the mental images had sprung right in front of the eyes. . . . It may turn vision science on its head, [Dario] Ringach [of the University of California at Los Angeles] says. It challenges 'the traditional view of the cortex as a pure stimulus-encoder machine.' Normally, when the eyes detect a tiny speck—a fly on the wall, say—a patch a few millimetres wide on the surface of the brain becomes excited. The activity of hundreds of thousands of nerve cells therein further refines what the speck looks like—dark, green, furry and vertical, for instance. Some nerve cells get extremely excited when a speck is vertical; others react more to horizontal or diagonal objects. . . . Neuroscientists call such cortical footprints 'orientation maps'. Until now the brain was thought not to produce these maps when the eyes are closed. Ongoing activity in the cortext was assumed to be random, like static on television. Intriguingly, the brain seems to scroll through its internal images methodically. It scans related orientation maps, one after the other. . . . It also shows strong biases. For example, the visual cortex dwells on maps that correspond to vertical or horizontal objects. . . . The findings strongly support theories of a 'topdown' mechanism of perception, says Ringach. The prevailing wisdom favours a 'bottom-up' concept—in which information flows only from the eyes to higher processing centres in the brain."

5. It is more than peculiar that the recurrence in almost all of Hitchcock's films of some variant of a name beginning *Mar-* has received no critical attention—where the work implants in some name or figure (central or minor), reference to a *marking* system that acknowledged the entire order of the visual in cinema to be immersed in a marking or marring event.

6. William Rothman, *Hitchcock: The Murderous Gaze* (Cambridge, MA: Harvard University Press, 1982), 33.

Introduction

1. Fredric Jameson, "Spatial Systems in *North by Northwest*," in *Everything You Always Wanted to Know about Lacan . . . But Were Afraid to Ask*

Hitchcock, ed. Slavoj Zizek (New York: Verso, 1992), 51; hereafter cited as *Everything.*

2. Thomas Elsaesser, "'Where Were You When . . . ?'; or, 'I Phone, Therefore I Am,'" in *PMLA* 118 (2003): 120.

3. Philip Rosen, *Change Mummified: Cinema, Historicity, Theory* (Minneapolis: University of Minnesota Press, 2001).

4. Aura implies not a narrative myth of originary presence but simply personification or anthropomorphism. What we call "film studies" has tended to restore mimeticism, ocularcentrism, the aesthetic ideology of the visual, light, the gaze, identification, historicism, and so on—for which the auteurial program has been something of a cover. In "The Work of Art in the Age of Mechanical Reproduction," Benjamin speaks not of film's power but "of the thoroughgoing permeation of reality with mechanical equipment." See *Illuminations,* trans. Harry Zohn (New York: Harcourt, Brace & World, 1968), 234. Moreover, for "the entire *spectrum* of optical, and now also acoustical, perception the film has brought about a similar deepening of apperception" (235).

5. Thomas M. Leitch, *Find the Director and Other Hitchcock Games* (Athens: University of Georgia Press, 1991); Tania Modleski, *The Women Who Knew Too Much* (New York: Methuen, 1988); *Film Sound: Theory and Practice,* ed. Elisabeth Weis and John Belton (New York: Columbia University Press, 1985).

6. In "I Wish I Didn't Have to Shoot the Picture: An Interview with Alfred Hitchcock," Hitchcock is cited typically: "When I've gone through the script and created the picture on paper, for me the creative job is done and the rest is just a bore." See Albert La Valley (ed.), *Focus on Hitchcock* (Englewood Cliffs, NJ: Prentice-Hall, 1972), 25.

7. See Sandy Flitterman-Lewis, *To Desire Differently: Feminisms and the French Cinema* (Urbana: University of Illinois Press, 1990), 15.

8. This view, derived from auteurist coding, is, given its long genealogy, deferred to the interventions of Bellour by Silverman: "It is therefore not surprising that the theory of authorship should have received fresh impetus in the late seventies through a theorist working closely with that director's films—Raymond Bellour." See *The Acoustic Mirror: The Female Voice in Psychoanalysis and Cinema* (Bloomington: Indiana University Press, 1988), 202. And again: "Bellour asks of Hitchcock's work the by now familiar question: 'Who is speaking (or, to be more precise, looking)?' However, he answers the question rather differently than the theoreticians who posed it before him, showing himself quite prepared to entertain the possibility that Hitchcock 'himself' might be said to speak *Marnie* or *The Birds.*"

9. Laura Mulvey, "Visual Pleasure and Narrative Cinema," *Screen* 16 (1975): 6–18.

10. Joan Copjec, *Read My Desire: Lacan against the Historicists* (Cambridge, MA: MIT Press, 1994); Anne Friedberg, *Window Shopping: Cinema and the Postmodern* (Berkeley and Los Angeles: University of California Press, 1993).

11. Marie-Claire Ropars, *Le texte divisé: Essai sur l'écriture filmique* (Paris: Presses Universitaires de France, 1981).

12. The hieroglyph points to a multiplaned aural-visual shuttle, as D. N. Rodowick summarizes: "The interest in the hieroglyph as a model for cinematographic signification would include its mixing of phonic, graphic, and figural matters of expression as well as its fundamental polyvalency. In the hieroglyph, a phonetic element can symbolize an object, transcribe an element combinable with other phonemes, or through juxtaposition of connected figures, formulate an entirely new concept." D. N. Rodowick, "The Figure and the Text," *Diacritics* 15, no. 1 (Spring 1985): 41.

13. Tom Conley, *Film Hieroglyphics: Ruptures in Classical Cinema* (Minneapolis: University of Minnesota Press, 1991), x. In a reshuffling of coordinates, Laura Oswald calls for a cinema-graphia "to describe both the textual deployment of film writing and the philosophical shift that it implies . . . a kind of writing freed from the tyranny of the image for its own sake." See "Cinema-graphia," in *Deconstruction and the Visual Arts: Art, Media, Architecture,* ed. Peter Brunnette and David Wills (Cambridge: Cambridge University Press, 1994), 250. Oswald sees her turn as a "more radical move" than that of "screen/play," because "it questions the very possibility of locating the site of the subject's construction in film space at all" (260). "Cinema-graphia," thus projected, "shatters the mirror in which the subject is held as a unity by defining the image as a trace for another image, a moment in the relentless movement of semiosis across the frame" (261).

14. Here would be one site to remark, again, the role of Zizek's neo-Lacanian "Hitchcock" with its hopes to move "beyond the wall of language"—with a resulting relapse into metaphor, auteurism, the displaced "gaze" (of the "thing"), an auteurism that upholds still the ocularcentric regime, however inverted. The theological nature of Zizek's "Cartesian" auteurism in addressing Hitchcock, which ends by dropping away all use of sound or dialogue as ocularcentric consequence, is criticized on other fronts by Claudia Breger, in "The Leader's Two Bodies: Slavoj Zizek's Postmodern Political Theology," *Diacritics* 31, no. 1 (Spring 2001): 91–104. Aside from inflecting his work with a totalitarian ethos reflecting institutional discursive origins, its theology involves a "holy Lacan": "the antidemocratic moment of Zizek's theory is created by the way in which Zizek reads Lacanian theory as an exegesis of a . . . totalitarian world" (74). For a further critique of Zizek's mapping of Hitchcock, see Tom Cohen, "Beyond the 'Gaze': Hitchcock, Zizek, and the Ideological Sublime," in *Ideology and Inscription: "Cultural Studies" after Benjamin, de Man, and Bakhtin* (Cambridge: Cambridge University Press 1998), 143–68.

15. Fredric Jameson, *Signatures of the Visible* (New York: Routledge, 1992), 210.

16. Peter Conrad, in *The Hitchcock Murders* (New York: Faber and Faber, 2000), wants to return to a purer auteurism from a glut of critical sophisti-

cations, yet instead is drawn into reading a web of repetitions and cross-cut patterns.

17. Christopher D. Morris, *The Hanging Figure: On Suspense and the Films of Alfred Hitchcock* (Westport, CT: Praeger, 2002), 193. This remarkably rich monograph opens the logics of figuration to Hitchcock criticism, which the latter has only gradually been prepared to absorb, largely because it precedes literary with visual divisions that remain politicized. As a mediazation of reading, however, it is a significant intervention, whether or not remaining itself spellbound by the central topos of "suspense" or "suspension." The entire book may be said to territorialize what Benjamin threw off as a "dialectics at a standstill" inherent to the image's citational field.

18. Cinema is only the most dubiously overt coalescence of every virtual manner of citationality, as is implied from the instant there is a camera shot—sound, image, number, letter, shape, enframe, remark. Allegory for Benjamin is said to *negate* what it *re*presents, and it turns back upon—represents and negates—its own archival inscriptions: which brings it, potentially, to the very rim of the archival grid, as when, speaking of translation, he posits the necessity of turning "the symbolizing" into the "symbolized," that is, raising the steps, traces, "material" vehicles—in short, media—to the desemanticized position of the designated agent. It would be here that inscriptions stand to be altered, temporal loops engaged or destroyed.

19. Benjamin describes the destroying implications of allegorical siting in the *Trauerspiel*: "(Allegory) means precisely the *non-existence* of what it (re)presents *[Und zwar bedeutet es genau das Nichtsein dessen, was es vorstellt]*." See Walter Benjamin, *The Origin of German Tragic Drama*, trans. John Osborne (London: New Left Books, 1977), 233; and *Ursprung des deutschen Trauerspiels* (Frankfurt am Main: Suhrkamp, 1963), 265. *Allegory* in Benjamin's sense is actantial. It is marked as a negating power at the *ante*site of (dis)inscription: a mnemotechnic.

20. Jameson runs up against "the paradoxes of the so-called neutral term (neither public nor closed)," "so that Hithcock's ingenuity lies in giving representation to what is somehow, by definition, *beyond* it" (*Everything*, 69). Cinema as the beyond of everything it adduces, a hyperbolization of tele-archival systems, is gathered and negated at once.

21. After a promising start investigating teletype machines in Hitchcock, Peter J. Hutchings relapses to a precritical *donnée*: "The point is that Hitchcock's understanding of modernity is that it is primarily experienced through vision—a vision that doesn't leave our other senses untouched—and that cinema is the art of telling stories through moving pictures." Hutchings, "Modernity: A Film by Alfred Hitchcock," *Senses of Cinema: An Online Film Journal Devoted to the Serious and Eclectic Discussion of Cinema* (May 2000), http://www.sensesofcinema.com. Hutchings adds: "Hitchcock's thinking through images exemplifies a Benjaminian perception (which treats everything, even words, as if they were images)."

22. After *Spellbound* discloses a fratricide as the purported referent of the bar pattern that pushes Gregory Peck into psychotic, teeth-grinding, razor-toting stares, and this to *undo* his identity-voided amnesia, the film proceeds to Murchison's autocinematic *suicide*—the giant spooled gun and hand, transparently mounted, turns into and shoots the camera or eye much as Dalí's dream sequence cuts an eye with scissors (even to permit an impossible flash of red, the first color exploding on the black-and-white screen of Hitchcock, like blood, but also tying the office-clinging Murchison as head of Green Manors to the dissolving regime of black-and-white cinema). The apparatus suicides, survives, migrates into a new machinal order or set.

23. Jacques Derrida, *Specters of Marx,* trans. Peggy Kamuf (New York: Routledge, 1993), 135.

24. Thus one critic writing under the aegis of "traveling concepts," after declaring Bellour and Metz to be dead-end examples of the mixing of text and image, returns again to the "hieroglyphic" model and the sponge-like ability of the always mute cinematic image to absorb all manner of semaphoric effect, letteral inscription, phonemic traversal. See Astrid Widding, "From Grammar to Graphics: The Concept of Text in Cinema Studies," in *Travelling Concepts I: Text, Subjectivity, Hybridity,* ed. Joyce Goggin and Sonja Neef (Amsterdam: ASCA Press, 2000). Mieke Bal's "Introduction" elaborates: "Many fear that speaking of the image as text turns the image into a piece of language. But shunning the linguistic analogy (as in many ways we should) in turn entails resistance—to meaning, to analysis, to close and detailed engagement with the object. . . . In its travels, *(text)* has become dirty; it implies too much, resists too much" (15).

25. Friedrich A. Kittler, in *Gramophone, Film, Typewriter,* trans. G. Winthrop-Young and M. Wutz (Stanford, CA: Stanford University Press, 1999), broods over these histories: "Before the end, something is coming to an end. The general digitalization of channels and information erases the differences among individual media. Sound and image, voice and text are reduced to surface effects, known to consumers as interface. Sense and the senses turn into eyewash. Their media-produced glamor will survive for an interim as a by-product of strategic programs. Inside the computers themselves everything becomes number: quantity without image, sound, or voice. And once optical fiber networks turn formerly distinct data flows into a standardized series of digitalized numbers, everything goes. Modulation, transformation, synchronization; delay, storage, transposition; scrambling, scannning, mapping—a total media link on a digital base will erase the very concept of medium" (1–2).

26. Eduardo Cadava, in *"Lapsus Imaginis:* The Image in Ruins," in *October* 96 (Spring 2001): 39–40, my emphasis. Cadava observes: "the image is always at the same time an image of ruin, an image about the ruin of the image, about the ruin of the image's capacity to show, to represent, to address and evoke the persons, events, things, truths, histories, lives and deaths to which it would refer. This is why, we might say, the entire logic of the world can be

read here, and it can be read as the logic of the image. Like the world, the image allows itself to be experienced only as what withdraws from experience. Its experience—and if it were different it would not be experience at all—is an experience of the impossibility of experience" (35).

27. On the interdependencies of war and photography, Cadava notes: "War not only names the central experience of modernity; it also plays an essential role in our understanding of technological reproduction in general and of photography in particular" (47). Again: "No *Blitz* without photography—and in part because both are a matter of speed. Like the rapidity of the blitz, the technology of the camera also resides in its speed. Like the instantaneity of a lightning flash, the camera, in the split-second temporality of the shutter's blink, seizes an image, an image that Benjamin likens to the activity of lightning. 'The dialectical image,' he tells us, 'flashes *(aufblitzendes)'*" (49). Cadava identifies one site of this war as the archive itself: "There could be no war, no destruction, without the archive: the archive ensures that violence will persist. This fact is all the more legible today when the militarization of technology corresponds to the textualization of its weaponry" (58). Kittler, in *Gramophone*, remarks this literally: "The history of the movie camera thus coincides with the history of automatic weapons. The transport of pictures only repeats the transport of bullets" (124).

28. For an exploration of the nonrelation between the image as information and the rhetoric of action, see Thomas Keenan, "Publicity and Indifference (Sarajevo on Television)," in *PMLA* 117 (2002): 111–15. Keenan points to this suspension both as a structure and as a political strategy of "Enlightenment" thought, implicitly mocking that the latter august program finds itself sustained, inversely, by the TV screen: "what can only be thought of as a failure in those terms is, in another sense, the success of a political strategy, and if we continue to think that images by virtue of their cognitive contents or their proximity to reality have the power to compel action, we miss the opening of the new fields of action that they allow" (113). On the ability of the photograph to convey the import of war, see also Susan Sontag, "Looking at War: Photography and Violence," the *New Yorker,* December 9, 2002, 82–98.

29. See McKenzie Wark, "Escape from the Duel Empire," in *Critical Secret No. 10,* http://www.criticalsecret.com/n10/temp.htm. This *Blitz* and thunderclap Hitchcock, in the second *Man Who Knew Too Much,* still deploys as such, but already fed into a prerecorded and rehearsed musical score, still pop "classical" in the Royal Albert Hall, which will have to be read, nonetheless, as so many bars on a page. In that work, however, it will display the formal requirement not just to mark a cinematic "excess" but to repeat, time, a recorded score to a precise instant, like an aerial bomb tracking its terrain, comparing and correcting against its programming, to strike the precise site or at the precise instant. The "time" that would be recast with an asymbolic phonetic crash (cymbals), involves one already caught in its own storage loop.

1. The Avenging Fog of Media

1. Peter J. Hutchings, in "Modernity," observes of geometrics, in Hitchcock, a multirelational, actantial space: "This geometry involves and addresses the audience, plays its part in the generation of suspense, *works as a narrative element on its own,* and is one of the most obvious aspects of Hitchcock's cinematic modernism" (my emphasis).

2. Morris, *Hanging Figure,* 216.

3. In *Saboteur,* there is the following odd reference to "golden curls," featured in *The Lodger,* albeit attached to boys and uttered by a fifth-column fascist named "Freeman." Freeman: "When I was a child, I had long golden curls. People used to stop on the street to admire me." Barry Kane: "Things are different nowadays. If you give a kid a haircut, it might save him a lot of grief."

4. If an endless pairing of *A* and *C* attached to proper names invokes this logic (or 13 trace), then as a 3 or third letter, for instance, *C* marks the first visible plane that emerges with the triangle itself. It cites a nonanthropomorphic logic of the *ca*mera, outside any possible pair: it abrupts, suspends hyperbolically, both gifting and voiding the position of the 1. A chain seems unable to escape the serial relays that generate it: triads, cinematics, nulls and ciphers, tele-graphics, animemes, citationality without reserve or return to any ground (auteur, character, "eye," subject).

5. This is apparent from the first, in the interface of real and performative: the "mannequin" Daisy is, in the credits or "life," presented as *June, a mannequin.* With *The Birds* Hitchcock literally appropriates a model into the act(ing) of the text, Tippi Hedren, recurring to the "half-cast(e)" premise begun in *The Lodger.* That Hitchcock experiences Hedren's stark blondness as a violent white is inversely echoed in the name Melanie, which connotes blackness.

6. The first major interlocutor opening *The Lodger* is the female bartender, or barmaid, female keeper of the "bar" (a trope reused about *Babs* in the Globe bar in *Frenzy*).

7. In a sketch presented in the Truffaut book that attends a discussion of the image, Hitchcock positions heads in the *Evening Standard* truck's round windows to present the image of a face with eyes as it pulls away.

8. For an exploration of the "materiality" of sound in one of Hitchcock's source oeuvres, see Tom Cohen, "Poe's *Foot D'Or*: Ruinous Rhyme and Nietzschean Recurrence," in *Anti-Mimesis from Plato to Hitchcock* (Cambridge: Cambridge University Press, 1994), 105–27. George Toles invokes Poe as a template in "'If Thine Eye Offend Thee . . . ': *Psycho* and the Art of Infection," in *Alfred Hitchcock: Centenary Essays,* ed. Richard Allen and S. Ishii-Gonzalez (London: British Film Institute, 1999), 159–78, hereafter *HCE,* where he uses Poe, crucial for Hitchcock, in an interrogation of seeing and sight, focusing on Poe's "Berenice." Pushing the eye as figure to expose its artifice, the predicates of ocularcentrism get rather elaborated than suspended by its own strategies of self-preservation: "With the sort of hideously perverse logic that we encounter

in Poe's most distressing tales, the eye must turn into the thing it dreads in order to be spared the sight of it" (160). The presence of Poe, in Hitchcock, can be turned an extra notch, once we gather that the metaphor of the "eye" does not guarantee a figure of seeing. It is "The Tell-Tale Heart," rather, that recalls the heart palpitations of *Young and Innocent's* blackfaced "drummer man's" sphincter-like eye twitching, that might draw attention, where the narrator is compelled to try to destroy a seemingly autonomous eagle eye attached to a man—only to find that the beating from beneath the floor compels him to externalize his crime and failed effort. Any trope of the eye here is as if detached to begin with, as if popped out of its frame or socket, become birdlike or animalized ("Eagle Eye"), yet also allied to Rothman's "bar series," here as aural drumbeat and rhythm, a parsing of space and time that subsists beyond any literal and personified "eye." What the narrator would entomb is the metaphorics of the eye, its power as a detached or prosthetic figure, an effect of the narrative or tell-tale syncopation for which it served as imaginary gaze and front. See Dana Brand, "Rear-View Mirror: Hitchcock, Poe, and the Flaneur in America," in *Hitchcock's America,* ed. Jonathan Freedman and Richard Millington (New York: Oxford University Press, 1999), 123–34.

9. François Truffaut, *Hitchcock* (New York: Simon and Schuster, 1967; rev. ed. 1984), 133 (my emphasis).

10. Lee Edelman, in *"Rear Window's* Glasshole," displaces the topos of face by turning, simultaneously, to what would be its obverse: "Suppose, however, one came at the question of vision from what a binary system construes as the 'other' side; suppose the redoubtable cut of castration that seems to star in each high-concept remake of cinematic theory—while pocketing, like its own wily agent, a cut of the profits for itself—were cut from the picture for a moment, became the face on the cutting room floor, so that theory could do an about-face in order to focus instead on what cannot be faced: the agency of a fundamental disturbance, a fundamental disorientation of vision, that must seem to vanish, to be foreclosed, for the visual field to open." See *Out-Takes: Essays on Queer Theory and Film,* ed. Ellis Hanson (Durham, NC: Duke University Press, 1999), 72.

11. This, as the formula of the double chase inaugurated here—of the lodger, a cipher, pursued (as the *Avenger*) while ostensibly pursuing this other as himself—in an intersection of circuits—revokes and suspends the circular mnemonics of any formal hermeneutics.

12. This, mock originarily, from a mark or mar(ring)—"Daisy" in French is *marguerite*—will also invoke the word *see* or *sea,* a mer, mère, or mar(k) that is also (a)material, excessive, the premetonymic displacement of a destroying maternity, a *mémoire,* or as *Psycho* might have it, "Mother."

13. One can suspend the numerous fronts the triad solicits to camouflage itself in symbolic phantasms, such as Chabrol and Rohmer's catholic Hitchcock, playing to an idea of the trinity.

14. Robert Kaplan, *The Nothing That Is: A Natural History of Zero* (New York: Oxford University Press, 1999), 132.

15. In the first *Man Who Knew Too Much,* the "secret" hidden in a shaving brush that designates the dangerous excess of knowledge, enough to clog the mouth and lead to the temple of sun worshippers, opens on an image: that of a corona or solar aura surrounding a pyramid that obliterates its sun, the emblem for the temple.

16. The intrusion of *thirdness* into studies of Hitchcock has been recurrent yet impressionistic, and the present analysis, locating its use at the site of a (failed) giving of face or voice, hopes to establish a new line of questioning. Examples would include Deleuze: "In the history of cinema Hitchcock appears as one who no longer conceives of the constitution of a film as a function of two terms—the director and the film to be made—but as a function of three: the director, the film and the public." See *Cinema 1: The Movement-Image,* trans. Hugh Tomlinson and Barbara Habberjam (Minneapolis: University of Minnesota Press, 1986), 202; Mladen Dolar: "the position of the third in the duality is occupied both by the fascinating and lethal object (which is also the object of exchange and circulation) and the mother's desire, Mother as the bearer of the law" ("Hitchcock's Objects," in *Everything,* 38–39); Stojan Pelko: "This 'thirdness' may, of course, be expressed in different ways. What is 'primary' on the cinematic level is no longer character (in this case we would have a whodunnit, scorned by Hitchcock) nor action, but the very multitude of relations" ("Punctum Caelum," in *Everything,* 112), as well as Zizek, who has identified thirdness either with a triangulation of the director's relationship to the audience or as the "big Other" of Lacanian mythography.

17. For an analysis of how, in the "dialogic" model of Voloshinov and Bakhtin, the triadic relationship, which supports it, involves both prosopopoeia and defacement, see Tom Cohen, "The Ideology of Dialogue," *Ideology and Inscription,* 56–98.

18. One need hardly elaborate the role of "laughter" as a personified agent of historical disruption, which shares a triadic structure with Freudian *Witz.*

19. In *The Lodger,* the title cards announcing "MUR/DER" repeatedly partition the two syllables, alternating white on black with its opposite on either side, which has the following effect: to identify the topos of this murder or death with a (reversible) split between white and black, presented here as lettering (the syllable *MUR* alone, which ellicits the French *mur* ["wall"], will echo in the numerous "Mar-" terms throughout Hitchcock, passing often through proper names to network marring, memory, "Mother," *mer, mère,* or materiality, the sea and sight [seeing], allied in *Rebecca,* in turn, to the letter *R,* and so on).

20. The *A,* before being converted into a *V,* also stands to initiate Hitchcock's signature, here bound again to the alphabet, to the triangle (Alfred,

which itself echoes alpha). In *Sabotage* Sylvia Sydney's Mrs. Verloc will be called "Mrs. V."

21. Since *Number Thirteen* was Hitchcock's first, unfinished, film, and *The Lodger* technically the third—the first having been effaced—it in a way assumes that figure (3, 13) preoriginarily as a (canceled) "first," or repetition: the triangle is thus borne into *The Lodger* already as its own repetition.

22. This impossible oneness spills into sheer numeration (the numberless "many" of the Greeks), like the single marksman's shot in the Royal Albert Hall sequence of the first *Man Who Knew Too Much* giving way to the innumerable chaotic shots of the police assault on the Wapping temple, the image at a standstill undone by its proliferation and acceleration in the celluloid band.

23. Thus in the film's "expressionistic" titles (of which Hitchcock had, reportedly, innumerably more), circles and sunbursts overtake the triangles; this inevitable and impossible translation of the triangle's explosive abruption into a temporal figure of circularity remains deferred. It is a translation of circularity heard in phrases like going "round the corner" *(Blackmail),* and the unbound figure of the ring (bangle, rope, circle, or sound). Indeed, the connection of a graphic sunburst—nonorigin of light, the "sevenfold ray"—with the triangle recurs in the first *Man Who Knew Too Much,* on the hidden message, namely, that excess of knowing that leads to the false temple of sun worshippers.

24. With that, we may say, a network of signature effects will be established whose import is affirmed by a moment in which different chains appear to cross: the 13, the *M* terms, the bar signature, all nominal dissolutions, the cameos and alternate surrogates and doubles, the play of letters.

25. Kittler, *Gramophone,* 211.

26. The figure of recurrence does not merely close or circulate, but breaks, as in *The Ring,* where cinema is interrogated as the *agonistic* boxing ring, and time as a malleable "bangle," ropelike, worn on the arm, an explosion ("bang"), a thing that cannot be rounded out.

27. We might say, rather than referring us to the "murderous gaze" of the camera, the camera's representable logic is an effect of what in Hitchcock is marked by the triangle.

28. These "hands," which anagrammatically inscribe A. H., get further reconfigured or even personified (in names like *Han*nay or *Hand*el Fane or Iris *Hend*erson).

29. The penultimate face morphing in Hitchcock, perhaps, occurs at the end of *Psycho,* where Norman, assuming Mother's face and voice, dissolves into a death's skull, and then becomes—with "Mother," as "Mother"—the grill of the sunken Ford or car-machine, the sunken tomb-machine reemerging.

30. Hitchcock's interview, "I Wish I Didn't Have to Shoot the Picture," in *Focus,* 23–24.

2. A User's Guide to Hitchcock's Signature Systems

1. Deleuze, *Cinema 1*, 203.

2. Zizek suggests, in *Looking Awry: An Introduction to Jacques Lacan through Popular Culture* (Cambridge, MA: MIT Press, 1991), that the "*sinthome*'s utter stupidity" (128), its material excess that can be likened to a "gift of shit," can be considered a "postmodern" theology. Thus Zizek offers a chapter in the middle of his collection *Everything* called "Hitchcockian *Sinthomes*." Here he begins to identify figures that traverse various films, breaking context, abrupting narrative interpretation, generating parallel universes of sense ("The postmodernist pleasure in interpreting Hitchcock is procured precisely by such self-imposed trials"; 127).

3. Zizek wants to inscribe his critical approach in the Cartesian tradition of auteurism: "one is even tempted to say that Hitchcock's films ultimately contain only two subject positions, that of the director and that of the viewer—all diegetic persons assume, by turn, one of these two positions." See "In His Bold Gaze My Ruin Is Writ Large," in *Everything*, 218.

4. It is not surprising that the "gaze" as personification figures prominently here—that is, what restores an auratic rhetoric, which Benjamin insisted on banishing. Zizek feels he can exploit the "psychotic" dimension of a desymbolic order to overleap the problematic of signs, yet he returns in doing so to the order of metaphor: "Lacanian theory provides a precise notion for this 'absolute Otherness': the subject beyond subjectivization . . . in other words: the subject *not* bound by the symbolic pact and as such identical to the Other's gaze" (*Everything*, 245). This recuperative arrangement can only return to a "subject itself," however vacated: "this subject dwells 'beyond the wall of language' . . . the 'impersonal' abyss we confront when we find ourselves face-to-face with Norman's gaze into the camera is the very abyss of the subject not yet caught in language—the unapproachable Thing which resists subjectivization, this point of failure of every identification, is ultimately *the subject itself*" (*Everything*, 245).

5. Edelman, "Hitchcock's Future," *HCE*, 240–41.

6. Deleuze, *Cinema 1*, 200.

7. Leitch, *The Encyclopedia of Alfred Hitchcock* (New York: Checkmark Books, 2002), 191.

8. One cannot address Hitchcock's signature system nor the "spies' post office" it sets up without addressing what Cadava, drawing on Benjamin, calls the "citational structure" of the image. In *Words of Light: Theses on the Photography of History* (Princeton, NJ: Princeton University Press, 1997) and elsewhere, Cadava links the "citational structure" of photography to Benjamin's contention that the practice of historiography is one of suspending and recasting historial trace chains.

9. The "string" would virally simulate mnemonic trace chains, DNA threads. One might require such a thread in entering a labyrinth. Throughout these

threads, strings, or intercut and viral lines, what leaps or traverses (so we are told) may be "a particularly vibrational pattern," a musical metaphor referenced to clangs, rhythmics, alternations: "According to string theory, the observed properties of each elementary particle arise because its internal string undergoes *a particular vibrational pattern.* This perspective differs sharply from that espoused by physicists before the discovery of string theory; in the earlier perspective the differences among the fundamental particles were explained by saying that, in effect, each particle species was 'cut from a *different fabric.*' Although each particle was viewed as elementary, the kind of 'stuff' each embodied was thought to be different. Electron 'stuff', for example, had a negative electronic charge, while neutrino 'stuff' had no electric charge. String theory *alters this picture radically* by declaring that the 'stuff' of all matter and all forces is the *same.* Each elementary particle is composed of a single string—that is, each particle *is* a single string—and all are absolutely identical. Differences between the strings arise because their respective strings undergo *different resonant vibrational patterns.* What appears to be different elementary particles are actually different 'notes' on a fundamental string. The universe—being composed of an enormous number of vibrating strings—is akin to a cosmic symphony. . . . Every particle of matter and every transmitter of force consists of a string whose pattern of vibration is its *'fingerprint'* . . . [E]very physical event, process or occurrence in the universe is, at its most elementary level, describable in terms of forces acting between these elementary material constituent, string theory provides the promise of . . . a theory of *everything.*" Brian Greene, *The Elegant Universe: Superstrings, Hidden Dimensions, and the Quest for the Ultimate Theory* (New York: Norton, 1999), 99 (my emphasis). One may suspend the metaphorization of a certain notion of music ("cosmic symphony") and its reassuring totalization ("a theory of everything"), and mark that "string theory's" value is tied to a semaphoric and prefigural model tied, nonetheless, to "event(s)." The dot of the atom is mutated into the temporal extension of the biomorphic line or duration trace while remaining irreducible: each twist is differentially monadic. Because negative, positive, and neutral values are generated from prefigural "vibratory patterns," binary content is suspended that "alters this picture radically." The picture is altered, alters itself, is indissociable in its phenomenalization from networking and proactive mnemonic strings. This is a "picture" of movement, departing from a vibration or oscillation. Its is also a matter of imprinting: "Every particle of matter and every transmitter of force consists of a string whose pattern of vibration is its 'fingerprint.'"

10. If it is metaphorized as a harmonic symphony to placate its theorist the model would be reassuringly unifying and maternal; if it is regarded as premetaphoric, void of aura or personification, such aleatory conflict might appear quite other, amaternal, viral webbings. Such can be claimed as a unity to be controlled by the police or its ocular detective, like Frank *Web*ber of

Blackmail, or compromised by a criminal blackmailer like *Trac(e)y* in the same work—whose access to a trace will imply all representational memory and writing systems in the chase through the British Museum: "everything."

11. Edelman, *"Rear Window's* Glasshole."

3. Espionage in the Teletechnic Empire

1. See Gayatri Chakravorty Spivak, *Death of a Discipline* (New York: Columbia University Press, 2003), specifically "Planetarity," 71–102. Masao Miyoshi, in a recent near abdication of leftist cultural studies, attempts to take in the looming impasses of the planetary, to cite an orientation to come (implicitly, beyond that of "globalization"), and personifies that, still, as the "planet." See Masao Miyoshi, "Turn to the Planet: Literature, Diversity, and Totality," *Comparative Literature* 53 (2001): 283–97: "Perhaps we need a new organization, one that is truly global and inclusive. . . . There is one such core site for organizing such an inclusiveness, though entirely negative at present: the future of the global environment" (295). Miyoshi's version recurs to a still Enlightenment model, and an inclusive utopian one at that: at issue is a de-anthropomorphization of the "human" sciences—what is without model to date, particularly if the latter are themselves produced by such sensorial regimes as ocularcentrism: what is indicated is a requirement of de-auraticization, a pan tele-technic shift in epistemologies that incorporates the laws of semaphoric systems and artificial memory.

2. In the original silent version of the film, the blackmailer's name was spelled Tracey, like some form of cinematic trace. I will retain that spelling, even though in the "talkie" the name was altered to Tracy.

3. See Satoshi Kanazawa, "Couch Potatoes Think 'Friends' Really Are," *New York Post,* May 9, 2002.

4. Blackmail in the Universal Reading Room

1. Jacques Derrida convincingly finds the figure of touch preoriginary to that of the ocular in *Le toucher, Jean-Luc Nancy: Accompagné de travaux de lecture de Simon Hantai* (Paris: Galilée, 2000).

2. In *The 39 Steps,* the museum is cited when Mr. Memory is said to be leaving his "brain" to the "British Museum."

3. Hitchcock uses the word *trouble* in the *Trouble with Harry* to designate something that will not stay in its place or frame, which ends up disclosing the autoconsumptive and atopos "logic" of (de)framing which is constitutive of the frame's legal fiction, and so on.

4. Leland Poague, "Criticism and/as History: Rereading *Blackmail,"* in *A Hitchcock Reader,* ed. Marshall Deutelbaum and Leland Poague (Ames: University of Iowa Press, 1986), 79. Hereafter cited as *HR.*

5. This van, which has a machine relaying transcribed code and directions and a curtain at its rear, cites the news truck from *The Lodger* and the figure

of flight—what will return, most notoriously, in the memorized formula for the silent plane, the flying or sublime trope for Hitchcock's cinema as war machine. The address taken down in the van from the wireless begins, as written out, to spell C-A-M- (like the "Camden Town" in the phone book in the second *Man Who Knew Too Much*), an address that also addresses the 3-1 or *C-A* of the triad, cameo logics, the camera, and so on.

6. This fall, or the British Museum, is recited frequently in earlier Hitchcock: the "British Museum" and the head as an "ivory dome" are featured in *The 39 Steps*, until the initials *B. M.* are complexly sported on the circulating ring in *Shadow of a Doubt* (by the time they turn up on John Hodiak's tattooed chest in *Lifeboat*, they are close to retirement).

7. The scene is also one that Annabella attributes to the Professor in *The 39 Steps*, who is missing a "joint": "He has a dozen names. He can look like a hundred people. But one thing he can't disguise. This part of his little finger is missing." The missing joint or digit condenses *Blackmail*'s point or pointing: touch as no touch, without hands or handcuffed, the digital deferred as preanalogic in essence.

8. Charles Laughton at his suicidal plunge ending *Jamaica Inn* declares, "Tell your children how the great age ended!" That age is both Hitchcock's British phase (in moving to America), or what is both antiquated, or forecast, by "cinema."

9. One might compare this to how "anagrams," a form of Scrabble, are played overtly in *Suspicion*, much as acrostics are in *The Lady Vanishes*.

10. We can ignore where the word *corona* mimes or cites the number 13 as well (*C*, third letter; *A*, the first), that is, the enumerative cluster associated with the predeath of the "I," his or her muting diremption by the materiality of language.

11. See Wai Chee Dimock, "Literature for the Planet," in "Globalizing Literary Studies," special issue, *PMLA* 116, no. 1 (2001): 178.

12. As Hitchcock tells Truffaut, an original idea of spy codes as writing on ice was abandoned as an opening for the first *Man Who Knew Too Much*: "From our window I could see the skating rink. And it occurred to me that we might start the picture by showing an ice-skater tracing numbers—eight—six—zero—two—on the rink. An espionage code, of course. But I dropped the idea" (*Hitchcock*, 61). He does not add that it was replaced by Louis Bernard's downward ski jump, ending in a snow-bursting fall as Betty's black dog runs out, a white dustup from which the limbs of the principals seem to disentangle. In turn, this whiteout or avalanche is the opening of *The Lady Vanishes*, associated with an obviously *model* train set—the set, and circuitry, of this cinema.

13. This political suspense can be taken as an aesthetic apprehension or a formal indictment and a looking beyond current programming. An example of the first might be Ina Rae Hark, "'We Might Even Get in the Newsreels':

The Press and Democracy in Hitchcock's World War II Anti-Fascist Films": "the director's inability to reconcile a belief in the desirability of preserving democracy's freedoms with his conviction that democratically constituted populations can't take on their enemies effectively without adopting those enemies' methods, inevitably sabotages his attempts to allocate to himself the mission of the democratic press" (*HCE*, 344).

5. The Archival Wars of "Old Man R"

1. DeLeuze, *Cinema 1*, 200.

2. If interpretation in its need for mimetic identification is part of this machinal problem, this historial vertigo confronting the cinematic, Zizek would be perhaps right to probe where something in the nonfigural epiphany of "the Thing" stands beyond interpretation. Except that in Zizek's hands, the interpretation is itself nothing if not metaphoric, personifying, symbolic, and hence reinscribed. Rather than mere "interpretation," Hitchcock seems to performatively short-circuit ocularcentric hermeneutics as a programmed perceptual field based on recognizing the already installed.

3. Hitchcock, in this regard, could be said to be explicitly positioned in the tradition of Poe, which he consciously recognizes. For a discussion of this tradition of cryptonymics see Shawn James Rosenheim, *The Cryptographic Imagination: Secret Writing from Edgar Poe to the Internet* (Baltimore: The Johns Hopkins University Press, 1997).

4. Rather than being a mimetic medium this cinema occupies the space Benjamin accords it in linking it to nonterms like allegory, translation, or materialistic historiography—the last as a reinscription of the history of a present that would recast inherited pasts to alter the course of a doomed historial program.

5. Dimock, "Literature for the Planet," 178. This will be reconfigured, following her example of Osip Mandelstam's reading of Dante, as a Soviet-style regime: "To anyone living under Stalin, relativity of simultaneity is not an esoteric idea. It is a living fact, a political fact, the only recourse against the absolute tyranny of an absolute synchronic plane. A long past and a long future are signs of hope. And hopelessness, conversely, is to be trapped in a time slot, changeless and dimensionless. Being thus trapped is the condition of hell" (183). The structure of the "Soviet" can be adapted, however, to any liberal democratic system that is the product of a history of representational decisions and exclusions, that of ocularcentrism generally or the association of the mimetic state with hypercapital and globalization. The imperialism of installed programs of perception and memory, time and definition, is at issue.

6. In *North by Northwest*, with the passage of Vandamm's microfilm, of a micrological reading of "cinema," the performative definitions of the political, the aesthetic, temporality, light, and memory would have been (already) recast.

7. In *Blackmail* the chase through the British Museum finds Tracey pur-

sued through the Egyptian room, past papyrus exhibits and the stone face of the giant Nefertiti, falling to his death through the glass dome into the universal reading room. Why *legibility,* though, in a huge dome head, through whose monumental history in storage the blackmailer will appear to crash—the storage of the museum transposed to that of the accelerated spool?

8. Rather than assuring the auteur of auteurism's signature or territory, the cameo dissolves that signature into a mobile outline, threading the serial productions, folding any behind the camera or outside of the frame into the set, borrowing the involuting logic of the MacGuffin understood as a performative black hole within narrative and mimetic pretexts. Since this process is murderous, it turns its death rays ("light") against its own representational premises, eviscerating the inherited inscriptions or mnemonic programs—as if void of personification or aura.

9. "Annabella Smith" in *The 39 Steps* inverts and caricatures (or redefines) the figure of an allegorical muse, while in *Sabotage* the detective Ted Spenser, who will be hunting down Verloc in his movie house, virtually names the standard bearer of English literary allegory as the saboteur's pursuer and the law. In *Secret Agent,* the long hunt for the German "secret agent" leads to a chocolate factory that is revealed to be the "spies' post office"—the site from which messages are transcribed and relayed across the espionage system of Hitchcockian writing, in which the agent is disclosed as "Marvin." At the heart of the postal system, then, is a system of marking, largely ignored among Hitchcock's critics, but recurrent in almost every film in an elaborate network of proper names bearing the syllable *Mar* itself (Marvin, Marlowe, Morton, Mark, Margot, Margaret, Martin, Marnie, and so on). Cinematic plotting occurs—rather, simply expounds its logic—in the name of a "foreign power" that is a nameless other as such, an alterity at the source of the familiar—like "Marvin," an English-speaking American. There would be a collusion between the Professor or Abbott or Verloc or Marvin and a certain Hitchcock that requires inspection, much as "England"—land of angels, from *angellein,* or hermeneutic sending, messaging—becomes the topos for a sort of hermeneutic. The stealth warplane formula to be smuggled out by Mr. Memory in *The 39 Steps*—which is to say, a figure of a new or antisublime identified with the cinematic apparatus or Hitchcock's writing—names his text as a virtual war machine, like the attack by the "birds" on the order of the visible and the mnemonic decades later.

10. *Espionage* is a privileged semaphoric arcade game lacing reading programs, one in which an "epistemological critique of tropes" (de Man) can politically be put into motion; hence the ironized return, in *The 39 Steps,* to the Palladium, the pursuit in *Secret Agent* to *Con*stantinople, the anatomy of "light" and the sun in the first *Man Who Knew Too Much.*

11. A Deleuzian might map this doubleness within a "nomadic" register. It might appear as a "dual empire" traversed by nonoriginary vectors, as McKenzie Wark topographizes in "Escape": "What confronts the world now is a dual

empire, not a unitary empire. The military-industrial complex of the cold war era has been replaced, not by a juridical empire of global law and trade, but by a new duality, a military-entertainment complex."

6. The Slave Revolt of Memory

1. Mr. Memory was Hitchcock's addition to John Buchan's novel.

2. Other MacGuffins pile up in viral fashion, gutted by a certain drift: the "thirty-nine steps," of course, but also Annabella, the missing digit, the flying helicopter that looks like a projector, and so on.

3. In this respect, the film offers yet another commentary on the ending of *Blackmail*: the fall of Tracey through the dome of the British Museum, into its reading room, an ending alluded to twice in the film. Mr. Memory is leaving his brain, we hear, to the "British Museum," and Hannay refers sparringly to Pamela's head as the "ivory dome," citing the dome of the reading room at the museum.

4. If the *aesthetic* will be associated with art, it will be an interrupted art, an interrupted and redirected *apoesis,* a making without hands (which distinguishes the *technē* of cinema, for which the fact of collaboration guarantees innumerable other hands and, for the director, none precisely)—what seems indicated by the first of a series of *names* hanging as placards in Hannay's apartment registry at Portland Place, *Por*lock (associated with the famous figure who interrupted Coleridge in heated inspiration and composition). It would, hence, be an interrupted or handcuffed (double-zero) *technē.*

5. The recuperations of William Rothman *(Murderous Gaze)* and Charles Silet ("Through a Woman's Eyes: Sexuality and Memory in *The 39 Steps,*" in *HR,* 109–22) are representative, suggesting that the dancing girls threaten the chaste couple with a rejected sensuality. The import of the legs is vaporized thereby, while the identificatory gaze is activated to foreclose Mr. Memory's disclosure.

6. In *Rich and Strange,* which combines silent film title cards with incipient dialogue, "crossing" is repeatedly used of a ship's transit, such as at various *ports,* among them "Port *Said.*"

7. If the recurrent "P" grounds this punning sequence in the encrypted triangle signature *(pi,* 3.1[4]), in the signature that sees "life" as an effect of a death associated with marking and representation, that too is allied with an (a)material grid of memory whose ordering the film aims itself against.

8. Kittler, *Gramophone,* 127. "Marey's chronophotographic gun" refers to the invention by the French physiologist Étienne-Jules Marey of the forerunner of the modern movie camera.

9. According to Kittler, this alertness to bodily atomization is in competition with the desire to identify with the mimetic image the photograph presents: "films anatomize the imaginary picture of the body that endows humans (in contrast to animals) with a borrowed I and, for that reason, remains their great love" *(Gramophone,* 150).

10. After noting Hannay's question to Mr. Memory ("What are the thirty-nine steps?"), Katie Trumpener points to and draws back from the consequences of the collapse of reference itself: "The physical space Hannay has been searching for throughout the move has become a concept, a plot with the same name as the movie he is in. The tangibility of the movie, too, is called into question at this moment in which the movie's mystery is solved, and Hitchcock must act quickly to prevent this proliferation of mirroring levels. Even as he is recounting the plot of the plot from memory, Mr. Memory, the man Hitchcock is shooting for his movie, must be shot, before everything is given away" ("Fragments of the Mirror: Self-Reference, Mise-en-Abyme, *Vertigo*," in *Hitchcock's Rereleased Films: From* Rope *To* Vertigo, ed. Walter Raubicheck and Walter Srebnick [Detroit, MI: Wayne State University Press, 1991], 177). Yet Trumpener puts the breaks on, in Hitchcock's name, assuming that everything is given away, or would be, drawing back from a certain *abyme*. Nothing, however, is given away by making this connection—which few enough, to date, have even remarked—since what is exposed ("the Thirty-Nine Steps is an organization of spies, collecting information on behalf of the foreign office of . . .") gives nothing away, is another MacGuffin within the MacGuffin that inverts the system further, folding into its trajectory, again, another putative exterior or outside.

11. For a more explicitly "Nietzschean" reading of the mnemonic in performance and retirement, here, see my "Hitchcock and the Death of (Mr.) Memory" in Tom Cohen, *Anti-Mimesis,* 227–60.

7. Contretemps

1. The *R* here would hark back to the secret formula of *The 39 Steps* for the silent warplane engine, presented to us as "R minus 1 over R to the power of *gamma*." The power of "gamma" here is a cinematic acceleration, gamma, the third letter, bearing the signature of the cinematic—hyperbolizing repetition; the "R minus 1" suggests the lack that attends imagistic repetition as initially encountered, that of a simulacrum.

2. The letter *R* recurs on the burning pillow of Rebecca or the tiepin of the killer Rusk in *Frenzy,* among other places (e.g., the name of the little boy "Arnie" in *The Trouble with Harry*).

3. Compare this to Hitchcock's final deployment of the trope of "con(stant),"
an arresting cognition, which is *Family Plot*'s opening kidnapping, in exchange for jewels, of the Greek tycoon Victor Constantine, a remarkably self-mocking trope: it suggests that the Grecian "cognitive" end—aesthetic and historial—is here portrayed by a vulgar CEO type, his kidnap and release not ends in themselves but yet more ploys for securing cinematic jewels.

4. It is a world-altering goal in which the first syllable, *con-,* marks a cognitive or epistemo-political critique within the "narrative" (R's reported advice to Ashenden on being given a "wife" as cover: "be very *con*nubial").

5. One might ask what Hitchcock meant by telling Truffaut it was a project

with many "ideas"—or in what sense the film performs a disarticulation of the idea itself, the external *eidos,* mock-visual prop of perception or *aisthanumai* whose repetitions spectrally generate idealities, generalities, identities, taking up quite differently a certain nameless site we have so far identified with the black sun, memory, or legs.

6. Thus the category of the *angel* appears. One hears the word *Engländer* in German, which stresses its etymology, as well as references to angels: "Angel, how well you're looking," "a good angel threw us together," "I'm no ministering angel." It connects this England to the Greek *angellein,* hermeneutic messenger, against which the spies' post office operates.

7. The letter *R* will be, in this sense, not only connected to the syllable *or,* with its earlike implications in the multilingual setting *(oreille),* but with the *R* as we find it in *Rebecca*—where it, and "she," will be linked to the surface of the sea, the crashing surface of signifying chains, and the recurrent word *see;* like Marvin, but otherwise, and indeed in seeming competition, "R" will network an entire system of relays. We are no longer dealing with "sound" as the technological element that can be manipulated and analyzed as an ingredient or effect (say, the way it is approached in film theory or by Elizabeth Weis), but rather as a prefigure of (a)materiality bound to a displaced series, a chain of substitutes whose false metonymy, presented in the image of the train or narrative itself, conceals a prefigural evisceration.

8. Go to *To Catch a Thief,* and one returns to this work via a coin toss or fake death or the initials S. A. ("South America"); go to *North by Northwest* and the telescopic iris shot; and so on—each thread activating a host of relays.

9. The Avenger's *triad* can never get back to the "previous" numbers that generate his serial murders, since they are posited from the third, which, if positioned by them, insinuates itself circularly, as the locus of the circuit, the circle, the zeroid endlessly: the "ground zero" of the visual.

10. R's address "84 Curzon St. W." echoes in the Swiss German *Kursaal* or casino. It suggests where a certain roll of the dice will be tied at once to R's offices and the manner in which the syllable *cur* or *car*—echoed in *Carroll* and her character's name, "*Car*rington"—will appear identified with the 3 *(c)* and 1 *(a, o, u),* or 13 signature. This sort of insignia or node runs throughout names like *Car*lotta Valdez and *Car*lton Hotel, or different *A-C* combinations alone, like *A*mbrose *C*happell.

8. Animation Blackout

1. In a recent piece, Susan Smith cannily connects "Hitchcock" to his series of saboteurs in this and other films (the Professor, Verloc, the schemers behind the movie house screen), but she seems to do so only by drawing psychological and equivocal parallels. In that hesitation, what is lost is the structural problematic that is not at all metaphoric, and more thorough than metaphoric analogy can penetrate: it returns to the definition and technicity of cinematic

"shock." See Susan Smith, "Hitchcock as *Saboteur*," in *HCE*, where she concludes: "Both Verloc and Hitchcock, it seems, engage in spoken acts of denial that are at odds with their cinematic impulses and aspirations" (49). For an earlier treatment that focuses on the revocation of the audience "contract" or the suspension of suspense see Cohen, "Sabotaging the Ocularist State," in *Ideology and Inscription*, 169–202.

2. Of Detective Spenser's greengrocer disguise, we hear of the open-air shop, which positions produce opposite the movie house's luring artifice: "It's one of a big chain—that shop. If you ask me, I believe he's the son of the man who owns them." The greengrocery is linked to a "big chain," itself like a celluloid strip, disclosing produce as more cinematic tropes. When a policeman nudges Spenser about a cabbage on the floor ("Suppose you or me were to break a *leg* on that"), the response is banter: "Can't tempt you, I suppose, with an orange . . . very nice today, *good for the feet.*" Why are *or*anges good for the feet, and what feet or shoes or *sabots*?

3. The phrase "*inner* history" is used of the Baring case, as it's called, in *Murder!* It is not accidental that Hitchcock's *next* work opens with a cinematic toy-train passing through a *whited-out* Babelesque Alpine village—as though a blizzard of signifiers, like an avalanche, lay as debris, turning the project back to the study of peasant dances, mnemonics, and vanishing childless "mothers" who turn out to be agents. This, by descending into the intrigue-filled vampire land, embellished with monster movie citations, the imaginary Balkan country with its own tongue, the cinematic Bandriki (naming the celluloid *band*). After Chatman's suicide bombing of the Bijou that ends *Sabotage*, Hitchcock must retool.

4. Susan Smith observes that the animation sequence lies at the core of the work—"In foregrounding issues of both authorship and spectatorship, the 'Who Killed Cock Robin?' sequence encapsulates the overall complexity of *Sabotage*'s metafilmic concerns" (*HCE*, 55), though not as a matter of "authorship and spectatorship" alone or necessarily. It focuses, above all, on animation as the "secret" of cinematic consciousness, a trace that traverses and splices animals and humans.

5. It is in commenting on the phantasmal collapse of Piccadilly Circus projected onto the aquarium tank, like a silent screen, that Conrad observes, "Cinema, like a bomb, is a device for dematerializing the world" (*The Hitchcock Murders*, 27). *Piccadilly* will be called "the center of the world," the omphalos of edifices from which dissolution world or history would again be reconfigured. Conrad expounds on Hitchcock's preference for the "buzz bomb" over the "V-2" as analog for cinema. Conrad's term *dematerializing* is indicative in other ways, as is that of "atomiz(ing) objects," since the process atomizes the components of image, citation, sound, phoneme, cut, and seems to reconstitute them as specters, gods, and wraiths in close-ups.

6. Indeed, the authorial name "Conrad" itself lies buried within the work,

under the pretext of a primary signature. Hitchcock will always associate this syllable, *Con*, with a figure of epistemological pursuit and evacuation—Jo Conway, Victor Constantine, Henrietta Considine, and so on—even as the *-rad* mimes the German word for wheel or circle, echoed in *Stage Fright* in the RADA (the Royal Academy of Dramatic Art), a logic of performance in which the model and simulacrum are technically reversed, the referent produced by the effect, the circular logic of cognition disclosed as a political issue.

7. Mladen Dolar, "The Spectator Who Knew Too Much": "It still produces contradictory and sharply opposed judgements, ranging from praise as Hitchcock's best English film and one of the most radical in his career to deprecatory verdicts that it is crude and in bad taste, 'academic, cold and phony' (Chabrol and Rohmer); its 'cruelty is unmatched until *Psycho*, and, perhaps, even by *Psycho*' (Durgnat)" (*Everything*, 129).

8. Katie Trumpener adds: "The constitutive elements of film itself—visual image, verbal messages, light, acting, sound, the movie-going consumers—are shown to us in terms of their function in the Verlocs' movie house. . . . The theme of consumption is introduced on the pavement outside the movie theater by the ticket-buying public waiting to consume this week's movie. Then it moves by stages to the grocery story next door, where a Scotland Yard detective, working undercover as a grocer, tries to get information out of Verloc's wife, wooing her with heads of lettuce and meals in fancy restaurants. Food in turn is connected to explosives (one saboteur keeps his dynamite in the larder in a bottle of catsup), explosivies which in turn become reconnected to film, reconnected to consumption and effect. . . . *Sabotage* examines the relationship of the technical processes and the commercial distribution of film to the finished work of art the audience sees on screen" (*Rereleased*, 178). Here the word *examines* falls back, fails to grasp a too-literal dimension by which the problematic of the *(Hamletian)* "act" is cited—that of the cinematic *event*.

9. When Spenser mocks the loss of electric power at the Bijou, he notes, "Blinkin' shame, robbin' the poor people like that." He links the felled cartoon crooner Cock Robin to the term *blinkin'*, invoking the blackfaced "drummer man" of *Young and Innocent*, whose accelerated eye twitch, like a camera shutter's metronomic or heartbeat, runs amok to reveal him as a murder.

10. The two taxidermist Ambrose Chappells of the second *Man Who Knew Too Much* traverse this logic, as do others (say, the Stevens women of *To Catch a Thief*).

11. Indeed, the boy may recall as countertype the bullying boy on the Underground train during Hitchcock's cameo appearance in *Blackmail*, a figure that repeatedly interrupts the director *reading* on the train—in the end staring him down, until the latter, cowed, lowers his book.

12. Akira Lippit's admirable *Electric Animal: Toward a Rhetoric of Wildlife* (Minneapolis: University of Minnesota Press, 2000) importantly argues, in this

regard, that the "animal" as a modern topos is invented with and by the cinematic, which also coincides with its virtual extinction. Extending this logic, the animeme is a trope for the cinematic, which is consistent entirely with its uses in Hitchcock—among other things as a trope of sheer technicity.

9. Solar Fronts

1. Foussard, in *To Catch a Thief,* will inherit Lorre's white streak across the hair (black-white-black), and add to it a "bad leg," a Hephaestus limp. This entire work, like *Secret Agent,* is cited (that is, activated and transmuted) in *To Catch a Thief,* which perhaps rewrites it more successfully than the then succeeding film—its overt "remake."

2. This scene will be rewritten, and accelerated at its own expense, in the travel service credit sequence of *To Catch a Thief.*

3. The exchange or theft of money for the cinematic is recurrently marked: on entering the Music Hall in *The 39 Steps* (the questioners of Mr. Memory as the filmgoers); the murder and theft of the ships following the light to their own shipwreck and murder in *Jamaica Inn*; the interrupted filmgoers at the Bijou in *Sabotage* bickering over their money's return or not (and the Londoners who merely "laugh" at Verloc's putting out of the lights, at his or Hitchcock's aesthetic sabotage to begin with), Mme Blanche's remunerated séances in *Family Plot.*

4. In Hitchcock the natural set is eschewed and every locale and public monument reconjured as semiotic beehives and cinematic terrain: Holland for its bicycles and black umbrellas, Switzerland for its snow and devastation of languages (and, finally, chocolate), postwar Riviera France for its affluent feast of simulation, the United States as a product of the cinematic.

5. The skit follows the certificate for the film issued by the state censor, stamped on the screen, the certification of viewability that will be defaced later, upstairs in the temple, when Hitchcock will visually *pun* on eating chocolate allied to excrement or black suns—that is, consuming the bonbon of film as entertainment, unwitting as to what sabotaging logic is being ingested.

6. The mountainscape will be cited in two other graphics: that of the forehead of Ramon entering the dentist's office with its parted black hair above the eye, and that of the parted curtains at the concert from which the gun protrudes—at the locus of the eye. The Griesalp outline simulates the *M* of St. *Mo*ritz, appropriating the nonanthropomorphic mountain within a triangulated pattern (white-black-white, peak-vale-peak), a near "maternal" graphics out of which Louis Bernard, ski jumper, will descend—and then fall (speaking later of his "last chance"). This fixed play of chance delivers us to and out of the M series in Hitchcock (mountain, murder, memory, music, mother), which activates a chain leading through memory and murder, music and "Mother," etching the site of the narrative in an evacuation of memory.

7. For Dolar, "The Spectator Who Knew Too Much," "knowing too much" is knowing about the Lacanian dominance of the "gaze," a knowledge that restores and economizes the ocularcentric tropology: "The surplus-knowledge is first and foremost the knowledge about the gaze as the agent of the cinematic image. But that surplus-knowledge also produces lack of knowledge, it confronts the spectator with his/her ignorance: if the initial setting was well known and predictable, then the surplus-knowledge makes it opaque and uncertain, the outcome becomes entirely unpredictable, beyond the reach of knowledge—it becomes the place where the subject is torn between his/her surplus and the lack of knowledge turns into lack. The objects lose their functionality, they become secret signs that have lost their (usual) meaning and are therefore open to multiplicity of significations" (*Everything*, 133).

8. Jacques Derrida, "From a Restricted to a General Economy," in *Writing and Difference,* trans. Alan Bass (Chicago: University of Chicago Press, 1978), 265.

9. Legs, through Hitchcock, may be heard as the convergence of legacy (anteriority) and the law (Lawrence), legitimation and legibility (reading)— the figure that dominates *The 39 Steps*.

10. That the name of "George" is used here, as with George Kaplan in *North by Northwest,* connects this name to the earth, to a node where that figure will resolve itself into the materiality of the bar motif.

11. Peter Conrad links the knockout scene of *The Ring* to the musical crescendo and failed assassinations of *The Man Who Knew Too Much*. At stake is an anatomy of the blackout as *Blitz,* a "crash" that knocks one out of the ring, a caesura mimed in the dissolution of the mimetic image. It is Hitchcock's anatomy, among other things, of the violence of "shock": "The same audience is in attendance. Socialites gossip in their boxes, and the dress code for the boxing match, as for the concert in the later films, is white tie. The referee, like the conductor of the cantata, bows to the crowd. Of course the spectacle is a little grubbier, and Hitchcock notices the water buckets in the corner of the boxing ring, the sponges and the sand, all intended to mop up the blood and sweat of the performers. But there is an equivalent to those brilliantly polished, deafeningly symbolic cymbals that give the gunman his cue and provide him with cover in *The Man Who Knew Too Much*. This is the gong, banged with a mallet in close-up to announce the beginning and the end of the match's rounds. Ian Hunter, playing Bob, aims a ferocious punch at the camera, which represents his opponent, Jack, played by Carl Brisson. A prize example of what Hitchcock called 'the free abstract in movie-making' follows: an uninhibited play of deforming fantasy, made possible by violence. Jack *blacks out,* and so does the Royal Albert Hall. *White flashes* like lightning *with black intervals* between them *scythe* across the screen. The arena swoons and swirls out of focus. The *ropes* of the boxing ring criss-cross like *railway lines* that head in *all directions* at once. *Disks* of fuzzy light swim through the air, then sharpen: they

belong to the *lamps* above the ring. The arm of the referee beats diagonally, like the conductor of the cantata. Then the gong is struck, with resonant finality" (*Hitchcock Murders*, 61–62).

12. The figure of an impression on a mattress will not perhaps return until Lila goes into Mrs. Bates's bedroom in *Psycho* to discover her absent shape in the featherbed.

13. One could extend this analysis of a *hyperbologic* enterprise by aligning it with another figure of excess, or overleaping, that of a Nietzschean "Overman," *Über* or hyper. Such a figure would not be understood as in the historical allegories or personalities that form its parody in Hitchcock (most literally in *Lifeboat* and *Rope,* where Nietzsche's name is mentioned). Rather, it can be heard as a hyperbolic rupture of the subject space, of "man" himself— the subject of the title "going under" with the bar series, so to speak—who is rewritten as a multiply surfaced network: a factor that makes Hitchcock's "psychopaths," including Norman Bates, failed allegories of a new personality type that evades binary inscriptions (among other things, of gender) and does not answer to a familial "I."

10. Zarathustran Hitchcock

1. The evocation is in the source text, David Dodge's novel *To Catch a Thief,* about which Peter Conrad notes that "[Francie] regards Robie, who shins up drainpipes as Nietzsche's Zarathustra vaulted over canyons, as 'a kind of superman'" (*Hitchcock Murders*, 112). Conrad, waxing autobiographical about his experience of Hitchcock as a kind of rape ("a Blooding"), inadvertently describes a type of shock or translation, even transvaluation: "*Psycho* had come to resemble a rite of passage, a visceral, constricted tunnel you had to pass through to get from one age to the next" (5).

2. The 3, strictly speaking, is hyperbolic—marked as such in phrases like "revolutionary *up*lift" or "pick *up*" or "catch *up* on my reading." The 3 lies behind the performative "zero" as a signature, too, for the *atopos* of the camera, also marked in the third letter, *c,* the machinal other witnessing and interrupting the mise-en-scène of human speech, dialogue, presentation. The zero passes into circuitry, circles, rings, and ringing—the "traveling circus" that Hitchcock will, in passing, name his cinematic operation, as if that too were a futuristic ray gun (*The Trouble with Harry*) or an atomic weapon (*Notorious*).

3. Raymond Durgnat, *The Strange Case of Alfred Hitchcock; or, The Plain Man's Hitchcock* (Cambridge, MA: MIT Press, 1974), 137. See also Carol Jacobs, *The Dissimulating Harmony: The Image of Interpretation in Nietzsche, Rilke, Artaud, and Benjamin* (Baltimore: The Johns Hopkins University Press, 1978).

4. Friedrich Nietzsche, *The Birth of Tragedy,* trans. Walter Kaufmann (New York: Random House, 1967), 52.

5. As a semaphoric atomization, Kittler allies this to a transvaluation of

signs, things, and relations: "A transvaluation of all values, even if it arrived on pigeon toes, as Nietzsche would have. . . . To mechanize writing, our culture had to redefine its values or . . . 'create a wholly new order of things'" (*Gramophone*, 187). Or: "*[Cabinet of Dr. Caligari]* frames the action in a way that represents not only the transvaluation of all values but their enigmatization" (147).

6. In George Collins's "Incidence of Instant and Flux on Temporal and Pictorial Objects, Listeners and Spectators" (*Tekhnema* 4 [1998]: 26–61), Nietzsche is linked to Hitchcock by addressing "Nietzsche's three throws at 'maintaining a sense' for 'God' in light of the will to power" (28). Or its dismantling? This association of Hitchcock with the thinking of technicity before a (Nietzschean) passage anticipates a next reading of his work that would move beyond those programmed by mimetic "relapse" of culturalist hermeneutics, identity politics, neo-Lacanian codes.

7. The accord between the bar series and rhythm is marked by its corollary in knocking, intervalled sound, but also by the blinking "drummer man" at the close of *Young and Innocent*—the eye as effect of blinking, of drum-like rhythm, associated with the agent of originary murder.

8. What Apollonian music opens with is the supplantation of a formalization, measure or rhythm, *before* the screen or metaphor of the originary—sheer alternation, or spacing, like the cymbalist's score in the Royal Albert Hall scene of the second *Man Who Knew Too Much,* where one pretends to read in close-up serial, spaced, mute bars.

9. The aesthetic emerges not as the discourse of the beautiful but as that of the mnemonic trace, out of which "perception" is projected or emerges.

10. From "On the Vision and the Riddle," *Thus Spake Zarathustra,* in *The Portable Nietzsche,* trans. Walter Kaufman (New York: Penguin, 1982), 158.

11. Extraterritoriality

1. On the "extraterritoriality" of literary effects, again see Wai Chee Dimock, "Literature for the Planet": "Literature . . . is extraterritorial in every sense" (178). Literature is meant here as encompassing figuration and the translation of reading events, yet is specifically cinematic by its dependence on motion, on travel: "Not stuck in any one national context—and saying predictable things in that context—a literary text becomes a new semantic template, a new form of the legible, each time it crosses a national border. Global transit extends, triangulates, and transforms its meaning" (177).

2. The figure of the "mummy" as the cinematic product—screen wraith, frozen (yet fluid) time, figure beyond death, eviscerated of interiors, spectral skin—is rooted in cinematic critical culture and, taken from Bazin, frames Philip Rosen's *Change Mummified.*

3. The bus is like that in which Hitchcock's cameo appears in the preceding work, *To Catch a Thief,* a cinematic bus that, in *Sabotage,* is exploded, time-bombed.

4. There is something curious when a Robin Wood suggests that the "shots of Doris Day's voice traveling up the stairs (so to speak) are among the most moving in the whole of Hitchcock" ("The Men Who Knew Too Much (and the women who knew much better)," in *Films Revisited,* 207). Does he "see" that this voice is with no body, the "shots" of a doubled absence, aphenomenal, bare *steps*? Drawing on Michel Chion's "Disembodied Voice," Pascal Bonitzer locates the film, surprisingly, as that closest to *Psycho.* He references a parallel use of the absent mother's voice and a "red herring" that forms a seemingly pointless hiatus in the plot: McKenna, misreading the name Ambrose Chapel as a person rather than a place (an "it"), visits the father and son pair by that name who run a taxidermy shop. Pascal Bonitzer, "The Kin and the Straw": "Thus *The Man Who Knew Too Much* is already, in filigree, *Psycho,* which seems, in retrospect, to derive from the burlesque scene with the taxidermist and, above all, from the motif of the mother's voice, which acts upon the son at a distance, through the incongruous song 'Que Será, Será'" (*Everything,* 179). Turning to the scene in which Stewart's hand is caught, as if bitten, in the stuffed tiger's mouth, Bonitzer suggests: "[Hitchcock's] aim was to create, on the cheap, an effect of strangeness and latent cruelty verging on the burlesque. But it was also because the stuffed wild animals, being at once wild and harmless, *symbolize* the double meaning of the whole scene" (183, my emphasis). Yet in a narrative of interruptions, the scene marks a pure hiatus, or *pause,* without use value.

5. That is, the name McKenna trades on the cognitive verb *to ken* (used in *The 39 Steps*) or the German verb *kennen,* as deployed elsewhere (Kenneth, Kentley, Kendall), whereas *Con*way (Jo's stage name), alternately, elicits a figure of *cogn*ition or conning, as also used elsewhere (Constance, Constantinople, Considine). It is part of what Paul de Man called an "epistemological critique of tropes," the emptying out of tropological pretexts en route to a certain act, translation, or event—here preferred as an (always missed) assassination.

6. This scenario is annotated by Hitchcock in his wartime propaganda short for the Free French, *Aventure Malgache,* which they found unusable, in part because of the unflattering parallels between French and German colonialism in Africa.

7. Egyptian implications of the solar poetics is developed not only by the pyramidal figures but by Ramon, who anagrammatically delivers the name not only of No-Mar(k) but Amon-Ra, the Egyptian sun god.

8. This is entirely different from the attempt on Ropa in the first version, where nonetheless that assassination and name conjure the image of an attempt to overleap narrative, temporal weaving, trope, or clothes itself.

9. *Interruptions* include the bus ride by Hank's accident, Jo's singing, Ben's dining, Bernard's whispering, the police interview by the telephone, the London hotel room visit, the Royal Albert Hall concert that is the text's seeming center piece, the visit to the Ambrose Chappells, the chapel sermon, even Drayton's final walk down the stairs, and so on.

10. Another peculiarity on the opening *bus* ride: while the McKennas later suspect "it was no accident" that Bernard approached them—looking for another, suspicious "married couple," the Draytons—there is a brief flash of a third couple (Anglo, she a blonde) sitting right next to the woman whose veil had been ripped off. They are glimpsed during the ruckus. Spectrally, they identify the McKennas with the Draytons—who, at the restaurant, will turn to be across from one another—and virtually seat each next to the source.

11. Bill Schaffer, in "Cutting the Flow: Thinking *Psycho*" (www.sensesofcinema .com), links this evisceration of interiority, manifest in the taxidermy tropes, to the insistence by the marking system that nothing can be in reserve, nothing not a sign, nothing "private" (the way Cassidy speaks of his own "private money"): "Bodies, faces, looks, cars, knives—all penetrate the zones of privacy and proxemic control Marion tries to establish around herself from moment to moment. And it doesn't stop with her death. There is still the Private Eye whose whole business is to conspire against the rights of privacy; the psychoanalyst who makes it his job to expose the intangible secrets of the unconscious; the penultimate scene where we penetrate into the devastated interior of a man unable to experience privacy even within his own head, the voice of his dead mother impossibly intoning 'they're probably watching me now'; the final scene where the car containing Marion's body is finally retrieved from the sludge and brought into the light of day."

12. One could certainly, using the ear as guide, follow traces of this word, this syllable or letter, throughout Hitchcock: as in Inspector Le*pic* in *To Catch a Thief,* or in the alliterative marking of the letter *p* in *The 39 Steps* (Portland Place, site of Annabella's murder; pips in poultry; pipe; and so on), or the "center of the world" to be bombed, *Pic*cadilly *Cir*cus *(Sabotage),* or in the emergence of the Greek letter pi, underfoot, etched hypogrammatically in the soil as a code of resistance, in *Torn Curtain* (the letter, too, of the Pythagorean theorem, numerically transposable as 3.14 . . . , another 3-1 combination, as if the letter *p* all along invokes this triadopheme associated with a blockage of speech, of the subject, mimed in Louis Bernard's passed "knowledge").

13. Ben thumbs the pages of a phone book, fanning the lists of names and numbers and letters and address, as though it were a dictionary in the Marrakesh police office when Drayton is talking to the hotel.

14. Maurice Yacowar, discussing repetitive figures across Hitchcock, focuses on the *X* figure, but, like Rothman interpreting the "bar series" as psychological containment, proposes a thematic and symbolic explanation: "Hitchcock often uses the X image to express his sense of man as a complex of good and evil" ("Hitchcock's Imagery and Art," in *HR,* 17). This would not begin to address its use, say, on the servant Germaine's back opening *To Catch a Thief* or the Prime Minister's flag in the second *Man Who Knew Too Much,* leaving all else aside (including *Strangers on a Train*'s "crisscross"). Even as we say that, according to the law that raises the symbolizing to the status of the symbolized (Benjamin), the bar series or *X* term re-mark themselves first, the formal

implications of the *X* begin as marking a rhetorical exchange, itself all but tropologically automatic, between performative polarities. After a while, like other tropological systems, the *chi* of *chiasmus* becomes target itself.

15. Compare the visit to the zoo and aquarium in *Sabotage*. Animemes in Hitchcock tend to enter the zone of prefigural traces swiftly, not as symbolic usage but, on the contrary, as an active voiding of mimetic associations that return, necessarily, to the "human" picture in the form of courier and critique.

16. This will not proceed as far, say, as the active vomiting marked in *The Birds,* of a turning inside out, of an "outside" without inside or out that will develop the logic of the taxidermists' shop, but a more intriguing suspension—of eating, of consumption, of Hank, a *pause,* a taking "stock."

17. A further complication adheres to invoking the name Benjamin in a way that, as in Hitchcock, puts the logic of generation in suspense. For when Joseph is sold into slavery, the father Jacob takes Benjamin, his other son by Rachel, as the former's substitute, while Joseph, in Egypt, assumes a paternal role (and even substitutes for Pharaoh), and at the end of his life, Jacob will bow to Joseph, reversing roles. Jacob, on the other hand, will bless Benjamin as a "ravening wolf" (Genesis 49:27), which is what Drayton will be called when presenting himself as pastor—"a *wolf* in sheep's clothing." In the same vein, Joseph's two sons while in Egypt and born of an Egyptian wife, will be acknowledged by Jacob as his own, collapsing generational difference. The box seat compartment of the marksman at the Royal Albert Hall is, inevitably if too precisely perhaps, number 33—double signature of the gun-as-camera logics, which are also those of, or within, number and logos as such.

18. One should recall, of course, that this evokes by proximity (connection) also Bloomsday in Joyce's *Ulysses (June 16)*—what invokes the entire panoply of antiapocalyptic cultural and pancultural, "literary" signifiers into play, as is the case, and puts them at risk.

19. The second *Man Who Knew Too Much* might be said to be doing within Hitchcock's oeuvre, by remaking the "first" version, what Scottie will do, perhaps, in re-creating "Madeleine."

20. Detour: the *natural* pretense of "generation" is suspended not only as a matrix of biological time and human reproduction, being before and after, which the photographematic brackets or allows to writhe and reformulate mnemonically; it is also a perspective of technicity that does not so much oppose cinematic prosthesis to natural "life" as insinuate the latter mirage as a mnemotechnic effect, too, of the former, like consciousness, the visible, and so on. To suspend "generation" or mark generations as awry simulacra cuts the dominant map of historicizing successions, Oedipal regimes, linear seriality, the empire of legislated times.

21. When Louis Bernard dies *Hank* disappears, establishing a parallel between them echoed in the words "little boy," with their "L. B." signature (*Louis Bernard*). Hank will, perhaps absurdly, be identified with the encrypted

knowledge itself—this, although his common response to every query is the wisely deferential, "I guess."

22. The shot references the giant ear in *Secret Agent,* at the Langenkirche. In that precursor, cited by McKenna's ear, there is a deafening effect of bells that makes it all but impossible to hear the words spoken into the ear (between Lorre and Gielgud).

23. This connection, that of pain and paint, is utilized obscurely in *"I Confess."* The Embassy of Vowels or O's, *zeroids* and *recurrence,* like Hank's "8," and at all events, of the circle or ring, is "extraterritorial." It is a placeless site identified, through its *kitchen,* with cinematic production—from which the person of the ambassador will, unlike the first version, plot against its own Prime Minister in a reflexive attempt at *auto*-usurpation, at hyperbolic overleaping. A fact that perhaps glosses the peculiar interview between the angered ambassador and the repentent Drayton on hearing of his assassin's failure, when the raging ambassador asks how the boy is to be gotten out of the embassy, an "extraterritorial" site of exteriority itself, what outside will accommodate what has no outside. He punctuates his questions with three ejaculations: "Eh!? EH!? *EH!?*"—each more emphatic and unnerving; each, like the vowels Ao——, a kind of apostrophe. Yet one may ask, particularly with the picture of the Prime Minister on the wall (a portly bald Hitchcock double, offers Truffaut), why the emphatic apostrophe, trope of personification that can only slide into the more proper *"Ah!"* which links Hitchcock initials (or that of the Albert Hall). The metaphorizations of the tourists on the bus have devolved, as it were, to a stripping of personification prepared for by the taxidermy scene.

24. Like Ambrose Chapel or Chappell, the two words in the title scroll that are capitalized—American and Cymbals—are *A* and *C,* 1 and 3. This multiply configured head, cut off like an "I" and hyperbolically disjunct, speaking and yet dead (of the chapel a bobby remarks, "No sign of life"), places the bodies of and in the text in conjunction with the figures at the taxidermists—one's own voice spoken by another in a reflexive catabasis, or visit to the underworld, that is at every point "life." Yet this de-capitalization, as we may call it, triggers another dislocation (a parallel relay is opened by the name George Kaplan—head of the earth, as witnessed, finally, in the Mount Rushmore figures in *North by Northwest*). The excessive knowing associated with the muted and detached head, whose noninterior seems partly anatomized in the Royal Albert Hall sequence, inescapably invokes a certain capitalism and *capo*-ism at once. The head, putative locus of perception, *aisthanumai,* or reading (we will see), also is cut off, adrift between the world of the north (affluent, touristic, formal) and the world of the south (impoverished, desert-like, yet imprinted as a scene of marring and solar excess, materiality and hyperbolism). A political subtext emerges in which a "knowledge" associated with decapitation links the formalist drift of cognitive allegory to a machinal (a)capitalism that runs from the sewing women of Morocco to the absurd "high" cultural display and expenditures of the Royal Albert Hall.

25. Unlike the first version's visit to the dentist George Barbor's office, which is transitional, the taxidermy scene is a visit to a *zoographic* underworld. It leads nowhere and has no place: it is an interruption, yet can only be broken off, a pocket, swirl, or momentary expenditure, which pretends to banally stumble into a cinematic preproduction toolshop for animemes and cinememes. The transposition, moreover, from the dentist's office in the first version—with its giant teeth hanging outside, citing the bar series motif at the place of the mouth (speech, ingestion), and linking that series nominally (Barbor) not only to unintelligibly foreign speech (barbaric) but the earth (George)—to the taxidermists' shop suggests where the latter refuses lending any utility whatever to the illusion of narrative progression.

26. Even "shock," if it enters legibility, cannot be located as other than a mnemonic catastrophe.

27. Indeed, the billboard advertises the concert's single absurd musical piece—a stand-in for all high-art music—on June 6th, which again makes the day on which the story opens two days before significant, not only for its Joycean resonances. D-day, again, when the Yanks *invaded* occupied Europe: Doris Day, who invades European parlor aesthetics with her singing, her acting, her packaged looks. Day, like the sun, only darkened, artificed, canceled in its ambassador the way the Prime Minister will almost be by his own ambassador, a *gift* (Doris), only reversely folded, like a "return" to Africa by McKenna, of the Americans to Europe, to originary England—only again not, because in another sense the Americans were already nonexistent, much as "Indianapolis, Indiana" reminds that even America was not theirs, and so on.

28. Events appear generated between and within male couples marking putative dominance or power: Drayton and the shooter, Ben McKenna and Louis Bernard, the ambassador and Drayton, the Prime Minister and the ambassador, the Ambrose Chappells, and so on.

29. Nor should too much be read into the hysteria Jo falls into before passing out, when the doctor sedates her before telling her of Hank's kidnapping: it is, after all, the pills from and of Stewart—whose hysteria we witness recurrently—that precedes the fit, acted to script, pills that operate like an injection, calling to mind what Hank is said to "spell" so well on the bus, the word *intravenously*.

30. A drummer if not the cymbalist has occurred, of course, elsewhere, and in blackface himself in *Young and Innocent*. This scenario cleans up the trope of the compulsively *blinking* "drummer man," heart problems and heartbeat mimed by a sphincter-like shuttering of the virtual eye blinking or *Augenblick*.

31. One can understand the camouflaged retreat in the "next" film. In *The Wrong Man* Hitchcock seems to return to a massively literal and mock-documentary subject void of "allegorical" temptations (though the opposite is the case).

Coda

1. Jean-Luc Godard, interview with Jonathan Rosenbaum in "Bande-annonce pour les *Histoire(s) du cinéma* de Godard," *Trafic* 21 (Spring 1997): 12.

2. The desideratum is what "you *remember*," and something happens: narrative gives way to things, objects become exploding beehives of signification ("the pair of glasses, or the windmill"). And if we read, instead, from the glasses or the windmill, from scenes of translation or the occurrence or naming of legs, suspending the penultimate MacGuffin: the film as "pictures of people talking," the mimetic narrative as such? One would here approach the event named "Hitchcock" as an allo-graphematic project, a translational exposure of sheer linguistic imaging beyond what is framed as "film" in film theory. If indeed Hitchcock again and again cancels the figure of the *eye*, of *sight*, or even *light*, then we must assume that this name, which inhabits a place at the center of film history, also puts cinema itself into question, embarks on a project that exceeds any single definition of a mimetic (or analogic) apparatus, such as sustains the history of film studies.

3. The *allographic* may be thought to produce the figure of a spectral event. Nicholas Royle's study of telepathy, *Telepathy and Literature: Essays on the Reading Mind* (Oxford, UK: Basil Blackwell, 1991), uses the term *allography* to suggest an alterity effect within the work of cryptonomy: "One might venture to call it an *allography*—a writing on behalf of another—but only if this 'other' is acknowledged as being non-human, unrepresentable and irremediably cryptic" (33). The term, however, is left inert and undeveloped, while the transposition ("a writing on behalf of another") remains precritical and minimal. Among current writers on Hitchcock, Jameson has been most acute in routinely marking a problem in language that traverses the production, down to marking as "genuine filmic 'sentences' these gestualities, whose syntax can thus be echoed or rhymed from film to film" (*Signatures*, 209).

4. The attempt to maintain Hitchcock's rhetorical mastery as a position with identifiable moves toward an engaged ideal viewer has been an ongoing critical assumption to stabilize the prospect of a "moralizing" auteur-master, a position that empowers and specularizes the interpreter. Such "moralism" persists through the neo-Lacanian use of Hitchcock as exemplar, and Zizek essentially ("one is even tempted to say that Hitchcock's films ultimately contain only two subject positions, that of the director and that of the viewer— all diegetic persons assume, by turn, one of these two positions" (*Everything*, 218). This blind spot is found too in Deleuze: "in the history of cinema Hitchcock appears as one who no longer conceives of the constitution of a film as a function of two terms—the director and the film to be made—but as a function of three: the director, the film and the public" (*Cinema 1*, 202). An interpretive version of this as rhetorical performance might be Thomas M. Leitch's *Find the Director and Other Hitchcock Games* (Athens: University of Georgia Press, 1991).

5. Kittler, *Gramophone*, 115. This approach accelerates Paul Virilio's analysis in *Cinema and War: The Logistics of Perception,* trans. Patrick Camiller (New York: Verso, 1989).

6. Alfred Hitchcock, "On Suspense," in *Hitchcock on Hitchcock: Selected Writings and Interviews,* ed. Sidney Gottlied (Berkeley and Los Angeles: University of California Press, 1995), 122. Cited in Morris, *Hanging Figure,* 46.

7. Rodowick observes that the ideology of the "mimetic" has been woven into the premise of cinema as such: "The historical development of cinema as a signifying practice has been dominated by an ideology of mimesis which, by determining the organization of images according to a schema of spatial continuity, linear exposition, and temporal irreversibility, has privileged film's realist vocation: the direct adequation of images to things. By posing visual representation as that which provides direct access to the real by short-circuiting symbolic expression or the mediation of 'writing,' the exploitation of film's mimetic faculty has tended to sublimate signification in favor of iconic presence." See Rodowick, "The Figure," 41.

8. Hitchcock, clearly, understood the "chase" as the mobilization of cinema, reading, hermeneutic pursuit, tracking, as he confirms in his interview, "Core of the Movie—The Chase." What is not remarked, however, is what is implied when he turns that back against itself to *implode,* immediately, or breaks it off (the opening of *Vertigo*) in sheer suspension. Thus he observes: "the chase seems to me the final expression of the motion picture medium . . . the movie is the natural vessel for the chase story because the basic film shape is continuous." In *Hitchcock on Hitchcock,* 125.

9. On the contrary: they may lead to a deanthropomorphizing scene that has all along been sabotaging and defacing the humanist, auteurist, anthropomorphizing, auratic, hermeneutic, ocularcentric, mimetic programs of the epistemo-aesthetic state of twentieth-century Euro-American culture.

10. In "The Work of Art" Benjamin links cinema to a technicity associated with the alteration of programs of memory and perception, hence of *aesthesis* and signification ("the mode of human sense perception changes with humanity's entire mode of existence," *Illuminations,* 222). It has a relation to an archival politics registered in the "shock effect" it induces: "This constitutes the shock effect of the film. . . . By means of its technical structure, the film has taken the physical shock effect out of the wrappers in which Dadaism had, as it were, kept it inside the moral shock effect" (238).

11. Like *cinema,* the concept of translation is translated from an at first strictly reproductive category—it assures reference back to an original text or meaning or content. Only in Benjamin's sense something called "pure language *(reine Sprache)*" intervenes: not, that is, pure meaning to which translation is responsible, but the nonhuman signifiers that comprise all possible languages, that traverse all signifying, and for that matter the possibility of "perception" organizing marks and sounds.

Index of Films

Tom Cohen is professor of literary, cultural, and media studies at the University at Albany, State University of New York. He has published widely on critical and cultural practices and is the author of *Anti-Mimesis from Plato to Hitchcock* and *Ideology and Inscription: "Cultural Studies" after Benjamin, de Man, and Bakhtin*. He is also contributing editor of *Material Events: Paul de Man and the Afterlife of Theory* (Minnesota, 2000) and *Jacques Derrida and the Humanities*.